Catholic Neurotheology

Andrew B. Newberg
Thomas Jefferson University, Philadelphia, Pennsylvania

Mary Clare Smith
Sisters of Notre Dame, Chardon, Ohio

Series in Philosophy of Religion

VERNON PRESS

In the Americas:	*In the rest of the world:*
Vernon Press	Vernon Press
1000 N West Street, Suite 1200,	C/Sancti Espiritu 17,
Wilmington, Delaware 19801	Malaga, 29006
United States	Spain

Series in Philosophy of Religion

Library of Congress Control Number: 2024932849

ISBN: 979-8-8819-0022-9

Also available: 978-1-64889-898-3 [Hardback]

Nihil obstat: Reverend Gerald Bednar, JD, PhD
        Censor deputatus

Imprimatur. Most Reverend Edward C. Malesic, JCL
        Bishop of Cleveland

Given at Cleveland, Ohio, on February 1, 2024.

The *Nihil* obstat and *Imprimatur* are official declarations that a book or pamphlet is free of doctrinal or moral error. No implication is contained therein that those who have granted the *Nihil obstat* and *imprimatur* agree with the contents, opinions, or statements expressed.

Cover design by Vernon Press. Background image by Freepik.

Table of Contents

	Acknowledgments	v
	Author Note	vii
Chapter 1	Introduction to Catholic Neurotheology	1
Chapter 2	Neurotheological Investigations in Catholic Thought	17
Chapter 3	Epistemological Considerations and Faith	45
Chapter 4	Methodology in Neuroscience and Catholicism	71
Chapter 5	Free Will and the Brain	93
Chapter 6	The Body's Response to Religious Experience	111
Chapter 7	The Neurophysiology of Catholic Rituals	125
Chapter 8	The Neurophysiology of Catholic Practices	159
Chapter 9	Psychology and Catholicism	179
Chapter 10	Spirituality from a Neurotheological Perspective	199
Chapter 11	Mysticism, Catholicism, and the Brain	231
Chapter 12	Catholic Theological Implications	263
Chapter 13	Holiness, Grace, Soul, and the Brain	283
Chapter 14	Critique, Clarifications, and Future Directions	305
	References	331
	Index	379

Acknowledgments

We are grateful to the colleagues who have provided helpful advice, support, contributions, and suggestions for this book.

We wish primarily to thank our consultants: Reverend Gerald Bednar, Ph.D., JD; James Beauregard, Ph.D.; Reverend Steven Payne, OCD, Ph.D.; Reverend Juan Jose Sanguineti, Ph.D.; Margarita Vega, Ph.D.; and Joel Johnson, Ph.D. They are also mentioned with their affiliations in our Author Note. The expertise and recommendations of our consultants have been invaluable. Any errors in this work are not attributable to our consultants or advisors.

Thanks are due also to my (ABN) colleagues, including Daniel Monti, M.D. and Nancy Wintering, M.S.W., and my wonderful mentors Abass Alavi, M.D. and Eugene d'Aquili, M.D., Ph.D. Dr. d'Aquili, who passed away 25 years ago, would have been particularly excited by this book since he was Catholic and loved all the Catholic rituals and ceremonies. We also want to thank the Sisters of Notre Dame, Linda Zagzebski, Ph.D., and Sofia Carozza, Ph.D. Finally, we owe thanks to Blanca Caro Duran, Maria Bajo Gutierez, Argiris Legatos, and the rest of the staff at Vernon Press for their excellent work and the high academic standards they have maintained in the production of our book.

Author Note

Andrew B. Newberg is a neuroscientist in the Department of Integrative Medicine and Nutritional Sciences, Thomas Jefferson University, Philadelphia, PA; Mary Clare Smith is a Sister of Notre Dame and counseling psychologist, Chardon, OH.

Consultants were: Gerald Bednar, former professor of systematic theology at St. Mary Seminary and Graduate School of Theology, Wickliffe, Ohio; James Beauregard, neuropsychologist and professor at Rivier University, Nashua, New Hampshire; Steven Payne, professor and president of the Carmelite Institute of North America at the Catholic University of America, Washington, DC; Juan José Sanguineti, professor emeritus of philosophy, Pontifical University of the Holy Cross, Rome, and current professor at Austral University, Buenos Aires, Argentina; Margarita Vega, professor of philosophy at Dominican School of Philosophy and Theology, Berkeley, California; and Joel Johnson, professor of philosophy at Borromeo Seminary College and John Carroll University, Cleveland, Ohio. Andrew B. Newberg contributed to the neurotheological aspects of the study. Mary Clare Smith and the consultants contributed primarily to aspects related to Catholicism and psychology.

Correspondence concerning this book should be addressed to Andrew Newberg, e-mail: Andrew.Newberg@jefferson.edu, and/or to Mary Clare Smith, mcsmith8920@gmail.com.

Abstract

The topic of "Neurotheology" has garnered increasing attention in the academic, religious, scientific, and popular worlds. Several books have been written addressing the relationship between the brain and religious experience, and numerous scholarly articles have been published on the topic. The popular press has also given significant attention to neurotheology, including major stories in *Newsweek, Time, The New Scientist, Readers Digest,* and *Popular Mechanics.* The scientific and religious communities have been highly interested in obtaining more information regarding neurotheology, how to approach this topic, and how science and religion can be integrated in some manner that preserves both.

However, there have been no extensive attempts at exploring more specifically how Catholic religious thought and experience may intersect with the brain and neuroscience. The purpose of *Catholic Neurotheology* is to engage this groundbreaking area fully. Topics are related to a neurotheological approach to the foundational beliefs that arise from Catholic learning from Scripture and Tradition, an exploration of the different elements of Catholicism, an exploration of specifically Catholic practices and rituals, and a review of Catholic mysticism. Specific Catholic scholars are considered in terms of the relationship between their ideas/teachings and different brain processes. *Catholic Neurotheology* engages these topics with the hope that readers, regardless of their background, will be able to understand the complexities and breadth of neurotheology from a Catholic perspective. More broadly, issues include a review of the neurosciences and neuroscientific techniques; religious and spiritual experiences; theological development and analysis; liturgy and ritual; epistemology, philosophy, and ethics; and social implications, all from a Catholic perspective.

Chapter 1

Introduction to Catholic Neurotheology

Catholicism and science

The relationship between the Catholic Church and science has a long and storied past. On the one hand, there has always been an embrace of science in the context of understanding the heavens, including astronomical events, as well as knowing the basic physics associated with building sacred structures such as St. Peter's Basilica. On the other hand, scientists, particularly those who are oppositional to religion, frequently point to the Church's problematic arrest of Galileo because of his astronomical findings or its strong opposition to Darwin's theory of evolution since both ideas removed humanity from the center of the universe, causing great theological consternation.

First, it would be helpful to clarify the terms. What do we mean by *science*? "Science is the pursuit and application of knowledge and understanding of the natural and social world following a systematic methodology based on evidence" (Science Council, 2023). Science follows a methodology that includes objective measurement of data through gathering evidence, formulating hypotheses, experimentation and observation, valid and reliable assessment, reasoning by induction from examples or facts to universal rules, repeating the experiments, analyzing them, and verification by peer review.

Secondly, what do we mean by *religion*? We can start by defining religion. Professor of philosophy, religion, and theology emeritus Robert C. Neville proposes: "human engagement of ultimacy expressed in cognitive articulations, existential responses to ultimacy that give ultimate definition to the individual, and patterns of life and ritual in the face of ultimacy" (*Defining religion: Essays in philosophy of religion,* 2018, in Simmons, 2019, p. 3).

Jesuit theologian, consultant for the *Catechism of the Catholic Church,* and author of the *Modern Catholic Dictionary* (1980), Rev. John A. Hardon defines religion as:

> The moral virtue by which a person is disposed to render to God the worship and service he deserves. It is sometimes identified with the virtue of justice toward God, whose rights are rooted in his complete dominion over all creation. Religion is also a composite of all the virtues that arise from a human being's relationship to God as the author of their being, even as love is a cluster of all the virtues arising from human

response to God as the destiny of their being. Religion thus corresponds to the practice of piety toward God as the Creator of the universe (Catholic Culture, 2023).

Thirdly, *Catholicism*. Christianity today numbers an estimated 2.4 billion adherents out of the Earth's population of 7.8 billion. Christians, including Catholics, Protestants, Orthodox, and other groups, make up 31.11% of the total population. Among Christians, the largest faith is Roman Catholic, with 1,250,319,000 members, second only to Sunni Muslims (Statistics and Data, 2022).

Are there variations within Catholicism? Catholicism is the same everywhere in that all members adhere to the basic beliefs expressed in the *Catechism of the Catholic Church* (*CCC*). This means acknowledging Jesus Christ as God, confessing one faith, initiated by one baptism, forming only one Body, enlivened by one Spirit, with one hope (cf. Eph 4:3-5), and finally overcoming all divisions (*CCC*, 866). The one belief system, communicating the rich and deep mystery of Christ, is expressed in a diversity of liturgical traditions (*CCC*, 1201). The early Church moved into three main communities: Rome, Antioch, and Alexandria, each with its liturgical practices and organization. Today, the *Catechism* names seven rites[1] with liturgical expressions passed down over generations, approved in that they meet the criterion of "fidelity to apostolic Tradition, i.e., communion in the faith and sacraments received from the apostles, a communion signified and guaranteed by apostolic succession" (*CCC*, 1209). For this study, we will consider "Catholic" to mean churches and individuals who accept the *Catechism of the Catholic Church*.

Although much has changed since the 1600s, topics such as evolution and the origin of the universe frequently put science and religion at odds. On the other hand, there are instances in which religion and science continue to find a productive dialogue between them. For example, the Vatican Observatory has been at the forefront of recent astronomical investigations. The dialogue between theology and science "should continue to grow in depth and scope," respecting the integrity of each field according to Pope John Paul II in his message to Director of the Vatican Observatory Rev. G. V. Coyne, S.J.: "Science can purify religion from error and superstition; religion can purify science from idolatry and false absolutes. Each can draw the other into a wider world, a world in which both can flourish" (1988).

In the prologue to his encyclical *Fides et Ratio* (Faith and Reason) (1998), the Pope called faith and reason two wings that lift the human spirit to the contemplation of truth—to wisdom, not just true things in specific domains such as physics, chemistry, neurology, or psychology, but to ultimate causes in light of the end or purpose of all things. Reason poses questions it cannot answer. Theologian Cardinal Joseph Ratzinger, Pope Emeritus Benedict XVI (1927-2022) pointed to faith as the capacity for a new kind of knowledge. Faith, he wrote,

> is not an act of (reason) alone, not simply an act of the will or feeling, but an act in which all the spiritual powers are at work together. It is only because the depth of the soul—the heart—has been touched by God's Word that the whole structure of spiritual powers is set in motion and unites in the 'Yes' of believing. (*Pilgrim Fellowship of Faith* [2005] as cited in Baglow, 2020, para.6)

Thus, many believe that there is room for a constructive interaction between science and religion. Perhaps the best opportunity for dialogue comes in the cognitive sciences. After all, it is reasonable to ask what is going on in the brain when people are religious or spiritual. If someone prays, they are using a variety of cognitive processes, including attention, memory, and language, as well as emotions such as love or joy. Thus, when we read a sacred text such as the Bible, we use our language abilities to read the words, cognitive processes to interpret them into a concept, and emotions that make these concepts personally meaningful. Specific cognitive processes such as causal reasoning, abstract thinking, holistic thinking, and binary thinking may all become part of a religious, spiritual, or theological endeavor.

Many fascinating questions can be engaged equally from both the religious and the scientific perspectives when it comes to how the brain and religion intersect. All of this comes together in the field sometimes referred to as *neurotheology*. This emerging discipline brings together a variety of other fields with the goal of understanding the relationship or link between the brain and religious and spiritual phenomena.

We should also emphasize at the outset that by *Catholic neurotheology* we do not mean that there is one part of the brain, or group of parts, that makes one Catholic. We also do not mean that Catholics have fundamentally different brains from adherents of other traditions. Rather, we mean that there are ways in which Catholicism itself—its doctrines, beliefs, rituals, practices, and experiences—specifically intersect with the human brain. Understanding this relationship in as much detail as possible could provide essential information for those who are Catholic, in addition to those who wish to understand Catholicism as well as possible.

Before going into a more thorough discussion about neurotheology itself, it is helpful to put neurotheology within a larger context of the science-religion relationship. As mentioned, scientists and theologians have often been at odds with each other. In *Religion in an Age of Science* (1990), scholar Ian Barbour systematically elaborates on several possible relationships between science and religion. For example, in addition to the more directly oppositional *conflict* relationship, science and religion sometimes can interact by not interacting. This is consistent with the famous statement by noted anthropologist Stephen J. Gould, who referred to science and religion as 'non-overlapping magisteria' (authorities). This perspective suggests that the domains of religion and science are separate and *independent* and, hence, should never interact on common topics.

While this is conceptually reasonable because the physical (or natural) world and the supernatural world can generally be regarded as separate, history has demonstrated that there are many topics in which both science and religion have something to say. The theory of evolution has been particularly problematic, as well as general cosmology. The idea that God has created both the physical world and human beings is clearly a religious perspective. Science, on the other hand, would argue that the world essentially created itself through the Big Bang and that human beings ultimately arrived on the planet through a complex process of biological evolution. In this case, both science and religion appear to have something to say about how the universe began and how it came to the present day. Keeping them as non-overlapping magisteria in this context appears to be problematic at best. Somehow, they seem to require a dialogue of some type, which enables them to discuss certain topics about which they both have something to say.

This is the third type of interaction described by Barbour: *dialogue*. Science and religion have frequently been able to dialogue about various topics pertaining to human activities and the nature of the world. The hope is that the dialogue might be fruitful and that both science and religion contribute to the discussion. Unfortunately, an oppositional approach frequently takes over, especially when scientific and religious perspectives are discordant.

The fourth type of interaction, *integration*, has not generally been the typical relationship between science and religion. However, there are many issues in which exploring ways of bringing science and religion together may yield interesting possibilities. For example, perhaps it is possible to find ways of linking the religious and cosmological perspectives on the origins of the universe, and some have certainly tried.

This brings us back to the topic of neurotheology, which might be a field ripe for an integrative approach between science and religion. While some may debate whether the brain creates God or God creates the brain, neurotheology can engage in far richer and more nuanced discussions, as we aim to show in the pages that follow.

Understanding neurotheology

Let us look a bit closer at what neurotheology is as a potential field of scholarship so that we can better understand where specific dialogues or integrations might occur.

Importantly, we intend to consider neurotheology from the Catholic perspective and, conversely, Catholicism from the neurotheological perspective. This point is critical as we intend to develop a dialogic or integrative approach that brings together science and religion. Neurotheology, to be effective, must be a true *two-way street*. It cannot be only a scientific evaluation of Catholicism, and it cannot be only a Catholic view of science. Neurotheology suggests that both science and its religious counterpart (e.g., Catholicism) might become part of an integrative approach that maintains the integrity of both.

A challenge for the dialogue or integration between science and religion stems from their different ways of knowing. The epistemologies of science and religion will be discussed more completely in Chapter Three. The epistemological differences mean that science begins with data in the natural realm and draws empirically verifiable rational conclusions. Catholic theology depends on revelation to answer ultimate questions. It begins with faith as the divinely inspired response to revelation, interpreted by magisterial teaching, and works heuristically to apply religious beliefs in context.

Several important points about neurotheology as a term should be considered before engaging in the broader discussion. While neurotheology appears to be the most widely used term currently to describe this field, there are other possibilities. "Bioreligion," "psychospirituality," and many others could be considered. Every possibility has its strengths and weaknesses. For a variety of reasons, both regarding the academic world and the broader public, *neurotheology* appears to be the term that has stuck.

In my (Andrew Newberg [ABN]) previous work on the *Principles of Neurotheology* (2010), several important points have been raised to make the term as accurate and useful as possible. We have already discussed one of the basic aspects, which is that neurotheology must be a two-way street, equally respecting and considering science and religion. Likewise, any conclusions derived from a neurotheological analysis must be accessible to both religion and science. In other words, if a study is designed to explore the effects of the rosary on the brain, it is essential to make sure that the rosary is recited as accurately and devoutly as possible. Similarly, brain science should be as rigorous and exact as possible to capture the power of the rosary for a given individual.

Another important point about neurotheology as a term is that both sides of the term must be considered broadly. The *neuro* side must include not only neuroscience and neuroimaging but a variety of other approaches that might help us understand the biological component of the human being. Thus, studies of various medical and neurological conditions, neurochemistry, psychology, and even anthropology can potentially contribute to neurotheology. Consciousness studies and the cognitive neuroscientific evaluation of the relationship between the mind and brain also play prominent roles in this discussion.

The second half of the term—*theology*-of course, is a specific discipline with the goal of exploring the fundamental concepts of any given tradition, such as Catholicism. Different religions can expand theology in a variety of directions. Catholicism has been particularly rich in its tradition of theology. There are many theologians throughout the past 2,000 years who have explored and debated the basis and concepts of the Christian tradition. Biblical exegesis is also fundamental to Christian theology. Neurotheology can certainly be applied to the entire array of theological principles and topics. After all, theology is also a cognitive discipline that utilizes a variety of brain processes to investigate, discriminate, and debate about the basis of Christian belief. In this regard, neurotheology can explore how the human person engages theology itself as well as religious and spiritual experiences, focusing specifically on neurophysiological correlates of human thoughts, feelings, and behavior. The theological side of neurotheology goes far beyond just an exploration of theology proper. It can conceptually ground neurobiological aspects of the religious and spiritual domain, which is the focus of neurotheology.

Neurotheology can make a broad exploration of rituals, practices, beliefs, behaviors, and experiences. The latter is particularly relevant to the field of neurotheology. A growing number of studies have tried to explore religious and spiritual experiences ranging from the mild experience one might have walking into a church and attending Mass to profound mystical experiences such as the *unio mystica.*

In fact, one might argue that neurotheology has been part of the Catholic tradition almost from its origins. The stories of Jesus and the development of Catholic rituals and practices always take into consideration how the human mind operates, even though specific knowledge of the brain and its functions had to wait until the twentieth century. The use of various rituals, images, songs, and writings all have an impact on the brain's sensitive experiences that help bring alive the basic elements of the Catholic tradition. Concepts such as good and evil, free will, morality, original sin, revelation, and salvation all include some aspect and understanding of the human person, whether it be our emotions, thoughts, or behaviors.

Although the early theological approaches were doctrinal for the most part, more recent explorations of Catholicism and Christianity have included approaches related to cognitive and emotional processes. For example, in the eighteenth century, German philosopher, theologian, and biblical scholar Friedrich Schleiermacher (1768-1834) emphasized religion as primarily a cognitive, visceral, or intuitive sense—*a feeling of absolute dependence.* German philosopher and theologian Rudolf Otto (1869-1937), in his book *Idea of the Holy* (1923), discusses the essence of religious awareness as awe, a mixture of fear and fascination—a *mysterium tremendum et fascinans.*

Professor of psychology and theology James Ashbrook, writing with professor of religion and science Carol Rausch Albright specifically from the Christian perspective in their book *The Humanizing Brain* (1997), expands on how various brain processes and behaviors are associated with religious and spiritual phenomena. *Whatever Happened to the Soul? Theological and Scientific Perspectives on Human Nature* (1998), edited by cognitive psychologist Warren Brown, professor of Christian philosophy Nancey Murphy, and professor of psychology H. Newton Malony, proposes a non-dualist, nonreductive physicalist explanation of the human person. With scholars in contemporary biology, genetics, cognitive science, philosophy, theology, ethics, and biblical studies, the book seeks consonance between the sciences of human nature and Christian anthropology (Spezio, 2000).

Catholicity and assimilation

What about "catholicity" in Catholicism? The still-living-and-effective mandate of Pentecost is to extend the good news to all peoples, times, and places. The Church was first called "catholic" (Greek *kath'holou*), "whole" or "universal" by Ignatius of Antioch in AD 115. The term was helpful over succeeding centuries in distinguishing the true/whole church from separated groups (Greek *hairein*, "take" or "choose" a part for the whole) and "heresy," meaning sectarian (Rausch, 1998, p. 26). "Catholicity" today is more complex and nuanced than it may seem at first. As Vatican II's *Lumen Gentium,* 13, states:

> In virtue of catholicity, the whole and each of the parts are strengthened by common sharing and by the common effort to achieve fullness in unity. The people of God is not only an assembly of different peoples, but there is diversity among its members. Some exercise the sacred ministry, those in the religious state stimulate others to sanctity by their example, and particular churches retain their legitimate variety of traditions and contribute to unity ([abridged] Galliardetz and Clifford, 2012, p. 129)

The Holy Spirit makes variation non-contentious. Pope Paul VI's Vatican II decree *Orientalium Ecclesiarum* (1964) recognized the theological significance of Eastern churches in the Roman Catholic communion. The Church supports whatever is good in human abilities, resources, and customs (*LG* 13, in Abbot, 1966). While evangelization historically followed European colonization, inculturation today has taken on new significance. The current expansion of Catholicism in the global South may be seen as "the most rapid and sweeping demographic transformation of Catholicism in its 2,000-year history" (cf. "Ten mega-trends shaping the Catholic church," *All things Catholic*, 2006, in Gailliardetz and Clifford, 2012, p. 136-137).

Inculturation means ecclesial permission for the Christian faith to find varied cultural expressions (John Paul II, *Catechesi Tradendae*, 1979, 53). Synodal governance goes back to the 1965 institution of the Synod of Bishops. Pope Francis, particularly with the Synod on Synodality (October 2021—October 2024), encouraged synodal consultation: "The world in which we live demands that the Church strengthen cooperation in all areas of her mission. It is this path of synodality which God expects of the Church, journeying together—laity, pastors, the Bishop of Rome" (*Ecumenical Review*, 2022, p. 3).

The Catholic Church acknowledges that being "catholic" is not equivalent to being "Roman Catholic." All Catholics must aim at Christian perfection. Falling short in terms of holiness and divisions among Christians prevent the Church from attaining complete catholicity. The Church represents both a sign of full catholicity and, unfortunately, a lack of sanctity to varying degrees. Outside the limits of Roman Catholicism are persons whose lives exemplify the gospel, even to martyrdom. Catholicity means that the Church's universal mission extends to all. "God's mercy and goodness are boundless for all creation. God's mind and energy are truly Catholic" (*Ecumenical Review*, 2022, p. 10).

> Catholicity includes a wide variety of theologies, spiritualities, and expressions of Christian life. It is pluralistic and follows a "both/and" rather than (Protestant) "either/or" approach. Not Scripture alone, but Scripture *and* tradition; not grace alone, but grace *and* nature; not faith alone, but faith *and* works. (Rasch, 1998, p. 26)

Catholicity refers to comprehensiveness. It is inclusive and erects a "big tent."

In the early Church, a major distinction between Christianity and the surrounding religions was that it claimed one origin for the revelation on which it was founded: "God, who at sundry times and diverse manners spoke in times past to the fathers by the prophets, in these last days has spoken to us by his Son" (Hb 1:1-2). The one Mediator had come to fulfill the prophecies. The Apostles alone guarded and passed on the sacred Message that was to "succeed in purifying, assimilating, transmuting, and taking into itself the many-colored beliefs, forms of worship, codes of duty, schools of thought, through which it was ever moving. It was Grace and Truth" (Newman, 1845, in Newman Reader, 2023, p. 2).

British theologian and philosopher Cardinal John Henry Newman (1801-1890), in his *Essay on the Development of Christian Doctrine* (1845), observed that doctrinal development can and has assimilated non-Christian philosophical concepts, customs, or rites, transforming them rather than the doctrine. The early Church, for example, integrated Greek philosophical categories and terms for doctrinal precision. "The more powerful, independent, and vigorous the idea, the greater its power to assimilate external ideas without losing its identity" (Murphy, 2023, p. 4).

Catholicism considers the human mind deferential to revealed truth and adherent to doctrinal faith. Truth founded in revelation is not a matter of opinion. The various sects had elements of truth, but Councils and Popes had to protect the dogmatic principle, carefully taking new true strands of thought into an existing body of belief. Over the centuries, this process enabled the creed to absorb and develop without distortion (Newman, 1845, in Newman Reader, 2023, p. 7).

Newman's plan for a university was to develop synthesizing minds that could distinguish essential specific expressions—in this case, what is essential to Catholic doctrine—from specific, changeable cultural instantiations. "Catholicism understands knowledge gained through the human sciences (natural revelation) to be consonant with and a component of supernatural revelation" (Kirsch, 2023, p. 33).

The catholicity/assimilating principle of the Church may be taken as a "method" for this study of the intersection of neuroscience with Catholic theology. Whatever is true in neuroscientific studies may be incorporated into Catholic catholicity. Where epistemological divergencies prevent integration, dialogue is welcomed for the reciprocal benefit of the two fields.

Neurotheology and definitions

We have already touched on several important concepts, such as mind, brain, consciousness, soul, spiritual, and religious, without defining what we mean by them. When we discuss terms that are challenging, rich, complex, and multi-layered and can be understood from a variety of perspectives—terms like soul, consciousness, person, mind, and self—we plan to define them initially as well as possible, then to discuss them cyclically, showing new dimensions as they arise within various chapter topics. Each of these terms can be approached from a variety of viewpoints. The first chapter of *Principles of Neurotheology* emphasizes the importance of definitions and the challenges therein. For example, we must consider where definitions come from. Should they come from the scientific or theological disciplines? Or should they come from a highly integrated approach that includes sociology, anthropology, and philosophy as well? Clearly, there will be differences in the way definitions are constructed depending on the definition's discipline of origin. Some terms are perhaps more appropriately defined from one perspective or another. *Soul* is perhaps better defined from the theological perspective, while *brain* would be from the neuroscience perspective. But what about terms such as *mind* or *consciousness*? These could be approached from either side. Hence, any definition is perhaps advised to include as many perspectives as possible. In the context of Catholicism, it is essential to consider some of the sacred texts and theological writings through the ages when it comes to complex terms such as *soul* or *mind*.

It is also important to note that whatever definitions we start with, we should expect there to be a dynamic process by which they evolve over time and as new data and concepts are brought to bear on them. Our approach will be cyclical: beginning with basic definitions of terms and seeing them from additional angles as they recur in the context of further topics. Regarding prayer, for example, if someday there is an experiment that finds prayer to activate important emotional areas of the brain, we will have to consider what prayer is and how it works. We might define prayer as a more emotional rather than cognitive process in this example. In the meantime, we need to keep an open mind regarding all these definitions and any future information that might suggest a modification. Throughout this book, we will utilize definitions based on extant philosophy and theology, but we will also encourage a broader exploration of all definitions to include various scientific perspectives.

The final point about definitions, for the moment, is that neurotheology would challenge us to explore how the brain itself functions to engage these definitions. In other words, are there some people who are more likely to seek spiritually based definitions while others are more likely to seek scientifically based definitions? And if so, what does this mean about the nature of the definitions themselves? We would hope that, at some point, the goal of neurotheology would be to help guide research and scholarship toward more accurate and universal definitions for these many complex concepts.

What would be a compelling reason to read this book? Pope Francis reflects on the importance of understanding basic terms like *body, mind,* and *soul,* which have long been fundamental to a Catholic Christian view of reality and the human person. We need to understand well the meaning of these and similar terms, as well as brain structure and functions for philosophy and theology, as well as science. A basic understanding of philosophy, theology, and neuroscience and how they interrelate can help persons of faith to interpret neuroscientific findings without uncertainty or confusion. Persons who identify as agnostic or atheist might better understand how neuroscientific results could impact their religious friends and associates.

Pope Francis writes:

> *Body, mind, and soul.* Thanks to interdisciplinary studies, we can come to appreciate better the dynamics involved in relationships among our physical condition, our psycho-physical well-being, and our spiritual life. Progress in medical-sciences research has also raised a number of anthropological and ethical issues. The dimension of the *mind* makes self-understanding possible. Our humanity even tends to be identified with the brain and neurological processes, although these do not explain all that defines us as humans. We cannot possess a mind without cerebral matter, yet the mind cannot be reduced to the mere materiality of the brain. Thanks to recent natural and human sciences, the relationship between material and nonmaterial dimensions of our being—the mind-body question, for centuries the domain of philosophers and theologians—is now of interest regarding the mind-brain relationship.
>
> In a scientific context, the term *mind* needs to be understood in an interdisciplinary way. *Mind* generally indicates a reality ontologically distinct from, yet interacting with, our biological substratum. *The mind* usually indicates the entirety of the human faculties, particularly regarding thought. There is question about the origin of human faculties like moral sensitivity, meekness, compassion, empathy, solidarity, philanthropic gestures, the aesthetic sense, and the search for the infinite and the transcendent.
>
> In the Judeo-Christian, as well as the Greek philosophical tradition, these human traits associate with the transcendent, immaterial dimension of the human person, our *soul.* The soul is understood to be the principle organizing the body and origin of our intellectual, affective, and volitional qualities, including moral conscience. Scripture and philosophical and theological reflection consider the *soul* to define our human uniqueness, including our openness to the supernatural and to God. This openness to the transcendent testifies to the infinite worth of each human person (Video message, Fifth International Conference: *Exploring Mind, Body, and Soul,* 2021, adapted).

Why Catholic neurotheology?

Given the broader perspective of neurotheology and its goal of understanding the relationship between religion and the brain, the next important step is to begin to apply neurotheological approaches to individual religious traditions. Catholicism is a particularly fruitful target because of its rich development in terms of its practices, rituals, beliefs, and theological perspectives. These highly developed elements of Catholicism lend themselves exceptionally well to neurotheology.

We will explore the many fascinating ways in which neurotheology may benefit from a treatment of Catholicism and vice versa. There are also some personal reasons for this exploration. While Andrew Newberg is not Catholic, his mentor in neurotheology, the late Eugene d'Aquili, was and introduced him to many of the complex and captivating rituals associated with Catholicism. d'Aquili was a devout Catholic throughout his life. This included participation in Mass throughout the liturgical year, particularly with the heightened pageantry of the Christmas and Easter seasons. It should be further noted that d'Aquili's family were nobility in Rome, and his family were administrators of an abbey such that he was able to trace records of his family's activities to approximately 750 A.D. Much of his early work was focused on the tenets of Christianity, and Catholicism in particular.

Sr. Mary Clare is a Catholic religious and counseling psychologist with a graduate degree in religious education. Contributing to this study in neurotheology was a Transfigured Brain course at St. Mary Seminary and Graduate School of Theology, Cleveland, that was offered from 2017 to 2021. The course was funded by a Templeton Science in Seminaries grant for courses across the United States incorporating science in seminary curricula. Andrew Newberg was a featured teleconference presenter for the course taught by Rev. Michael Woost[2] and the late Edward Kaczuk. This book also explores other topics related to neurotheology from a Christian perspective, including some work of Patrick McNamara, professor of psychology at Northcentral University and of neurology at Boston University, and Patricia Bennet, scholar at the Iona Community in Scotland. Bennet proposes a locus for neurotheological exploration in linking "the experience of human relationality and health outcomes, . . . to bring together various neurobiological and theological perspectives on human relationality and health as a way of expanding understanding of the connection between them" (2019c, p. 103). She proposes "a model for a possible pathway connecting relational experience and health via immune signaling mechanisms" (p. 104).

Essential to this study was the invaluable help of consultants: Rev. Gerald Bednar, professor of systematic theology for 31 years at St. Mary Seminary and Graduate School of Theology, Cleveland; James Beauregard, neuropsychologist, author (2019, 2023), and professor at Rivier University, Nashua, New Hampshire; Rev. Stephen Payne, OCD, author, professor, and president of the Carmelite Institute of North America at the Catholic University of America, Washington, DC; Rev. Juan José Sanguineti, author and professor emeritus of philosophy, Pontifical University of the Holy Cross, Rome, and professor of philosophy at the Austral University, Buenos Aires, Argentina; Margarita Vega, professor of philosophy at the Dominican School of Philosophy and Theology, Berkeley, California; and Joel Johnson, professor of philosophy at John Carroll University and Borromeo Seminary College, Cleveland.

Given these historical, personal, and professional backgrounds, the exploration of Catholic neurotheology seems most appropriate. With this in mind, we plan to explore the wide range of topics associated with Catholicism, from its rituals and practices to its beliefs and theological principles.

Overview

With regard to the overall approach we take in this book, we will develop and explore many ideas associated with Catholicism and consider how the rituals, practices, experiences, and beliefs associated with the tradition may be related to the brain. Chapter One (Introduction to Catholic Neurotheology) considers broadly some of the ways that Catholicism and science can interrelate. It introduces the potential field of neurotheology, particularly from a Catholic perspective. There is an overview of the chapters and book.

Chapter Two (Neurotheological Investigations in Catholic Thought) reflects on the human person as the focus of science and theology, the goals of neurotheology, and the necessary attitude of humility. It explains a hylomorphic understanding of human mind-body unity. There is a review of neural physiology and a Catholic view of the soul, consciousness, and the spiritual person. Therapies to enhance well-being are briefly considered.

Chapter Three (Epistemological Considerations and Faith) orients neurotheology to metaphysics and again considers basic terms, particularly *mind*. Epistemology is presented through Maritain's theistic realism and Lonergan's levels of consciousness, offered as two examples of possible ways to sort through some contemporary challenges of neuroscience in its dialogue with Catholicism. Among current cognitive science theories is the notion that cognition can be described with 4Es: embodied, embedded, enactive, and extended. Theology is considered as it relates to the human mind, grace, and spiritual experience.

Chapter Four (Methodology in Neuroscience and Catholicism) looks at paradigms and methods in science and religion and the challenges of measuring subjective experience and imaging the brain. *The soul* is again focal, now as it relates to neuroscientific methodology.

Chapter Five (Free Will and the Brain) defines free will in view of Catholicism, distinguishing the domains of philosophy and neuroscience. Morality, responsibility, and virtue are related to neurotheology.

Chapter Six (The Body's Response to Religious Experience) discusses physiological/neural response to religious experience, health outcomes associated with religious practice, and mechanisms for assessing effects, all primarily from a Catholic perspective.

Chapter Seven (Neurophysiology of Catholic Rituals) offers a synopsis of Catholic sacramental theology and reviews *the matter and form* of the sacraments of Baptism, Confirmation, Eucharist, Reconciliation, Anointing of the Sick, Holy Orders, and Matrimony. Neural areas and networks are associated with the sensory, linguistic, and decisional elements of the sacraments.

Chapter Eight (Neurophysiology of Catholic Practices) considers the neural correlates and brain functioning for Catholic prayer and practices, including Liturgy of the Hours, Scripture reading, meditation, Benediction, sacramentals, relics, and pilgrimages.

Chapter Nine (Psychology and Catholicism) discusses relationships between psychology and neuroscience regarding disorders and spirituality/religiousness. Psychology is seen from a Catholic perspective on philosophical anthropology and theology, particularly regarding the human relationship with God.

Chapter Ten (Spirituality from a Neurotheological Perspective) studies spirituality from a neurotheological perspective and explores spirituality's potential for providing a bridge for science-theology dialogue. The focus is on self-transcendent experience, interpersonal neurobiology, and theological dimensions. There is a review of principal Catholic spiritualities.

Chapter Eleven (Mysticism, the Brain, and Catholicism) defines and describes mysticism specifically from the Catholic perspective, the neurophysiology of mystical states, connaturality, and the experience of grace with neuroscientific considerations.

Chapter Twelve (Theological Implications) looks at revelation and its relation to neurobiology, a Catholic view of the soul, and Catholic neurobiological ethics regarding moral reasoning, exemplars, brain death, and resurrection.

Chapter Thirteen (Grace, Holiness, Soul, and the Brain) considers the universal call to holiness, grace, connaturality and attunement, second-person perspective, and growth in holiness.

Chapter Fourteen (Critiques, Clarifications, and Future Directions) revisits principal critiques of the evolving potential field of neurotheology regarding its theoretical assumptions. Some current possibilities for course correction are described. Challenges for attempting to integrate neuroscience and theology are reviewed. Promising theoretical possibilities such as coordinated pluralism and transversal spaces are considered. Suggestions for developing graduate scholars in neurotheology are considered.

We hope that such a treatment of neurotheology will be beneficial to its development as a scholarly field while also attending to our understanding of the Catholic faith. As with all neurotheological explorations, the goal is to help better determine how the various elements of a religious tradition like Catholicism can be more deeply understood with new knowledge currently available about the human brain. We similarly hope that scientific investigations, particularly of religious phenomena, including religious experience, will also benefit from the interaction as we explore neuroscience as it relates to Catholicism.

The Catechism of the Catholic Church (*CCC*, 1995) is structured on the four pillars of catechesis or handing on the faith: *CCC* Part 1: the creed; Part II, the sacraments; Part III, the life of faith; and Part IV, prayer.

Part I reflects philosophically and theologically on the human person, integrating insights and methods of neuroscience. Broadly, it would be possible to relate *CCC* Part I (the creed) with Chapters One (Introduction to Catholic Neurotheology), Two (Neurotheological Investigations in Catholic Thought), and Three (Epistemology).

CCC Part II (the sacraments) corresponds with Chapters Seven (Neurophysiology of Catholic Rituals) and Eight (Neurophysiology of Catholic Practices) on the seven sacraments, devotional practices, and sacramentals.

CCC Part III (commandments and beatitudes) associates with Chapters Five (Free Will and the Brain), Six (The Body's Response to Religious Experience), and Nine (Psychology and Catholicism).

CCC Part IV (prayer) might be said to correspond with Chapters Ten (Spirituality from a Neurotheological Perspective), Eleven (Mysticism), Twelve (Theological Implications), and Thirteen (Holiness, Grace, Soul, and the Brain). Chapter Fourteen (Critiques, Clarifications, and Future Directions) may be said to draw from the *CCC* generally, on the dialogue between neuroscience and Catholic theology that is Catholic neurotheology.

Study questions:

1. How did Popes John Paul II and Benedict XVI see the relationship between Catholic faith and science?

2. Which of Barbour's science and religion relationships (conflict, independence, dialogue, or integration) do you think best characterizes the interaction of neuroscience with Catholicism?

3. Why are terms like *mind, brain,* and *soul* crucial in a field like neurotheology?

Endnotes

[1] The seven rites are: "Latin, Byzantine, Alexandrian or Coptic, Syriac, Armenian, Maronite, and Chaldean. (All Catholic rites) are of equal right and dignity" (*Sacrosanctum Concilium* [*SC*] 4) and validly express the common faith (*CCC*, 1203). Attendance at any rite fulfills the Sunday obligation.

[2] Rev. Michael Woost is now Bishop.

Chapter 2

Neurotheological Investigations in Catholic Thought

Science and theology with respect to being human

Neurotheology represents a fascinating nexus for dialogue between science and theology. By this, we mean that neurotheology represents the potential for finding productive ways of enabling the Catholic Church to interact with science that is ultimately beneficial to both. Neuroscience, and more specifically neurotheology, is an approach that can enable Catholicism to maintain the strength of its philosophical, theological, and spiritual perspective while still finding value in the biological dimension regarding religious beliefs, experiences, and practices. Of course, at present, neurotheology is not yet a fully defined discipline with generally accepted positions and approaches. The views expressed here are mine (ABN) about possibilities for this potential field. For the dialogue between neurotheology and Catholicism, since both neuroscience and the Church focus on "what it means to be human," this would be a good place to start.

The history of philosophy and theology frequently considers the constituents of the *human person*. The physical or biological part of the human person typically refers to the blood, organs, and sinews of the body that hold our physical being together, plus the sensory dimensions of sight, hearing, touch, taste, and smell. And, of course, the biological aspect of the human person includes the brain with its billions of neurons and quadrillions of interconnections that, at least from a scientific perspective, are the physiological source of human imagining, interior senses, emotions, desires, and memories.

The chariot allegory of Greek philosopher Plato (428—348 BCE) in the *Phaedrus* provides a metaphor important to the Western philosophical and spiritual tradition. Ancient even in his time, possibly from Egypt or Mesopotamia, the myth that Plato reworked portrays a charioteer, representing reason or intellect, the aspect of the soul that guides the soul to truth and drives two winged horses to celestial heights. One horse is white—spirited, bold, irascible—representing the positive, rational, moral inclination of human nature. The black horse—appetitive, desiring, concupiscible—represents the soul's irrational passions. According to Socrates, chariot processions in heaven are led by Zeus. The white horse tries to ascend, and the dark horse pulls the chariot back to earth. Immortal souls that are successful come close to seeing divine reality and grow in wisdom and goodness. Other souls are unable to rise and, in discordant striving, do not achieve a glimpse of eternal reality. The chariot falls to earth, the horses lose their wings, and the soul is embodied in human flesh. Souls that have seen more truth will be born as a philosopher or artist; those that have seen less truth will be less favored. Those who have not seen the truth at all will not pass into the human form (Jowett, n.d.).

Platonic philosophy provided a foundation for the Christian mystical tradition. The Church Fathers introduced a distinct new trajectory based on the Genesis account of creation *ex nihilo*, on the Incarnation, Scripture, liturgy, and graced relationship with God (Louth, 2007, in Howells, 2002, p. 322).

Thomas Aquinas (1224-1274), the Italian Dominican philosopher and theologian whose doctrinal system and developments by his followers are known as Thomism, called the biological side the *actus hominus*. This was distinguished from the *actus humanus* with our human qualities, such as language, thought, and decision-making. Both sides unite us in a single human person. With René Descartes (1596-1650), French philosopher and scientist, seminal in the emergence of modern philosophy and science, there was a clear separation between the body and soul, or body and mind. Today, neuroscience tends to hold a materialistic view of the brain, that everything is finally reducible to the physical. This preserves the validity of the scientific method and empirical experimentation in studying human beings. However, if consciousness and the mind are completely reducible to the biological functions of the brain, the psychological and spiritual dimensions of a person nearly evaporate. There are numerous theories about ways that the body and mind interrelate. There is the dualistic perspective that the body is a material substance and the mind is a separate immaterial one. Some current scholars argue that consciousness and the mind are emergent properties that require the biological processes of the brain but are not simply reducible to them.

Neurotheology takes an open stance to these different possibilities, given the present state of science and analysis. For this study of the way that Catholicism relates to neuroscience, materialistic reductionism is problematic. Neurotheology encourages full exploration of the spiritual and psychological dimensions of the person. In the pages that follow, we intend to do this. We will explore an integrated approach to the person, considering the biological, psychological, and spiritual dimensions as all contributing to who we are as human beings. We also acknowledge that how we assess the relative importance of each of these dimensions may depend on our understanding of the way things are, our philosophical and religious convictions, or our background and interests. If you are a deeply religious individual, the spiritual realm is likely to seem most important. If you are a scientist, you might consider the biological dimension most important. If you are a psychologist, emotions, desires, personality, thoughts, and behaviors might be your principal interests.

These different perspectives might be incompatible and present a challenge for neurotheology. Several possible hybrid approaches might be considered. Neurotheology would ask us to explore the possible, reasonable options that are available and use a combination of neuroscientific as well as philosophical and theological approaches to understanding them. Since this current study focuses on Catholicism, we try to present clearly and cogently a philosophical understanding of the human person that is compatible with Catholic belief and practice. We would argue that neurotheology should attempt to be consistent with Catholicism in considering the various dimensions of the human being, including the notion of the soul or, as Aquinas would argue, the *actus humanus*.

Goals of neurotheology

As neurotheology develops as a field, several overarching goals have been previously described, derived in large part from the primary principles of neurotheology elaborated in the book of the same title (Newberg, 2010). These principles cover definitional, methodological, clinical, and conceptual elements of the field. Furthermore, neurotheology encompasses other fields, such as psychology, anthropology, and sociology, and encounters specific religions, such as Catholicism, philosophy, and theology. Some aspects of the goals will pertain more to the fields secondarily associated with neurotheology. We should also note that the goals stated here are based on a current analysis of the field. They are likely to be modified in the future to meet objectives yet to be discovered, especially as neurotheology develops in dialogue with experts in contributing fields.

The four foundational goals for scholarship in neurotheology are (Newberg, 2010):

1. To improve/advance our understanding of the human mind and brain.
2. To improve/advance our understanding of religion and theology.
3. To improve/advance the human condition, particularly in the context of health and well-being.
4. To improve/advance the human condition, particularly in the context of religion and spirituality.

The first two goals we would consider to be both esoteric and pragmatic regarding scientific and theological disciplines. The second two goals refer to the importance of providing practical applications of neurotheological findings toward improving human life. For Goals Two and Four, it is crucial to be clear that they do not suggest an underlying assumption that theology will ultimately be subsumed under neuroscience. It is recognized that theology's goals are ultimate, overarching, metaphysical, spiritual, and derived from revelation, not simply pragmatic or utilitarian or intended to improve/advance the human condition, although that would be included. Further, in the dialogue with theology, these goals are likely to be revised to incorporate the more comprehensive, existential, revelation-derived goals of theology beyond the bounds of neuroscience.

The first goal (to improve/advance our understanding of the human mind and brain) is scientifically oriented. It indicates the possibility that neurotheology can aid substantially in the exploration of the mind, brain, and consciousness. This includes the importance of utilizing an approach combining science and religion to help ascertain the most accurate definitions of critical terms such as mind, brain, consciousness, soul, spirituality, religion, and other terms that pertain to this area of study. Definitions may come from sources including scientific, psychological, philosophical, theological, sociological, and other fields. For example, the term *mind* might be explored from the neuroscientific perspective as mental processes that relate to the brain. *Mind* and *consciousness* can be debated from various philosophical perspectives. The term *mind* in traditions such as Buddhism or Hinduism can be different still. Neurotheology will hopefully be able to help sort through these definitions and contribute relevant scientific and spiritual perspectives on many of these terms.

This first goal also encourages the development of new or improved techniques for the scientific study of the mind and brain. The development of such techniques, specifically in the study of religious and spiritual phenomena, will undoubtedly be a cornerstone for neurotheology in the future. And neurotheological research can potentially improve upon current methods in cognitive neuroscience. Religious, spiritual, and mystical phenomena are notoriously difficult to evaluate from any scientific perspective. Since some aspects impinge upon and may be expressed neurophysiologically, reworking neuroscientific methodology will hopefully lead to a better overall understanding of such neurobiological manifestations. Psychology has, in recent decades, developed a plethora of assessments regarding spiritual and religious dimensions of human experience. Theology will undoubtedly affirm that grace cannot be measured. It is understood that authentic apophatic and kataphatic mystical experiences, at their core, will have to be respectfully allowed to remain in the realm of mystery.

In addition to improving cognitive neuroscience, neurotheology can help develop new perspectives regarding the human mind itself. Current research studies frequently explore morality, love, compassion, and various complex behaviors (Lee and Newberg, 2005).[1] Neurotheology, with its analysis of religious and spiritual phenomena, will advance our understanding of these complex brain processes. Religion and spirituality have tremendous effects on behavioral, sensory, emotional, and cognitive processes within individuals, communities, and society. Furthermore, evaluating how the brain and mind consider profound philosophical ideas such as causality, teleology, and epistemology could be essential for understanding how human beings understand and explore the world.

The second goal (to improve/advance our understanding of religion and theology) is intriguing since the implication is that theology has something to gain in interacting with cognitive neuroscientific research. This does not in any way reduce or eliminate the true theological nature of discussion but helps us frame the ways in which the human brain can engage in such a discussion. For example, while theology proceeds from foundational tenets of a given religious tradition, and these tenets are believed to come from God or some absolute reality, the human mind must acknowledge its limits and accept in faith what it will never fully comprehend. Neurotheology can help explore how the human person, acknowledging their intellectual inadequacies, attempts to understand theological ideas. In other words, we might ask how we use our thoughts, feelings, or experiences when debating the meaning of a particular passage in the Bible or the relevance of a specific story about Jesus' life or actions.

The third goal of neurotheology (to improve/advance the human condition, particularly in the context of health and well-being) would encourage people to invoke religious and spiritual beliefs or practices to meet practical needs. Specifically, neurotheological studies might assess which practices—meditation or prayer—are most useful for helping combat depression or anxiety. Neurotheology would encourage exploring therapeutic interventions that combine current psychological approaches with religious and spiritual content to enhance the effectiveness of treatment for patients. Practically, we might also wonder how religion and spirituality can contribute to better health and well-being. It should be noted that this goal derives from the first in that improving our understanding of the relationship between religion and the mind should ultimately yield information that will have practical applications. For example, there is strong and expanding research literature regarding the potentially beneficial relationship between religion and both physical and mental health (Lucchetti, Koenig, and Lucchetti, 2021; Roberts, 2019; Koenig, 2012). Studies have shown that religion might contribute to improved physical health by reducing stress, helping with coping, and improving compliance with medical interventions. Studies have also shown that specific practices such as meditation or prayer can have important health-related effects on the cardiovascular system, digestive system, and immune system.

Neurotheological research might also identify potentially negative consequences of religious and spiritual beliefs, such as times when people feel that God is punishing them or when they reject God. Another area that would lend itself well to neurotheological study is the problem of terrorism and fundamentalism, which leads to destructive behaviors such as killing others in the name of God. It is not clear what goes on in the minds or brains of individuals who end up following extreme religious or spiritual views.[2] Neurotheological research can thoroughly evaluate which type of individual is most likely to follow such a path and perhaps offer methods for appropriately redirecting them.

The fourth foundational goal (to improve/advance the human condition, particularly in the context of religion and spirituality) suggests that through neurotheology, it might be possible to guide augmenting religious and spiritual beliefs, practices, and behaviors for both individuals and groups. Neurotheological research might find practical applications to enhance the ways in which individuals pursue their spiritual objectives. While it is not clear precisely how such a goal might be achieved, it could be argued that whenever there is improved knowledge, especially if a new perspective is offered, there is an opportunity for growth. We would argue that "In the context of theology and religion, spiritual growth is always encouraged, and neurotheology should be supported as another mechanism by which such growth might occur" (Newberg, 2010).

Humility and discovery

While neurotheology argues for taking an integrative approach to the person, it makes a similar argument for a variety of topics that can be accessible to both neuroscience and theology. These can include challenging topics such as the existence of a soul, the nature of free will, and even the existence of God.

To address these from an integrative approach, it is essential to engage all these acts of discovery with a strong sense of humility. Ideally, humility derives from both scientific and religious viewpoints. While both science and religion may harbor strong beliefs about the nature of reality, they must engage these topics with some degree of openness. Even if certain topics cannot be reconsidered, that does not mean that the entire enterprise is without merit. Neurotheology can find many avenues to explore the relationship between the brain and our religious and spiritual selves.

It is also important for neurotheology to sometimes consider topics from a "meta-level" perspective sometimes. By this, we mean that neurotheology can first engage a topic such as humility psychologically to try to understand what character traits contribute to a sense of humility as well as a lack thereof. Then, we might find that certain brain processes contribute to a sense of humility and other processes that contribute to a sense of certainty that might seem to care little for humility when engaging someone with a different point of view. Similarly, there may be other brain processes that lead people to be open and tolerant of alternate perspectives.

There has been research on the character trait of humility (e.g., Tangney, 2009, 2011; Exline and Geyer, 2011). Generally, it is associated with a sense of being secure in oneself without arrogance. It is associated with an openness to other ideas. And perhaps most important, it is associated with a non-reactive approach to alternative ideas. By this latter point, we mean that when a person approaches a new idea with humility, they are not likely to have a strong fear reaction (usually mediated by the autonomic nervous system's fight or flight response). It is not just about other ideas, but rather, how one feels about their ideas. To be humble means that you do not hold your own beliefs to the exclusion of openness because, for scientific ideas, you recognize that you might be wrong.

For faith-based beliefs, as in Catholicism, since they derive from divine revelation rather than human judgment, we would be certain that our beliefs themselves are true but acknowledge that there may be some aspects of them that we do not yet fully understand. "Humility involves the full knowledge of our status as creatures, a clear consciousness of having received everything we have from God" (von Hildebrand, 2001). As we will consider in more detail, the Catholic Church holds that faith and science will not ultimately be at odds. Since God is the Truth and the Author of both creation and revelation, science and faith will finally coincide and complement each other. New ideas or proven scientific discoveries might need to be integrated into current beliefs and our understanding expanded.

It is interesting to note, from a psychological perspective, that an overreaction to the possibility of being wrong might lead to or derive from depression and negativity. Humility is different. It asks about current beliefs in a positive, growth-oriented way. A theological perspective acknowledges with humility that humans will not fully comprehend either the divine Revealer or revealed faith-based beliefs.

Neural substrates for the character trait of novelty-seeking might contribute to keeping reactivity at a minimum, which could lead to humility. As we will consider throughout this book, a neurological perspective extends beyond biological brain structure to chemical functioning in specific neurotransmitter molecules. Some neurotransmitters turn on certain neurons, while others turn them down or off. One might speculate that humility is derived from a brain that keeps neuronal function at lower, better-regulated levels rather than higher, reactive ones. People might inherit a proclivity to character traits that support humility or develop that quality with contributions from both nature and nurture. Such hypotheses would be testable using a variety of intriguing psychological or neuroimaging techniques. Of course, Catholicism would note with Thomas Aquinas that "grace does not destroy nature, but perfects it" (*ST* I, 1. 8 ad 2) and that humility, as well as any virtue, derives primarily from grace, from God rather than oneself. The question would be how this religious perspective might or might not correspond to anything we might learn from a neurological perspective. Such an approach and result would be the type of goal that can arise from a neurotheological perspective.

In the end, humility is essential for both science and religion. Scientists must always regard their data and theories as making the best possible conclusion, given their current evidence-based understanding of the nature of reality. In fact, every scientific discovery or theory might in the future be replaced should new data or new theories emerge. In the medical field 200 years ago, it was believed that bleeding people would benefit their health. Today, we laugh at that concept. One cannot help but wonder whether treatments such as radiation or chemotherapy will be viewed similarly 200 years from now. In cosmology, 200 years ago, the universe was believed to be static, and today, we understand the universe to be expanding. Who knows what cosmologists may comprehend 200 years from now?

Religions, too, have changed over time. The Christian religion, several hundred years after Christ walked the Earth, was different in some ways from medieval Catholicism and today. The "deposit of faith" remains the same. Still, some doctrines can develop into something more mature and more complete in the context of changes in culture, science, and technology over time (see *An Essay on the Development of Christian Doctrine* [1878] by important English theologian and intellectual John Henry Newman [1801-1890]). Furthermore, the Christianity of one thousand years ago did not have to deal with concepts such as evolution, the origin of the universe, or the contentious issue of abortion. In today's world, traditions such as Catholicism continually address the present day while maintaining a belief system that assists in mutually relating human beings and God.

While both science and religion require dispositions of humility, there are also contrasts between them regarding certainty in the knowledge of the truth. We have noted that science is open-ended, searching, hypothesizing, experimenting, judging, and determining the validity of its conclusions. Catholicism, grounded in revelation, provides for believers certitude in knowing religious truth and obliges to adherence of faith (*CCC*, 88). Pope John Paul II in *Veritatis Splendor* (*VS*) (1991) explains that truth, for example moral truth, can be known:

The *morality of acts* is defined by the relationship of man's freedom with the authentic good. This good is established by Divine Wisdom, which orders every being toward its end. This eternal law is known both by man's natural reason and—integrally and perfectly—by God's supernatural revelation. Activity is morally good when it expresses the voluntary ordering of the person to his ultimate end and the conformity of a concrete action with the human good as it is acknowledged in its truth by reason (*VS*, 72).

The Pope adds that:

In the context of today's prevalently scientific and technical culture, exposed as it is to the dangers of relativism, pragmatism, and positivism, from the theological viewpoint, the affirmation of moral principles is not within the competence of formal empirical methods. While not denying the validity of such methods, moral theology, faithful to the supernatural sense of the faith, takes into account, first and foremost, *the spiritual dimension of the human heart and its vocation to divine love.* In fact, while the behavioral sciences, like all experimental sciences, develop an empirical and statistical concept of 'normality,' faith teaches that normality itself is affected by sin. Only Christian faith points out to man a way that is often quite different from that of empirical normality. Hence, the behavioral sciences, despite the great value of the information they provide, cannot be considered decisive indications of moral norms. It is the Gospel that reveals the full truth about man and his moral journey. (*VS*, 112, adapted)

Given that science and some aspects of religion are perpetually in motion, humility seems the most appropriate course to take when addressing scientific and religious questions or topics. We hope that neurotheology can foster a powerful synergy of humility with science and religion. We do not pretend to have all the answers but hope to contribute to engaging these questions as openly as possible.

Body, mind, and soul

How does the brain relate to the person? And neuroscience to theology? To find an answer, we need first to consider the biblical view of the human person. Men and women are unique among creatures in being in "the image of God" (Gn 1:27), uniting in human nature spiritual and material dimensions, and established in friendship with God (*CCC*, 355). Being in the image of God, humans can know and love their Creator (*Gaudium et spes* [*GS*] 12.3). They are the only creatures "God willed for their own sake" (*GS* 24.3), and called to share through knowledge and love in God's own life (*CCC*, 356). With the dignity of a person, a man or woman is not something but someone equipped for self-knowledge and self-possession and able to unite in communion with other persons and by covenant with their Creator (*CCC*, 357). In the mystery of Christ, Word made flesh, the mystery of human beings is made clear (*CCC*, 359).

We also need to consider philosophy or metaphysics, the study of what is. To understand the human person, Catholic faith, and theology by preference, use Aristotle and Thomas Aquinas. Pope Leo XIII, in the encyclical *Aeterni patris* (On the Restoration of Christian Philosophy, 1879), reintroduced Thomism into Catholic education to bring faith and reason back into beneficial dialogue. Aristotelian Thomism explains the unity of body and mind as (Greek: *hyle* [matter] and *morphe* [form]) a hylomorphic explanation. Hylomorphism sees the person as a single being composed of two principles, not substances—matter and form. "Matter" here means "primary matter," not something, but the *possibility of being* something. A lump of clay, for example, might become a vase or a bowl by changing shape (accidental change), but it could not become something substantially different, like a cat. That would require a substantial change. If we had a cat and it died, the cat would have made a substantial change. "Form" means the principle *by which something is* what it is. Aristotle called the form of living plants and animals their "soul." Living things are composed of primary matter and soul or substantial form. A human individual, then, is a person, a single unified being composed of two principles: a material body and a living, substantial form or soul.

A substantial form determines that the single body-soul being will operate as an ontological whole with unity of being and action. This means that the parts of the person depend on the whole person for their existence and structure. As Aquinas explains:

> The substantial form perfects not only the whole but each part of the whole. The soul is a substantial form, and therefore, it must be the form and the act (actualization of its potency), not only of the whole but also of each part. (*De anima* 2.1.412b5, in Dodds, 2019, p. 905)

The soul explains not only the being but also its characteristic activities (Aquinas, *Summa contra gentiles* [*SCG*] III, ch. 7, no. 4; Wallace, 1985, *The Thomist 49*, 612-648).

We can see, then, why Thomistic philosophy is key to understanding the relations between brain, soul, and person. Thomistic philosophy also demonstrates how the study of the brain—neuroscience—relates to the philosophy of mind. Catholic theology, often employing Neo-Aristotelian Thomistic philosophy, begins with faith in divine revelation and seeks understanding. Thomistic philosophy shows that the brain is part of the person, one important physical aspect of the principle of the body. The brain would seem to be part of the person in a more fundamental sense than other body parts. You can amputate your foot and would still be the same person, not in the case of the brain. Neuroscience needs to consider philosophy to find its place in overall Thomistic metaphysics. When neuroscience links to theology, as in neurotheology, that field interacts with the Catholic faith, which responds to revelation seeking understanding of God and divine-human interaction.

Neuroscience, being empirical, cannot directly study a religious concept such as the soul. The soul is an ontological principle that cannot be quantified or measured. Neurotheology can study the soul, not directly, but by considering it through the lens of philosophy, which deals with ontological principles. In addition, neurotheology can evaluate how the brain helps us consider the soul.

To recall, the person for Aristotelian-Thomistic hylomorphism is comprised of both body and soul, a unity of the two principles of intellect and will. *Hylomorphism* refers to the unity of spiritual and material dimensions in a single person. The spiritual dimension, or *soul* for Thomistic philosophy, consists of a unity of intellect and will. Then what is *mind*, and where did the notion originate? Considering Western philosophy of mind broadly on this topic, *mind* comes from *De trinitate* of theologian and philosopher Augustine of Hippo (354-430). Looking for the *imago Dei* (image of God, Gn 1:26-27) in the human person, Augustine finds traces of the human image of the trinitarian God in three powers of the soul: memory, intellect, and will.

Aquinas' reflection on the soul begins by respecting the authority of Augustine, and Aquinas refers to the powers of the soul as memory, intellect, and will. In *Quaestiones disputate de veritate* (*QDV*) 10.1 ad 2), Aquinas notes that the *mind* denotes the powers of the soul (O'Callaghan, 2000). In *De veritate* 10, q. 22, Aquinas refers to the will and intellect as particular powers of the soul; in Article 11, he does not mention the mind. In Q 22, in response to objection seven, Aquinas writes that (the mind) is not a power *over and above* the other powers. It is simply a power of the soul. *Mind* properly speaking names a potential whole constituted by the powers of memory, intellect, and will ... while the *subject* of any power is the soul" (p. 6). Memory, intellect, and will might be thought of as three fingers of a hand; they can only function as parts of a hand. "The power of the *mind is* the powers of memory, intellect, and will; it is not a power over and above them" (p. 7). "Aquinas, in *De veritate*, distinguishes will from intellect and both from the sense powers. But he never tells us what it is that the mind does. Augustine's mind is absent from the *Summa*" (p. 9). If the mind were a distinct power, it would have a distinct object. Aquinas looked for a specific object of the mind and did not find one. He finally kept to two properties of the soul: intellect and will.

While a healthy degree of questioning has been part of philosophy since the ancient Greeks, in the seventeenth century, skepticism was more formally introduced into philosophy, with an emphasis on science rather than metaphysics. Descartes' *cogito ergo sum* ("I think, therefore I am") based certainty on psychology rather than metaphysics.

> The old dichotomies of body and soul now became a three-way contest between body, soul, and mind. Mind now existed somewhere between scientific discourse with its prerequisites of materialism, mechanization, and quantification and the metaphysical credos of immaterial human essence. (Krebs, 2016, p. 540)

Other influential thinkers in modern philosophy of the past three hundred years, including Enlightenment philosophers Hobbes, Locke, and Kant, and founder of neurology Willis, effected a "turn to the subject," promoting a scientific worldview (Krebs, 2016). Not sharing Descartes' focus on the human mind or consciousness, Aquinas presented the person philosophically and contributed to the unity of human life, clarifying that the soul unites two principles of intellect and will. Tensions from contending views of human nature still characterize the contemporary world (p. 542).

Recent Catholic philosophies

We might ask whether Catholicism embraces a philosophical approach other than Thomism. Phenomenology may be, after Thomism, Catholic philosophers' most popular philosophy (Vincelette, 2011, p. 14). Phenomenology describes the immediate data of experience of phenomena to find what is essential. Representative phenomenologists include Polish Jewish philosopher Edith Stein (1891-1942), author of *Individual and Community* (1922). Stein was a convert to Catholicism and a Carmelite saint martyred in World War II. German Catholic phenomenologist Deitrich von Hildebrand, author of *Christian Ethics* (1953), controverting moral relativism, was called by Pope Pius XII a "twentieth-century Doctor of the Church."

Existentialism, focusing on the concrete existence of the human being, stresses meaning in life and freedom to choose. Gabriel Marcel (1889-1973) was a French Catholic existentialist author of *The Mystery of Being*, two vols. (1949-1950). Marcel described inner life experiences phenomenologically. He observed that human life could be understood not by scientific problem-solving but through reflection on encounters with the mystery of the spiritual.

Analytical philosophy uses linguistic analysis to solve philosophical problems. Irish lay convert to Catholicism, Elizabeth Anscombe (1919-2001), author of *Intention* (1957) and *Modern Moral Philosophy* (1958), helped found the philosophy of action and contemporary virtue ethics. Canadian Catholic analytical philosopher Charles Taylor, author of *Sources of the Self* (1989) and *Varieties of Religion Today* (2003), developed the notion of human "epistemic gain" when one is able to articulate a cogent account of what they believe, particularly regarding moral agency and personal identity (Vincelette, 2011, p. 197).

Personalism may be represented by Maurice Nédoncelle (1905-1976), author of *Reciprocity of Consciousnesses* (1962) and *Toward a Philosophy of Love and the Person* (1946). Nédoncelle defined the person as a center of self-awareness and free will, a reciprocal benevolence received and afforded in knowledge and love. God is understood as a supreme personal consciousness that encompasses the human person as the Source and energy of charity.

Neo-Thomism, as we have seen, developed in the early twentieth century following Pope Leo XIII's *Aeterni Patris,* encouraging Catholic philosophers and theologians to model their work on Thomas Aquinas. The Congregation of Sacred Studies gave Catholic seminaries "Twenty-Four Thomistic Theses" (1914) as key to their education. Etienne Gilson (1884-1978) is the author of *The Spirit of Medieval Philosophy,* two vols. (1932) and *God and Philosophy* (1941), focused with Jacques Maritain on Thomist metaphysics from an existential perspective. They emphasized epistemology, opposing with "critical realism" Descartes and Kant's idealistic supposition that the subject is essentially imprisoned in their mind. Thomists held that the human subject can reliably know the external world of reality.

Neo-Thomist Jacques Maritain (1882-1973), author of *The Degrees of Knowledge* (1932) and *Approaches to God* (1953), understood Thomism to be a perennial philosophy that needed to develop by assimilating contemporary thought. Maritain observed that knowledge might be both natural (philosophy and science) and supernatural (faith and mysticism) (Vincelette, 2011, p. 60). Natural knowledge may also be connatural, an emotionally toned grasp or intuition through sympathy that is elicited by morality, poetry, understanding oneself, or spirituality. The person of faith may understand what they believe through supernatural connaturality grounded in charity.

Transcendental Thomism, founded by Jesuit Pierre Rousselot (1878-1915), was essentially Thomist but incorporated notions from modern philosophy, giving it a subjective, epistemological rather than objective metaphysical starting point. Transcendental Thomism takes as fundamental to the dynamic act of knowing that God is always present as infinite horizon. Some proponents (Bernard Lonergan) held that an at-least-implicit *desire* for an Absolute Being is an impetus for human knowing. Others (Karl Rahner) contended that humans attain knowledge because we have in every act of knowing the a priori apprehension of the Absolute Being. These approaches constitute an anthropomorphic principle in natural theology rather than the traditional cosmological one. Rather than seeking God as the originating cause of the universe, transcendental Thomists regard God as "the basic thrust of our intellect and will" (Joseph Donceel, *Logos* 1, 1980, p. 53, in Vincelette, 2011, p. 83).

Karl Rahner, S.J. (1904-1984), author of *Hearer of the Word* (1941) and *Spirit in the World* (1968), based his transcendental philosophy on the process of human knowing. He contended that in the perception of an object, the agent intellect by pre-apprehension (anticipation) extends beyond individual objects to being itself, the ultimate limit of potential objects with implicit awareness of the infinite dimension of reality. This permits humans to know the grasp of universal concepts and points to a propensity toward the infinitely True, Good, and Beautiful God.

Transcendental Thomist Bernard Lonergan, S.J. (1904-1984), author of *Insight: A Study in Human Understanding* (1957) and *Method in Theology* (1972), was influenced by epistemological notions of John Henry Newman. Lonergan developed cognitional dynamics of human knowing. As a Thomist, Lonergan showed that insights detect real qualities of data; they are not derived solely from the human mind but disclose the character of external reality. Lonergan showed that philosophy and science point to the need for theology's transcendent knowledge of ultimate realities. Supernatural faith perfects the search for truth, and grace perfects the desire to pursue moral rectitude.

Neo-Thomist Karol Wojtyla (1920-2005) integrated the Aristotelian-Thomist philosophy of being with Husserl's phenomenology of consciousness in his philosophy of the person and ethics. Wojtyla authored key philosophical works *Love and Responsibility* (1960) and *The Acting Person* (1969). Pope John Paul II, a canonized saint (2004), explained his natural-law moral views in philosophical encyclicals *The Splendor of Truth* (*Veritatis Splendor*, 1993) and *Faith and Reason* (*Fides et Ratio*, 1998). He observed that the transcendent dimension of the human person comprises self-consciousness and self-determination that renders each one unique, intrinsically valuable, and irreproducible.

Pope John Paul II steadfastly held to St. Thomas for metaphysics and theology: "He continues, in fact, to be the master of philosophical and theological universalism" (*Crossing the Threshold of Hope*, ed. Messori, p. 31). Still, studying phenomenology, Karol Wojtyla (the Pope's name prior to being John Paul II) appreciated its method for understanding subjectivity and lived experience. He recognized that consciousness, or subjectivity, "was a kind of synonym for the irreducible in the human being" (*Person and Community: Selected Essays*, trans. Sandok, p. 211). In his 1975 article "Subjectivity and the Irreducible in the Human Being," he observed that the categories of Aristotle and Aquinas (substance, quantity, quality, place, time, and so on) could explain but not fully capture human subjectivity. At the same time, the descriptive phenomenological method could not be regarded as a philosophy of the human person. The Pope considered that Thomistic metaphysics "supplies the worldview and phenomenology supplies a method which can supplement that view" (Flippen, 2006, p. 16).

"Even though the intuitive and descriptive approach of phenomenology remained subordinate to reasoning (in) metaphysics, consciousness had been uncovered by the modern approach, despite its often-erroneous views of the nature of man and reality" (Flippen, 2006, p. 18). John Paul II observed that traditional ancient and medieval thinkers might have explored consciousness more deeply with something like a phenomenological approach. He found no problem with incorporating insights regarding human subjectivity in an Aristotelian-Thomistic view of the human person.

A quick review of the brain

When it comes to the brain itself, it is worth reviewing important structures and functions so that we have a basic understanding for the remainder of the book. We should emphasize at the outset that the brain works as an integrated unit. While we may consider the function of specific structures in the brain, they all work together to give us our full perception of the world. In fact, recent cognitive neuroscience has focused on brain networks. These networks incorporate multiple areas of the brain that work together to support distinct functions. For example, there is an attention network that helps us to focus our minds on specific tasks or ideas. There is also a salience network that helps us to identify things that are important to us.

Let us take a moment to review essential areas of the brain involved in religious and spiritual phenomena, at least based on current research. As we review these areas, recall that each area has its basic functions that extend beyond the religious and spiritual. However, we are going to focus on those functions and processes that are specifically relevant to our discussion of religious and spiritual phenomena.

One way of understanding the neural structure of the brain is according to its three axes: (1) top-down and bottom-up, (2) front-back, and (3) left-right (Afford, 2020). First is the top-down and bottom-up neural architecture. The top is the cortex; the bottom is the assortment of structures, such as the hippocampus, amygdala, and brainstem, that make up the subcortex. Generally, the subcortex produces potential actions, and the cortex chooses among them for coherent behaviors. In the body itself, billions of neurons work their way up through the spinal cord and cranial nerves into the lower parts of the brain. These sensory nerves provide all sorts of information to the brain, including our body position and motion, sensations of pain, feelings of pleasure, and input from our primary sensory organs of the eyes, nose, ears, mouth, and tongue. Some of these nerve pathways reach the brain stem and basic core areas of the brain, such as the hypothalamus and thalamus. The brainstem contributes to basic body functions such as breathing and heart rate. The hypothalamus is also a major regulator of the body, controlling most hormone systems as well as the autonomic nervous system.

Second is the cortex's front-back axis. The back posterior lobes—parietal, temporal, and occipital—receive sensory information from the ears, eyes, and viscera or bodily organs. The frontal lobes accept sensory signals to combine them into higher-order processing. In general, the posterior lobes activate quick, routine reactions, and the frontal lobes generate slower, deliberate responses (Afford, 2020).

Third is the left-right axis corresponding to the left and right cerebral hemispheres. The left hemisphere mainly focuses attention on the foreground, details, and specific tasks. In contrast, the right hemisphere generally provides open attention to the background and a felt sense of the whole.

The autonomic nervous system has two basic parts: the sympathetic and the parasympathetic. The sympathetic nervous system is our arousal system and is best known for generating the "fight or flight" response in the face of danger. This all works automatically. When a car cuts you off on the freeway, you do not have to think about reacting. Your autonomic nervous system takes over; your eyes dilate, your heart races, and your entire body is ready for action. The sympathetic nervous system becomes activated during life stressors but also by positive emotions. Seeing a loved one or winning the lottery elicits a strong arousal response.

The parasympathetic nervous system is our calming or quiescent system. It is activated to help us rejuvenate our energy stores, digest our food, and help us sleep to restore body functions. The parasympathetic nervous system slows down the heart and respiratory rates. The sympathetic and parasympathetic nervous systems typically balance each other. When confronted with an emergency, you want your arousal system turned on to maximum while your quiescent system should be shut off. Similarly, we have all experienced the difficulty of falling asleep when worrying about a problematic issue at work because the arousal system continues to be activated. At the same time, we need our parasympathetic system to turn on to help us sleep.

The autonomic nervous system may be quite important regarding religious and spiritual phenomena. Calming experiences associated with meditation or prayer, as well as listening to slow religious chanting, can induce profound feelings of blissfulness. On the other hand, rapid religious dancing or even reminders of awe or fear of God can elicit an arousal response in the brain. Ultimately, intense religious or spiritual experiences, including mystical experiences, have a combination of powerful blissful and arousal elements and may evoke activity in both dimensions of the autonomic nervous system.

American psychologist and neuroscientist Stephen Porges' polyvagal theory explains how persons thrive relationally when their nervous system works in sync with others' nervous systems. A three-way classification involving the vagus nerve describes autonomic states as they affect relationships with a sense of safety, danger, or life threat. The ventral vagus, directed by the cortex, seeks a sympathetic-parasympathetic balance, facilitating a sense of *safety* and rewarding social interaction. The sympathetic nervous system, set off subcortically, generates a sense of *danger* and instigates fight or flight reactions, struggle, and defensiveness. The dorsal vagus, controlled by the brainstem, evokes a sense of *life threat* and induces shutdown, freezing, shame, and dissociation. The three states can and do interact and overlap (Afford, 2020).

The thalamus is a central structure that is a key relay in the brain connecting many different parts and allows us to have complex thought processes about the world. Some have even suggested that the thalamus may be a principal player in human consciousness. It is an important relay, particularly for auditory and visual input into the brain. Thus, the thalamus likely plays a fundamental role in how we perceive the reality around us. Another small but central structure that recently has been implicated in religious and spiritual experiences is called the periaqueductal gray region near the brain stem. This small area is generally involved in integrated responses to internal and external stresses. Recent brain imaging research (Ferguson et al., 2022) has shown that damage to this area reduces the sense of the spiritual.

The next set of structures as we move up into the brain is called the limbic system (see Figure 2.1). The limbic system surrounds the previously mentioned core structures of the brain. The limbic system consists of several important and well-known structures involved in emotional responses, such as the amygdala and hippocampus. The amygdala is activated when something of motivational importance enters our sensory field. This has frequently been associated with fearful or negative stimuli. Hearing a fire alarm or almost being in a car accident will activate the amygdala because of the intense fear reaction. The amygdala is connected to the hypothalamus, which will activate the sympathetic nervous system in such a situation. The amygdala also turns on when positive things occur in our environment. Seeing a loved one or a new puppy will activate the amygdala as well. One can easily extrapolate the importance of the amygdala when it comes to religious phenomena. Having intense emotional reactions to the notion of Jesus or God is likely to activate the amygdala based on their importance and meaning.

Figure 2.1. Structures of the limbic system. Structures of the limbic system are shown, including the cingulate cortex, amygdala, hippocampus, and hypothalamus.

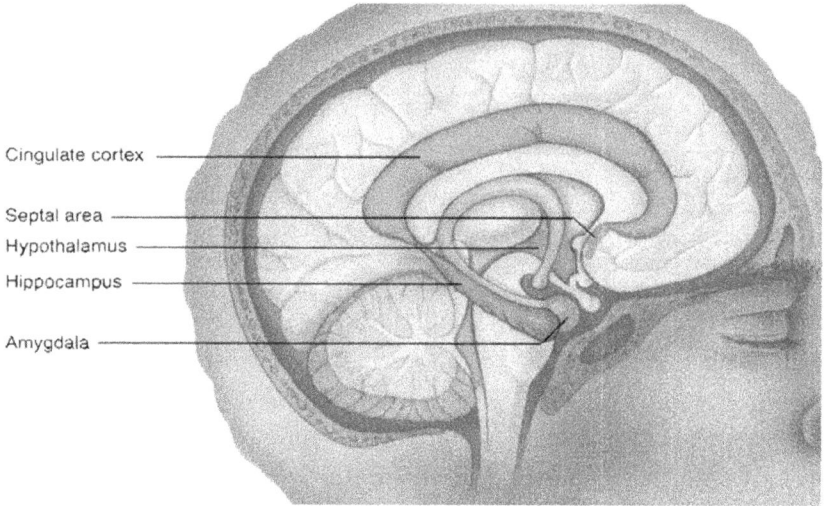

Figure 2.2. Structures of the neocortex of the brain. Brain structures involved in higher cognitive and sensory processing, including the frontal, temporal, parietal, and occipital lobes. Areas more specifically involved in attention, orientation, verbal, conceptual processing, and visual processing are shown.

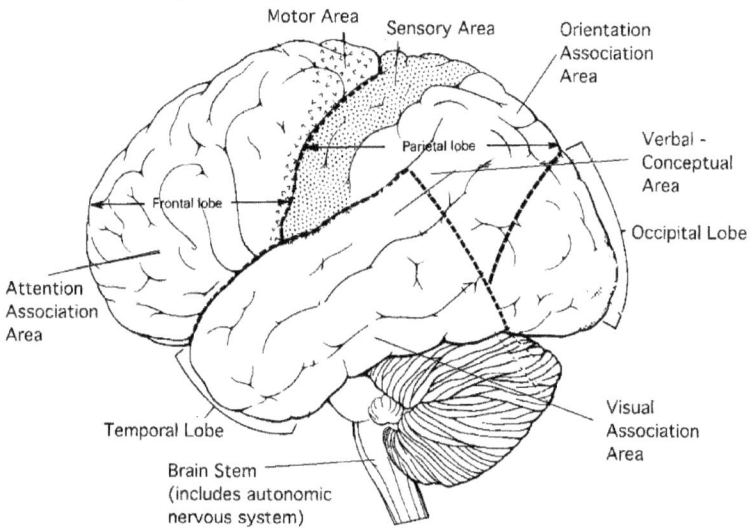

The hippocampus tends to balance the activity in the amygdala in terms of emotional responses but also helps to write various events into our memory (in fact, the hippocampus is particularly affected in diseases such as Alzheimer's dementia). It makes sense that the emotional centers of the brain would be closely tied to memory because our brain wants to remember emotionally important things, both positive and negative. In the context of religious practices and beliefs, it is important to remember the essential elements and tenets of a religion. In addition, rituals and prayers will activate these limbic areas to evoke strong emotional responses and consequently help us to remember them.

The primary cognitive processes are linked with the four main lobes of the brain's outer part or neocortex, the most recently developed brain regions (see Figure 2.2). In many ways, these are the parts of the brain that make us human. The frontal lobes are primarily involved in concentration and attention. Many brain studies have shown that these areas become active when we focus our attention on a given task, such as solving a math problem or finding our way when we are lost. The frontal lobes are also involved in executive processes that have to do with planning our day as well as our lives.

Parts of the frontal lobe, particularly Broca's area, are involved in the generation of language. When we have thoughts, this part of the brain translates our thoughts into language that we can express verbally. Finally, the frontal lobes are involved in regulating our emotional responses. When we feel a strong emotional response in our limbic system, the frontal lobes help to balance that response. In fact, a simplistic way of thinking about this relationship is to consider the frontal lobes and limbic system on opposite sides of a balance beam. When one tends to go up, the other tends to go down. The fulcrum appears to be a structure that is between the frontal lobes and the limbic system called the cingulate gyrus. When people have disorders of the frontal lobes, such as an attention deficit disorder, they are unable to concentrate; with frontal lobe dementia, they are unable to plan their day; or with anxiety disorders, they are unable to regulate their emotional responses. As we will discuss in some detail later in this book, the frontal lobes have some important functions regarding religious and spiritual practices and experiences. For example, concentrating on the theological meaning of a certain story in the Bible or repeating a certain prayer, such as the rosary, is typically associated with the activation of the frontal lobes.

The temporal lobes located along the sides of the brain, which also house the limbic system, have numerous cognitive functions, including the reception of language, memory, and various aspects of abstract thinking. Some of these functions appear to be linked to the upper part of the temporal lobe, which is right next to the parietal lobe and is located more toward the back of the brain. It is to this region that a lot of abstract thought processes appear to be associated. Thinking about concepts such as morality, ontology, epistemology, and theology likely are associated with activity in these areas of the brain.

The parietal lobe is primarily involved in sensory perception, but importantly, it is also involved in the spatial representation of the self. This area of the brain is involved in helping us navigate through a crowded room so that we do not bump into people as we walk through the doorway. Many of our brain imaging studies have shown that decreased activity in the parietal lobe is associated with decreases in the spatial representation of the self. This might be associated with common religious and spiritual experiences such as the loss of the sense of self or the sense of connectedness or oneness with God.

The occipital lobe is particularly involved in visual processing. It receives most of the primary visual input from the eyes and helps us to construct a three-dimensional representation of the world around us. One of our (ABN) studies showed the importance of the occipital lobe in helping us perceive and understand religious and spiritual symbols.

All these areas work together, as we said at the outset, to provide a complex representation of the world around us, as well as self-awareness. There are many avenues for understanding how our brain is related to various religious and spiritual phenomena, and this is, in large part, what we intend to pursue through the rest of the book, particularly regarding the Catholic tradition.

Brain-soul interaction

We noted that the parts of an entity depend particularly on the substantial form or soul of the being. This means that the part of the mind that is the brain depends on the whole being, the person (Dodds, 2019). It is the person, not the brain, who thinks, acts, and has mental states, traits, and attributes. Mechanisms and neural functions of the brain may correlate with mental operations, but it is the person who reasons, feels, and chooses. This points to a tendency in neuroscience to attribute to the brain functions, qualities, and mental states that belong to the person—a category mistake. Parts of the brain, areas, or networks may correlate neurologically with thoughts or mental states, but the brain does not think, feel, or decide—the person does. To ascribe to a part (the brain) what the whole (the person) does may be a way of speaking but easily confuses a mereological fallacy or *the hazard of the disappearing person* (De Haan, 2020, pp. 66, 57; Bennett and Hacker, 2003). The brain provides a neural substrate for spiritual powers that exist beyond space and time, spiritual capacities that correlate with but transcend the physiological structure and function of the brain. It is the person, not their brain, who maintains an identity, consciousness, and responsibility for their life and actions.

Interestingly, although in the Catholic Aristotelian-Thomistic view, the spiritual dimension of the person—the soul, or intellect and will—cannot be reduced to the neurophysiological, in this life, the person's thoughts and decisions leave neurological traces. The new mechanist philosophy (NMP), a recent movement in the philosophy of science, takes a stance in reaction to reductionist logical empiricism, looking for ontological connections between spiritual and physiological levels. Theorists such as Daniel De Haan (2018), a research fellow at the Centre for Science and Religion, University of Oxford, U.K., conclude that "there are no principled reasons for taking Neo-Aristotelian teleology and the mechanisms of the new mechanistic philosophy to be incompatible" (p. 25). The search for connections between the physiological and the spiritual intersecting in the human brain will undoubtedly explore this complex, intriguing theme.

The soul associated with the brain

Soul is a thought-provoking term with a long and varied past. Hinduism believes that the soul reincarnates, passing on from one body to the next. Egyptians buried their dead with artifacts to take along to the next world. For the ancient Greeks, the soul was the essence or core of the human being, with uncertain existence after death. Plato thought that the soul comprised desires and emotions, as well as reason. Western notions, notably from St. Augustine, considered the soul immortal, designed to influence and guide the body (Newberg, 2010, p. 29). The *Catechism of the Catholic Church* (1995) refers to the soul as "the innermost aspect of humans, that which is of greatest value in them (cf. Mt 10:28; 26:38; Jn 12:27; 2 Mac 6:30), that by which they are most especially in God's image. Thus, 'soul' signifies the *spiritual principle* in humans (*CCC*, 363). The soul, the form of the body, appears distinct from the brain, but the brain is closely associated with the soul.

To make sense of an immaterial principle affecting material physiology, as we saw in Chapter One, Brown, Murphy, and Malony propose "non-reductive physicalism," where "the person is a physical organism whose complex functioning, both in society and in relation to God, gives rise to 'higher' human capacities such as morality and spirituality" (1998, *Whatever Happened to the Soul*). By virtue of a soul, humans can engage in processes of language, abstract thinking, memory, projection to the future, empathy, and unregimented behavioral choice, all capacities irreducible to the simply biological. Neuroscience, in fact, can investigate each of these human capacities. Non-reductive physicalism does not consider the soul separate from the body but still claims ontological materialism, which puts it at odds with Catholicism. Neurotheology, respecting theological traditions regarding the soul, might explore the relationship between the soul and body and ways that an immaterial principle might affect and interact with a material one (Newberg, 2010, pp. 244-245).

Catholic stance toward the soul

We noted that neurotheology attempts to bridge the gap between science and theology. Then what about Christian beliefs regarding the human person? Belief in a rational soul is central to the difference between neuroscientific and Christian views of the person (McGoldrick, 2012). "The foundation of the Catholic position rests on the methodology that moves from effects to an underlying cause. (The soul) is a conceptual construct from the data of the shared experience of human life" (McGoldrick, 2012, p. 496). The Catholic view of the human person as spiritual begins with concepts of a rational soul and mind. These are observable in free will and the experience of consciousness.

Humans made in God's image express their spiritual principles in intellect and will, knowing and loving. Through human consciousness, the person strives to understand and then freely chooses the goods they will pursue, making self-determination in social relationships the means to self-identity. "Because of freedom, human beings are a product not only of their genes, but also of their self-conscious, free, and deliberate choices" beyond neural processes (McGoldrick, 2012, p. 497). While animals act through instinct or respond to stimuli, humans deliberate and decide their moral objectives, whether to seek and adhere to the good, the true, and the beautiful. The moral value of human life depends on the goals and objectives one follows. Consciousness and free will contribute to the spiritual principle of the human person who becomes who they choose to be by choices, large and small. Choices affect not only individuals but also societies and cultures, moving humanity along in progress toward ideals. "And finally, the inner life, where one encounters God in prayer, the very sense of oneself with awareness of one's dignity, is experienced in the ever-present moment of consciousness" (p. 485).

As we have seen, Catholic philosophy and theology follow Aristotle and Aquinas in understanding the soul metaphysically as the substantial form or foundational essence that makes the living person. Even if the human being is not fully developed, such as a fetus, or is in some way incapacitated, such as the physically or mentally disabled, if they have what is essential—a soul—they are human, made in God's image, and carry human dignity. The *Catechism of the Catholic Church* teaches that "the unity of body and soul is so profound that one has to consider the soul to be the 'form' of the body (Council of Vienne, 1312: DS 902): i.e., it is because of its spiritual soul that the body made of matter becomes a living, human body; spirit and matter, in humans, are not two natures united, but rather their union forms a single nature" (*CCC*, 365).

This observation connects to the field of neurotheology. Since the spiritual soul is united with the body, including the brain, studying the biological processes of the brain is studying an aspect of the body that correlates with the soul. This may be particularly relevant in understanding how people come to make life choices moral decisions, and determine which religious faith to follow. For example, as we shall describe in more detail below, numerous studies have tried to determine how the brain of a religious person differs from that of a non-religious person, particularly in terms of making decisions or observing the external environment.

For believers, conscious, intelligent life is more than biochemistry and needs to include the spiritual dimensions of life. Transcending physiology are the intellectual abilities to abstract from the particular to the general, to imagine past and present events and to project into the future, to generalize and make inferences, and to judge and come to conclusions. The human person includes a rational soul and mind manifest in free will. "Free will and consciousness are at the nexus of mutual influence of body and soul, that argues for a spiritual dimension to personality" (McGoldrick, 2012, p. 498).

St. Thomas Aquinas, in his *Summa Theologica*, called the soul one principle of the human person, the other principle being the body. From this assertion, he concluded since the intellectual soul can comprehend material things, it must not be corporeal itself, must operate separately from the body, could subsist without a body, and cannot be destroyed as can material things (Newberg, 2010).

> Since existence belongs to the form of the soul (since the soul is, in fact, subsistent because it is formed), it cannot be corrupted. . . . Since it is part of the essence of a soul to exist, corruption cannot occur. Therefore, the soul is incorruptible. (*ST* I, q. 75, art. 6) (Daniel, 2013).

Can we know that mind or soul must be more than material other than Aquinas, from more contemporary thought? "The British geneticist J. B. S. Haldane (1892-1964) reflected:

> It seems to me immensely unlikely that the mind is a mere by-product of matter. For if my mental processes are determined wholly by the motions of atoms in my brain, I have no reason to suppose that my beliefs are true. They may be sound chemically, but that does not make them sound logical. I am compelled to believe that the mind is not wholly conditioned by matter (1927, 1932, p. 209) (Grassie, 2008, p. 144).

What does theology say about the soul? According to the *Catechism of the Catholic Church*:

> Every spiritual soul is created immediately by God—it is not 'produced' by the parents—and it is immortal: it does not perish when it separates from the body at death, and it will be reunited with the body at the final Resurrection (366).

Consciousness in neuropsychology

In neuropsychology, consciousness generally has two meanings: (1) physiological, based on neuroanatomy, in terms of a wakeful brain state, and (2) a subjective awareness of the self and reality. The latter meaning is taken to be more abstract and subtle since it is quite possible to be awake and at the same time unaware of the environment and even one's internal condition. Consciousness as awareness or self-awareness is a mystifying capacity that is "far more difficult to investigate with cognitive neuroscience or, for that matter, with any other methods" (Purves et al., 2019, p. 625). Most neural processing in the nervous system tends to be automatic, working below the level of cognizance. Changes in brain activity when attention is redirected are recordable with fMRI and electrophysiological methods.

Neuroscience observes perceptual disruptions with impairment to higher-order regions of the brain that have something to do with awareness. And there is an interesting finding that in sensory processing when consciousness is involved, it takes longer for an initial feedforward signal to return to the relevant sensory processing area. This longer latency movement, called *recurrent* or *reentrant* neural activation, might be a neuronal mechanism for perceptual awareness. EEG studies suggest that "recurrent activity in visual processing regions correlates with reported awareness of a visual stimulus, although the tightness of the link between the activity and awareness is still unsettled" (Purves et al., 2019, p. 626).

It is generally acknowledged that in perception and thinking, consciousness is associated with altered cortical neurons in the association cortices, which combine information from other sensory systems and environmental input. Regarding vision, neuroscience finds action in the visual association cortices *necessary* but not *sufficient* to cause awareness, "and no defining neural signature of awareness has been discerned" (Purves et al., 2019, p. 626).

Clinical data have contributed to our understanding of physiological awareness in the phenomena of blindsight, split-brain conditions, phantom limb syndrome, and hallucinations.

Blindsight is a pathological situation in which a patient verbally reports that he does not see objects presented in the blind region of his visual field (referred to as the 'scotoma'). Still, when forced by the experimenter to respond to visual stimuli presented to their scotoma, the patient's correct responses are significantly higher than chance. The implication is that there is some preservation of sight even if it is not conscious. Electrophysiological and functional neuroimaging readings in patients with blindsight show that the unperceived stimuli do evoke some neural activity in primary visual regions of the brain (called the extrastriate cortex and located in the back of the brain in the occipital lobe). This suggests that these regions are necessary for appropriate performance without awareness of having seen the objects. Blindsight may be due to visual processing at the unconscious level, even though it is ultimately sent in some form to the conscious parts of the brain. "This interpretation accords with other evidence that subliminal (unconscious) information processing influences behavior of all sorts" (Purves et al., 2019, p. 626).

With so-called 'split-brain' patients, the corpus callosum connecting neural fibers between the right and left hemispheres is surgically cut, for example, to relieve severe epileptic symptoms. This logically would render for the individual two relatively independent spheres of consciousness. Surprisingly, researcher and psychology professor Yair Pinto at the University of Amsterdam found, despite such surgery, that individuals function as one conscious perceiver with a unified awareness. However, if presented with stimuli that isolate one hemisphere or the other, a different response occurs. If you present the image of a hammer to the left hemisphere that houses our language abilities, the person can say, "I see a hammer." However, if presented to the right hemisphere, the person cannot make the same statement but could produce the hand motion of hammering if asked how to use the object presented. In some sense, people can act as if they have two separate consciousnesses.

Finally, it is possible to be aware of something that does not exist. A remarkable example is the amputee who is subjectively aware of an absent arm or leg, particularly the pain from it, even though the physical limb and its sensory input are missing. The phantom limb phenomenon demonstrates that the brain can actively construct perceptions even if there is nothing there to perceive (Purves et al., 2019).

Blindsight, split-brain, phantom limb, and hallucinations all point to neural mechanisms for physiological consciousness. But these answers are unsatisfying for philosophers and theologians, as well as some neuroscientists. It may be that neuroscience might not ever find the neural correlates of consciousness as awareness or self-awareness, as distinct from attention and wakefulness (Purves et al., 2019, p. 629). Wherever this data leads, we might imagine how these results affect the notion of the soul, a unique part of every person, but something that also must interact with the brain and human consciousness.

Academic psychology has generally seen consciousness from a materialistic perspective as a neurobiological mechanism formed by genetic heredity, developmental factors, and cultural influences. A problem with materialism, of course, is that if consciousness derives entirely from the brain when the brain dies, so should consciousness. Interestingly, some consciousness researchers, traditions such as Buddhism and Hinduism, and data from near-death experiences (Spitzer, 2015) argue that consciousness extends beyond the brain. In fact, some make the argument that consciousness pervades the universe, and the brain merely taps into that universal mind. The range from materialist to postmaterialist perspectives of consciousness can have a dramatic influence on understanding religious ideas of the person and the mind and consciousness. Neurotheology would ask us to look at these different possibilities, but also how the mind and brain consider them in the first place. Is there something about one person's psychological profile that might incline them toward a materialist rather than a spiritual perspective, due partially in some way to their brain's neurological substrate?

To sum up this section, consciousness research explores one of the most elusive dimensions of the brain. By engineering consciousness, spiritual traditions such as Hinduism and Buddhism contend that humans can attain a higher psychological or spiritual state. They might even reach enlightenment, a transcendent goal for human interaction with the world (Newberg, 2018b, p. 39). Consciousness seems essential to being human, even though science finds it difficult to clearly explain what it is, how it originates, or why we have this amazing capacity.

Jesuit philosopher and theologian Bernard Lonergan (1904–1984) asks about the brain and mind as interactive for the person. He wonders what it is that integrates the constitutive elements of a human being. "The answer must be the intellectual consciousness, the constant between brain and mind." Linking mind and brain is "intelligibility—order, coherence" (Helminiak, 2015, pp. 135-136). Within the mind, sensations, images, and emotions belong to a perceptual level of reality. But at a higher level are insights. "Consciousness fully transcends space and time and is *spiritual*. Intelligibility accounts for transcendent experiences" (p. 242).

The spiritual dimension of the person

It is not uncommon today for people to say they are *spiritual* but not religious. Spiritual in this context is not easily defined. From Latin, it derives from *spiritus*, or the verb *spirare, to breathe or blow*. The idea of being *spiritual, not religious*, seems to pursue a "return to an original, unmediated, pure connection with a foundational moment, a mystical experience, or the teachings of a charismatic leader" (Grassie, 2008, p. 129) without the accouterments or commitments of formal religion. Spirituality is inherently subjective and experiential. It might mean:

(1) a set of personal opinions about the meaning of life and/or as being part of something greater, (2) experiences of transcendence and/or feeling a sense of oneness with everything, or (3) beliefs about the actual existence of a greater spiritual reality. (Schwartz, 2012, p. 584).

A definition used by many is that the term *spirituality* refers to "the existence of consciously striving to integrate one's life in terms not of isolation and self-absorption but of self-transcendence toward the ultimate value one perceives" (Schneiders, 1986, p. 266, in Payne, 2022). A group of approximately 80 scientific researchers exploring the relationship between spirituality and health defined the criteria for spirituality as the subjective feelings, thoughts, experiences, and behaviors that arise from a search or quest for the sacred. *Search* refers to attempts to identify, articulate, maintain, or transform. *Sacred* refers to what the individual perceives as a divine being, ultimate reality, or ultimate truth (Larson et al., 1998).

Pope John Paul II observed that spirituality is a fundamental aspect of every human mind, those who commit to religion and those who do not. Scientists, as well as members of faith-based religions, perceive in the human person a spiritual dimension:

> which transcends cerebral physiology and appears to direct all our activities as free and autonomous beings, capable of responsibility and love, marked with dignity. (For Catholics) it includes the interpretive and evaluative work of the human mind, the foundation of that spiritual dimension proper to a special relationship with God the Creator (cf. Gn 2:7) in whom every man and woman is made (cf. Gn 1:26-27) (Address to the Pontifical Academy of Sciences, 2003). (Grassie, 2008, p. 157)

It is also hoped that a link between the spiritual dimension and the person might be important not only from the theological perspective but from a practical or therapeutic one as well.

Therapies to enhance consciousness and well-being

The Catholic tradition refers to the human person as a spiritual being. This contrasts with the views of scientists such as Edward O. Wilson, who holds the human person to be the product of material evolution, resulting in "organic machines" that can make "transcendent achievements" (Wilson, 1998, p. 121). According to Catholic philosophy and theology, body and soul make a composite unity, with each impacting the other. Consciousness blends physical and spiritual elements. Love, for instance, begins with appreciation for good in the higher spiritual dimension of the rational soul. The corresponding neurological activity would register in the brain's frontal lobes and then affect emotions in the brain's limbic system. There are physiological changes in blood chemistry and other bodily systems. Love would have to be more than a feeling; it must be spiritual because love can lead to free choice of self-gift to the loved object, another person, or a purpose, even to the point of virtuous self-sacrifice (McGoldrick, 2012, p. 488).

Therapies such as cognitive behavioral therapy (CBT) show by an abundance of supporting research that cognition can be reframed to better approximate the truth so that behavior can be re-shaped in a healthier direction. Addicted individuals can overcome powerful compulsions through coping strategies, assistance from sponsors, attending meetings, and staying away from circumstances likely to lead to relapse. According to the CBT approach, if the mind can reason, the will can make free choices. However, it might be constrained by ignorance, disorder, fear, force, or passion. Valuable work is in progress to integrate the Catholic stance on the human person with clinical psychology (Brugger, 2009; McGoldrick, 2012, p. 488) (cf., Vitz, Nordling, and Titus, 2020, *Catholic-Christian Model of the Person*).

Study questions

1. Do you think that contemporary culture tends to prioritize findings of neuroscience over principles of theology? Explain.
2. Why is humility necessary for a subject like neurotheology?
3. Noting that we will return to basic terms cyclically, building on definitions from various vantage points, what is *mind*? Explain philosophically in a historical context.
4. What are the principal lobes of the brain and their predominant functions?
5. What is the Thomistic understanding of the *soul*?
6. How is the soul related to the brain?
7. What is *consciousness*? Explain with physiological data.
8. How would you explain the spiritual dimension of the person?
9. Explain how psychological therapies might enhance well-being.

Endnotes

[1] See d'Aquili, E. G., & Newberg, A.B. (1999). *The mystical mind: Probing the biology of religious experience*. Minneapolis, MN: Fortress; Moll, J., & Oliveira-Souza, R. (2007). Moral judgments, emotions, and the utilitarian brain. *Trends in Cognitive Science, 11*, 319-321; Gazzaniga, M. S. (2005). *The ethical brain*. New York: Dana; Talbot, M. (2007, July 2). Duped: Can brain scans uncover lies? *New Yorker*, 52-61; Fisher, H. E., Aron, A., Mashek, D., Li, H., Brown, L. L. (2002). Defining the brain systems of lust, romantic attraction, and attachment. *Archives of Sexual Behavior, 31*, 413-419; Bartels, A., & Zeki, W. (2000). The neural basis of romantic love. *Neuroreport, 11*, 3829-3834.

[2] For further reading, see Juergensmeyer, M. (2000). *Terror in the mind of God: The global rise of religious violence*. Berkeley, CA: University of California Press.

Chapter 3
Epistemological Considerations and Faith

Neurotheology and metaphysics

Central to neurotheology from a Catholic point of view is the way that the soul relates to the brain. In this chapter, we will consider how neurotheology can be situated within a metaphysical framework. For epistemology and the theory of knowledge, we will follow French Catholic philosopher Jacques Maritain (1882-1973). There are other contemporary virtue epistemologists whom we might consider. We are focusing on Maritain as one Catholic Thomistic philosopher whose exposition of the *degrees of knowledge* helps us understand how neuroscience and theology relate to the overall order of being. We will explore realism and orders of knowledge, natural science, and natural philosophy. We will then follow Lonergan, whom we introduced in Chapter Two as one Catholic Thomistic philosopher relevant to our study for his distinctions in human consciousness: organism, psyche, and spirit. Maritain and Lonergan represent two Catholic philosophers whose thinking might help to orient current findings in neuroscience within a Catholic philosophical perspective[1].

Neurotheology is a recent endeavor that is not yet fully established as a field. To our knowledge, prior to this study, neurotheology has not yet been considered extensively in conjunction with Catholicism. Aquinas, Maritain, and Lonergan appear to be among the well-known Catholic philosophers who might contribute to a neuroscience-theology dialogue. They may or may not be the best choices for demonstrating a Catholic perspective. Suggestions from other Catholic thinkers are welcome. This chapter may seem overly technical. It is necessary to define terms and explain fundamentals. Hopefully, the effort with patient endurance will pay off in a rewarding sense of clarity in areas where ambiguity and perplexity may otherwise reign. If an explanation of metaphysical basics is too tedious, the reader might want to skip to Lonergan's Thomistic anthropology and epistemology.

We have seen in Chapter Two (Body-soul and mind) how the *mind*, from Augustine's reference in *De trinitate*, did not appear in Aquinas' *Summa Theologica*, where the soul is said to comprise intellect and will. We also briefly addressed the soul-body (or, commonly, the mind-body) problem.

Defining terms

Some basic terms need to be clarified from a Thomistic perspective for this study. *Soul, body, intellect, will, affectivity/emotions, mind, person,* and *self* take on a variety of meanings today according to context. We will settle on the following simple meanings, though more could be said.

The soul is the formal principle of the actuality of the living human person, the substantial form uniting two principles—intellect and will (Dodds, 2014). *The body* is the physiological material principle of the human person, including the brain as the primary integrating organ.

Classical and Christian thought understands *intellect* to consist of *ratio* and *intellectus. Ratio* is an active, logical, discursive reasoning that works to define, form concepts, and reach deductions. *Intellectus* passively receives a philosophical, spiritual, or contemplative view of reality-oriented toward truth. Genuine knowledge of reality requires both *ratio* and *intellectuals* (Pieper, *Leisure as the Basis of Culture,* 1952, pp. 6-11, in Trepanier, 2017). *Intellect* is the spiritual capacity of the human soul with the abilities to reason, make tools, use language, make art and poetry, participate in religion, establish the culture, follow moral codes, and engage in self-reflection (Dodds, 2014, pp. 40-43).

Will is the decision-making capacity, dependent on the intellect and oriented toward the good.

Affectivity or *emotions,* according to Aquinas, are movements of the soul. They may react through cognition to seeming sensory good or evil (concupiscible) or to arduous sense of good or evil (irascible). Aquinas classified emotions as love, desire, pleasure or joy, hate, aversion, pain or distress, hope, despair, fear, courage, and anger. Essentially psychosomatic, they cause behavioral change and are not possible for bodiless beings like angels or God (*ST* I-II.22.3, Aquinas, trans. 1948) (Knuuttila, 2022). "Emotion" (Dixon 2003) was an early nineteenth-century term by psychologists. The general Christian psychological tradition distinguished passions and affections. Passions are feeling responses to sensory stimuli shared with animals, associated with temptation or moral baseness. Affections derive from the intellectual appetite or will and psychological capacities shared with angels and God. Examples are compassion, joy, hope, gratitude, contrition, and other religious movements of the soul (Roberts, 2021).

Mind is a power of the soul. With modern philosophy since the seventeenth century, emphasis has been on empiricism, intentionality, and consciousness rather than soul. In the latter half of the twentieth century, philosophy of mind has become one of the most active subjects of philosophical interest (Crawford, 2011, p. 2). Today, discussion of the mind often has an empirical aspect and may include "areas such as psychology, neuroscience, linguistics, evolutionary psychology and biology, and computer science" (p. 5).

Person and self

Person and *self* are terms that represent each of the "two greatest ideas," according to Catholic philosopher Linda Zagzebski (2021), that have shaped Western perception of the world and the individual from ancient and medieval times to the present. The terms *person* and *self* as we understand them today developed in the context of large historically conditioned ontological and theological movements that Zagzebski sees as the two greatest ideas.

The first great idea throughout the premodern Western world, based on metaphysics and theology, was that "there is an Eternal Law of the divine reason for governing the entire universe" (*ST* I-II, q. 91, one corpus)" and that the universe comprises a structure of forms for the physical and non-physical world (Zagzebski, 2021, pp. 54-55). Doctor of the Church Pope Leo the Great (c. 400-461) extended the Roman Empire's designation of *person*s as male citizens of quality to all humans because all are made in the image and likeness of God (Sermon 21) (Zagzebski, pp. 105-106). Philosopher Boethius (c. 470-524) defined a *person* as "an individual substance of a rational nature" (Zagzebski, p. 5). Aquinas (1225-1274) agreed: "'Person' signifies what is the most perfect in all of nature, and that is rationality' (*ST* I, q. 29, art. 3 corpus). (We will discuss later the case of "persons" who do not exercise rationality.) Rationality, distinctive of human beings, extends preeminently to God and acknowledges a status of ontological, social, and moral dignity.

Italian philosopher Pico della Mirandola (1463-1494), in *Oration on the Dignity of Man,* associated human dignity primarily with the power of free choice and self-determination. Emphasis on autonomy laid the groundwork for the second great idea, that reason mattered primarily not in the mind of God but in the individual human mind (Zagzebski, pp. 90-91).

The Reformation and Scientific Revolution (sixteenth to eighteenth centuries), preceded by social disintegration with the (fourteenth century) Black Death, contributed to a philosophical shift where theology was no longer central to the Western conception of the world and the individual. With his method of doubt, Descartes was certain only of his mind and consciousness. Reversing the fundamental order of knowledge, he knew his mind, then God, then the world (Zagzebski, 2021, p. 67). Art and literature now focused on the individual rather than subordination to the metaphysical and theological order of being. Empirical science followed suit, as did the political notion of a social contract comprised of self-governing autonomous individuals. Although a person is always a self, *self* has attained preeminence. The self-conscious individual attained "dignity because of the value of (their) unique subjectivity" (p. 18).

We saw in Chapter Two that Catholicism uses Aristotelian-Thomistic hylomorphic metaphysics to understand the human person as composed of two principles united in a single person. The two principles are "primary matter" and "substantial form." *Primary matter* means the *possibility of being*—a body. *Substantial form*—soul—is what makes the person a particular substance. The soul and body interact as one entity. Of course, this raises the larger philosophical, theological, and scientific question as to how the concepts of soul and body are related. We are considering similarities and distinctions from a Catholic perspective. Neurotheology also includes other religions and perspectives that would describe the soul from different points of view.

Interpreting the data

How does metaphysical explanation affect the interpretations of neuroscientific experimental results? Neurotheology finds that brain scans show distinctive activation patterns during spiritual practices or when people have spiritual experiences. It is possible to conclude, as some do, that what we attributed to God's activity was, in fact, only electrochemical effects. One interviewer put the question to me (ABN). "Some people might think that reducing spiritual states to brain circuitry is reductive—that it diminishes these states to chemical firings rather than experiences that reveal the truth and refer to some high reality. What do you think?"

> --I think it depends on how you interpret that data. Some people say, 'Okay, here's the brain scan; there's nothing more to these experiences than what's happening in the brain.' And others say, 'Of course, you can see these experiences in the brain. If God is talking to you, it will show up in the brain.' I don't think reductionism is necessary. So it goes back to how we experience reality—and what reality really is" ("How does the brain experience God? Interview on neurotheology with Andrew B. Newberg" in Smith, 2017, p. 37).

Brain scans look at the physical functioning of the brain. It is important not to make the purely scientific assumption that what cannot be perceived and measured does not exist or that science is the only legitimate way of acquiring knowledge. References to God need to come from another knowing. Neurotheology attempts to extend interpretation beyond neuroscience to philosophy and theology. We have seen in Chapter Two and continue in this chapter an effort to clarify ways to interpret and understand neurophysiological data from a Catholic perspective.

Epistemology: Theory of knowledge

How do we experience reality? How do we know what is real? Epistemology is generally understood to flow from metaphysics—how we understand what reality is and how it is structured and ordered.[2] According to Jacques Maritain, arguably at his death in 1973, the best-known contemporary Catholic philosopher, all human questioning has "being" as the formal object of the mind (*Preface to Metaphysics*, 1939, p. 25, in Sweet, 2019).[3] Influential in restoring Thomism for contemporary times, Maritain authored more than 60 books and was prominent in developing the United Nations Universal Declaration of Human Rights (1948). His contribution to the Universal Declaration that the U.N. General Assembly adopted unanimously demonstrates that a contemporary worldview with an emphasis on common human rights need not conflict with the premodern metaphysically grounded first great idea (Zagzebski, 2021). Maritain differentiated among the levels of being that the human intellect attains. First grasped is sensible being—the work of the empirical scientist—then the levels of mathematics, philosophy, theology, and mysticism. Metaphysics seeks and explores the *cause* of being—God, the subsistent act of existing. Maritain emphasized the precedence of metaphysics over epistemology and held that the object to be known determined the organization and methods of the different sciences (Sweet, 2019).

As we have seen, epistemology from a Catholic perspective is preferentially Aristotelian-Thomistic. Maritain contended that metaphysics studies first principles and the ultimate causes of things (*The Twilight of Civilization*, 1942, p. 27). In analyzing nature and sensible beings, human beings included, Maritain followed Aquinas in distinguishing matter and form. Form designates nature or essence; matter determines individuality. Flowing from metaphysics, epistemology addresses the nature of the knowing person and relationship with the known world, as well as how persons know themselves and others (Crawford, 2011, p. 2). Epistemology may be characterized as the theory of knowledge, how it is attained, and whether opinions and beliefs are justified (Stanton, 2023).

Neuroscience generally depends on the empirical method rather than philosophy. Empiricism holds that experience alone—sense experience involving our five senses or reflective experience including consciousness of our mental operations—provides information and knowledge. The problem is that our notion of causation derives from expectation based on the experience of the consistent concurrence of similar causes and effects (Markie and Folescu, 2021, pp. 1, 15). Causation can be experienced because our senses are informed by intelligence, in the same way as when we see a human being, we understand that they are a person. However, with the pure external senses, we only see an empirical configuration. Science generally, as we have seen, proposes hypotheses and experiments with measurable variables to determine and validate conclusions about the observable world.

Theology is generally associates with philosophy rather than empiricism. By considering epistemology–our way of knowing–we hope to gain insights that are helpful for understanding the mind and brain from a philosophical point of view in order better to explore possibilities of neurotheology from a Catholic perspective. We begin with the consideration of realism, an Aristotelian-Thomistic view of human knowing[4].

There are other philosophical positions and traditions operative throughout the modern era that might support neurotheology. Catholic philosopher Zagzebski reflects that "almost all forms of epistemology on offer today are compatible with Catholic doctrine, with the exception of purely naturalistic approaches" (personal communication, September 20, 2022). For one example, as we have seen in Chapter Two, Pope John Paul II noted the current emphasis on consciousness and advocated a phenomenological approach to supplement Thomistic philosophy. Realist phenomenology investigates conscious experience "from the subjective or first-person point of view" (Smith, 2013, Introduction, para. 1). Experience may include:

> temporal awareness (within the stream of consciousness), spatial awareness (notably in perception), attention, self-consciousness, self-awareness, the self in different roles, embodied action, purpose or intention, awareness of others (in empathy, intersubjectivity, collectivity), linguistic activity (involving meaning, communication, understanding), social interaction, and everyday activity in our cultural life-world (Section 1, para. 7).

Philosophy of mind has recently focused on ways that conscious experience and intentionality are grounded in a neural substrate.

Realism

Maritain maintained a position that he called "critical realism," the view that what the mind knows is the same as what exists. This countered rationalist and empiricist systems of knowledge, such as the *modern philosophies* of Kantianism and, more generally, idealism, which holds that the mind creates its universal notions. Maritain held that we know reality through the *concept* by passively receiving sense impressions and actively constructing knowledge from the impressions. Intellect abstracts from sense impressions, the immaterial essence of the thing that then exists in the mind (see Deely, 1997; Munoz, 2012). Maritain held that knowledge is based on the object to be known within the various *orders* of knowledge—sensible, mathematical, philosophical, or mystical—and the *degree of abstraction* involved (Sweet, 2019). Understanding the order of knowledge helps us see, from an overall perspective, where and how our knowledge applies to various fields of study.

Orders of knowledge

First natural science. Knowledge of sensible nature, the field of experimental science, is distinct from metaphysical knowledge. Science strives to articulate laws that reflect regular features of sensible objects, using what Maritain calls an *empiriological* approach (cf. *Degrees of Knowledge*, 1932/1959, pp. 178-180; *Philosophy of Nature*, 1935/1951, p. 49). "An empiriological analysis is a non-philosophical, non-ontological approach to understanding natural beings that do not seek to know them 'in terms of their type of being or reality,' but only 'in terms of their empirical manifestations' (Carlson, 2012, p. 37)" (Sweet, 2019).

Second natural philosophy. Philosophy of nature ranges from knowing the individuating characteristics of natural objects to a discipline that investigates essential causes and relationships. The philosophy of nature focuses on not only the physical but also on the essence. Natural philosophy does more than study the physical sciences in their approaches and findings. It considers the natures or essences of things, categorizes them into classes, and looks for underlying principles. This is knowledge at the first *degree of abstraction* (Sweet, 2019). Philosophical knowledge is distinct from natural science and mathematics and is a discipline with established ways of supporting this type of knowledge (*Range of Reason*, 1948/1952, p. 5).

Maritain observed that the philosophy of nature is speculative in seeking the first principles of its objects—corporeal, conscious, *moving beings*. It particularly focuses on movement, bodily substance (matter and form), life, and the basic elements of organisms. Natural philosophy is a speculative branch of philosophy that addresses sensible beings, different from the empiriological sciences as observable and measurable. Its conclusions require confirmation by sense data. Its reflections extend beyond science but do not reach metaphysics. Philosophy of nature involves "knowledge whose object, present in all things of corporeal nature, is mobile being as such and the ontological principles which account for its mutability" (*Degrees of Knowledge*, 1932/1959, p. 197). Maritain asserts that:

> it belongs to the philosophy of nature to instruct us about the nature of the continuum of number, quantity, space, motion, time, corporeal substance, transitive action, vegetative and sensitive life, of the soul and its operative powers (1932/1959, p. 186, in Sweet, 2019)

and so is at the same level of abstraction as the natural sciences.

Since humanity is included among natural objects, psychology is the category at the high point of natural philosophy. And the question of the soul emerges. Maritain writes:

> A spiritual soul cannot be corrupted since it possesses no matter; it cannot be disintegrated since it possesses no substantial parts; it cannot lose its unity since it is self-subsisting, nor its internal energy since it contains within itself the source of its energies. The human soul cannot die. Once it exists, it cannot disappear; it will necessarily exist forever and endure without end. (1953, p. 60)

Maritain reflects the Catholic position:

> The Church teaches that every spiritual soul is created immediately by God—it is not "produced" by the parents—and that it is immortal: it does not perish when it separates from the body at death, and it will be reunited with the body at the final Resurrection. (*CCC*, 366)

Empirical science is concerned with the observable and measurable; metaphysics deals with purely intelligible beings. To attempt to use scientific demonstration to ascertain or critique metaphysical knowledge would result in a category mistake. Maritain took issue with empiricist epistemologies that do this (Bennet and Hacker, 2003, p. 406). Neurotheology attempts to find points of convergence among the levels of abstraction—empirical data about the central nervous system and natural philosophy, including the soul and psychology. Neurotheology, as it relates to Catholicism, looks for an epistemology that will open to a comprehensive metaphysics that can accommodate revelation-based Christian theology. Catholicism holds that there is no real contradiction between science and faith. The challenge is to find common ground among levels of abstraction and to reflect and generate beneficial new knowledge while avoiding a category mistake.

Lonergan's Thomistic anthropology and epistemology

Canadian Jesuit philosopher Bernard Lonergan developed an epistemology or theory of knowing based on Aristotelian-Thomistic metaphysics, a universal process of human knowing that could come to know reality as it is correctly. As noted above, Lonergan is relevant to this study of neurotheology for his distinctions in human anthropology and epistemology: organism, psyche, and spirit, and his levels of consciousness.

Dimensions of mind: Organism, psyche, and spirit

Lonergan formulated "a process of knowing that is natural to our minds, (that) pertains to any instance in any application to any reality" (Helminiak, 2021, p.

3). It can apply across all disciplines, rooted in a phenomenological description of human thinking. Lonergan's anthropology and epistemology are relevant for his distinctions regarding human knowing: organism, psyche, and spirit. We will revisit Lonergan's transcendental method in the next chapter on methodology. For now, we would like to consider his helpful insights as a grounding for Thomistic epistemology.

As we considered briefly above, it is important to distinguish the *soul* from the *mind*. We have seen in Chapter Two that the Aristotelian-Thomistic understanding of the human person is a single entity composed of two principles—body and soul. "The soul is considered the core of human identity" (Garcia-Valdecasas, 2005, p. 292). Where does the mind fit in? According to Aristotle, our soul is characterized mainly by rationality—the property that expresses the human ability to think, including, in the medieval context, also freedom and the will (p. 298). The soul is a principle of the human person, and the mind or intellect is a property of the soul. Aquinas followed Aristotle, who ruled out the belief that the soul was the subject of activities:

> To say that the soul is angry is as if one were to say that the soul weaves or builds. For it is surely better not to say that the soul pities, learns, or thinks, but that the man does this with his soul' (Aristotle, *De Anima*, p. 6).

Thinking is not attributed to a soul but to a person *with* his soul. Then what happens at death? Aquinas indicated that "the separated soul will retain after death the habit of knowledge acquired while it was united to its body (Garcia-Valdecasas, 2005, p. 306), although clearly not in the same way with senses and phantasms (*ST* I, Ia, QQ 1-19).

"Since the soul is immaterial, the intellect is immaterial too. Whenever Aquinas attributes to the intellect a certain property, this should also be attributed to the soul" (Garcia-Valdecasas, 2005, p. 299). "Despite the fact that the body is largely cooperative with the mind, especially by supplying suitable impressions, cognition (itself) does not concern the body" (*ST* I, Ia, QQ 1-119). Intellect depends on the body, but it perceives more than sense impressions. The intellect pierces through to the universal de-individualized object, to the essence of what a thing is. The intellect knows spiritual natures and participates in being or truth (Maritain, 1953). Intellect uses the brain, "yet the brain is not an organ of intelligence; there is no part of the organism whose act is intellectual operation. The intellect has no organ. Since intellectual power is spiritual, the subsisting principle from which this power proceeds (the soul) is also spiritual" (Maritain, 1953, p. 6).

Aquinas says that "the human soul, by reason of its perfection, is not a form (completely) merged in matter, or entirely embraced by matter (*ST* I, Ia, QQ 1-119)" (p. 300). We know, of course, that our knowledge comes through the bodily senses and brain. Aquinas here refers to the acts proper to intellect itself. As Lonergan concluded, acts following experience or encounter with perceptible data are proper to the intellect: understanding the data that the senses experience, judging or verifying the truth of our conjectures, and deciding to pursue the good. According to Aquinas, we do not have direct access to self. We only indirectly come to self-knowledge and knowledge that we have a soul by perceiving that we exist, sense things, understand, and conduct other activities (*ST* III, IIa-Iiae, QQ 1-148).

Contemporary psychology, particularly Freud's theories about the impact of unconscious drives on human choice and personality, tends to emphasize self-consciousness. From the mind's self-awareness derives the sense of *ego* or *I*. Aquinas, however, observed that the soul is not a whole human being; I am not identical to my soul. "My soul is not I" (Aquinas, 1953, Super primam epistolam ad Corinthios lectura. In R. Cai (ed.), *Super Spistolas S. Pauli lectura*, Vol. 1, p 411, in Kenny, 1988, p. 27). Aristotle and Aquinas observe that from the experience of the data of reality, mental acts give rise to self-consciousness, but self-consciousness is not equivalent to intellect. Neither egos nor self-consciousness are souls.

We need to distinguish between *egos* and *selves*. *Ego* can refer to a center of conscious thought, while *self* means person, a single entity with two principles, body and soul. "The person we are is the singularized unity of spirit/body, which with consciousness is subjectively experienced as a self (a phenomenological identity), with a story (narrative identity), who is always a corporeal person while alive (ontological identity)" (Sanguineti, 2022, p. 8). The human person has a soul with a property of intellect, which sometimes engages in self-consciousness, but some humans are not able to think. They may be embryos not yet ready to be born, or they might be in a coma from severe brain damage. They would not be self-conscious or even rational but would be human beings. Aquinas would likely agree that humans are *selves*, but not that we are always self-conscious *egos* (Garcia-Valdecasas, 2005, p. 55). We also distinguish between external and internal, first- and third-person dimensions of self. In religion, the standard model of the human person is 'body and soul,' and in psychology, 'body' and 'mind' (Helminiak, 2015, p. 250). Aquinas' philosophy and psychology are helpful for making these distinctions.

We turn now to Lonergan's Aristotelian-Thomistic epistemology, which is helpful because it is based on Thomistic philosophy. Lonergan attempted to extend the scientific method to all areas of human inquiry, considering both externally derived sense data and interior information from consciousness. He developed four transcendental precepts, not culturally constricted, that pertain to all domains of reality: *be attentive, intelligent, reasonable, and responsible* (Jones, 2015). And he makes anthropological distinctions that clarify levels of human consciousness.

Neurotheology, in the juxtaposition of neuroscience with theology, asks whether an anthropological foundation in the dynamics of the human soul would support such a theory. Lonergan's theory shows how it does. His *generalized empirical method* (GEM) offers insights into a set of cognitive activities, followed by personal verification of insights and ways that we use values to make moral decisions (Dunne, 2003). Lonergan reflects on levels of consciousness. His GEM considers a tripartite model for the mind: organism, psyche, and spirit. "Animate and sensate reflexivity and sensation pertain to the human as an *organism*; perceptual responsiveness, as *psyche*; and intentional consciousness, as *spiritual* (italics added)" (Helminiak, 2015, p. 251). All three levels pertain to some form of *consciousness.*

The primary dimension of the mind for all living organisms (animals) is *animate reflexivity*—their sensitivity to stimuli. Animate reflexivity may be either (1) *sensate reflexivity*, as for specific sense organs in some animals, and (2) *perceptual responsiveness*, that higher animals share with humans: emotions, imagery, conation (innate inclination, urge, or desire), and memory. On the level of *organisms*, including the neurophysiological brain, humans share an extraverted sensitive consciousness with animals.

There are distinctions in cognition between humans and animals. Microscopic study of the human brain at the cellular level has found "neural structures, enhanced wiring, and forms of connectivity among nerve cells not found in any animal" (Premack, 2007, p. 13861). Cognition is evaluated not by microscope but by comparing cases. Large human-animal dissimilarities have been found in areas such as causal reasoning, teaching, planning, short-term memory, and theory of mind. The next challenge is to find cellular-level differences between human and animal brains (p. 13867). In human beings, the *psyche* is closely associated with some specific level of the organism—the brain—in that sensitive perception encounters data. These data are then used to develop our levels of knowing.

Levels of knowing

Lonergan observed that our attentiveness to our intellectual functioning, our "self-appropriation" (1957/1992, pp. 2-21) reveals these components: experience, understanding, and judgment (1957/1992, 1980-1990), followed by a fourth implicit in his later works (Dadosky, 2010, p. 768), valuation and ethics in behavior. He based his epistemology on what might be regarded as four levels of consciousness: experience, understanding, judgment, and decision. In other words, pay attention to the data of experience, try to understand the meaning inherent in reality, determine whether your conclusions are accurate, and pursue the good.

First, *experience.* The human experience of the data we encounter corresponds to the first levels of consciousness. Lonergan (1967d, 1957/1992) follows Aristotle in showing that in the first level of human consciousness (*experience* of encounter with data), perceptions are formed by the mind into *images,* a term that includes more than visual, all perceptual phantasms, psychologically known as "representations" (e.g., Pylyshyn, 1973; Podgorny and Shepard, 1978). From representations of the data perceived, the psyche seeks insight through inquiry. Lonergan held that *the data of consciousness* (1957/1992, p. 299) are as valid in the domain of the mind as are *the data of the senses* in the natural sciences for physical entities (Helminiak, 2015, pp. 18-19). Experience works on data that identify whatever is to be known or understood, which could be anything a human being encounters. We have access to experience only through consciousness working on the data of experience (p. 19).

The second level of consciousness is *understanding.* In understanding, insight that is drawn from the data is intellectually grasped and understood. According to Helminiak, insight's actualization of intentional consciousness is a *spiritual* act (2015, p. 251):

> Lonergan's epistemology can (make sense of non-material reality) because it identifies the real not as the palpably experienceable but as the meaningful/intelligible. We do not sense the intelligibility of anything, but we understand and affirm it. The same is true of the human mind and consciousness: unlike the brain, it cannot be looked at, but it can be understood and affirmed. (Traska, 2017, p. 282)

From experience of data, the human being seeks understanding through verification of meaning. "Insight discerns patterns, order, coherence, interrelationship, systematization, explanation where earlier none was available. Intelligence grasps a new whole, an integrated unity" (Helminiak, 2015, p. 45). By finding coherence and explanation, we discover intelligibility and meaning. Intellect takes its object into itself, unbounded by temporal or spatial limitations. "To experience insight is to quintessentially engage the consciousness or spiritual dimension of the mind" (p. 54). In grasping relationships within the experience of data, the conscious mind uses spiritual mental activity to generate meaning. Through perceptions, insights, and ideas, human knowledge attains reality as it is. "Lonergan's theory presents human knowing as an ongoing process, ever open to new data, ever facing new questions, ever correcting past mistakes, ever adding splinters of knowledge to a growing synthesis" (p. 55) toward knowledge of being, correct understanding of reality.

Central to the human dimension of consciousness called *psyche* is an elusive, amazing key transition: In the act of cognition, the human mind makes use of *phantasms* (common also to animals) or *representations* emergent from sensate physiological data in the brain. With a spiritual capacity (i.e., *understanding*), the person intellectually comprehends the meaning or intelligibility of the data.

> Inquiry affects the transition from empirical consciousness to intellectual consciousness. Inquiry manifests itself in 'questions for intelligence,' such as 'What? and Why? and How often' (Lonergan, 1957/1992, p. 298). 'Insights are expressed in concepts, suppositions, definitions, postulates, hypotheses, theories (p. 278). (Allen, 2016, p. 452)

What is understood ultimately is reality as it is, including the metaphysical realm. It is not some concept or construction that is invented by the mind, even though we can make things up as well.[4]

Third, *judgment* (veridicality). On the foundations of *experience* and *understanding*, the third level of consciousness—*judgment*—can build. *Judgment* determines whether one has understood correctly by consulting the evidence (as in science). "Reflective understanding 'grasps the sufficiency of the evidence for a prospective judgment' (Lonergan, 1957/1992, p. 304)" (Allen, 2016, p. 452).

According to Lonergan's epistemology, science belongs to the second level of consciousness, *understanding*. Empirical science begins with data and derives a hypothesis from explaining it. The task of science now is to verify through experimentation whether the hypothesis is verifiable and can be considered a matter of fact, whether it squares with reality as it is (Helminiak, 2015, p. 60). Openness and honesty regarding the evidence are needed for this process. The idea elicited by insight needs judgment based on pertinent evidentiary support. This third element of consciousness—*judgment*—is, like *understanding*, a mental, spiritual power that builds on data from sensitive perception but is not limited or constrained by it.

Lonergan asks what is the force that drives the person to affirm or deny what is or is not true. He concludes: "At the root of the cognitional process, there is a cool, detached, disinterested desire to know, and its range is unrestricted" (1957/1992, p. 376). He means that the process is, at least by intention, unimpeded by bias, desires, and drives (p. 404). The desire to know "unrestrictedly intends a correspondingly unrestricted objective named being, or all, or everything about everything, or the concrete universe" (p. 380). (Allen, 2016, p. 453).

It is interesting to note that some of the original work in the field of neurotheology proposed a similar concept, the "cognitive imperative" (a new term not found in standard neuroscience), that had to do with the inherent human drive to use our cognitive processes. This occurred in an almost automatic fashion. For example, if you hear a noise in your house, your brain immediately begins thinking about what it is and what you should do about it. The brain does not need to be told to start working. Similarly, we use our minds to solve all types of problems, from the everyday issues we face at work to complex metaphysical questions. The important point is that there appears to be this natural drive, just as Lonergan suggested, to use our cognitional processes.

Fourth is a *decision* (action/behavior). *Decisions* can determine whether or not to act on what has been understood. In the fourth level of consciousness, *decision,* "one is responsible if one asks questions about the value and makes decisions on the basis of authentic judgments of value" in pursuit of the good (Traska, 2017, p. 284). A movement from knowing to acting completes the capacities of consciousness. Decision corresponds to a sense of responsibility. "This precept relates to a judgment of value and pertains to ethics" (Helminiak, 2015, p. 61).

In the domain of decision, Lonergan refers to a *transcendental exigence* that is finally grasped by ultimate concern and gives rise to religiously differentiated consciousness. This concept ties into the conceptualization of religion by theologian Paul Tillich as being involved in things of ultimate concern. There is "a vertical relation with a transcendent Other and the horizontal commitment to one's neighbor" (Dadosky, 2010, p. 772). The person ideally grows into a dynamic state of unrestricted being-in-love and (vertically) affirms the transcendent Other. For Christians, there is an acknowledgment that God's love is bestowed in the Holy Spirit (Rm 5:5), and the person pursues holiness (Lonergan, 1972/1990, p. 240-241). The decision requires surrender and commitment also (horizontally) to the welfare of family, society, and humankind (Dadosky, 2010, p. 771).

In future sections, we will explore different levels of consciousness that expand on this conceptualization of Lonergan's and consider how these levels are associated with brain processes. From our initial ability to receive information from the world through our senses to our ability to understand and make decisions about the world, to mystical awareness, we would argue that there are important reciprocal relationships between the brain and these different levels of awareness or consciousness.

Epistemological distinctions: Descriptive and explanatory knowing

"Lonergan's key contribution to epistemology was to sort out and interrelate two basic kinds of knowing" (Helminiak, 2015, p. 157). Sensate-based, common sense knowing describes things as they appear to our senses; intellectual, scientific knowing explains things using intelligence to show how they relate to one another. Lonergan (1957/1992) calls these two approaches descriptive and explanatory (pp. 107-109, 201-203, 316-317, 320-321) (p. 158).

The person as one material/spiritual entity

Experience, understanding, judgment, and decision are properties of intentional consciousness, so they are constituents of the mind. These are properties of the human being that define awareness and belong to the person who has intentional consciousness (Helminiak, 2015, pp. 157-158). "The human being comprises organism, psyche, and spirit yet is one thing. Epistemology is the crux of the matter" (p. 159). We would also argue that while these are a combination of biological and spiritual properties of the person, there is always an important interrelationship that can be studied. This ability to evaluate both the spiritual and biological can be considered from the perspective of neurotheology.

The person acts as one body and soul entity. Since *action follows being* and the person can act spiritually, with insight transcending space and time, the person must be partly spiritual. The soul, with its intelligibility, is not identical to the brain, although it cannot function in earthly life apart from the brain.[5] "If we transcend the limits of matter in our *actions*, we must also transcend matter in our very *being*, since action follows being" (Dodds, 2019, p. 908). The biological emphasis of neuroscience considers the material physiological level, assuming also higher levels. For philosophical anthropology and psychology, higher levels infuse and confer meaning on the whole human body, as well as the brain (Sanguineti, 2022, p. 8).

The rational, volitional soul

According to Thomistic anthropology, the intellect operates independently of matter, so because action follows being, the intellect must not be material. Intellectual and spiritual activities include knowledge of universals, having universal ideas of specific concrete things (like *house* or *yard*), abstract ideas (like *justice*), and immaterial cognitive operations (like *mathematics*). And the intellect can engage in self-reflection and consider itself and its behaviors. The whole intellect reflects upon not extended material parts of sensitive data but a whole spiritual entity (its being and action). It follows, Aquinas concludes, that the intellect must be immaterial (*SCG* III, c. 49, no. 8). The soul, being spiritual, cannot be generated materially. The brain is essential to the person, necessary but not sufficient for intellectual, voluntary, and spiritual functioning. "Thought is not caused by a brain connection; on the contrary, a thought triggers a brain connection" (Sanguineti, 2022, p. 8). "Since the rational soul does not depend in its existence on corporeal matter, and is subsistent, and exceeds the capacity of corporeal matter, it is not educed from the potentiality of matter (*ST* 1, q. 90, a. 2, ad 2)." The spiritual soul must be created individually by a purely spiritual Entity. "The rational soul can be made only by creation (*ST* 1, q. 90, a. 2, resp.)." (Dodds, 2019, p. 909).

With the separation of the substantial form and primary matter at death, the spiritual soul does not decompose, as do the physical components of the body.

> As to its destiny, the human soul does not cease to be when the human being dies. Since the human soul transcends matter, it may continue to exist even without its material co-principle of primary matter. In this continued existence, however, the soul is not a complete human being. (Dodds, 2019, p. 909)

Catholic belief looks to a final resurrection at the end of time when soul and body will be reunited (*CCC*, 1015-1017). Jesus, after his resurrection and while still in his time on earth, could appear and disappear and walk into locked rooms. After his resurrection, he was not easily or readily known by his close associates. It is not clear whether he could choose at will to hide or disguise his appearance or whether it was the disciples' spiritual obtuseness that prevented them from recognizing him. The Catholic anticipation of a new heaven and new earth (Rv 21:1f) includes a new immortal body/soul unity without sadness, fatigue, sickness, disease, and the temporal limitations we experience now.

How does a Catholic hylomorphic understanding of the human person understand the soul?

> As a principle, the soul is a concept that explains the unity of consciousness and its powers. Human consciousness is something different from other forms of consciousness or awareness (in animals), and the soul is one way to articulate the difference. (Hess and Allen, 2008, p. 166)

For neuroscience, the soul is generally assumed to be associated primarily with the brain, the central integrating organ for the body. "The soul is a concept that designates the agency that marks the brain in operation" (p. 166). According to Thomistic anthropology, however:

> the soul does not reside in any part of the body. The soul uses the brain, yet the brain is not an organ of intelligence. The intellect has no organ. The body does not contain it but rather contains it. (Maritain, 1953, p. 6)

To summarize, according to one Thomistic Catholic understanding, the soul is directly created individually by God, united to the body at the moment of conception, and held in existence from one moment to the next, as is all contingent creation. The mind is the immaterial rational property of the subsistent soul, connected to but not derived from the brain. The mind operates with consciousness when, as Lonergan explains, it experiences, understands, judges, and decides. The brain is the physiological integrating/organizing organ of the body. The brain can be generated physically, but to function with consciousness, it needs the immaterial rational mind, a property of the soul.

Consciousness: Conscious and intentional

Human consciousness has dual poles: the self-aware subject and the object with which the subject is concerned, reflecting on, or involved with (Helminiak, 2015, p. 245). Ontologically fundamental is the originating point: one must be self-present, aware that one is aware as the starting point of experiencing, the experiencer. And secondarily, the experience is simultaneously intentional in subjectively tending or orienting attention toward some object. While writing this, the experiencer may be both aware of seeing fruit trees outside their window and concomitantly aware of engaging in the subjective act of looking out the window. "Within human sight are both the seen and the seeing. The seen is experienced in the seeing which is present 'to' the seer" (p. 255).

The same is true for intellectual understanding. I can both seek the solution to a problem and be conscious that I am seeking it. I can both find a solution and know that I have found it. My consciousness is both directed toward the object of my perception or inquiry and aware of myself as the subject who is acting, the experience of the object I am tending toward. The *I* who is acting is always more than can be said. I am always potentially acting again, looking for more content for reflection—about the data of reality and my subjectivity.

> This presence *to* oneself constitutes data not only on any intentional object of interest but also on oneself, the subject who is intending the object. This presence *to* oneself constitutes (a) the data of consciousness into which (b) inquiry can provide insight and interpretation and (c) against which judgment can test the interpretation. (Helminiak, 2015, p. 257)

We can become aware of our manner or style of knowing. We can have our sense of self as an ongoing identity. The psychological experience of self may be the core of transcendent experiences (p. 319).

Challenges for consciousness

Psyche includes *perceptual responsiveness*, including emotion, imagery, conation (desire or volition), memory, and, for humans, personality. If the four levels of consciousness functioned in an ideal manner, we would smoothly grasp the truth and pursue the good. But as with all things human, such is not always the case. *Psyche*—dependent as it is on a body and working brain—makes an impact that may not always be fully beneficial. Positively, the psyche provides the data that consciousness experiences to know reality. Negatively, the psyche can interject biases, and human desires and drives, as well as neurologic deficits, can distort and mislead the workings of consciousness.

Humans are unique among terrestrial beings in having access also to the *spirit*, the mental realm of intellectual consciousness by which lower levels become accessible to human self-conscious attention, inquiry, and cognition. Challenges for seeking truth and pursuit of goodness can also arise from dimensions of the spiritual level.

Intentional consciousness, Lonergan, refers to the aspect of the human mind (in levels two, three, and four: *understanding, judgment,* and *decision*) that makes meaning, abstracts from temporal-spatial data, comprehends universals, and decides. Intentional consciousness refers to the human capacity to be present to oneself and concomitantly aware of other objects of attention (Helminiak, 2015, p. 243). Intentional consciousness is a form of responsiveness directed not simply to the physical data of experience but to the realm of being, to all that human beings may know and love (p. 247).

We will see in the next chapter how Lonergan's transcendental precepts (each matching one of the levels of consciousness): *be attentive, intelligent, reasonable, and responsible,* assist the human individual and collective in striving for authenticity (Helminiak, 2021, pp. 2-3).

To summarize, humans are comprised of an organism, psyche, and spirit—a single hylomorphic entity with two principles: body and mind. The mind is closely connected to the body, including and principally the brain, but is not identical with it. The human mind has a consciousness that engages in experience, understanding, judgment, and decision. From the physiological aspect of the mind comes animate reflexivity. From the psyche with perceptual responsiveness, we derive emotion, imagery, conation, memory, and personality. From spirit comes intentional consciousness with intellectual and decision-making capacities. Some elements of these processes also connect with the biological aspects of the brain. It is important to consider a neurotheological perspective to emphasize the person, the soul, consciousness, and faculties as they may relate to the physiological rather than beginning with the neural substrate and risk neglecting the spiritual dimension ontologically unique to the human person.

Understanding that relationship could be essential in better understanding how the organism, psyche, and spirit, much like the brain, mind, and soul, are intimately interconnected.

Cognition: Embodied, embedded, enactive, extended

Philosophical questions about what minds are and how to understand concepts and representations have been raised, particularly since the 1990s, by the theory that intelligent behavior emerges from the interaction of brain, body, and world. One cognitive science theory is that the brain does not operate on its own but is embodied, embedded, enactive, and extended (4Es). From a notion beginning with Plato and Aristotle, through Augustine and medieval times to the present, thinkers have considered the mind *embodied*. Perception, spatial navigation, theory of mind, and action all depend on embodied, real-time interaction with the environment. They can be localized to specific networks in the brain. Spatial navigation, for example, utilizes the parietal lobes, and the hippocampus has been found to be essential in developing spatial maps. At the same time, it is the person and not the brain that engages in these actions.

Embedded cognition means that an individual succeeds better cognitively when they interact—embeddedly—with an appropriate physical or social environment. Children are better with arithmetic, for example, when they use manipulatives, e.g., visualizing a fraction by cutting a pie.

Enactive cognition observes that problem-solving and all intelligent operations involve active engagement with the environment through dynamic coupling to tools or other persons. *The Embodied Mind* (1991) was developed by Chilean biologist, philosopher, and neuroscientist Francisco Varela (1946-2001), professor of philosophy Evan Thompson, and psychologist Eleanor Rosch. Their work holds that enactive cognition means that an organism actively uses its sensorimotor processes to match its actions to the difficulties of the situation. Perception, cognition, and emotion are thought to be tightly integrated in the person's sense-making. In the enactive approach, though, the mind is not confined to the individual's brain. "Mind is defined as a meaningful activity in the world" (Froese, 2015, p. 1). Enactive cognition studies the intricate discrepancies between phenomenological subjective and biological experience. Sense-making combines sensation, interpretation, and valuation to enact in context a meaningful perspective on the world, which may also encompass other subjects and their perspectives (Froese).

Cognition is *extended* when affordances facilitate thinking: environment, tools, another person, information, opportunity, or concepts. Clark and Chalmers in *The Extended Mind* (1998) suggest that external instruments, such as a computer, journal, or whatever stores information, could belong by extension to cognition, actively driving the mind in its thinking process.

Epistemological questions about the 4E theory are around how to decide whether a cognitive process is constituted by or depends on extracranial processes

(Newen, Gallagher, and De Bruin, 2018). We will consider methodological issues around 4E cognition in the next chapter.

Theology: Built on revelation

Beyond natural knowledge with its orders and degrees, there is suprarational knowledge—theological wisdom or the *science of revealed mysteries*—and, above that, *mystical theology*. Distinct from metaphysical knowledge that depends on reason, theology draws on faith and focuses on revelation. Mystical knowledge, by connaturality, depends on the supernatural capacity (*Degrees of Knowledge*, 1932 [1959/1995], p. 253) and can be pursued through the practice of charity and contemplation. Mysticism, of course, can be found also outside of Christianity.

Catholic theology builds on the revelation of the Persons of the Trinity and the Person of Jesus to understand human life and its purpose. In his encyclical *Fides et Ratio* (1998), Pope John Paul II expounds on the fundamental Church position that faith and reason are interdependent and both are essential for answering life's ultimate questions (McGoldrick, 2012, p. 484). For most Christian believers, faith is not grounded on exceptional mystical experiences. Everyday faith is generally based on belief in the simple, profound truths of revelation, trust in a benevolent Creator, obedience to guidance by the Holy Spirit, in the revelation of Jesus as Lord, and meaning found in joining with His suffering, charity, and cooperation with others, confidence in prayer, and putting beliefs into practice (Clarke, 2015, p. 190). The record of revelation in the New Testament, Hebrew Scriptures, and Church Tradition, together with the Magisterium, the Spirit-guided teaching authority, provide a context for Catholics in interpreting religious as well as life experience.

Theology, based on the revelation of God and accessible by faith, proceeds through the light of reason. Since it rests on truths that faith understands to be divine, theology emphasizes Mystery. Human understanding of the truths that we believe about Mystery will always be inadequate, yet also more solid than what metaphysics can offer. Theology considers God in aspects otherwise unknowable, things pertaining to himself alone, as he will be seen and known in the Beatific Vision (Maritain, 1932 [1959/1995], p. 265). "No one has ever seen God; it is the only Son, who is close to the Father's heart, who has made him known" (Jn 1:18).

> If God himself had not revealed it, never would we have known that the notions of generation and filiation, or the notion of three having the same nature, or the notion of being made flesh and of the personal union with human nature, or the notion of participability in deity by the creature and the love of friendship with it, could be valid in the proper

order of the deity itself, and in regard to the intimate life of God. (Maritain, 1932 [1959/1995], p. 257)

For human reason to explore the tenets of revelation, there needs to be in the soul intellectual virtue proportionate to the divine object. The supernatural light of faith penetrates beyond where natural philosophy might go and guides and directs the natural light of reason (Maritain, 1932 [1959/1995]). "The theological virtues (faith, hope, and charity) relate directly to God. They encourage Christians to live in a relationship with the Holy Trinity. They have the One and Triune God for their origin, motive, and object" (*CCC*, 1812). "God infuses them into the souls of the faithful . . . . They are the pledge of the presence and action of the Holy Spirit in the faculties of the human being" (*CCC*, 1813). "Faith is the theological virtue by which we believe in God and believe all that he has said and revealed because he is truth itself" (*CCC*, 1814). God infuses the theological virtues (faith, hope, and charity) into those who accept the grace of faith. The theological virtues empower the faculties of the human soul with the action of the Holy Spirit (*CCC*, 1812-1814).

Sanctifying grace and Divine Indwelling

Catholicism holds that the human person who receives the gratuitous created gift of sanctifying grace begins to participate as an adopted son or daughter in the life of God. The calling to eternal life is "a stable and supernatural disposition that perfects the soul itself to enable it to live with God, to act by his love" (*CCC*, 2000).

> Since it belongs to the supernatural order, grace *escapes our experience* and cannot be known except by faith. We cannot rely on our feelings or our works to conclude that we are justified, but reflection on God's blessings can spur us on to trustful poverty (*CCC*, 2005).

Maritain makes an interesting observation about epistemology as it relates to Catholic theology, perhaps approaching a central aspect of the relationship between neuroscience and theology. "Both science and religion claim to give a description to the same world and the human experience thereof, and thus the primary locus for tension between them is usually perceived as being epistemological" (Bennet, 2019a, p. 91). Maritain reflects:

> No science or wisdom exists unless, within the soul, there is a genuine intellectual virtue proportioning the light of discrimination and judgment to the proper level of the object. To an object which is the depths of revealed divinity, insofar as it can be exploited by reason, there must necessarily correspond, as its light in the soul, not the light of philosophy, but a proportionate light, the light of supernatural faith

taking up and directing the natural movement of reason and its natural way of knowing. (1932 [1959/1995], p. 269)

Supernatural sanctifying grace is necessary beyond our natural way of knowing so we can grasp God with understanding and love in a real, though limited, way. We need "a new root of a spiritual operation whose proper and specifying object is the Divine Essence itself (John of St. Thomas, *Theol.*, I-II, q. 110, disp. 22, a. 1 [Vives, t. VI, pp. 790ff])" (Maritain, 1932 [1959/1995], p. 271). Catholic theology understands sanctifying grace as gratuitously, lovingly bestowed by God on the person who is open and receptive. Grace is an inherent ontological capacity, quality, or habit placed in the soul as the seed or root principle of the Beatific Vision.

> This supernatural spiritual principle (has) as its connatural object the subsistent Supernatural and (renders) us proportionate in the depths of our being to an essentially divine object. . . . With charity, this new nature develops within us a whole organism of supernatural energies— theological virtues of hope and faith, gifts of the Holy Spirit, and infused moral virtues. These establish our conversation in heaven. (Maritain, 1932 [1959/1995], p. 272)

In the order of being, human recipients of grace remain human, infinitely distant from the Divine. Nevertheless, according to Catholic theology, in spiritual operation and its object, informed by grace, they participate in the Divine Nature. This is more than a metaphor; it is a metaphysical reality known by supernatural faith, a radical transformation that may not register or be perceived on the natural level. Grace makes the recipient a son or daughter of God who lives with divine life. This "distinction between the natural order and the supernatural order is at the very heart of the Catholic faith" (Maritain, 1932 [1959/1995], p. 272). The recipient of sanctifying grace is supernaturally ordered to the Divine Essence in the soul and its faculties by "infused qualities to possibilities absolutely inaccessible to their nature alone" (Maritain, 1932 [1959/1995], p. 273).

The effect of human elevation to the state of grace consists in a new form of the presence of God within the soul: the indwelling of the Trinity in the soul. According to Catholic theology, God is always present in all creation and every part of it, including humans. Simply because God is necessary and everything else is contingent, he must be present, holding everything in existence all the time. This presence, due to his immensity, means that at the core of all that exists is God conferring being to creatures by his infinite efficacy, being, and action. But grace is something other than this common presence of immensity. "It is a question of a special presence peculiar to souls in the state of grace . . . as term toward which the soul is inwardly turned . . . and ordered as to an object of loving knowledge" (Maritain, 1932 [1959/1995], p. 273). This loving knowledge is:

> a fruitful, experimental (John of St. Thomas, *Curs. Theol.*, IP., q. 2, disp. 17, a. 3, n. 10 [Vives, t. IV]) knowledge and love which puts us in possession of God and unites us to him not at a distance, but really. For if the Divine Persons give themselves to us, it is in order that we may possess them, that they may be *ours* (John of St. Thomas, In *I Sent.*, dist. 14, q. 2, a. 2, ad 2) (Maritain, 1932 [1959/1995], p. 274). Thus, it is clear that mystical experience and infused contemplation are, indeed, seen to be the normal, rightful end of the life of grace. They could even be said to be the summit toward which all human life tends. . . . Christian life itself . . . tends to the mystical life. (Maritain, 1932 [1959/1995], p. 175)

Neurotheology

The epistemological question for neurotheology arises around dissimilar methodologies for science and theology. We will explore methodology more carefully in the next chapter. Science proceeds by observation and experiment, testing by induction and deduction of the data around physical phenomena, and coming to rational conclusions with reasonable certainty or (as in psychology or neuropsychology) statistically significant probability. Theology works heuristically with faith-based reason, building on tenets of revelation around the Divine and ultimate questions. While there is clearly an overlap between science and theology, particularly as they both importantly affect the human condition, there can also be differences of opinion about how they ought to relate. According to Ian Barbour, as we noted, science and theology relate through "theories of conflict, separation, dialogue, or integration" (Stone, 2000, p. 417).

A key question in the relationship between science and theology involves attention to the metaphysical and epistemological challenges to authentic collaboration and development of knowledge (Bennet, 2019a, p. 88). A valuable aim of neurotheology could be to combine theology's profound comprehension grounded in philosophy and faith with insights from current neuroscientific studies of the central integrating organ of the human person for a fuller understanding of the human condition (p. 95). Catholic philosophers and theologians might find a good dialogue partner in neurotheology. In some matters, such as the immortality of the soul, where faith assists in a definitive conclusion, agnostic scientists might not be so readily convinced. Still, scientists studying the neural concomitants of religious experience might wish to explore the Catholic perspective.

Christians would easily agree that the experience of God has neural correlates. Natural processes can impact the person who has religious faith. God might have designed the brain so that neural processes might be the material basis of knowing that he exists and concerning his attributes (McIlhenny, 2011). In the next chapter on methodology, we will consider some challenges and opportunities for convergence between neuroscience and theology.

Neurotheology considers spiritual life beyond the physiological brain, including the soul, meaning, freedom, morality, and purpose. Characteristics of spiritual experience for the human person necessarily have neuronal and neurotransmitter correlates. Such spiritual experiences include qualities of unity, intensity, clarity, surrender, transformation, and a sense of realness. The encounter of neurotheological themes with Catholic theology highlights the philosophical fields of metaphysics and epistemology. Catholic theology uses philosophy and faith to explore mysteries of revelation as they relate to human knowing and willingness. Sanctifying grace and the Divine Indwelling, with the theological virtues and gifts of the Holy Spirit, promotes a life of virtue that may flourish in mystical knowing by connaturality. Epistemological methodology for the neuroscience-theology dialogue is an area in the process of exploration and development.

Study Questions

1. The *soul* is comprised of intellect and will. For intellect, how is *ratio* distinguished from *intellectus*?

2. What is *will*?

3. What are types of affectivity: emotions, passions, affections?

4. What is the current emphasis in philosophy of mind? What might the various fields contribute to understanding the *mind*? From a Catholic perspective, what might the current emphasis overlook?

5. According to Zagzebski, what are the "two greatest ideas"? Why does this matter?

6. Thomist philosophy grounds epistemology in realist metaphysics— first principles and God as the ultimate cause. Why does this matter for the Catholic understanding of the human person and how we know what is real?

7. What is a Thomist/Catholic understanding of the *soul*?

8. Why would scientific empiricist epistemologies be problematic for interpreting neuroscientific data?

9. What is the epistemological challenge for neurotheology? Explain.

10. Distinguish among Lonergan's dimensions of mind: organism, psyche, and spirit.

11. How does the self differ from ego and person? Why are these distinctions significant?

12. Lonergan's generalized empirical method (GEM) attempts to extend the scientific method to all areas of inquiry. What are his four transcendental precepts?

13. What are Lonergan's four levels of consciousness? How do they correspond to his four transcendental precepts?

14. What is Lonergan's understanding of transcendental exigence?

15. How does Thomism/Catholic belief explain the spiritual principle of the human person? The origin of the human soul? Its immortality?

16. How does neuroscience generally understand the soul as it relates to the brain?

17. How does Thomistic anthropology, Catholic hylomorphism, understand distinctions among the soul, mind, and brain?

18. How is consciousness both conscious and intentional?

19. What are some challenges for consciousness? Explain.

20. Why is it important for neurotheology to emphasize the spiritual (person, soul, consciousness) rather than focusing only on the physical brain to neglect the potential spiritual dimensions of the human being?

21. How can cognition be understood as embodied, embedded, enactive, and extended?

22. Why is it important to keep in mind that it is the person, not the brain, that engages with the environment?

23. Explain how theology builds on faith and revelation, as well as reason, for answering ultimate questions in everyday life.

24. What are some aspects of Christian theology, beyond what reason could attain, that revelation and theological virtues provide?

25. Can grace be reliably perceived or experienced? How does this pertain to neuroscientific brain scanning of religious experience?

26. How does Catholic theology understand sanctifying grace?

27. Metaphysical transformation by supernatural faith may not register or be perceived on the natural level. Is this always true, or to varying degrees in individual cases? Explain.

28. What about scientific or empirical measurement or experiential evidence of the effects of grace?

29. According to Catholic theology, besides God's presence by immensity in all creation, including humans, God dwells by special presence in souls who respond to grace, tending even to mystical life. What does this mean?

30. Why is the relationship between science and theology challenging epistemologically? Or, how do science and theology differ in their approach to truth?

31. What might neurotheology contribute to understanding the human condition, particularly from a Catholic perspective?

Endnotes

[1] An alternate twentieth-century movement, empirical theology, requires religious ideas to be justified through human experience.

[2] Contemporary epistemologists include William Alston, Robert Audi, Paul A. Boghossian, Laurence BonJour, Stewart Cohen, Keith DeRose, Richard Feldman, Jane Friedman, Alvin L. Goldman, John Greco, Maria Lasonen-Aarnia, Sarah Moss, Ram Neta, Duncan Pritchard, Suzanna Rinard, Miriam Schoenfeld, Ernest Sosa, Matthias Steup, and Crispin Wright (Steup & Neta, 2020). Contemporary virtue epistemologists include Mark Alfano, Jason S. Baehr, John Greco, Duncan Pritchard, Wayne Riggs, Ernest Sosa, John Turri, and Linda Trinkaus Zagzebski (Turri, Alfano, and Greco, 2021).

[3] Today, the "new" metaphysics develops theories about modality (pertaining to the possibility of necessity; space and time; persistence and constitution; causation, freedom, and determinism; the mental and the physical; the methodology of metaphysics; and whether metaphysics is even possible (van Inwagen, 2014).

[4] This is one way in which Thomistic realism differs from Kant. In his *Critique of Pure Reason*, "scholars generally agree that for Kant, transcendental idealism encompasses at least the (claim that) in some sense, human beings experience only appearances, not things in themselves. 'All our intuition is nothing but the representation of appearance . . not (things) in themselves. . . If we remove our subject. . . then all constitution. . . would disappear, and as appearances, they cannot exist in themselves, but only in us. . . We are acquainted with nothing except our way of perceiving them, . . . which does not necessarily pertain to every being (A42/B59-60)" (Rohlf, 2020, pp. 9-10).

[5] After death, the person's soul continues to function. "Heaven is the blessed community of all who are perfectly incorporated into Christ " (*CCC*, 1026). "In the glory of heaven, the blessed continue joyfully to fulfill God's will in relation to other men and to all creation" (*CCC*, 1029). Since the human person comprises both body and soul as a single entity, the human deceased exists in a state of imperfection until the final resurrection, when body and soul are reunited at the end of time. "I believe in . . . the resurrection of the dead and life everlasting" (The Apostles' Creed).

Chapter 4

Methodology in Neuroscience and Catholicism

Methods and paradigms in science

At the outset, it must be admitted that when there is a conflict between science and religion, it relates partly to the methodological approaches of both. In some ways, there are important similarities, and of course, there are important differences as well. The scientific method generally starts with a hypothesis based on some observation or idea by the investigator. The hypothesis pertains to some aspect of the natural world and is hopefully amenable to evaluation through some experimentation. The experimentation should provide information or data to either support or refute the initial hypothesis. Once an experiment is performed, the new information obtained is blended with the initial hypothesis to either strengthen it or weaken it. If the new data does not support the original hypothesis, a new or revised hypothesis must be derived. Thus, science is based on a continual ebb and flow of new ideas and new data that push ideas and hypotheses forward and vice versa.

While religion has been around since the origin of human beings, science itself has been around for thousands of years.[1] However, it has been only in recent times that more sophisticated methods have been developed. That is why, in ancient times, when people observed the sun transiting across the sky, they naturally assumed, or hypothesized, that the sun was circling the earth. It required thousands of years and special instruments such as telescopes to be able to determine exactly how the solar system is arranged with the earth circling about the sun.

Relevant to the discussion between science and religion are the various paradigms that science follows. Philosopher of science Thomas Kuhn (1922-1996) describes the issue in his well-known book *The Structure of Scientific Revolutions*[2], which is about a new lens to interpret the data. The new lens shifts the paradigm.

Paradigms have to do with overall perspectives on the natural world. Importantly, though, these paradigms are hypotheses in and of themselves. For example, the original scientific paradigm regarding the nature of the universe was static. It was not until astronomer Edwin Hubble (1889-1953) used special measurements that the universe was determined to be, in fact, expanding. This ushered in a new paradigm based on the Big Bang theory. The Big Bang theory itself is a term that describes a general notion of how the universe came to be, at least from a materialistic perspective. However, there are multiple theories and hypotheses about how exactly the universe came to be. Some of these even require a virtually infinite number of universes in order to produce the one singular universe, our universe, that has the exactly right physics constants and forces that lead to the development of our universe as we see it. In science, paradigms do not shift easily. In fields as diverse as cosmology, chemistry, biology, and medicine, it often takes a multitude of experiments to overturn a prevailing paradigm. But sometimes, even in the face of new and compelling data, scientists, who are all human beings in the first place, frequently struggle to accept that data when they believe in a different paradigm.

One of the best examples of how difficult it can be to challenge paradigms arises from one of humanity's greatest geniuses, theoretical physicist Albert Einstein (1879-1955). When quantum mechanics was developed to help explain the nature of the atom, Einstein was wholly opposed to its concepts. He did not like the randomness of quantum mechanics and its implications for how the universe works. This led him to his famous line about God not playing dice with the universe. Try as he might to discredit quantum mechanics, every time he threw up a challenge or critiqued why quantum mechanics does not work, new experiments demonstrated that it did work. What was it about quantum mechanics that stymied even the greatest scientific genius of all time? From a psychological perspective, one can only conclude that it *just didn't make sense to him.* But therein lies the problem. When any person holds a particular belief or paradigm about the natural world, those beliefs bias how we view new information.

This is an important point because it affects how we look at new data. Often in history, initial scientific data were declared poor or inaccurate when they contradicted the prevailing paradigm. From a psychological perspective, we could ask a similar question. How much contrasting data is required to change our minds? It is also important to state here what is meant by data. Data and scientific methods can be vastly different depending on whether they relate to physics, chemistry, biology, or other fields. Accuracy refers to how closely a sample estimate matches the population on average. Physics may require an accuracy of 0.000001, while a medical study may only need an accuracy of 0.01.[3]

The scientific method is effective for experimentation and for reasonable empirical conclusions in the natural domain (Cohen and Nagel, 2007). Professor of philosophy and theology Michael Dodds (2017) brings the metaphysical assumptions of the scientific method into dialogue with Aristotelian-Thomistic metaphysics. Causality for the latter has four dimensions: *material, efficient, formal,* and *final* (Aristotle, *Metaphysics II;* Aquinas, *On the Principles of Nature,* ch. 3). Simply, for example, a *material* cause could be the physical materials to build a car; the *efficient* cause could be the company that produces it; the *formal* cause would be the kind of car that is made; and the *final* cause, the purpose of the car. Compared to Thomistic metaphysics, with four philosophically comprehensive causes, modern science generally does not claim to deal with metaphysics—only reasonable evidentiary conclusions in the realm of nature—and tends to narrow the meaning and scope of causality (2017). Causality in modern science is characterized by:

> (a) the restriction of causation to *natural* causation (naturalism); (b) the further restriction of all varieties of natural causes to *efficient* causation; (c) the endeavor to reduce efficient causes to *physical* ones (mechanism); (d) the requirement of *testing* causal hypotheses by means of repeated observations and, wherever possible, through reproduction in controllable experiments; (e) an extreme *cautiousness* in the assignment of causes and ceaseless striving toward the minimization of the number of allegedly ultimate natural causes (parsimony); (f) the focusing on the search for *laws,* causal or not; (g) the *mathematical* translation of causal connections. (Bunge, 1979, p. 206; Dodds, 2017, p. 48; in Alexander, 2018, p. 114)

When it comes to religion, the question of what constitutes *data* is essential to answer. Famous atheists such as British evolutionary biologist Richard Dawkins have questioned why anyone would believe in "god" when there is no "evidence" that god exists. A prior question is, "What is god?" Believers clearly do not share Dawkins' view of God.[4] But this misses an important scientific point. Suppose one speaks to a church congregation or a group of theologians. In that case, they will all describe a range of evidence that points to the existence of a loving, omnipotent, infinite, generous God, from sacred texts such as the Bible to personal experiences. In fact, most religious individuals perceive evidence of God all around them, whether in a sunset, the birth of a child, or the origin of the universe.

Similarly, scientists, as well as religious individuals, all take in data of various types to conclude the nature of reality. The free-standing, theory-free empirical data obtained through scientific methods can be contrasted against the religious data obtained through religious traditions. A theologian will evaluate a wide array of knowledge regarding God and the universe through biblical exegesis and hermeneutics.

Neurotheology asks us to consider how a person attributes meaning to various pieces of data, particularly wondering whether the neural substrate of their beliefs may be measurable physiologically (Newberg, 2010). Questions might arise like: Why is it that someone might believe in the Big Bang but not God? What type of data is necessary to convince any given individual that their own beliefs and paradigm accurately reflect the world around them? To which domain would these questions pertain? Would they be addressed by neurobiology, personality theory, psychology, or religion?

As we have seen, science deals with the realm of nature and sensory phenomena, working inductively, proposing hypotheses, and using exploration and investigation to come to understanding and attain knowledge through rational conclusions. The sciences follow empirical methods, looking for proof of significant statistical differences and evidence to support reasonable results. Science is concerned with the empirically demonstrable and stays within the domain of nature and reason. The fund of scientific knowledge flows from diligence in following the scientific method and building on the rational conclusions of former generations.

Religious paradigms and methods

Religion fits humans into a larger order of things. Catholicism builds on revelation and uses philosophy as a tool. Recently, theology has made progress by drawing on anthropology. Religion answers ultimate questions: Where did we come from? Where are we going? What is the meaning of life? Why is there misfortune and suffering? These questions are not answerable using sensible phenomena, experimentation, and rational conclusions.

Catholic theology begins with revelation and uses philosophy to understand and apply what is revealed. There are several approaches to philosophical considerations. John Paul II's encyclical *Fides et Ratio* (1998) reflects on the early Church encounter between faith and reason (nos. 36-42): "What does Athens have in common with Jerusalem?" (Tertullian, in no. 41). Early Christians had to contend with two currents—first, a radical incompatibility of Christianity with pagan culture, and secondly, openness to constructive dialogue with Greek philosophy. Generally, the pre-Nicene (325 CE) Church tended to harmonize philosophy and the Gospel through apologists, including Justin, Clement of Alexandria, and Origen. For theologian Clement (150—c. 213), the *Logos* was revealed, although imperfectly, in Greek philosophy as well as the Jewish Law. Philosopher Justin (c. 100—c. 165) anticipates Rahner's "anonymous" or implicit Christianity, respecting the secularity of Greek philosophy but showing that the truth found there supports the Gospel (dal Covolo, 1999, p. 3). Scholar and theologian Origen (c. 185—c. 253)

> proposes a spiritual journey in which faith and reason, knowledge, contemplation, and the mystical experience of God are not divergent

but penetrate each other and are continually offered to every Christian so that he can advance on the way to perfection. (p. 4)

The Fathers of the Church recognized that many paths lead to truth:

They fully welcomed reason, which was open to the absolute, and they infused it with the richness drawn from revelation. This was more than a meeting of cultures. Reason attained the supreme good and ultimate truth in the person of the Word made flesh. Faced with the various philosophies, the Fathers were not afraid to acknowledge those elements in them that were consonant with revelation and those that were not. (John Paul II, *Fides, et al.*, 1998, no. 41).

The Pope encourages theologians to "recover and express the metaphysical dimension of truth in order to enter into a demanding critical dialogue with both contemporary philosophical thought and with the philosophical tradition in all its aspects" (no. 105).

There are several approaches to philosophical reflection in Catholic theology. Thomism is typically recommended. The *Code of Canon Law* (1983) indicates that "seminarians are to penetrate more deeply into the mysteries of salvation, with St. Thomas as their teacher" (252.3). However, there are also other valid theologies, such as liberation theology, process theology, existential theology, and so on. Thomism demonstrates that the universe is objectively real. Human perception can accurately know reality as it is. Catholic theology based on realist philosophy takes God to be the Creator of all that is and reality to be naturally knowable. There must be a necessary, uncaused Cause in relation to which all else is contingent. Reality is understood to include an invariant order of being, hierarchically arranged from angels to humans, animals, plants, and inanimate objects. Humans are embodied organisms with spiritual capacities of intellect, will, and personal identity that survive beyond death.

As mentioned, the Catholic faith derives from revelation expressed in Scripture and Tradition.

The Tradition here in question comes from the apostles and hands on what they received from Jesus' teaching and example and what they learned from the Holy Spirit. . . . Tradition is to be distinguished from the various theological, disciplinary, liturgical, or devotional traditions, born in the local churches over time. These are the particular forms, adapted to different places and times, in which the great Tradition is expressed. In the light of Tradition, these traditions can be retained, modified, or even abandoned under the guidance of the Church's magisterium. (*CCC*, 83)

Tradition includes magisterial teaching, and "liturgy is a constitutive element of the holy and living Tradition" (*CCC*, 1124). There are also traditions with a small *t*: practices, such as Byzantine, spiritualities, works of charity, praying with an Advent wreathe, erecting a nativity scene during Christmas, chalking a door on Epiphany, fasting during Lent, receiving palms on Palm Sunday, and so on.

Faith requires a God-given ability to respond to revelation. The tenets of faith do not contradict reason but go beyond it. Theology uses reason to reflect on the experience of faith, including that humans are made in the image of God for the moral pursuit of goodness, truth, and beauty, with a destiny of eternal life and happiness with God.

Methods for theology derive from its being an interpretive/hermeneutical discipline where there is a "two-way movement or interdependence between data and explanatory theories" (Clayton, 2000, p. 620). Theology reflects on faith as it comes to expression in sacred Scripture, Tradition, experience, and the like.

Influential theologian Bernard Lonergan, as we have seen, considered a transcendental Thomist, developed an epistemology of human knowing with levels of experience. His four steps of intentionality and consciousness: (1) experience, (2) understanding, (3) judgment, and (4) decision—are universally applicable across all disciplines. Considering the scientific method, the scientist gains access to data (step 1: *be aware:* experience); develops a hypothesis (step 2: *be intelligent:* understanding); does experiments to test the hypothesis (step 3: *be rational:* judging); then acts accordingly (step 4: *be responsible:* deciding).

Building on this epistemology, he offered a transcendental method for theology, as well as science or any other domain. "If the definition of theology is faith-seeking understanding, then human knowing is the place to begin. The dynamic process of knowing always operates the same way: experiencing, understanding, judging, and deciding" (Lonergan, 1972, p. 13, n4) (Mueller, 1984, p. 14). The methods for theology, in eight functional specialties, correspond to the operations of human knowing.

> Research corresponds to *experience* (gathering data); (2) interpretation corresponds to *understanding* (what is meant by the data); (3) history corresponds to *judgment* (specifying human activities in time and place); (4) dialectic corresponds to the *decision* (seeking a comprehensive viewpoint to examine conflicts); (5) foundation corresponds to *decision* (Christian conversion that enables acceptance of doctrine); (6) doctrine corresponds to *judging* facts and values; (7) systematics works toward a comprehensive *understanding* of theology; and (8) communications is

concerned with external *communication* of theology. (Mueller, 1984, pp. 17-18)

Using Lonergan's universally applicable four levels of consciousness, the only difference between scientific and theological methods is the data experienced. Judging (step 3) will require that scientific and theological data be treated appropriately to the discipline.

The open-ended, transcendental levels of consciousness applicable to any field of study specify the line of reasoning that any seeker of truth and meaning will necessarily follow (Gregson, 1988, p. 80).

Scientific method and religious method

Taking this discussion a step further, we can more directly explore how scientific methods are similar to or different from religious methods. Both science and religion use reason and faith. Scientific methods use reason in the natural realm and are empirical, based on experimentation to attain scientific knowledge. Scientists put faith in the paradigm they use to collect data and develop hypotheses. They apply reason to verify or disprove the hypotheses. Theological methods in Catholicism tend to be more explicit about faith than science, but theology also applies reason to achieve knowledge of faith. In fact, the goal of theology is to attain an understanding of faith.

One might argue that appropriation of religion in individual religious experience is personal and subjective, while science strives to be impersonal and objective. Regarding subjectivity, it is important to keep in mind that a religious experience that an individual reports is not generalizable to religion itself, a much more comprehensive, complex dimension of human life. Some aspects of scientific studies, such as neurophysiological measurement of electro-chemical processes in the brain, may pursue impersonal objectivity, although other aspects of the process require subjective human judgment. For example, "most techniques of (brain scan) data analysis implies a sort of separation between 'signal' and noise' (while) the exact meaning of the notions 'signal' and 'noise' is not always clear" (Kotchoubey et al., 2016, p. 6). Psychological assessments of mental states or symptoms, even with scientifically oriented norm-referenced testing, are also still, to some degree, personal and subjective.

If we push the meaning of human consciousness to its extreme, we must acknowledge that all scientific data is ultimately filtered through the brain. Operating through the brain are two of Lonergan's levels of consciousness— *understanding* and *judgment*. The first level of consciousness—*experience*— derives from objective reality. The data of reality do not derive from the human mind unless one is the Creator (Helminiak, 2015). Objectively, the data that the person does not know about still does exist. The human person and brain are always subordinate to reality as it is; the human mind always perceives in a limited way the much larger reality that is out there.

It is important to consider the relationship between human consciousness and the acquisition of scientific data. Studies are designed by human beings who, on the level of the psyche, may have various biases and more or less accurate perspectives on the nature of the universe. To recall, according to Lonergan, the psyche derives from the organism (brain) and is influenced by emotion, imagery, conation, memory, and personality.

Biases drive hypotheses that become the basis for future experiments. Even the execution of various experiments can be heavily biased, which has led the scientific community, particularly in the medical realm, to utilize the randomized, controlled, double-blind study design. The hope is that by randomizing patients and blinding not only the patients but the researchers as well, the data will be as unbiased as possible. But even in these instances, many study designs suffer from the researchers' biases. It is not surprising that attempts at replicating research studies have often demonstrated an overall inability to achieve consistent results, whether they are studies on cancer treatment, psychiatric disorders, or other biologically related processes.

The realm of physics is perhaps a bit more robust from an objective perspective. But even these types of experiments have met with substantial differences between study designs, leading to discrepancies in important cosmological values that challenge current theories. Thus, science is not exempt from the impact of biases and beliefs.

Returning to our understanding of the brain, one can see that science is obligated to develop appropriate methods for investigating brain function. We can see that the challenges facing science are quite similar to those facing religious and theological explorations. The biases of scholars color their approaches to the objects of their endeavors. The perspective of a Christian theologian is vastly different from that of a Buddhist scholar. Discussion of free will, for example, first needs to find a common starting point. Similar challenges affect neuroscientific studies of free will. One must agree about how free will works in the first place, perhaps initially from the philosophical or theological perspective, and then design a study accordingly. Is free will a purely conscious decision? Or can it be substantially influenced by unconscious processes? Depending on the answers, researchers may come up with quite different study designs.

Similarly, questions about the soul can be just as problematic for scientists as for theologians. Both fields of investigation must start with certain definitions and perspectives about what the soul is and how it relates to the brain. If one takes the position that the soul and brain are distinct constructs, the soul encompassing spiritual as well as physiological capacities, the direction of one's investigation will be quite different from that of a scholar who believes that the soul is reducible to the brain.

For these reasons, neurotheology makes the bold argument that both scientific as well as spiritual perspectives are necessary for addressing these profound questions. Questions about the brain and soul, consciousness, free will, and determinism all require philosophical and theological perspectives to inform scientific investigation. We saw in the last chapter that Lonergan's domain-universal Aristotelian-Thomistic epistemology offers helpful distinctions about organism, psyche, and spirit; brain and soul; the consciousness with experience, understanding, judgment, and decision; valuation and ethics; the conscious and intentional poles of consciousness. Science can also inform philosophical and theological perspectives. Hence, neurotheology acknowledges the mutual interrelationships and complexity involved in addressing these profound questions.

One might ponder how well religious belief systems can support scientific investigation. Theology is a highly rational, inductive process that starts with a given paradigm. Catholic theology is based on revelation (as recorded in Scripture and expressed in Tradition). It is supported by philosophy, Aristotelian-Thomistic metaphysics, and epistemology, working heuristically to answer ultimate questions about divine and human reality as it is. Science is similarly a highly rational, inductive, and deductive process that starts with a given paradigm, based on the scientific method seeking reasonably verifiable conclusions through experimentation, seeing answers to specific questions in the physical, natural domain that can be answered empirically. The main difference is how both approaches evaluate and find data and information. Religion accepts various types of evidence to support ideas and concepts, just as science does. Thus, one might expect the Catholic tradition to bring forth great scientists, as it does, striving to understand God's universe more deeply. The search for truth is completely consistent with religion in exploring the physical aspects of the universe.

In the end, one would hope for a coalescence of ideas and concepts. We would argue that this coalescence occurs prominently in the realm of neurotheology.

Measuring the immeasurable

An important aspect of the relationship between science and religion has to do with how we might measure the immeasurable. Many of the elements of religion — beliefs, experiences, and the supernatural — are difficult to evaluate scientifically.

A similar difficulty exists within the fields of psychology and psychiatry. After all, there is no way to measure how depressed someone is. We cannot apply a blood test or some instrument around the head to assess the level of depression someone feels, as it is subjective. The only way to ever measure something subjective, such as an emotion or experience, is by asking the individual. But even then, we cannot understand depression unless we have felt it ourselves. We all know what it is like to feel sad, so when someone tells us that they feel depressed, we have a frame of reference.

Another common problem in the field of medicine is how to assess the perception of pain. We have all felt pain, but how any given person deals with pain depends on many different factors. Pain itself is highly variable. Two people can have the same injury, with one feeling great pain and the other feeling only mild pain. But the pain goes beyond the actual feeling. Pain can limit a person's functioning in variable ways. If someone has hip pain, how much does that affect the way they walk? We can observe their stride to see where they appear to be limited, but we never truly know how much the pain is causing that limitation.

Despite these problems, fields like psychology and psychiatry have made tremendous advances in methods for assessing subjective experiences. Numerous questionnaires and scales ask all kinds of questions about how people feel. For example, one of the best-known scales for depression is the Beck Depression Inventory. It consists of questions about the person's mood, but also items about behaviors such as crying and sleeping. The presumption is that someone who is more depressed will cry more and have poor sleep. But this can be problematic at times since a person who works the night shift may have slept poorly because of their schedule, not because they are depressed.

Of course, there are more complex psychological assessments, such as the Wechsler cognitive tests and the Minnesota Multiphasic Personality Inventory, both of which have hundreds of questions and are rigorously authenticated to meet scientific standards of validity and reliability. With any human endeavor, there will likely be some element of subjectivity. Also, no single test is considered without reference to demographic information as well as additional measures of the person.

Religious and spiritual beliefs and attitudes have also been explored with a wide variety of questionnaires and scales. In the book *Measures of Religiosity*, psychologists Hill and Hood (1999) provide over 100 such scales. These scales assess dimensions including the strength of one's religious beliefs, the motivations for those beliefs, related feelings such as the fear of death, and the intensity of various spiritual or even mystical experiences. As with the scales in psychology, these religious scales have certain pros and cons. They appear able to get some sense of the religious, but they are purely subjective, depending on the respondent to provide the answers. Frequently, the experiences that a person has are not adequately captured by a questionnaire, which makes responses more problematic. Another approach is to obtain narrative descriptions of beliefs and experiences. In our (ABN) Survey of Spiritual Experiences, approximately 2,000 responses enabled an analysis of common words to help better understand the nature of religious experiences.

It must always be acknowledged that the words people use may depend on multiple factors. In deep spiritual experiences, some people describe the sense of a force, the sense of love, the sense of God, or the sense of energy, to name a few. An important neurotheological question would be whether these experiences were all the same yet described differently by different individuals or whether these experiences were distinct. It becomes even more challenging when one begins to explore beliefs and experiences across religious traditions. If a Catholic has a mystical experience of love and a Buddhist has a similarly intense experience of love, can they both be attributed to God? And how would either of these individuals incorporate this experience into their beliefs and subsequent behaviors? A Catholic might try to become more altruistic in their community, while a Buddhist might try to meditate more deeply.

It is important to take a neurotheological perspective that strives to combine subjective experiences with scientific approaches. An essential part of this approach requires active questioning on many levels. For example, if we wish to understand the nature of the soul, we must certainly ask well-known theologians and religious scholars what they think the soul is. But perhaps it is equally important to ask thousands, if not millions, of "regular Catholics" to find out what they think about aspects of the faith that fall within their direct competence or experience, such as the schooling of their children, the requirements of a good marriage, or the effect of certain practices at liturgies.

We also must engage a wide variety of methods for asking such questions. Do we need open-ended questions or specific ones? For example, we might want to understand whether people equate the soul with the mind. The simplest approach would be to ask the question: Is the soul the same as the mind? On the other hand, we might ask people what they think the soul is and see what words they use and whether they are the same or different when a person responds to the question regarding what the mind is. We can then take those words and use them to develop questionnaires to explore other populations, including other Christians, as well as adherents of other traditions. Such sampling would not be intended to develop an accurate understanding of terms like soul or mind but would yield popular perceptions of their meanings.

Neuroscience "is based on a heterogeneous set of concepts, methods, paradigms, and theories. . . . (It studies) electrically active molecular structures, i.e., ion channels (*physics*), gene expression (*genetics*), synaptic processing (*molecular biology, pharmacology*), growth and wiring of neurons (*histology*), structure of brain areas (*anatomy*), (and) plasticity of circuits (*physiology*). The great challenge for neuroscience is related to neural mechanisms of 'higher' or 'mental' information processing (*psychology*)" (Kotchoubey et al., 2016, p. 3).

Distinctions and definitions among the various disciplines, as well as clarification of their assumptions, are necessary to integrate multiple fields effectively. Regarding methods, in neurobiology, there are advanced, objectively accurate physico-chemical measurement technologies. Sociology or psychology may rely on subjective Likert-style ordinal-scaled (with no specified measure between the levels) or verbal reports. Included may be behavioral observations, which may range from qualitative direct observation to strict mathematical analyses. Quality of data collection may span interval data for empirical sciences like physics to qualitative or ordinal data for social sciences like sociology (Kotchoubey et al., 2016, p. 3). These and other fine-tuned distinctions, clarifications, and domain specifications are needed even to work in the field of neuroscience. When neuroscience combines with theology, methodological challenges abound.

The sciences can be classified as natural or social/cultural. This would mean for neuroscience, a basic version that would study the brain in isolation, and an alternate version—behavioral, affective, and cognitive neuroscience (BACN), which investigates dimensions of the brain as part of an organism-environment system (Kotchoubey et al., 2016). The former studies the structure and function of the nervous system using methods of the natural sciences—a third-person objective perspective for data based on experimentation. The latter asks how these physiological neural processes relate to mental and psychological processes and incorporates first-person-perspective subjective accounts. Findings on electrochemical neuronal processes are much more easily accepted than conclusions associated with human feelings, decisions, and behaviors. When the topic of study is social neuroscience, a hybrid methodology incorporates both investigation of the brain networks involved and BACN and questions such as what happens in the brain when the subject is involved in cultural affairs (Han et al., 2013). There are, of course, always social components in every neuroscientific study, if only from the fact that the experimenter's dialogue with the experimental subject, explaining the study for informed consent, already affects the results of the experiment (Kotchoubey et al., 2016). The study of neurotheology would seem perhaps to fit this integrative third-and-first-person, objective-and-subjective, natural-science-and-social-science model. Of course, such an integrative approach also complicates the methodology for neurotheology since it requires an appropriate blending of objective and subjective perspectives.

European and American scholars Kotchoubey et al. (2016) suggest for such an interdisciplinary study, three possible strategies: (1) reduce everything to neurobiology, although we may use empirical and subjective reports; (2) take a transdisciplinary attitude, that the objective and subjective be equally respected with pluralistic methodology (Mittelstrasse, 2011; Nicolescu, 2014); (3) develop integrative neuroscience, showing theoretically how the various concepts and methods overlap epistemologically. Following are examples of journals striving to "synthesize results of brain research with understanding complex behavior (*Frontiers in Integrative Neuroscience*, 2015)" (Kotchoubey et al., 2016) or integration otherwise (World Scientific *Journal of Integrative Neuroscience*, 2015), and universities conducting integrative research including humanities or computational science (Universities of Tubingen, Binghamton, and Fordham) (Kotchoubey et al., 2016, p. 5).

The goal of the current book is to explore many approaches to understanding how neuroscience relates to religious beliefs and experiences from the Catholic tradition. This is why it is essential to understand the ways we can measure these immeasurables.

Statistics . . . the good and bad

Once we have a set of data, such as questionnaires or quantitative scales, another fundamental question to ask from both a religious as well as scientific perspective is, how do we analyze it? Science typically uses statistics to assess large groups of individuals. The advantage of this approach is that when a significant finding is obtained, one can feel confident that it is substantial. For example, suppose we reviewed 1,000 descriptions of spiritual experiences and found that 800 of them use the term *oneness*. In that case, we might feel relatively confident that spiritual experiences are associated with an experience of oneness. Statistically, this might be an accurate statement. The problem is that 200 individuals did not use that term.

The first question is whether they felt a sense of oneness, or if they did feel a sense of oneness, did they decide not to count it as important to the experience? Perhaps they had a different kind of spiritual experience altogether from those who did experience oneness. This is where the religious perspective becomes important because it can emphasize the power and uniqueness of individual experiences that statistics sometimes are insufficient to help us understand.

In the Catholic tradition, God has a personal relationship with each person, and each one relates to a community. That is not something that can ever be measured with statistics. But if we cannot measure it with statistics, are there other ways of understanding that relationship—scientifically as well as religiously? We could just as easily ask this question in the context of human personal relationships. There is no statistical analysis that can show how much a married couple love each other. We can ask them about their feelings, but there is no numerical or statistical analysis that we can do. And for those individuals who suffer from various psychological problems or difficulties with interpersonal relationships, there is no unified way of managing such problems. There are standards of care based on peer-reviewed research literature, where studies about interventions supported by recognized psychological theory are validated by at least $p = 0.05$ statistical probability. The field of psychology requires that practitioners adhere to guidelines supported by quantifiable data regarding the likelihood of success. Still, each client is unique, and their presenting problems are usually multifaceted. Thus, psychotherapy relies on human interaction and is an art as well as a science. Statistics can tell us that a certain antidepressant works in many people with depression, but it can never tell us whether it will work for a specific person. Thus, in science as well as religion, we must struggle with how to understand the individual as well as the group when it comes to feelings, attitudes, and experiences.

Imaging the human brain

Much of the discussion so far in this chapter has dealt with the subjective. But neurophysiology also has an interesting objective approach for measuring various religious and spiritual phenomena: neuroimaging. In the past 30 years, there has been a growing number of research studies that have used brain imaging to explore an array of religious and spiritual phenomena, mostly practices and experiences. Early studies tended to look at intense meditation or prayer practices. In fact, there are brain-imaging studies of practices across many different traditions, including Christianity, Islam, Buddhism, and Hinduism.

As stated above, it is essential to connect the physiological measurements obtained with neuroimaging techniques to the actual experiences people report. After all, unless we understand what someone was thinking or feeling while undergoing a brain scan, we don't know how to interpret the results. Asking someone to pray in a brain scanner only works if they are saying prayers. One way of confirming this is to have them do the prayer out loud, but we still don't know what they feel unless we ask them. Of course, this is a fundamental challenge of all cognitive neuroscience. We never truly know what the subject is thinking. However, neurotheology tasks us with trying to develop better and better methods of observing the brain in action, especially when it comes to elusive religious experiences.

An important critique of current neuroimaging studies related to religious and spiritual phenomena is that many have focused on practices. There is a reason for this. It is much easier to study a person while they are doing a given practice, especially if it has specific elements that the investigator can follow. It is much more challenging to examine the brain while a person ponders a simple belief or while people are having a mild prayer experience, such as while praying the rosary. The larger challenge at times is how one obtains a brain scan during various mental states, especially states that are not amenable to being near a brain scanner. It clearly would not be an easy task to be anointed while in an MRI scanner.

With that in mind, it is worthwhile to briefly review some of the primary methods for imaging the brain to understand better how they might be used in the context of neurotheology and inform our understanding of the Catholic brain.

Functional magnetic resonance imaging (MRI) is one of the principal tools of cognitive neuroscience. It works by using large magnets to modify various molecules in the brain that can be observed while they function in different ways. One of the most common approaches is to measure changes in blood flow or oxygen concentration. This is a useful approach since the brain uses more oxygen and blood flow when it is active. If you are concentrating on solving a math problem, areas of the brain involved in concentration and mathematics will have increased blood flow and oxygen usage. These functional changes can be observed using MRI, also called functional MRI.

Functional MRI has now been used to study thousands of brain states ranging from pathological conditions such as depression or schizophrenia to spiritual practices to tasks involving free choice. It is an outstanding technique for observing these different states because images can be acquired over seconds and explore all the different areas of the brain that might be activated. fMRI also has an excellent spatial resolution, which means that we can see fairly small areas, usually on the order of several centimeters in size, seeing with great detail areas of the brain that might be involved in various mental states. A variety of brain images can be found online at *The Human Brain Project*.

Multiple fMRI and diffusion tensor imaging (DTI) techniques have also been developed to assess measures of functional and structural connectivity. DTI aligns magnetic fields of water molecules in axon tracts to picture axon pathways. Genetic disorders, for example, can result in major modification of axon tracks.

By these means, we can see how different parts of the brain are connected and how they work together during different tasks. One of the most studied networks is called the *default mode network*, which is what turns on when our brain is doing nothing. When you start to pray, the default mode network starts to quiet down as other parts of the brain turn on to engage in the activity.

Perhaps the biggest downside of studying religious phenomena using fMRI is that you must be in the scanner when you're doing it. Thus, you would have to pray or meditate while in the scanner. The scanner environment is not particularly conducive to these practices because you must be lying down in a very narrow tube while having up to 100 dB of banging noises all around you. Some studies have utilized expert meditators to reduce the impact of this highly artificial and distracting environment. In one of our own (ABN) studies, some expert meditators indicated that during certain meditation practices, the cadence of the practice matched the rhythm of the scanner noises so that it was easier to perform than other practices that were out of sync with the scanner. Other challenges for brain imaging research include small samples—groups of subjects who may not generalize to a larger population, lack of appropriate control or comparison groups, and level of significance that can be adjusted for processing and interpreting brain scan results.

MRI scans do not always have to be done during specific practices but sometimes can be used to observe the after-effects. We might be able to determine how an intense prayer program over weeks or months changes the resting state of the brain and alters emotions or cognitive processes. In fact, multiple studies have explored the impact of religious symbols, beliefs, and attitudes on a variety of brain processes using MRI.

Another group of brain imaging methods comes from the field of nuclear medicine. Nuclear medicine involves studies in which a radioactive tracer that follows some part of the physiology is administered to an individual. There are nuclear medicine scans for the heart, lungs, kidneys, and essentially, every organ of the body, particularly the brain. There are two main types of nuclear medicine scans of the brain: positron emission tomography (PET) and single-photon emission computed tomography (SPECT). They are similar in that they require the injection of a radioactive tracer that goes into the brain. However, the tracers themselves are slightly different because of the radioactive isotopes involved. PET and SPECT tracers have primarily been used to evaluate blood flow and metabolism in the brain. Much like the MRI scans, these PET and SPECT scans can determine areas of the brain that turn on or off during various religious or spiritual phenomena.

One of the main downsides of these scans is the radioactivity required, although it is typically a very low amount and generally considered safe. The other downside is that uptake of the tracer can be anywhere from minutes to hours. Therefore, we usually cannot observe multiple states during a single scan session. By contrast, fMRI scans can be obtained over three seconds so that we can observe many different states during the same imaging session.

On the other hand, one of the most important benefits of nuclear medicine scans is the ability to observe changes not only in general brain activity but also in specific neurotransmitter systems. The ability to measure neurotransmitters is an important advantage. After all, it is this array of chemicals, such as dopamine, serotonin, and endorphins, that mediate most activity in the brain. These neurotransmitters are not only essential for neurons to communicate with each other but are also often associated with specific processes. For example, dopamine is part of the reward system that makes us feel euphoric when something good happens to us. There is evidence that dopamine is released when people are deeply engaged in meditation practices. One of our (ABN) studies of the Spiritual Exercises of Saint Ignatius revealed that an immersive one-week retreat led to an alteration in the dopamine system that made the brain more sensitive to dopamine effects (Wintering et al., 2021, p.23). This means that religious practices can change the way the brain responds to the world and can change our thoughts and emotions as well. Similarly, the serotonin system was also sensitized in our study.

Of course, as in all things brain-related, at the level of neurotransmitters, a one-to-one relation between a molecule and a mental function would oversimplify the matter (Kotchoubey et al., 2016). We are speaking in general terms. Still, this not only helps us understand how religion may be protective against disorders that affect the serotonin system, such as depression, but it may also help us understand the relationship between intense religious experiences and those mediated by psychedelic drugs that primarily activate the serotonin system.

These neurotransmitters may be important not only for understanding specific practices and experiences but also for understanding the brain of a person who practices religion. Perhaps those individuals who are predisposed to atheism rather than religious beliefs have different concentrations or sensitivities of specific neurotransmitter systems. Many questions can be asked from a neurotheological perspective that helps us understand the relationship between the various brain processes, various structures, and neurotransmitters.

There are also other methods for measuring brain function. One of the older techniques, but still able to provide interesting information, is electroencephalography (EEG). EEG studies look at the electrical activity in the brain and can monitor moment-to-moment changes associated with various practices. Some of the earliest studies of meditation practices in the 1960s used EEG to observe different types of electrical patterns in the brain. Contemporary research not only observes these electrical changes but can help isolate the areas of the brain that they come from. Some methods involve infrared imaging, magnetoencephalography, and others that all have their advantages and disadvantages when it comes to the study of religious and spiritual phenomena.

The last two approaches that should be mentioned are not so much about imaging the brain but about directly affecting the brain's function. One ancient approach comes from the use of various psychedelic substances. The current research on the use of psychedelic compounds such as psilocybin demonstrates that the intense experiences under their influence are frequently described as *spiritual.* In fact, our own (ABN) research has shown that psychedelic experiences are described with the same words and intensity as religious and spiritual experiences (Yaden et al., 2017). A serious theologian, to be fair, would probably not consider a drug-induced experience spiritual or religious. As mentioned above, psychedelic drugs affect specific neurotransmitter systems, particularly the serotonin system. Thus, it makes sense that as these drugs induce very intense experiences, they provide interesting information that might relate to ways that *natural* religious experiences arise in the brain.

Another approach affecting the brain has to do with various stimulatory methods, such as transcranial magnetic stimulation. Using strong magnets, areas of the brain can be turned on or off, changing the way a person thinks, feels, or behaves. Some studies have explored whether transcranial magnetic stimulation can help induce spiritual experiences or, at least, augment spiritual practices.

On the other hand, brain scans are processed representations of neural activity based on various physiological processes (e.g., blood flow or glucose metabolism), which do not necessarily correspond to a mental state. And behavioral correlates are normally distributed over several areas. The brain is a "non-linear dynamic system with parallel processes and redundancy with brain regions that overlap and are multifunctional" (Weissenbacher, 2015, pp. 48-49).

Neurotheology is a new, multidisciplinary research field. It is in the process of developing realistic, attainable goals supported by specific strategies for collaboration between neuroscience and theologies. Challenges for any neuroscientific focus on spirituality include the need to address "subjective states, small samples, test bias, level of significance, lack of controls, and levels (the general issue)" (Jastrzebski, 2018, p. 522). While the data is certainly not conclusive, there are intriguing possibilities for understanding how different parts of the brain function during spiritual mental states.

Soul as organizing form

From the scientific perspective, the brain appears to be intimately involved with our thoughts, feelings, and experiences. From the philosophical perspective, the soul can be understood as life that animates the body, "a formal principle that causes a living being to be what it is and accounts for its characteristic structure and proper activity" (Dodds, 2014, p. 15). When the Hebrew Scriptures refer to one's *nefesh*, some modern scholars translate the term as "soul." The Hebrew writers mean, not an immaterial substance, but a living corporeal animal or human being as that living being experiences life as vulnerable, as needy" (Wolff, 1974, *Anthropology of the Old Testament*). Aristotle and Aquinas, after him, took the *soul* to be the *substantial form* of the body. To Aristotle and Aquinas, every creature consists of *primary matter* (possibility of being) and *substantial form*, a partner with matter that makes a living thing what it is (Dodds, 2019, p. 904). Matter and form are two inseparable principles that together constitute a living entity. The form is the organization or configuration of a being that defines it and enables it to function (Oomen, 2003, p. 381).

For a living entity, the form is the soul. Since we now know that it is, in fact, the brain with the soul that accounts for the functions of the human person, should we replace the *soul* with *neurons* and say that it is really neurons that account for human functioning? No, for the following reason. The soul is not separate from the body. The soul is the body's organizational arrangement, and the organization is not reducible to its neuronal components.

> It is not the neurons as such but their very mutual organizational structure, their network structure, that makes them a functioning conceptual and emotional organ. According to neuroscientists, it is thanks to neuronal organizational structures in networking contact that our brains produce our minds (Swaab, 2001, p. 80). (Oomen, 2003, p. 382)

Neuroscientifically, the brain is a complex and networked organizational structure that significantly impacts the functioning of the mind. From a Catholic perspective, speaking ontologically, the brain alone does not produce the mind. Form, or soul, adds a new dimension to matter, the neural substratum, as its sculpting. Also, the soul—or "mind" in scientific terms—is more than the brain and also comprises a spiritual dimension distinct from its neural substrate.

For an analogy, we might have a collection of components—a building, an online address, some books, people, and computers. If we add an organizational form, taken together, these components might constitute a library. "Neural activities are the physical basis of what we call the mind (i.e., perception, consciousness, personal identity, thinking, willing). The mind is not separate from neurons, but the mind has properties that cannot be reduced" to neurons (Oomen, 2003, p. 380).

Aquinas differentiates distinctive human capabilities, including intellect and will (*ST* I, q 78). For Aquinas, "willing implies being attracted by that which is perceived as good, and thus ultimately, albeit indirectly and in a veiled manner, by God" (Oomen, 2003, p. 381). In a living person, the soul is the substantial form connected to material neurons, and for Aquinas, it is attracted ultimately to God.

Pope John Paul II reinforced that within the human soul is a spiritual dimension that scientists perceive "which transcends cerebral physiology and appears to direct all our activities as free and autonomous beings, capable of responsibility and love, marked with dignity," and includes "the interpretive and evaluative work of the human mind, foundation of that spiritual dimension proper to a special relationship with God the Creator (Gn 2:7) in whom every man and woman is made (cf. Gn 1:26-27)" (2003, Address to the Pontifical Academy of Sciences) (Grassie, 2008, p. 157).

Catholicism, the soul, and neuroscience

Pope Francis remarks on the role of neuroscience in understanding the soul:

> The Church calls for a synthesis between the responsible use of methods proper to the empirical sciences and other areas of knowledge such as philosophy, theology, as well as faith itself, which elevates us to the mystery transcending nature and human intelligence. Faith seeks and trusts reason since both come from God and cannot contradict each other. The Church rejoices in acknowledging the enormous potential that God has given to the human mind. (*Evangelii Gaudium*, 2013, par. 242)

We are looking at relationships that may inform us about how Catholicism might affect us as human persons and how our humanness might engage the Catholic faith. We hope that the discussions that follow provide some exciting perspectives on these complex relationships and hopefully will enrich liturgy, theology, and overall engagement in the Catholic tradition.

Study Questions

1. What is the scientific method?
2. What are the four dimensions of Thomistic causality? Explain each.
3. Which causes are addressed by science? By theology?
4. Distinguish method in science from method in theology.
5. What are the challenges to methods in science and theology?

6. How do science and theology each find and evaluate data and information?

7. What are some methodological challenges in measuring subjective information in fields like religion, psychiatry, and psychology? How are the challenges attempted to be met?

8. What are some challenges for methods in the study of neurotheology?

9. Neuroimaging can be said to make physiological data measurable, changing as it does from one mental state to another. Can physiological data showing neural correlations measure mental states? Explain.

10. What are some difficulties with engaging in prayer or religious experience while in an fMRI scanner?

11. What are some disadvantages of using nuclear medicine PET or SPECT scans to evaluate brain function? What are the advantages?

12. What can electroencephalography (EEG) contribute to the study of religious and spiritual phenomena?

13. How might the effects of psychedelic substances on the brain contribute in some way to the study of religious or spiritual experience?

14. What about transcranial magnetic stimulation (TMS)?

15. What are some challenges for the neuroscientific study of spirituality?

16. How is the human soul understood as an organizing form of the person with cerebral physiology?

17. Can spiritual dimensions like mental states, thoughts, concepts, and decision-making be captured by cerebral neural measurement?

18. What might neuroscientific study contribute to theology, particularly the Catholic tradition?

Endnotes

[1] "Studying nature to understand it purely for its own sake seems to have had its start among the pre-Socratic philosophers of the 6th century BCE, such as Thales and Anaximander" (history of science.www.britannica.org).

[2] For more details, see Kuhn, T. S. (2012). *The structure of scientific revolutions.* Chicago, IL: University of Chicago Press.

Researchers use 3 p (probability) values to say whether a measurement is statistically significant, that is, small enough to indicate that the hypothesis can be empirically supported. A p-value of 0.05 indicates that there is a 95% chance that the hypothesis is supported. $P = 0.05$ or $p = 0.01$ is generally acceptable for human sciences. $P = 0.01$ accuracy would suffice for medicine. Natural sciences require considerably higher accuracy. The human person studied in *soft* sciences like psychology, sociology, and philosophy is too complex to be measured with the precision of the *hard* sciences like physics, math, or chemistry.

[4] "The God of the Old Testament is arguably the most unpleasant character in all fiction: jealous and proud of it; a petty, unjust, unforgiving control-freak; a vindictive, bloodthirsty ethnic cleanser; . . . a megalomaniacal capriciously malevolent bully" (*The God Delusion*, 2006).

Chapter 5

Free Will and the Brain

Defining free will

To discuss the relationship between the brain and free will requires an initial consideration of what exactly free will is. The definition of free will is likely to depend on a scholar's prevailing beliefs. Some might see free will as the ability to choose a given situation consciously. Others might see free will as a combination of conscious and unconscious processes, whether related directly to the brain or not.

If one takes a religious or spiritual perspective, some might view free will as inherently endowed by God. If one takes a Buddhist or Hindu perspective, individual human beings have free will through their connection with universal consciousness. There are also multiple philosophical perspectives on the potential existence or non-existence of free will and how free will might actually occur. Catholic theologians like Karl Rahner (1904-1984) thought that freedom lies in the ability to make a decision that is so enduringly valid that it becomes permanent. In fact, free will is at the intersection of time and eternity.

> "Freedom is the capacity for the eternal" (*Theology of Freedom*, 186). But we have access to our total being only in the self-transcendence made possible by the self-offer of the infinite mystery of God (*Foundations*, 39). We decide definitively who we will be, therefore, only as we utter a *yes* or a *no* to this offer. Deciding about God and deciding about the totality of our being is the same act of freedom. (Highfield, 1995, p. 487)

Not everyone agrees that humans can be this definitive with their freedom. "God's being is freely willed. God is fully what God wills. Humans, however, have neither being nor freedom (to an) absolute (degree). Humans have freedom insofar as their willing and their particular 'having-being' coincide' (Highfield, 1995, p. 503). Following his theology of grace, Rahner highly emphasizes human freedom.

For Michael Polanyi, not just the brain but "the body becomes the ultimate faculty for all external knowledge (1966)." Polanyi (1891-1976), a Catholic Hungarian-British physical chemist and philosopher, regarded the mind as embodied. He observed that we perceive the world from our body, in some context, against a particular background. We rely on tacit knowledge of particulars in a comprehensive, active process to understand the whole. This does not equate our vantage point with subjectivism because in knowing, we recognize and strive to achieve objective standards. Knowing itself cannot avoid being self-referential (Korzybski, 1958, in Scott, 2004) since every concept and meaning is derived from our situated context (von Glasersfeld, 1991, in Scott, 2004). Personal and contextual aspects are always involved in acquiring knowledge and developing knowledge over time, as happens in apprenticeship toward mastery (Dillern, 2020). Only about 20% of the neurons that contribute to vision originate in the retina (Robson, 1983; Varela and Singer, 1987); at least 40% derive from the visual cortex. "Hence, any visual interpretation . . . is dependent on conclusions drawn from past experiences, rather than on current sensations (Maturana and Varela, 1992, in Umpleby, 2016)" (Dillern, 2020, p. 582).

From a neuroscientific perspective, understanding free will begins with an exploration of its elements. The study of free will would require the ability to evaluate a given choice to be made and then determine what parts of the brain are involved in making a given decision. Areas such as the frontal lobes have been particularly implicated in purposeful or willful processes. Hence, several brain scan studies have found frontal lobe activity associated with free-choice tasks.

However, it is also important to determine whether the processes in the brain represent free will or make a choice based on pre-existing conditions of the brain or necessary responses to environmental situations. In other words, we might make a decision but have no choice in making that decision.

One of the most famous studies that tried to assess what happens in the brain during free choice was performed by neuroscientist Benjamin Libet in 1988 (Libet, 1999). In these experiments, he asked subjects to make voluntary movements with their wrist or fingers and to record the time of the conscious urge to move while their brain activity was monitored. Findings showed that "neurons in the supplementary motor cortex that are related to a particular physical movement of the hand started firing 500 ms before the impulses arrived at the muscles involved in moving. However, the feeling of intention, want or urge to move the hand, as reported by the subjects, occurred only 150 ms before the movement was executed" (Bennet and Hacker, 2003, p. 229). A *readiness potential* in the brain a fraction of a second before subjects reported conscious awareness of having decided to move was interpreted as the brain, rather than the person, making the decision. While Libet did not claim the experiments disproved free will, some did. Some neuroscientists noted that the readiness potential could have been the brain preparing to initiate the movement rather than unconsciously deciding. Some philosophers remarked that free will is typically associated with actions of moral import or significance. To be valid as a test of free will, the experiment would need to have included content commensurate with agents consciously weighing competing decisional reasons. The experiment with neutral, inconsequential wrist movements did not meet that criterion.

There have been other critiques of that study both in terms of how it was designed and how the results were interpreted. For one, the study was very small in terms of the number of subjects, and thus, it is hard to know whether the results are generalizable to all people. But more important, there have been concerns about the study design. Subjects were asked to make a conscious decision to push a button and then were also asked when they were aware of their decision. One of the issues with this design is that the brain is constantly interacting with the world. So, the preceding brain activity may have just had something to do with how the brain was responding to the external or internal environment without having anything to do specifically with the actual decision. The other issue has to do with whether willful processes are directly connected to brain function or vice versa.

Several follow-up studies have demonstrated the complexity and controversy of neuroscientific studies of free will. A study by New Zealand psychology professors Judy Trevana and Jeff Miller suggested that the early signal observed in Libet's experiments was merely related to the brain paying attention (Trevana and Miller, 2010). In their experiment, they used Libet's basic design but added an audio tone, at which point test subjects had to decide to move their finger. Interestingly, the same early brain activity was observed whether or not subjects decided to move their finger. The results from this study suggested that the decision to move the finger was not the basis for early brain activity but rather the surveillance of the environment.

There are also other developments in the study of free will, such as the use of a device called transcranial magnetic stimulation (TMS), which applies magnetic fields to the brain to turn either up or down the activity in a particular area. The important point is that this device can theoretically modify how the brain works, which can be applied to decision-making. For example, one study used TMS to influence which hand people move by stimulating the frontal lobe regions involved in the generation of movement (Ammon and Gandevia, 1990). Under normal circumstances, right-handed people normally choose to move the right hand about 60% of the time. However, in this study, if the investigators stimulated the right frontal lobe controlling the left side of the body, the subjects now chose to move their left hand approximately 80% of the time.

Most importantly, test subjects continued to perceive that they were freely making their own decisions about which hand to move. The brain continued to perceive it was acting on its own free will even though it was being externally manipulated. Studies such as this do not necessarily exclude the possibility of free will but certainly show that free will can be a complex process that might have factors affecting it. Adding to the controversial nature of these studies, one follow-up study of TMS was unable to replicate these findings. Overall, more research will be necessary to assess how the brain might be involved with the origination of intentional or willful behaviors.

In the end, it is not surprising that there are a number of perspectives and controversies regarding the relationship between the brain and free will and what neuroscience has to say about it. Adding the Catholic voice to this conversation can be quite enlightening and provide a theological perspective that contributes to future neuroscientific investigations of free will.

Catholicism and the spiritual dimension of the person

What about free will for Catholicism? According to the *Catechism of the Catholic Church* (1995), "Freedom is the power to act or not to act, and so to perform deliberate acts of one's own. Freedom attains perfection in its acts when directed toward God, the sovereign Good" (*CCC*, 1744). For traditional Catholic theology, the human person is spiritual as well as physiological. The spiritual dimension consists of a rational mind and free will. The physical processes mutually interact with spiritual aspects of the personality—consciousness, dignity, a moral sense, and freedom. Arguing for a spiritual dimension are the person's capacities to engage in the arts; to find meaning in disparate sensory fragments, such as music from tones, narrative from words, experience from a flood of data; to find coherence in perceptions; to discriminate good from bad; and to read into, discern, and evaluate phenomena and circumstances (McGoldrick, 2012).

Regarding free will, we notice that what distinguishes human action from that of, say, rocks is that human movements happen for *reasons*. Rocks that are let loose due to some meteorological impetus and tumble into a valley may constitute an avalanche *event*. If a human handsets off the cascade for a *reason*, we have something different, intentional, with an *end* in view. Unintended movements may happen, while intentional ones are purposeful. "Movement can be called an intentional action only if it originates from a cognitive state with meaningful content, and this content defines the cognitive state's causal influence" (Schall, 2009, p. 177).

In distinguishing voluntary actions from involuntary motions, it is important to ask about intention: what did the person want to do? And why? The answer will show how the action reflected objectives, ideas, and inclinations. A persistent dilemma for neuroscience and psychology is to tease out the relationship between mental realities like reasons or emotions and physiological processes among nerve cells. The brain's neurons and glial cells are physiological entities; reasons are mental events. How can they smoothly and mutually interact?

"Recent cognitive neuroscience research has described particular brain circuits that register errors and success. Such signals can adjust behavior and provide the basis for distinguishing *I did* from *it happened*, which is needed to feel like we are acting with freedom and responsible power" (Schall, 2009, p. 178).

Humans are capable of learning from the consequences of their actions. Doing so requires circuitry that can evaluate the outcomes of decisions and update the control systems that regulate the connections between stimulus inputs and behavioral outputs. Presumably, such feedback signals influence brain regions, like the dorsolateral prefrontal cortex, that are involved in control processes that mediate flexibility. Such monitoring is most strongly associated with the anterior cingulate cortex (ACC). Activity in the ACC is also consistent with the evaluation of outcomes and generation of feedback signals useful in updating behavioral goals and the adoption of new cognitive rules (Purves et al., 2019, p. 696).

Certainly, the brain does not always act with full freedom. Sometimes, a bodily movement is reflexive, caused by a particular stimulus. Overlying these reflex circuits are higher-order neuronal pathways in the cortex that are instrumental in human awareness of a sense of agency. When a movement is directed toward a purpose to achieve a goal, the person is likely to perceive owning the action. The same action may be reflexive in some situations and deliberate in others, depending on reason or will (Schall, 2009). Physical factors, of course, may impact and direct our thoughts and decisions. According to Catholic thought, material elements do not totally determine what we think and choose to do. If they did, we would not be responsible for what we believe and decide (Society of Catholic Scientists, 2023).

Moral psychologists like Jonathan Haidt have recently drawn attention to debates about free will. Haidt suggests that we function according to dual-process neural networks, both fast and slow cognitive systems. The speedy, spontaneous, intuitive network associated with the limbic system is non-conscious, and an unhurried, laborious, rational network through the frontal lobes is deliberate, intentional, manageable, and conscious. "The typical function of moral reasoning, Haidt maintains, is not to guide moral judgments, but to provide post hoc justifications for judgments made intuitively" (Messer, 2017, p. 43, in Haidt, 2001, p. 814). This (social intuitionist approach) tends to support group and community intuitions on moral issues.

If there are non-material elements to free will, how can we hope to evaluate free will from a neuroscientific perspective? Perhaps one approach would be via distinction, meaning that if we can distinguish all the biological processes that lead to some decision, perhaps we might be left with something willful and non-material. Whether such a capability is ever going to be possible is another question. Still, it seems important to try to define what the elements of free will are in order to design the most effective future studies.

Domain clarification between philosophy and neuroscience

It is important to clarify the domain distinction between philosophy and neuroscience. Philosophy deals with concepts associated with the mind, psychology, and person, while neuroscience focuses on the structures and functioning of neural processes and events. Neuroscience can examine the neural substrate of emotional, psychological, and behavioral abilities and their operations. Failure to discriminate between the two domains can lead to confusion. Neuroscience can scan brains with PET and fMRI and investigate synapses and neurotransmitters. Conceptual connections of consciousness or volition need to be investigated by the conceptual domain of philosophy. There is a categorical, logical difference between the two domains (Bennet and Hacker, 2003, p. 402-405).

> We have a wide range of concepts of volition and the will: felt inclinations, felt desires, wanting in all its confusing conceptual complexity, purpose, goal and aim, decisions and reasons for acting, intention, and so forth. Hence, we also have various volitional categories of action, such as voluntary, involuntary, non-voluntary, intentional, unintentional, deliberate, and impulsive. The attentive and the careless, rash or negligent, and so forth. We have manifold forms of explanation of human behavior in terms of reasons and motives, intentions and purposes, habits, tendencies or inclinations, as well as in terms of dispositions and character traits. (Bennet and Hacker, 2003, p. 224)

In his book *Self Comes to Mind* (2012), Portuguese-American neuroscientist Antonio Damasio sees the neuron, rather than a rational soul, as fundamental to the conscious human mind. Self is considered the result of physiological processes that begin with molecular-level stimuli susceptible to emotional influence, which are combined into feelings and attended by thoughts for self-guidance and reflection on coordination of actions for community benefit, incipient ethical evaluations. He writes:

> Could it be that our very human conscious desire to live, our will to prevail, begins as an aggregate of the inchoate wills of all the cells in our body? That single voice does exist in the form of the self in a conscious brain. But how does one transfer the brainless, mindless wills of single cells and their collectives to the self-conscious minds that originate in the brain? For that to happen, we need to introduce a radical, game-changing actor in our narrative: the nervous cell or neuron. (The

neuron's) ability to produce electrochemical signals capable of changing the state of other cells is the very source of the activity that constitutes and regulates behavior, to begin with, and that eventually also contributes to making a mind (pp. 36-37). (McGoldrick, 2012, p. 490)

But consciousness and intention cannot be found in neurons as such, though brain areas and circuits can be animated by sensitive powers (Sanguineti, 2019, p. 27). A reductionist view of the person equating neurobiology with freedom effectively eliminates the self.

Philosopher of mind Alva Noe in *Out of Our Heads* (2010) suggests that consciousness does not originate in our brains. It is what we actively do in interaction with the world around us. To understand how the brain plays a part in consciousness, we need to see how the brain contributes to the rest of the body and the environment. "It is a body- and world-involving conception of ourselves that the best new science as well as philosophy should lead us to endorse" (p. 24). Thus, there are philosophical and theological perspectives that observe that voluntary human acts of will, volition, desire, intentions, or decisions originate with the human person rather than exclusively with the physiological mechanics of neural pathways and patterns.

One of the problems with a neural-substrate-oriented approach is that it leads to a perspective that begs the question of how the human person, or more precisely the human mind, is separate from the physiological processes of the brain. What controls what, and what influences what? Such questions and their answers lie at the heart of the free will argument. If there is something beyond the brain that makes our willful decisions, then how is that translated into the corresponding brain processes? On the other hand, is it possible to conceive of the capacity to decide being derived from the brain itself without the need for an external consciousness, yet still considered *free* will?

Morality: Original and personal sin

Free will is foundational for morality and for Christianity, a religion that aims to rectify the human relationship with the divine after deliberate disobedience in the Fall at the dawn of human history—original sin. Free will is regarded as foundational for personal morality. If, as Libet's experiments are taken to hold, the brain decides prior to the person, or as Damasio contends, it is the neuron and neuronal patterns that choose, not the person, either way, free will is in jeopardy. "If everything is predetermined, a sinful act cannot be ascribed to the person committing the act since they had no choice" (Newberg, 2010, p. 213).

Most recently, the well-known behavioral neuroscientist Robert Sapolsky attempted to tackle the free will issue, stating that neuroscience proves unequivocally that we do not have it. His position starts with the primary challenge: "Find me the neuron that started this process in (a person's) brain, the neuron that had an action potential for no reason." This is a standard neuroscientific argument against free will since there have been a number of scientific experiments that have documented neuronal activity occurring prior to conscious decisions being made. However, it does miss an important larger neuroscientific point—current research cannot point to any place that explains how neurons create consciousness or even subjective thoughts and experiences. Meanwhile, sodium and potassium ions crossing the neuronal membrane result in the depolarization of those neurons. There is the release of dopamine, serotonin, and many other neurotransmitter molecules. There are billions of interconnected neurons firing in different ways. However, in all of that, we have no idea how thought actually originates and becomes part of our consciousness. At this point, we can ask the same "Where does it start" question about everything involving human mental processes. There are also other challenges to this question, though. For example, there are a number of studies that demonstrate neurons firing spontaneously (Uddin, 2020). So, that potentially answers the question about whether there might be some ways in which spontaneous brain activity that could be part of free will might occur. Finally, there are many traditions and philosophical ideas about consciousness not being reduced to material or neuronal processes. If consciousness itself does not require the brain, then all bets are off regarding free will being constrained by neuronal activity. Thus, it is important to consider what science has to say about free will, but other approaches must also be considered.

According to Aquinas, a broad conception of freedom of will demands sourcehood – that the source of an action be the acting person. A narrow notion of free will requires that, along with sourcehood, there be alternative options. Praise or blame can only be ascribed to the actor if they might not have done the action (*Liberum Arbitrium* 2, 3, in Hoffman and Michon, 2017, pp. 3, 8). For Catholicism, sin is something other than "a developmental flaw, a psychological weakness, or the necessary consequence of an inadequate social structure" and so forth. A record of revelation in the Hebrew Scriptures and New Testament explains the divine plan for humanity and sin as a misuse of freedom given to human creatures for loving God and others (*CCC*, 387).

In Genesis 3, Scripture describes a primeval event accepted in faith as an original sin freely carried out by the first human ancestors (*CCC*, 390).

> God created man in his image and established him in his friendship. A spiritual creature, man can live this friendship only in free submission to God. The prohibition against eating 'of the tree of the knowledge of good and evil' symbolically evokes the insurmountable limits that man, being a creature, must freely recognize and respect with trust. Man is

dependent on his Creator and subject to the laws of creation and to the moral norms that govern the use of freedom. (*CCC*, 396)

The first sin is understood to have been mistrust and disobedience with abuse of freedom. All subsequent sin follows the same pattern of distrust and disobedience toward God (CCC, 396-397). Originally, human persons were created in a condition of holiness. God intended for humans their "divinization," participation by grace in divinity that is natural to the three divine Persons. The devil's seduction led our first ancestors to attempt to take likeness to God by force, irreverently preferring self-assertive willfulness over loving deference to the Creator (*CCC*, 398).

The sad consequence of that original disobedience was the immediate loss of original holiness. Adam and Eve distorted their image of God, thought of God as possessive of his prerogatives, and began to fear God as threatening, tyrannical (*CCC*, 399). The unity of their original justice was now demolished: the body was no longer easily subject to the spiritual faculties of the soul, man and woman did not relate so harmoniously as before, and tensions began to arise. The rest of creation could be antagonistic and harsh toward humans, and all were subject to decay. Death came into human history (*CCC*, 400).

What Scripture records is frequently verified by human experience. People find themselves inclined to what is wrong and subject to hostility and tribulations that cannot be attributed to the good Creator. Frequently not alluding to God as his origin, "man has also upset the relationship which should link him to his last end and has broken the right order that should reign within himself as well as between himself and others and all creatures: (*GS*, 1)" (*CCC*, 401).

Each contracts original sin with birth, although not as a personal culpability. Original justice and holiness are absent. Nevertheless, Catholicism holds that humans are still made in God's image and are not totally corrupted. Natural human capacities are deficient; people find themselves exposed to ignorance and pain, inclined to evil, and destined to eventual death. Baptism imparts grace, eliminates original sin, and turns the human person toward God. Remaining, however, are original sin's natural consequences, weakness, and inclination to evil that call for persistent spiritual struggle (*CCC*, 405).

German Lutheran pastor and theologian Deitrich Bonhoeffer (1906-1945) emphasizes the Christian position that the Fall's human striving to become like God on human initiative has resulted in alienation from the original order of creation. Humans face internal division regarding the choice of good over evil. Neuroscientific findings about a self-serving bias should come as no surprise to Christians. Research seems to suggest that we have a "deep-seated capacity for self-deception about what is actually going on in our moral psychology and a falsely inflated sense of the power and reliability of our practical reason" (Messer, 2017, p. 58). Protestant rather than Catholic, Bonhoeffer proposes a position on the effects of original sin that is consonant with Catholicism—"a profound theological suspicion of ethics-as-human-project: the attempt to know about the good on the strength of our resources of reason and insight" (Messer, 2017, p. 59). Christian theology insists that natural ethics needs to be transformed and reconstructed through the Gospel. Christian faith opens the person to the reception of the grace of the Holy Spirit that operates through charity (*CCC*, 1978, 1983).

Personal sin has been defined as "an utterance, a deed, or a desire contrary to the eternal law" (St. Augustine, St. Thomas Aquinas) (*CCC*, 1849), a failure in love toward God and others. *Mortal* sin is a grave violation of a serious matter with complete knowledge and considered consent (*CCC*, 1857). *Venial* sin does not fully destroy love but wounds and offends charity (*CCC*, 1855).

The moral use of free will, in the Catholic view, entails living in truth and loving what is good in the quest for the fullest possible consciousness. "Freedom attains perfection in its acts when directed toward God, the sovereign Good" (*CCC*, 1744, in McGoldrick, 2012). Our actions, choices, and experiences all depend on neurobiological functioning, among other things. Neurons, with their trillions of connections and their chemical neurotransmitters, are necessarily linked to changes in brain activity. There are even brain scan studies that have revealed the areas of the brain in positive and negative moral behaviors. In particular, emotional areas such as the amygdala and insula, as well as areas involved in social interactions such as the precuneus, are involved when people make certain decisions that might be more compassionate and altruistic versus those that are more selfish. There are changes in the brain associated with moral processes. Still, we would consider sin, as well as virtue, to be mental constructs rather than physiological ones. Sin and virtue are more than entities that can be empirically scanned or measured. We can ask the question, "Is it the person who commits a sin or their brain?" We do not fully understand the link between subjective mental events and discernable brain processes—only that neuroscience affirms a close connection between the two (Jeeves and Ludwig, 2018).

Degrees of responsibility, predestination, and Providence

All behaviors, of course, are associated with the brain. Complex behavior, particularly volitional activity, is contingent on distributed neural networks that access memories, cognitions, biases, environmental and relational input, and other factors, any or all of which might disrupt freedom and decision-making. Lesions in the ventromedial prefrontal cortex have been found to correlate with antisocial behavior, but only in rare cases (Adolphs, Glascher, and Tranel, 2018). Studies have pointed to an imbalance between the emotional centers of the limbic system and the prefrontal cortex in people who have committed violent crimes or other immoral acts (Sohn, Kaelin-Lang, and Hallet, 2003). In addition, areas of the brain involved in social perceptions and empathy, such as the parietal lobe and insula, seem to be particularly involved with sociopathic or psychopathic behaviors (Van Dongen, 2020).

While some instances of criminal behavior seem to be associated with genetic or environmental changes in the brain or cerebral injury, attributing criminality to a brain defect is often difficult to determine.

> In order for neuroscience to provide insight into the extent to which criminals act freely and are morally responsible and accountable for their actions, scientific advances must go hand-in-hand with improved philosophical insight into and consensus about the link between brain activity and free will. (Roache, 2014, p. 37)

Since no one determines their genetic inheritance and youngsters have limited control over their developmental environment, extenuating circumstances seem to affect the degree of moral responsibility (Clarke, 2015).

Catholicism holds that unintentional ignorance can diminish or even cancel responsibility for a serious offense.

> But no one is deemed to be ignorant of the principles of the moral law, which are written in the conscience of every man. The prompting of feelings and passions can also diminish the voluntary and free character of the offense, as can external pressures or pathological disorders. (*CCC*, 1860)

Catholic moral philosopher G. E. M. Anscombe (1919-2001), in her book *Intention* (1957), which is regarded as foundational in action theory and philosophical psychology, reinforced intention as crucial in determining the moral culpability of an action. Objecting to the University of Oxford's plan to honor U.S. President Harry S. Truman with an honorary degree for the bombing of Nagasaki and Hiroshima, Anscombe considered the nature of agency through intention and came to ethical evaluations of such actions. Neuroimaging is able to observe brain changes associated with cognitive or emotional intention. However, whether the intended action has morally positive or negative outcomes is not inherently related to what is going on in the brain.

Alasdair MacIntyre, a preeminent Catholic Thomistic political philosopher defines virtue as a quality of character that emerges in a social context from one's role in a life narrative (Darr, 2020, p. 7).

> The narrative of an individual life can be understood as the pursuit of various internal and external goods. The rational integration of life

involves continually asking and answering the question of what constitutes a good life. The virtues sustain us in the quest for the good by enabling us to overcome the harms, dangers, temptations, and distractions we encounter, which will furnish us with increasing self-knowledge and increasing knowledge of the good. (MacIntyre, 2007, pp. 218-219, in Darr, 2020)

In *Ethics in the Conflicts of Modernity* (2016), MacIntyre stresses that an effective narrative directs to an ultimate end beyond all limited goods (pp. 230-231, in Darr, 2020, p. 16). Given these arguments, one might ponder whether there are certain brain processes or states that are involved in the cultivation of virtues, such as these processes involving compassion, forgiveness, and empathy. Perhaps one might argue that the cultivation of certain brain processes is part of the moral direction of humanity.

Aquinas' defense of free will, conceived narrowly as freedom of choice among alternative options, meets a major challenge in the doctrine of the divine, efficacious will. God is necessary, while creatures are contingent. God is omnipotent, while creatures are totally dependent on his power. And since God is goodness and love, God only acts for the welfare of his creatures. It follows that everything that happens is either willed or not hindered by God. Physical evil, such as destructive forces of nature, exists "as long as creation has not reached perfection (Thomas Aquinas, *SCG* III, 71)" (*CCC*, 310). God does not directly or indirectly cause moral evil (Augustine, *De libero arbitrio* 1, 1, 2; Thomas Aquinas, *ST* I-II.79.1). God does not hinder the evil acts of people (Ia.IIae.79.1, reply to obj.1), however, "because he respects the freedom of his creatures and, mysteriously, knows how to derive good from it (Romans 8:28)" (*CCC*, 311). As Vatican Council I (1869-1870) stated:

> By his providence, God protects and governs all things that he has made.... For 'all are open and laid bare to his eyes, (Hb 4:13)' even those things which are yet to come into existence through the free action of creatures" (Pius IX, *Dei Filius*) (*CCC*, 302).

"Divine providence is universal in that all events, even the most personal decisions of human beings, are part of God's eternal plan" (Hardon, 1980, p. 448).

How humans can have free will while God's will is all-encompassing has been debated for millennia without a fully satisfying resolution. Aquinas sorts through the congruence between the divine, efficacious will, and human free will in his treatment of divine providence and predestination. Providence means that God orders all creatures to their ultimate end. Predestination is a particular aspect of providence by which God guides creatures endowed with reason, humans and angels, to a supernatural end of eternal happiness with him (Hoffman and Michon, 2017, p. 18). From the neurotheological perspective, we again might wonder if the relationship between human free will and God's providence somehow comes together in the brain. The brain may be set up by a combination of genetics and divine intervention through grace and environmental learning to be more optimistic or pessimistic, more moral or less moral. The question is how free will interacts with the brain and engages its limitations and possibilities.

Similarly, according to Aquinas (*ST* I, q. 22, a. 2), everything is subject to divine primary causality, which depends on God's will, including secondary, created causes like the human will. Creatures all depend on divine providence. However, divine providence works in and through secondary causes (*CCC*, 308). At the transcendent level, the final source of human acts must be the divine will, but human will nevertheless retains its sourcehood, incorporating functions of the brain. God confers secondary effectiveness on the human will so that humans maintain responsibility for their free choices (Hoffman and Michon, 2017, p. 18).

Professor of philosophy Peter Kreeft explains it this way:

> Since human life is (God's) story, it must have *both* destiny and freedom. Predestination is a misleading word, for it concedes too much to our temporal way of thinking. God is not *pre-* or *post-*anything. He is present in everything. He does not have to wait for anything. Nor does he wonder what will happen. Nothing is uncertain to him, as the future is uncertain to us. There is no *predestination* but *destination*. This follows from divine omniscience and eternity. The oneness of love and power is why we need not fear God's power: it is his very love. Therefore, it cannot be used lovelessly. And it is also why we need not fear that his love will ever fail, for it is omnipotent. It *is* power. The One who loved us even unto death, the supreme weakness, is infinite strength. (2011, p. 2)

Neuroscience can look for the sourcehood of the human will within the various functions of the human brain and has explored this to a very limited extent. We have considered studies such as those by Libet. The Catholic position is that free will, along with the conceptualizing capacity of the intellect, belongs to a mysterious spiritual dimension of the will that constitutes the image of God in the human person. "God created man a rational being, conferring on him the dignity of a person who can initiate and control his actions" (*CCC*, 1730). "Freedom is the power, rooted in reason and will, to act or not to act, to do this or that, and so to perform deliberate actions on one's responsibility" (1731). "Because of freedom, human beings are a product not only of their genes but also of their self-conscious, free, and deliberate choices. This belief represents a stark contrast with any science that reduces human choices to neuro-processes" (McGoldrick, 2012, p. 497). "It is true that *imputability* and responsibility for an action can be diminished or even nullified by ignorance, inadvertence, duress, fear, habit, inordinate attachments, and other psychological or social factors" (*CCC*, no. 1735). But then, free will is not free, at least not fully free. A search for sourcehood in the brain would find associated neurological processes preceding or subsequent to decision-making but not free will itself. Just as regards intelligence, the brain can yield evidence of sensation, perception, imagination, emotion, and behavior, but not universal abstract conceptualization. Thus, it might be possible to characterize free will as well as intellect as spiritual rather than empirically measurable dimensions of the soul.

If neuroscience finds evidence that pre- or unconscious brain activity is the driver of personal decision-making at times, free will, in those cases, will have been affected by some constraining factor(s) that render it at least less than fully free. Perhaps free will is dependent on all our brain processes, conscious as well as preconscious. On the other hand, perhaps neuroscience will be unable to find any specific neurological cause of human decision-making. If that is the case, then perhaps willfulness is a non-biological process that somehow affects the brain's initiating thoughts and behaviors. However, this returns to the problem of how something non-physical affects the physical and whether there is a mysterious immaterial or spiritual dimension of the human soul that impinges upon neurological processes. Neuroscience may not be sure. Catholicism answers in the affirmative.

Virtue and the brain

For Catholicism, human life and, therefore, free will are oriented to God and eternal beatitude with him. "Virtue is a habitual and firm disposition to do good" (*CCC*, 1833). The theological virtues are capacities that God gratuitously infuses at baptism. Supernatural faith, hope, and charity enable and incline Christians to live in a relationship with the trinitarian Persons. These virtues originate in God, orient and move toward God, known by faith, trusted, and loved for himself (*CCC*, 1840). Also bestowed at baptism are the moral virtues— of prudence, justice, fortitude, and temperance. These develop through education, intentional choices, and perseverance. Grace elevates the practice of natural virtues (*CCC*, 1839). Human virtues are consistent tendencies of intellect and will that guide our conduct according to reason and faith (*CCC*, 1834). Specific virtues like prudence or fortitude might correlate with the functioning of the brain. It may be that the study of brain processes that effect decision-making facilitates a better understanding of functions that support deliberate judgment, grit, and fortitude. For example, it has long been known that some individuals appear to have to have these characteristics to a greater or lesser degree. It is conceivable that such qualities correlate with neurotransmitters. Interestingly, individuals not known to gamble can, with the progression of

Parkinson's disease, begin to gamble excessively. Since Parkinson's affects the dopamine system, that neurotransmitter appears to help regulate gambling's risk-taking and decision-making behaviors.

Scottish-American Catholic philosopher Alasdair MacIntyre observes that each human person throughout their life continually asks, "'What is the good for man'? This narrative quest is always an education both as to the character of that which is sought and in self-knowledge" (*After Virtue*, 1984, p. 219). MacIntyre holds that virtues and morality need to fit within what he calls a practice with "a shared end, shared rules, and shared standards of evaluation by which we define our relationships to other people with whom we share purposes and standards. We have to accept as necessary the virtues of justice, courage, and honesty" (p. 191).

For Aquinas, the individual needs to self-orient toward the end, toward God and the common good. Additionally, every person uses practical reason to direct their decisions toward objects of their love—friends, family, nation, politics, arts, sciences, religion, and so on—with actions to be done or things to be acquired. Among possible objects, we often base our priorities on natural inclination, personal beliefs, or socio-cultural trends (Sanguineti, 2011). The person may be left to choose for him- or herself among possible goods and to determine their purpose (MacIntyre, 1984). "The typical modern self has no home (tradition) in which to learn the virtues" (Bergman, 2008, p. 13). Catholic thought regarding human rights is grounded in a communitarian rather than individualist vision (p. 19). Here, too, we might ask how the brain enables us to be social and recognize what behaviors and ideas support the common good compared to those that move human beings toward immorality.

Neurotheology and free will

First, we need an agreed-upon understanding of free will. Then, we can attempt to consider relevant empirical and theological notions about it (Newberg, 2018b). Neurotheology provides a middle ground regarding free will since it can and should be considered from scientific, philosophical, and religious perspectives. Questions regarding morality and ethics can be considered neurologically on multiple levels. At a "meta" level, we might try to understand how and why the human brain can even think about morality in the first place. What parts of our brain help us to consider that some behaviors are right and some wrong?

Interestingly, our brain is designed in large part to help us survive in the world. To do this, the brain has to continuously identify things in the world that are good or bad. We need to distinguish between food and poison and between a good home and one that will not protect us. From the communal perspective, we need to understand which individuals belong to our safe group and which might be enemies and try to steal from us or hurt us. The brain does this through emotional centers such as the amygdala and the autonomic nervous system. The brain automatically elicits a fight-or-flight response when something threatening our survival enters our sensory environment. Thus, our basic notions of good and bad, right and wrong, have to do with human pain and survival.

From these rudimentary biological processes, the higher cortical areas can begin to understand *the good* and *the bad* as part of a larger and more complex moral philosophical system. We can hypothesize why some things are good or bad, especially those that do not specifically pertain to survival. Where does this notion originate: in God, the brain, consciousness, or some metaphysical realm?

More practically, we also can recognize that our beliefs and behaviors contribute to what is good and bad. Thus, we can do some things that help others or ourselves and some things that harm others or ourselves. By incorporating these concepts into our memories via the hippocampus, each of us can develop a moral system dependent on both heredity and environment: our genetically established neural sensitivity to moral good and evil and our environment where we might encounter an abundance of positive or negative stimuli. Some people, having been raised in horrific environments with abuse and violence, still become highly successful and happy. In contrast, others raised in supportive environments might nevertheless end up pursuing immoral behavior.

Experiments might assess how the brain intervenes as a material cause to know what is good and bad for the individual, for others, or even on a universal scale. We can also consider how baseline brain processes help to predict future moral decisions.

> The brain is an intrinsic dimension of psychosomatic acts—human sensitive acts, cognitive and affective, vegetative and intentional, to cause intentional behavior. These acts need a neural 'systemic architecture' which is the material cause of the sensitive and intentional behavior" (Sanguineti, 2011, p. 16).

Following Aquinas, the *embodiment* of spiritual functions occurs through *higher sensitive intentional operations* (p. 17).

Christian theology contends that through conscious resolve, we can choose to become a moral and spiritual person. An interesting neurotheological possibility would be to evaluate a range of moral beliefs and behaviors. Human beings might be limited regarding their capacity for meeting specific standards of morality. This has important theological implications. Arguably, the more we follow the Commandments and other biblical teachings, the more our mind habituates to morally elevated decision-making. Neurotheology would challenge us to explore how beliefs and actions change the structure and function of the brain. Studies show that the individual's prevailing beliefs shape both their perception of and response to the external world. In other words, we might ask whether a person has a positive, optimistic outlook and whether it affects their moral or religious evaluation of others (Rao, Asha, Rao, and Vasedevaraju, 2009).

In the end, one can see how many fascinating moral and ethical questions can be addressed using not only traditional Catholic theology but also neuroscience.

Study questions

1. What is free will?
2. Are Libet's experiments conclusive regarding free will? Explain.
3. What did TMS studies find regarding free will?
4. Why are intention and purposefulness significant in matters of free will?
5. How do dual-process neural networks affect the exercise of free will?
6. How might neuroscience evaluate free will with its spiritual dimension?
7. Why would neural-substrate-based decision-making pose a problem for the *person* and *free will*?
8. What is the Catholic understanding of original sin?
9. How do neuroscience and psychology verify the effects of original sin in human persons?
10. How does neurobiological functioning indicate the specific direction of moral choices?
11. Are sin and virtue mental constructions or measurable physiological ones? Explain.
12. How does Catholic theology understand moral responsibility.
13. What are some factors, neurophysiological as well as psychological, that could diminish or eliminate moral culpability?
14. How might knowledge of brain processes or states contribute to the cultivation of virtue?
15. What is the Catholic understanding of Providence?
16. How might neurotheology consider the longstanding unresolved debate about free will and providence?

17. Why does Catholic theology affirm that free will cannot be reduced to neural processes?

18. How does Catholicism understand theological and cardinal moral virtues?

19. How might neuroscience contribute to understanding some aspects of moral behavior?

20. What are challenges in contemporary culture, according to MacIntyre, for the person self-orienting toward their end, God and the common good?

21. How might neurotheology contribute to the Catholic understanding of free will and moral dimensions of human life?

Chapter 6

The Body's Response to
Religious Experience

Religion and health

As we have seen in Chapter Three on epistemology, the soul and body together comprise a fundamental, ontological unity. We have already explored the response of the primary part of the body that responds to religious experience—the brain. However, the body itself also has a significant response to religious practices and experiences. We have also seen in Chapter Three that the cognitive science theory of cognition observes that the brain does not operate on its own but is embodied, embedded, enactive, and extended. Studies in the physiological response to religious experience have ranged from trying to understand the basic physiological mechanism of religious phenomena to clinical outcomes in terms of overall health and well-being.

It should come as no surprise that there have been hundreds, if not thousands, of research studies exploring the relationship between health and religion or spirituality. While the overall results seem most promising in terms of a generally positive association, there is much to learn by exploring these studies, determining their overall quality and results, and assessing the implications for health as well as religion.

While Catholicism itself has not been a specific target of many studies, it has frequently been noted that in the United States, since Christianity is prevalent, most studies of the relationship between religion and health are about Christianity and health. An important question, then, is whether the results of the existing studies can be interpreted more broadly to include those of other religious traditions. However, for our explorations, we will focus on the effects of the Christian tradition on physical health and well-being.

While most studies, as we just mentioned, tend to show a beneficial effect of religion on physical health, there are certain circumstances in which religion can have a detrimental effect. From a neurotheological perspective, it is relevant for us to understand both positive and negative effects. Understanding the negative effects may be particularly important if we are to help redirect individuals to positive outcomes.

Understanding the relationship between religion and physical health may be beneficial from a health perspective, but there also could be important religious implications. In fact, studies of near-death experiences or intercessory prayer may be particularly revealing in terms of understanding the nature of the human person and whether our consciousness or soul—prior to death, in this mortal life—might extend beyond the physical body.

Although we have previously discussed the importance of definitions at some length, it is worth mentioning that definitions are equally important for comprehending the relationship between religion and health. When we say that there is an association[1], are we talking about religious rituals, practices, feelings, beliefs, experiences, or all of these? How can we differentiate religion from spirituality in the context of physical health? Perhaps it is spirituality rather than religiousness that is the key factor. Thus, it is essential to define these terms as well as possible for an accurate, thorough investigation of the relationship between religiousness and health.

Targets of exploration

When it comes to physical health and well-being, there are multiple avenues for exploring the impact of religiousness and spirituality. In early research studies, as well as for clinical healthcare patients, the primary question asked is, "What religion do you belong to?" referring to religious preference or affiliation. However, a patient's self-identifying as Catholic does not necessarily say much about their practice. Some may be devout Catholics who refer to their faith as a basis for making a variety of healthcare decisions. Others may mean that they were raised Catholic even though they are not committed to Catholic belief or practice, particularly in the context of healthcare. The problem is that a study of patient health that tries to take their religion into account if only by self-report, might completely miss the mark.

If one were to dig a little deeper into individual affiliation, we might take a religious history. For example, there may be two patients who both identify as Catholic. One Catholic may have been raised Catholic from birth, attended Catholic schools, married a Catholic, and may attend church weekly and adhere wholeheartedly to the Catholic faith. A second Catholic may have been raised in a reformed Jewish family, dabbled in agnosticism and atheism in college, married a Catholic, converted to Catholicism, and then became deeply adherent to the religion. Both these individuals might describe themselves as devoutly religious Catholics, but we might wonder about the effects of their distinct religious journeys.

Another target of exploration has to do with the ways in which people engage their religious traditions. For example, one Catholic might go to church weekly and be deeply involved in all aspects of her religion, participating in Bible study, church outings, and various church programs. Another Catholic might feel quite strongly about her faith but engage it on a more private level. Perhaps she prays the rosary every day. And while she might go to church regularly, she might not engage in social activities to the same extent as the first person. How do we evaluate the distinction between those for whom religion is mainly social versus those who engage their religion more privately?

We might also wonder how much any given individual turns to their religious faith for support and coping. When faced with a serious health problem or terminal illness, how much do the religious beliefs of a given patient affect their medical decision-making? Does a patient pray to God when confronted with significant health problems? And how much does a patient seek out their faith community or clergy to help cope with their health problems? A meta-analysis review of 464 articles on the impact of spiritual care services on patients' quality of life, spiritual well-being, and level of satisfaction found that older age, severity of illness, and longer stay were indicators of greater need. The provision of spiritual care resulted in improvement in perceived patient quality of life, spiritual well-being, and level of satisfaction (Kirchoff et al., 2021).

Another related concept in the context of religiousness has to do with a person's commitment to their religion. In fact, how does one determine the level of commitment of any given person? Early studies tried to approach this question by asking people how often they went to church. The presumption was that people who went to church more often were likely to be more committed to and influenced by their religion. However, this is not always the case. Specifically, those individuals who have a deeply private religious life may be highly committed, even though it does not relate directly to direct participation in their church.

Health usually does not motivate religious participation, but for religiously committed individuals, attending religious services at least once weekly was found to impact health positively. Longitudinal data from three large U.S. cohorts was taken from questionnaires on religious service attendance (9,862 subjects for a questionnaire in 2007; 68,376 subjects for 2008, 2009, or 2013; and 13,770 subjects for 2014 and 2016). Attending weekly services was found to lower the risk of drinking, smoking, depression, anxiety, loneliness, and mortality. Beneficial psychosocial outcomes included positive affect, social integration, life satisfaction, and purpose in life (Chen, Kim, and Vander Weele, 2020).

Finally, regarding targets, we can explore the effects of various religious practices on physical health and well-being. These might include going to church, singing hymns, saying prayers, and a variety of other practices. It is particularly challenging to know how to compare practices both within and across traditions. How, in the context of physical health, do we distinguish the effects of receiving Communion from saying the rosary? And to what practice might we compare the rosary in Judaism or Islam?

Many other religious or spiritual interventions can be associated with Catholicism, as well as with other traditions. Some of these are specific to a religion, while others are incorporated into formal interventions. Many different meditation practices have been developed and used to help people with high blood pressure, cancer, heart disease, and other medical disorders (Hummer et al., 1999; Levin, 1994, 1996; Matthews et al., 1998; Murphy et al., 2000).

Thus, there are many possible targets that we can explore for fascinating data in terms of the relationship between religiousness and physical health.

Current measurements of spirituality and religion

As mentioned, one of the most common measures of religiosity has been to ask about the frequency of church attendance. The hope is to create some relative scale by which people might indicate their degree of religiosity based on how often they go to church. Those who go weekly are presumed to be more religious than those who go monthly, who are more religious than those who go once a year. While this can be problematic, one advantage is that it represents an objective[2] measure, at least to some degree. Researchers realized, however, that it was more important to focus on people's religious attitudes and beliefs rather than how often they attend church.

Many researchers set out to develop scales of religiosity to assess the intensity of a person's feelings. The value of such questionnaires is that they more accurately measure participants' feelings about religion. An individual is asked to report how strongly they feel about God or religion on a scale of 1 to 10. The downside is that these scales are highly subjective. Mother Teresa, for example, might have described herself as a 3 out of 10 because she was so humble. But her 3 out of 10 might be equivalent to someone else's 8 out of 10.

Further, subjective questions must use specific terms that may or may not correspond to how a given person understands their religious beliefs. We mean that a question such as, "I feel God's presence all around me," might not capture what a person actually feels. Perhaps a person knows that God is all around him even though he doesn't feel it as a presence. It can be quite complex and challenging to develop adequate questions.

Several hundred scales have been developed to date to explore various parameters of religiosity and spirituality. Some scales focus on beliefs, while others may address various attitudes or motivations. Some scales try to assess religiously oriented concepts such as fear of death. But should someone with a strong sense of religiosity fear death more or less? And is this a religious or psychological question?

The ideal would be to have some approach that combines objective and subjective components to assess a person's sense of religiosity as accurately as possible, particularly how their sense of religiosity might affect physical health. This will continue to be a challenge for neurotheology, as well as for the broader field of spirituality and health.

Health outcomes and religion

As mentioned in the introduction of this chapter, there are thousands of research articles about the relationship between religion and health, focused primarily on health outcomes that may be disease-specific. Thus, a study of heart disease may determine whether religious individuals are more or less likely to have a heart attack. In fact, in the United States, in a Maryland County, an early study of 91,000 people found that those who regularly attended church had a lower prevalence of cirrhosis, emphysema, suicide, and death from ischemic heart disease (Comstock and Partridge, 2008). Several other studies have found that people who are more religious or attend houses of worship more regularly may have better outcomes after major illnesses or medical procedures (Koenig et al., 1999). Religion and spirituality represent patients' seeking meaning, purpose, and transcendence, connecting to family, community, or nature (Rura, 2022).

A systematic review of 15 studies showed that 75% of these studies found lower heart disease or cardiovascular mortality among the most religious individuals (Abu et al., 2018, p. 2777). Another study of heart surgery patients revealed that stronger religious belief was associated with shorter hospital stays and fewer complications. In a small study of 30 older women after hip repair, religious belief was associated with lower levels of depressive symptoms and better ambulation status (Pressman et al., 1990, p. 758).

Other studies focus on symptoms such as pain or disability. These studies have generally shown that those individuals who are the most religious are able to cope with illnesses more effectively and report lower levels of pain and disability (Koenig, 2001, p. 321). This appears to be the case for both acute as well as chronic conditions.

Still, other studies focus more broadly on mortality, showing that those individuals who are the most religious using some measure, tend to have reduced death rates both for specific diseases such as cardiac surgery and cancer, as well as all-cause mortality (i.e., Hummer et al., 1999, in Pearce, 2013, p. 528). This latter measure has to do with death from any cause.

While the data seem to suggest a generally very positive relationship between religiosity and health, there are certainly negative effects as well. Sometimes, religions or religious ideas can lead to an overall negative perspective that can be detrimental to health. For example, suppose a person believes that God is punishing her with cancer because she lived an immoral life. In that case, she may be less likely to engage in appropriate medical therapies and more likely to have a poor health outcome. It is important that a physical problem not be attributed to a lack of spirituality. Numerous studies have found associations between spiritual struggles and health. A study at a Polish university (180 subjects, average age 24) found religious struggle to correlate positively with anxiety and negatively with life satisfaction. The link between religious doubt and satisfaction with life was mediated by meaning-making (Zarzycka and Zietek, 2019).

It is interesting to note that sometimes, even positive experiences may result in increased anxiety and depression, leading to poor outcomes. For example, a cardiac patient having a near-death experience during a sudden cardiac arrest might be viewed negatively by his friends or clergy. Even though the negative reaction seems to stem from others' skeptical attitudes rather than the patient's positive experience per se, it could evoke substantial religiously based anxiety and fear.

Finally, there are obvious negative health outcomes associated with religiousness in the form of terrorism or cults. Individuals willing to kill themselves or others for their beliefs represent the ultimate in poor outcomes. In 1978, Peoples Temple founder Jim Jones led his followers in a mass murder-suicide at their agricultural commune in Guyana. Many willingly ingested poison-laced punch, while others were forced to do so at gunpoint. The final death count was 909, a third of them children. The cult leader had promised they would build a socialist utopia in a tract of jungle. It is important to understand how and why some individuals engage in destructive behaviors with strong religious undertones. Certainly, there is an important effect of various rituals. But there seems to be something specific that draws people to beliefs that can potentially be very detrimental, either for the individual or for the larger society. Individuals who join cults are found to have predisposing factors, including emotional vulnerability or feelings of loneliness, low-income family and social relationships, insufficient means of meeting basic needs, history of abuse or neglect, and debilitating circumstantial stress (Curtis and Curtis, 2016). By understanding the basis of behaviors with negative health outcomes, we hopefully can find effective ways of redirecting people to more positive perspectives and outcomes.

On the other hand, neurotheology would also remind us that religious beliefs can potentially be more important than poor physical health outcomes. After all, many early Christians were martyred. This laid the foundation for the development and expansion of the Christian faith. As Tertullian, the third-century Christian apologist, put it, "The blood of martyrs is the seed of Christians." Negative health outcomes lead to positive spiritual outcomes. Which is better? That is a fascinating potential neurotheological debate.

Mechanisms

When it comes to understanding the relationship between religion and health, it is important to consider the potential mechanisms by which that interaction occurs. We have typically divided mechanisms into two basic types—indirect and direct. Indirect mechanisms have to do with participating in certain aspects of a religious tradition that also happen to have health benefits. Direct mechanisms have to do with the performance of specific practices or even the inherent effect of belief itself.

Expanding on these concepts, we can first consider indirect mechanisms. As mentioned, these are effects of participating in various elements of a religion that indirectly lead to positive health benefits. Perhaps the most important and prominent benefit is enhanced social interaction. Any time you go to church or participate in a group religious function, there is value and benefit. The human brain has many areas responsive to social connection. It is well known that individuals who have a strong social support network frequently do better health-wise, both in terms of overall health as well as when confronting a specific illness (Kok et al., 2013, p. 1123). For example, women with breast cancer have significantly extended survival if they have a strong social support network (Krenske et al., 2006, p. 1105). These findings support clinicians' asking their clients about their spirituality or religion.

Churches provide a strong social support network, from the clergy to the church leaders to the congregation. Ideally, everyone is there to support one another. If an individual develops cancer, she might be visited in the hospital by her priest or fellow congregants. This social support network not only lifts the patient's mood but can help them handle other aspects of life, such as childcare, getting groceries, or managing their home. Relieving these stressors can be enormously helpful. With the relief of stress, a patient's physical health rallies. When social support reduces anxiety and depression, a patient's physical and mental health can substantially improve. Christians with liturgical traditions revert to prayer and sacraments in times of suffering. As we will see again in Chapter Seven, Baptism and Eucharist are foundational sacraments of healing, orienting the Catholic toward friendship with God, with implications regarding medical decision-making. The sacraments of Reconciliation and Anointing of the Sick bring peace and support at challenging times on the journey. The Eucharist transforms perceptions of painful circumstances through meaning—God's lovingly sharing human suffering (Henson, Morrill, and Barina, 2023).

In the context of social support, many churches provide health screenings for their congregants. Whether to help detect high blood pressure or diabetes or to encourage regular screening for diseases such as colon or breast cancer, health services through the church can significantly enhance a person's health. Of course, sometimes, this can backfire. Dr. Daniel Amen has frequently noted that churches will often have doughnut or ice cream drives, which encourages poor eating habits and obesity. Dr. Amen even quipped that not only will a church teach you about heaven, but it sometimes might send you there more quickly. However, when churches support healthy living, not only regarding eating but through exercise programs or the intellectual stimulation of Bible study, they generally have a positive impact on health and well-being. Together with Pastor Rick Warren, Dr. Amen developed a program called the Daniel Plan with the goal of getting churches to encourage healthier living habits (Amen, Warren. The Daniel Plan).

A healthy diet is another example of an indirect mechanism linking religion and health. In our (ABN) Jefferson University integrative medicine center, we encourage patients to follow a plant- and protein-based diet. Religious traditions such as Hinduism that promote vegetarianism indirectly improve health by recommending an overall healthy diet. In Catholicism, the season of Lent, a time of religious conversion, including penance, could bring a secondary benefit of healthier living.

A more specific yet indirect mechanism by which the Catholic Church promotes healthy practices has to do with the overall approach toward many high-risk behaviors. Encouraging church members to avoid drugs, alcohol, and promiscuity are goals consistent with those of physicians around the world. Research has generally shown that frequent church attendance is associated with less drug and alcohol abuse and fewer sexually transmitted disease cases (Grim and Grim, 2019, p. 1713). Spirituality can serve for recovery among persons who have lower rates of substance use disorder when they are closely connected with religion (Galenter et al., 2021). Church-based activities and safe social spaces are likely to promote positive peer interaction.

Direct mechanisms of action have to do with participation in practices that directly affect the body and brain. In previous chapters, we discussed how practices such as meditation or prayer affect the brain. Multiple studies demonstrate that reduced high blood pressure, improved heart rate variability, and better immune function are associated with practices such as meditation and prayer (Black and Slavich, 2016, p. 13).

Prayer can have considerable bearing on the autonomic nervous system.[3] Prayer exercises can enhance or diminish the arousal (sympathetic) or quiescent (parasympathetic) systems. Heart rate and blood pressure can down-regulate. Decline in stress can reduce cortisol[4] levels in the blood, counteracting harmfully elevated cortisol effects such as neuronal damage and immune suppression. Research shows that meditation and prayer reduce cortisol levels (Newberg and Waldman, 2009, p. 222). Studies in neuroplasticity[5] find that meditation practice can help decrease anxiety and beneficially alter neuronal pathways (Bingaman, 2013, p. 549). Meditation can develop, over time, a mindful awareness, an observing self that becomes non-reactive to the brain's negative bias toward life and human relationships. The limbic system's amygdala, programmed to detect and overreact to stress and danger, is down-regulated to allow trust in God and peaceful optimism to emerge and gradually form a calmer, more spiritually attentive, faith-based attitude.

Researching the effects of medication, studies have focused on evoked potentials (EPs—the electrical signals produced by the nervous system in response to an external stimulus) to assess sensory pathways and event-related potentials (ERPs—the measured brain responses that are the direct result of cognitive processing). Long-term meditators were found to have enhanced "frontal top-down control over fast automatic salience detection. (They showed) increased attentional engagement after meditation, enhanced perceptual clarity, decreased automated reactivity, and increased efficiency in the distribution of limited brain resources and switching attention" (Singh and Telles, 2015, p. 9). Meditators reported increased emotional acceptance with decreased anticipation of pain, and they were less affected by emotionally adverse stimuli. Meditation was found to foster a mental state with enhanced emotional regulation and more effective apportionment of neural resources (Singh and Telles).

Dr. Singh Khalsa and I (ABN) have introduced a term called *spiritual fitness*. The point of this term is that by optimizing the spiritual self, we also optimize the physical self and vice versa. Practices such as meditation and prayer, eating in moderation, and engagement in positive attitudes and practices, including altruism and charity, all lead to enhanced spiritual life. But all of these have also been associated with improvements in physical health and well-being.

There is a growing international interest in arts therapies, such as visual arts therapy, music expression, movement-based therapy, and expressive writing, in healthcare settings. Arts interventions enhance the medical practice with a holistic view of the person. A review of research studies (1995-2007) on the association between creative arts engagement and health found evidence that such interventions effectively reduce adverse physiological and psychological outcomes" (Stuckey and Nobel, 2010, p. 254). The success of arts interventions relies largely on cooperation by clinical staff. A review of the literature (2004—

2014) found that most staff perceive patient engagement in arts interventions to impact their stress, mood, pain level, and sleep positively (Wilson et al., 2016).

Finally, simply having a religious or spiritual outlook may have inherent health value by fostering *dispositional optimism*. Several studies have shown that optimistic individuals have improved overall health, particularly regarding heart disease. Optimism may be comparable to belief in a positive future. Positive thinking has been found to reduce stress and risk of sickness, as well as stress-eliciting cortisol levels, and to improve coping skills. Optimists generally show increased longevity. People with faith and optimism are likely to engage in life more actively and have overall better physical well-being (Newberg and Waldman, 2009, pp. 164-165).

Pope Benedict XVI takes faith to the level of answering ultimate questions like, What is the meaning of life? Does my life have a purpose? What is our communal destiny? Does suffering have value? What happens at death? The Pope observes that:

> Faith is the substance of hope (*Spes salvi* [*SS*], 10). Man's great, true hope, which holds firm in spite of all disappointments, can only be God who has loved us and who continues to love us "to the end" until all "is accomplished" (cf. Jn 13:1 and 19:30). From faith I await "eternal life"— the true life, whole and unthreatened, in all its fullness. Life in its true sense is a relationship with him, who is the source of life (27). The great hope can only be God, who encompasses the whole of reality and who can bestow upon us what we, by ourselves, cannot attain. God is the foundation of hope, the God who has a human face and who has loved us to the end, each one of us and humanity in its entirety. His love alone gives us the possibility of soberly persevering day by day, without ceasing to be spurred on by hope, in a world which by its very nature is imperfect. (31)

For those with strong faith, being connected to God may lead to improved health. In the book of Daniel, we find evidence of the first controlled trial about the health effects of being religious.

> Daniel had determined not to incur pollution by food and drink from the (pagan king's) royal table. . . . To the guard assigned to Daniel, Hananiah, Mishael, and Azariah by the chief eunuch, Daniel then said, "Please allow your servants a ten-day trial, during which we are given only vegetables to eat and water to drink. You can then compare our looks with those of the boys who eat the king's food; go by what you see and treat your servants accordingly.' The man agreed to do what they asked and put them on ten days' trial. When the ten days were over, they

looked better and fatter than any of the boys who had eaten their allowance from the royal table. (Dan 1:9,11-16).

Eventually, as Daniel and his colleagues remained faithful to God, the king threw them into a fiery furnace. They emerge unharmed, saved miraculously by God.

The Catholic Church believes in miracles—"signs or words, such as a healing or the control of nature, which can only be attributed to divine power. The miracles of Jesus were messianic signs of the presence of God's Kingdom" (*CCC*, 547). Miracles, at times, occur by the power of God through the intercession of the Virgin Mary and other saints. Some of the faithful, after their death, are *canonized* as saints—recognized by the Church for having practiced heroic virtue through God's grace. Saints are proposed to the faithful as intercessors and models of virtue in challenging times (*CCC*, 828).

Faith, spirituality, and religion are nurtured by prayer. What is prayer? For a theist, it is communication with the transcendent Being who creates, sustains, and ordains or permits the providential events and circumstances of human life in view of eternal life beginning here and opening into heaven. Love, in Christianity, is the primary attribute of God (1 Jn 4:8) and the primary obligation of Christians (1 Co 12:31—13:3). For Catholics, prayer may occur at any time because God is always present, bestowing natural life from one moment to the next. God surrounds and permeates the human existence of each individual and confers supernatural grace. He precedes and enlivens every intention and animates every movement (Ps 139). He is more profoundly present to the person than the soul to the body. Each human being is immersed in God: "He penetrates all that we have and all that we are by His active presence and His vivifying power" (Grialou, 1986, p. 2). "In Him, we live and move and have our being" (Acts 17:28).[6]

Catholics (and Christians generally) might appreciate the physiological and psychological advantages of prayer, meditation, or contemplation. They would probably not be comfortable with stopping there. Communication with God means much more than neurological, psychological, or emotional benefits for human health.

With any discussion of prayer, spiritual supernatural dimensions need to be primary. "No deliberate attempt should be made to reach the contemplative state, either by emptying the mind of all thoughts and ideas or by fixing the mind on any object without discursive thought. Contemplation is the gift of God" (Scaramelli, 1913/2015, p. 33). In fact, communication with God in some way leads to the willingness to do what God wills, which, since God is all goodness and love, will be to the ultimate advantage and welfare of the human person. Conformity to God's will can be attained without contemplation or mystical union. The Church teaches that "all states of contemplation are gifts of God" (p. 68).

> "The wonder of prayer is revealed beside the well where we come seeking water: there, Christ comes to meet every human being. It is he who first seeks us and asks us for a drink. Jesus thirsts; his asking arises from the depths of God's desire for us. Whether we realize it or not, prayer is the encounter of God's thirst with ours. God thirsts that we may thirst for him (St. Augustine, Sermon 56). (*CCC*, 2560)

In the end, being religious is enough to keep one healthy. Overall, there are a great number of associations between physical health and religious beliefs. Most of them are positive, although occasionally they can be negative. Hopefully, this review demonstrates the powerful relationship between religion and health, another dimension of the neurotheological exploration of the Catholic tradition.

Study Questions

1. What are some discriminating factors in self-reporting about religious affiliation?

2. What do studies show about the effects of religious practice on physical and mental health?

3. What are some study targets of intervention regarding religious or spiritual practice and health?

4. What are some challenges regarding scales of religiosity and spirituality?

5. What are examples of positive findings regarding the association between religiosity and health?

6. What are examples of religiosity having a negative impact on health?

7. How might even a positive religious experience lead to poor health outcomes?

8. Some individuals appear to be drawn to cast in religious terms factors that are destructive rather than life-giving. Explain.

9. What are some direct and indirect benefits of religious practice on health?

10. What is meant by "spiritual fitness"?

11. According to Pope Benedict XVI, how might precarious health be associated with faith?

12. What is the Catholic stance on miracles and saints?

13. What is prayer for Catholicism?

14. What do you think about health benefits as a motive for religious practice?
15. What essentially constitutes union with God?
16. What is the place of contemplative prayer on the trajectory toward union with God?

Endnotes

[1] Association is a statistical relationship between two variables. They may be associated or co-occur without a causal relationship. Causation means that exposure to one variable produces an effect on the other (Boston University Medical Center). When correlations between variables are consistently high, causative factors may be suspected. Most of the literature on the association between religion and health seems to suggest that ordinarily, the more persons engage intrinsically in religion, the better their health outcomes.

[2] An objective measure can provide a source for a semi-structured qualitative interview to elicit a deeper understanding. The qualitative aspect gives the subject the opportunity to say what they might have thought during the objective measure but that its questions did not capture.

[3] The autonomic nervous system (ANS) is part of the peripheral nervous system, in contrast to the central nervous system (CNS: brain and spinal cord). The ANS regulates involuntary processes like breathing, heart rate, and digestion. The ANS's three divisions include the sympathetic nervous system (SNS), parasympathetic nervous system (PSN), and enteric nervous system (ENS). The SNS initiates a state of elevated arousal and attention: *fight or flight*. The PSN fosters a quiescent, restful state. The ENS primarily regulates digestion and blood flow.

[4] Cortisol is a hormone secreted by the adrenal glands (on top of the kidneys). Cortisol regulates the stress response, metabolism, blood pressure, and blood sugar, suppresses inflammation, and helps to control the sleep-wake cycle. Elevated cortisol levels can be harmful to health.

[5] Neuroplasticity refers to "the ability of the nervous system to change its activity in response to intrinsic or extrinsic stimuli by reorganizing its structure, functions, or connections after injuries, such as a stroke or traumatic brain injury (TBI)" (Puderbaugh and Emmady, 2022).

[6] Among other authors, Deitrich von Hildebrand (*Transformation in Christ* [2001] and *Liturgy and Personality* [2016]) has written perceptively about the spiritual life in modernity.

Chapter 7
The Neurophysiology of Catholic Rituals

We now begin an exploration of specific Catholic rituals from the neurotheological perspective. This requires an evaluation of a variety of rituals and practices in terms of their elements and the experiences that arise from them. There are cognitive, emotional, and experiential effects that each potentially associates with specific brain processes. Catholic rituals and practices help connect the individual and community to God the Father, Son, and Spirit through Jesus. We begin with an exploration of the sacraments and liturgy in this chapter, then consider various practices in the chapter that follows.

Sacramental theology

According to Canadian philosopher and theologian Bernard Lonergan, S.J. (1904-1984), sacraments are cognitive and affective symbols and activities that support individuals and communities in their intention to contact and be contacted by God in Jesus Christ (Happel, 1989).

Reflecting on the sacraments, Lonergan emphasized the importance of embodied knowing. Symbols or images of sight, sound, touch, taste, and smell are captured by perception in conscious imagination and provide matter for understanding or insight. They belong to human cognition and affective life. This means that they also have potential neurological correlates. Neurological underpinnings include areas of the brain that support emotional, cognitive, and sensory processing and are highly interconnected. Thus, some images and symbols encountered in the ins and outs of life are charged with emotional and ethical value. Symbols are necessary in the religious domain since we are embodied with intellect and will to evoke and communicate religious experience. Lonergan saw symbolic activity as primarily about events and actions rather than objects. Jesus' self-donation at the Last Supper is extended in service to his relationship with the believer in the Eucharist (Happel, 1989).

For Lonergan, the Catholic sacraments symbolically express religious conversion. He orients the salvific meaning of worship and prayer to being in love with God. For Lonergan, the person is already, primordially, a word in the Word, although fallen, a created effect of divine Love who pursues the human person. Conversion for Lonergan means an ultimate being-in-love that involves self-surrender to the Transcendent Other. The sacraments flow from the loving self-sacrifice of Jesus and operate at the value level of human functioning. The value of Jesus' self-gift supersedes his truth, goodness, and authenticity, as well as the human moral inadequacies that will also be present.

Similarly, we might consider how feelings and thoughts are associated with the brain and with physical reality that is incorporated into God. In this way, the connection of the biological with the spiritual adds another layer to creation's connection with God. How does this happen biologically? We might ask how religious conversion or salvation impacts the brain. What part of the person is affected? How do the biological effects yield changes in behavior or beliefs?

Theology of spiritual senses

Since the human person embodies a paradoxical union of matter and spirit, reflection on the sacraments leads to the consideration of spiritual senses. "The doctrine of the spiritual senses asserts that there are 'five spiritual sense faculties' that bear 'some likeness to the exterior senses' (Teresa of Avila) 'by which God's presence in the various states of union is detected'" (Pike, 1992, p. 42). The spiritual senses may mean that 'in Christian mystical encounter God can be recognized through 'sensations that at least are similar to the bodily perceptions usually identified with these terms' (p. 44). Philosopher Nelson Pike's descriptions in *Mystic union: An essay on the phenomenology of mysticism* closely follow the work of Poulain (Wainright, 2011, p. 21). Using corporeal senses, images, symbols, and rituals, the human individual perceives, experiences, and responds to the immaterial Transcendent. "Faith allows the divine to be perceived according to the sensory forms of experience" (Fields, 1996, p. 227). Whenever the soul, self, person, or consciousness is involved with sense perception, opening to transcendent meaning and human choice, there may be some level of challenge for understanding what happens neurologically.

Neurotheology would argue that the spiritual senses are deeply connected with our standard senses, as we will elaborate on below. It is important to mention here that our senses of vision, hearing, smelling, tasting, and touching all connect our inner selves to the spiritual world. Furthermore, our senses connect our body to our brain. Each sensory system has complex pathways from the sense organs themselves (e.g., the eyes or ears) through various processing steps and to the cortical areas of the brain that integrate all the sensory information we receive. And ultimately, our entire conceptualization of reality builds from the senses by which we establish a mental picture of the reality around us. This is critical since our mental picture of reality establishes our sense of the Divine and the Divine presence in the world and our lives.

"The concept of the spiritual senses has played a significant role in the history of Roman Catholic and Eastern Orthodox spirituality" (Wainright, 2011, p.

21). At least as far back as Origen (185-254) and then Augustine (354-430), there were allusions to vision, sound, smell, taste, and touch to describe Christian perception and experience of God. Bonaventure (1217-1274) relates the intellect to vision and hearing and the will and emotions to touch, taste, and smell (p. 26). Twentieth-century Swiss theologian and priest Hans Urs von Balthasar (1905-1988) and German theologian Karl Rahner, S.J. (1904-1984) addressed the doctrine of spiritual senses as the interchange among human sensory, intellectual, and volitional faculties in pursuit of encounter with God. How can the human person radically engaged in sensation and imagination attain union with God, who totally transcends the finite?

Balthasar grounded his answer in faith, in theological anthropology that understood religious experience as "perceiving the non-sensuous sensuously. . . . Faith reconstitutes the human person according to its object Christ, the humanly visible form of God's definitive self-revelation. Through faith, human nature becomes transformed so that the intellect is rendered capable of receiving the forms of grace (and) insofar as the intellect is transformed, so are the will, the imagination, and sensation, the subordinate faculties that serve it" (Fields, 1996, p. 226). Balthasar noted that faith establishes an incarnational metaphysics that allows the Christian to perceive in the image of Jesus more than his humanity, in Christ the divine Logos. Sensible forms are associated with Jesus. They "become vehicles of grace because the Word of God, the very principle of Being through whom 'all things were made' (Jn 1:3), has taken corporeal form unto itself (*The Glory of the Lord* [*GL*]1, pp. 419-420, 423-424)" (Fields, p. 228).

Even more than the Incarnation, the Trinity becomes, for Balthasar, the ontological foundation for sensation and imagination mediating spiritual forms of faith. Since the Son is the Image of the Father (Col 1:15), and through him all is made and saved, the Son is the formal cause, 'the archetype, idea, exemplar of all things outside God' (*GL2*, 1989, p. 293). It follows that sensory reality expresses him implicitly, and when sensate and imaginative content are incorporated into Christ, faith mediates grace. According to Balthasar, the universe flows forth from the generation of the Logos, which draws it back to its origin (*GL1*, pp. 419-420; 2, p. 296) (Fields, 1996, pp. 228-229). "The spiritual senses for Balthasar constitute the range of the continuum that, once elevated by the virtues, the gifts, and the beatitudes, perceives the supra-sensuous, transcendent world within the sensuous, empirical world (*GL*, 1989, pp. 317-318)" (Fields, 1996, p. 238).

Rahner grounds his theology in Mystery. He expounds on the nature of mystery through his reflections on reasoned judgment. According to hylomorphic (spirit-body) anthropology with matter-and-form body-and-soul unity, the body, with its operations of sensation and imagination, works closely with the soul and its powers of intellect and will. Rahner considers the human person a hylomorphic "spirit in the world" that can make sensible forms intelligible (*Spirit in the World* [*SW*], 1957, pp. 406-407) (Fields, 1996, p. 229). Since affirming an infinite Being transcends what sense perception presents to the intellect, the intellect must include the capacity to open onto a wider ontological range. Rahner proposes that the goal (final cause) of human intelligence is infinite Being (*SW*, pp. 393-395).

> Naturally constituted by an ontological dynamism, the human spirit, through finite, yearns for an intuition of unrestricted Being as its end. This yearning means that the human person possesses an openness to the divine that constitutes a 'preapprehension' of it. Preapprehension (means) an intellectual 'horizon:' a preconceptual, nonobjective grasp of the Absolute. . . . (There is) a contrast between the intellect's pre-grasp of infinite Being on the one hand and the (conversion-to-the phantasm's) grasp of sensible form of the other. This contrast causes a sensible form to be determined when the intellect sees it as finite against its preapprehension of the infinite (*SW*, 1957, pp. 395-400). (Fields, 1996, p. 230)

Rahner distinguishes implicit from explicit revelation. Implicit revelation is what he calls *transcendental* revelation: it implicitly affirms that God exists. Explicit or *categorical* revelation is a revelation to which Christians assent by faith. According to Rahner, transcendental or implicit revelation happens in the *supernatural existential.*

> This means that categorical (or explicit) revelation shows that human intelligence reaches its full term, not in the merely implicit drive of the preapprehension for the Absolute (God), but in faith's explicit (impetus toward) the God who reveals himself in Christ (*Theological Investigations* [*TI*] 1, 1961, pp. 297-317 at 312-313). (Fields, 1996, p. 233)

Rahner claims for humanity an end beyond itself in the Absolute. The preapprehension of the Absolute (supernatural existential) is the metaphysical basis for a mystical consciousness that can begin in an implicitly known horizon and develop into consciously perceived proximity to the triune Infinite (*TI* 18, 1961, pp. 173-188 at 176-177, and *The Spirit in the Church*, 1977, pp. 11-14) (Fields, 1996, pp. 233-234).

Neurotheology would challenge us to consider how mystical consciousness relates to brain functions. Our research (ABN) has long been involved with exploring the biology of mystical states and the practices that lead to them. Areas of the brain involved in decision-making and spatial representation of the self appear to be particularly involved in such experiences. Neurotheological investigations might expand understanding of ways that spiritual experiences affect the brain and body and connect the experience to fundamental reality.

The Catholic sacramental system

"The liturgy is the summit toward which the activity of the Church is directed; it is also the font from which all her power flows' (*Sacrosancto Concilium* [*SC*], 10)" (*CCC*, 1994, 1074). The liturgy presupposes evangelization, catechesis, conversion, and good works that support the mission of the Church (*CCC*, 1072).

Catholics understand that God speaks through creation. Humans can discern in the cosmos evidence of the Creator (Ws 13:1, Rm 1:19f, Acts 14:17). "Light and darkness, wind and fire, water and earth, the tree and its fruit speak of God and symbolize both his greatness and his nearness" (*CCC*, 1994, 1147). Human persons, body and spirit, grasp and communicate spiritual realities through physical signs and symbols. We need signs and symbols to communicate with others through language, gestures, and actions. And it is the same for relating with God (*CCC*, 1146).

Catholics have seven sacraments, many sacramentals, and various practices for sanctifying time and space. The sacraments are Baptism, Confirmation, the Eucharist, Penance, Anointing of the Sick, Holy Orders, and Matrimony. The Catholic sacramental system includes pilgrimages and processions, shrines, and churches—bridging the physical and spiritual, earth and heaven, the human and divine. Perceptible realities become means for God to sanctify human persons and for humans to worship God. Words and actions express the sanctifying presence of God and human gratitude to the Creator (*CCC*, 1148). "The liturgical celebration involves signs and symbols relating to creation (candles, water, fire), human life (washing, anointing, breaking bread), and the history of salvation (the rites of the Passover)." Incorporated in expressions of faith, these elements, rituals, and gestures become instruments for sanctification in Christ through the Holy Spirit (*CCC*, 1189). Perceptible signs in the sacraments—words, symbols, and actions—express and strengthen faith and efficaciously make present the grace they signify (*CCC*, 1084, 1123, 1127). The fruits of the sacraments depend on the dispositions of the recipient (*CCC*, 1128).

Symbolic cognition and associative learning

Symbols are derived from the cognitive ability to generate representations. In other words, symbols intentionally make something in the physical, social, or psychological/experiential world stand for something else, either actual or imaginary (Noble and Davidson, 1996, p. 63). Concepts and meanings derive from sensory information and higher-order abstraction (Mesulam, 1998). Several cognitive processes support the use of symbols. (1) Symbolic cognition incorporates associative learning, the emotional and reinforcing associations that symbols represent. (2) Through meta-cognition, we can reflect on our thoughts and feelings. We can monitor our monitoring (Harre and Secord, 1972). (3) We can mentalize: *decouple* an imagined meaning or condition from reality to be able to keep more than one situation in mind at the same time (Gallagher and Frith, 2003). And (4) we can manipulate symbols offline—words, concepts, representations. This is necessary for creativity, for inventing new concepts, objects, or events that may be completely imaginary (Deeley, 2004, p. 246).

Through the dopaminergic neurotransmitter system, religious symbols can invest concepts with a sense of heightened reality (Geertz, 1993, p. 90; Kapur, 2005; Deeley, 2004, p. 260). "A dysregulated, hyperdopaminergic state, at a 'brain' level of description and analysis, leads to an aberrant assignment of salience to the elements of one's experience, at a 'mind' level" (Kapur, 2003, p. 13).

Both brain hemispheres assist with meaning-finding in symbolic processing. The right hemisphere tends to give a generalized perspective on semantic concepts, in contrast to the left's more focused view.

> Right hemisphere language processing is characterized by a widespread, or coarse, as opposed to a focused activation of semantic concepts, . . . the appreciation of metaphorical or connotative as opposed to literal or denotative aspects of language, and a preference for remote as opposed to close associations. (Taylor et al., 2002, p 251; Taylor et al., 1999; in Deeley, 2004, p. 261)

In the symbol-rich ritual setting, supernatural entities and events evoke analogical interpretation. Right hemisphere processing focuses primarily on emotion and indirect meaning (Davidson and Irwin, 1999). Religious symbols need to engage with semantic meanings to be regarded as real and meaningful objects outside the realm of ordinary everyday life. "The analogical mode of salient, loosely associative thinking is the mode of 'cognitive fluidity,' 'mapping across domains,' and 'representational re-description'" (Michen, 2000, in Deeley, 2004, p. 262).

Sacraments of initiation: Baptism, Confirmation, and the Eucharist

Laying the foundation for Christian life are the sacraments of Christian initiation: Baptism, Confirmation, and Eucharist. "The sharing in the divine nature given to men and women through the grace of Christ bears a certain likeness to the origin, development, and nourishing of natural life" (Paul VI, 1971, *Divinae consortium naturae* [*DCN*], 657).

The *sign of the cross* marks with the imprint of Christ, the one who is going to belong to him, and signifies the grace of the redemption Christ won by his cross. The proclamation of the Word of God enlightens the candidate and the assembly with the revealed truth and elicits the response of faith, which is inseparable from Baptism. (*CCC*, 1235, 1236)

The *baptismal water* is consecrated by prayer so that those who will be baptized may be 'born of water and the Spirit' (Jn 3:5) (*CCC*, 1238). The *essential rite* of the sacrament follows:

Baptism signifies and brings about death to sin and entry into the life of the Trinity through configuration to the paschal mystery of Christ by triple immersion in the baptismal water (or) by pouring the water three times over the candidate's head. (*CCC*, 1239)

The minister of the sacrament says: "*N.*, I baptize you in the name of the Father, and of the Son, and the Holy Spirit."

The anointing with sacred *chrism*, perfumed oil consecrated by the bishop, signifies the gift of the Holy Spirit to the newly baptized. The white garment symbolizes that the person baptized has "put on Christ" (Gal 3:27) and has risen with Christ. The *candle*, lit from the Easter candle, signifies that Christ has enlightened the neophyte. In him, the baptized are "the light of the world" (Mt 5:14). (*CCC*, 1241, 1243)

A priest was recently called out for having celebrated the sacrament of baptism over more than 20 years using "We" instead of "I" baptize . . . . The Vatican's Sacred Congregation for the Doctrine of the Faith declared that this incorrect formula rendered his thousands of baptisms invalid. They needed to be redone with the correct words. Many asked why such a small mistake with no ill intent mattered so much. The Vatican explained that it was necessary to use the formula handed down by Tradition. St. Thomas Aquinas ruled out more than one person baptizing an individual at the same time. Vatican II's *Sacrosanctum Concilium* (*SC*) notes that "when a man baptizes it is really Christ himself who baptizes . . . . No one may add, remove, or change anything in the liturgy on his own authority" (22). Through their ministry, the one who baptizes (even a layperson in an emergency) acts in the person of Christ. The matter and form, words, actions, and intent of each of the sacraments must conform to what is approved in the Church's liturgical rites (Allen & Trestman, 2020, pp. 1-3). This may come across as legalistic. Merely legalistic mistakes are routinely forgiven through the doctrine of *ecclesia supplet*, which means the Church supplies. To imagine a hypothetical case of the minister of a sacrament not following the sacramental rite, a greater fault would be not simply using a wrong word but attempting to redefine what the Church was doing.

For Catholics (Christians), the profession of faith with baptism initiates the believer into the mystery of Jesus' death and resurrection and communion with the Church. Neuroscience finds that through the physical action of washing, the inner 'experience' of God becomes concrete and communicable by being fixed within symbolic discourse using language that tries to fuse feeling and knowing (McGinn, 2001, p. 156) (Anderson, 2012, in Lamm [ed.], pp. 604-605).

> In the Latin rite, 'the sacrament of Confirmation is conferred through the anointing with chrism on the forehead, which is done by the laying on of the hand, and through the words: 'Be sealed with the Gift of the Holy Spirit.' (*CCC*, 1300)

"The sign of peace that concludes the rite of the sacrament demonstrates ecclesial communion with the bishop and with all the faithful" (*CCC*, 1301). "The effect of the sacrament of Confirmation is the full outpouring of the Holy Spirit" (*CCC*, 1325). Confirmation then,

> roots us more deeply in the divine filiation, unites us more firmly to Christ, increases the gifts of the Holy Spirit in us, renders our bond with the Church more perfect, and gives us a special strength to spread and defend the faith (by) 'the spirit of wisdom and understanding, right judgment and courage, knowledge, and reverence, holy fear in God's presence.' (*CCC*, 1303)

"The Eucharist is the heart and the summit of the Christian life" (*CCC*, 1407). "The other sacraments, and indeed all ecclesiastical ministries and works of the apostolate, are bound up with the Eucharist and are oriented toward it. For in the blessed Eucharist is contained the whole spiritual good of the Church, namely Christ himself, our Pasch" (*CCC*, 1324). "Under the consecrated species of bread and wine, Christ himself, living and glorious, is present in a true, real, and substantial manner: his Body and his Blood, with his soul and his divinity" (*CCC*, 1413). "Jesus' passing over to his Father by his death and resurrection, the new Passover, is anticipated in the (Last) Supper and celebrated in the Eucharist" (*CCC*, 1340).

> The Eucharist is the efficacious sign and sublime cause of that communion in the divine life and that unity of the People of God by which the Church is kept in being. It is the culmination both of God's action sanctifying the world in Christ and of the worship men offer to Christ and through him to the Father in the Holy Spirit" (*CCC*, 1325).

"Finally, by the Eucharistic celebration, we already unite ourselves with the heavenly liturgy and anticipate eternal life, when God will be all in all (cf. 1 Co 15:28)" (*CCC*, 1326). In brief, the Eucharist is the sum and summary of the

Catholic faith: "Our way of thinking is attuned to the Eucharist, and the Eucharist, in turn, confirms our way of thinking" (*CCC*, 1327).

Sacraments of healing: Reconciliation and Anointing of the Sick

Since the grace of new life can be weakened or lost, the Church provides sacraments of healing and salvation: Penance or Reconciliation and Anointing of the Sick. Repentance involves sorrow for sins and a firm intention not to sin again. Supporting conversion is hope in divine mercy (*CCC*, 1490). The sacrament of penance consists of the penitent's disclosure of sins to a priest (by the penitent's choice, anonymously or not) and intention to make reparation (*CCC*, 1491). The confessor proposes the performance of 'penance' for the penitent to repair the harm sin has caused and to re-establish Christian virtue (*CCC*, 1494).

The spiritual effects of the sacrament are:

> reconciliation with God by which the penitent recovers grace; reconciliation with the Church; remission of the eternal punishment incurred by mortal sins; remission, at least in part, of temporal punishments resulting from sin; peace and serenity of conscience, and spiritual consolation; an increase of spiritual strength for the Christian battle. (*CCC*, 1496)

The sacrament of Anointing of the Sick confers grace in difficulties experienced in serious illness or old age (*CCC*, 1527). Only priests and bishops can administer anointing of the sick, using oil blessed by the bishop or, if necessary, by the presiding priest (*CCC*, 1530). The celebrant anoints the sick person's forehead and hands (in the Roman rite) or other parts of the body (in the Eastern rite) with the liturgical prayer (*CCC*, 1531).

> The special grace of the sacrament has as its effects: the uniting of the sick person to the passion of Christ for his own good and that of the whole Church; the strengthening, peace, and courage to endure in a Christian manner the sufferings of illness or old age; the forgiveness of sins, if the sick person was not able to obtain it through the sacrament of Penance; the restoration of health, if it is conducive to the salvation of his soul; and preparation for passing over to eternal life. (*CCC*, 1532)

Sacraments at the service of communion: Holy Orders and Matrimony

Sacraments directed toward salvation for others are Holy Orders and Matrimony. Although Baptism confers a common priesthood of the faithful, priesthood confers a specific ministerial role. The sacrament of Holy Orders bestows a sacred function to serve the faithful, teach, offer divine worship, and provide pastoral care (*CCC*, 1592). The ordained ministry is exercised by bishops, priests, and deacons (*CCC*, 1592). A bishop confers holy orders by laying on of hands and a solemn prayer of consecration for graces of the Holy Spirit required for this ministry (*CCC*, 1597).

The sacrament of Matrimony symbolizes Christ's union with the Church. It confers on the spouses grace for an elevated Christian love for each other. The sacrament perfects the spouses' human love, fortifies their unbreakable union, and sanctifies them for eternal life (*CCC*, 1661). "Marriage is based on the consent of the contracting parties, that is, on their will to give themselves, each to the other, mutually and definitively, in order to live a covenant of faithful and fruitful love" (*CCC*, 1662). "Unity, indissolubility, and openness to fertility are essential to marriage" (*CCC*, 1664).

Liturgy as character formation

Cross-culturally speaking, ritual is central to all religions (Durkheim, 1912/2016; Eliade, 1968; Rappaport, 1999). Participation in ritual forms believers (Sosis, 2003b), giving emotional emphasis and motivation to a shared symbol system and religious beliefs (Alcorta and Sosis, 2005, p. 344) that then affect life choices and behavior (Dehaene and Changeux, 2000). Liturgical practices build habits that direct intentionality toward an ultimate end (Smith, 2009, p. 40; Strawn and Brown, 2013, p. 4).

Knowledge, skills, and attitudes that are important for religion are woven into ceremonial rituals that are primary ways of passing on a worldview, imbuing it with a sense of factuality and motivational impact (Knight, 1999; Lambek, 2002, in Deeley, 2004, p. 256). The structure of the liturgy—gathering for praise, expressing and responding in faith, sending out—is intended to form persons and the Church into the likeness of Christ. Liturgy is intended to encourage participation and involve the whole person (Strawn and Brown, 2013, p. 13).

Fowler (1991) observes that liturgy addresses the sensory experience of faith, evoking "images that represent our convictional knowing" (p. 181). Rituals and ceremonies of a worshipping church are intended to influence faith and character formation. "Liturgical practices give expression to the particular beliefs, values, and feelings of a specific faith community and in that way to their identity (Anderson, 1997, p. 361) (de Klerk and Kruger, 2017, p. 2). The aim of the Christian life is more than simple conversion. It is insight, discernment, and judgment about how to behave in a range of circumstances toward ongoing maturity in wisdom and virtue (Strawn and Brown, 2013, p. 11).

Liturgical mysticism

For Catholics, liturgy can be called mystical—that is, liturgical mysticism—because it is "the Paschal Mystery liturgically celebrated, the Church's self-experience as the communion of the Holy Spirit" (Fagerberg, 2019, pp. 2, 3). Liturgical mysticism belongs both to the mystical body of Christ and to each member waiting to join the eternal liturgy of heaven. The liturgy of the Church incorporates rituals and symbols to enable the faithful to receive the living water overflowing from heaven into the Church and the world (p. 30). Liturgical mysticism catches light from divine Mystery. Ritual celebrated in chronological, linear time participates in mystery. "Because of the presence of the eternal, it is also eschatological" (p. 146). Humans engage consciously, freely, and purposefully in the ritual mystery that originates in the Father, expresses the redemptive death of the Son, and, through the Holy Spirit, incorporates human participants to have them return with Jesus to the Father.

"The mystical life of believers is their immersion and assimilation into the mystery that Christ accomplished and that they continue to encounter in a liturgical cult" (Fagerberg, 2019, p. 148). Ritual liturgy is animated by the Holy Spirit given to believers to enable them to welcome Christ as he approaches. God must draw men and women for them to come to faith (Jn 6:44). This drawing is the mystical aspect of the liturgy (p. 148).

Neuroscience for sacraments

When considering a more specific relationship between the brain and the sacraments, we can begin with the basic relationality that is key to the Catholic sacramental system—that humans are made in the image of God, who is relational in the Trinity. It follows that grace, incorporation into the family of God, and development in divine likeness would be relational. The following reflections are arranged arbitrarily for this discussion to suggest a possible correspondence between the brain and the sacraments of initiation, healing, and service. For each sacrament, we will consider one specific instance; other examples of brain-sacrament correspondence can be inferred, with some variation.

Baptism: The rite of Baptism points to welcoming the newly baptized into a new communion, incorporating them into divine life and the Mystical Body of Christ. "The effects of Baptism are signified by the perceptible elements of the sacramental rite. Immersion in water symbolizes not only death and purification but also regeneration and renewal" (*CCC*, no. 1262).

> The person baptized belongs no longer to himself but to him who died and rose for us. He is called to be subject to others, to serve them in the communion of the Church, and to "obey and submit" to the Church's

leaders, holding them in respect and affection. (And the newly baptized) enjoys the right to receive the sacraments, to be nourished by the Word of God, and to be sustained by the other spiritual help of the Church (cf. *LG* 37). (*CCC*, 1269)

Present at the ceremony are godparents who assume responsibility for guiding the newly baptized in the Catholic faith.

For the catechumen (the young person or adult who has prepared for baptism by instruction and formation), the various sensory components of the sacrament (its matter in water, verbal formula and rite, chrism for anointing the senses, white garment, and lighted candle) will register neurologically in the brain's sensory systems of sight, language, hearing, and touch. The form of the sacrament (its meaning) will affect the mind, perceptions, emotions, decision-making, and behavior of the candidate. A neuropsychological aptitude that develops with the preparation and reception of baptism is empathy, seeing, and understanding through the eyes and minds of others. Empathy originates genetically and is closely associated with emotional development and self-other differentiation as cognition matures (Roth and Dicke, 2005). Austrian-American psychoanalytic psychologist Kernberg theorizes that affective initiation begins in areas associated with emotion: "brainstem regions, periaqueductal gray, amygdala, striatum, the septal region, hypothalamus, and the autonomic nervous system." Cognitively oriented regions then become more involved: "the paralimbic region, cingulate cortex, insula, and orbitofrontal region" (2015, p. 41).

Confirmation: The principal sensory systems involved in the sacrament of Confirmation to which the brain is neurologically responsive are sight, language, hearing, and touch. Since incense is usually part of the Confirmation liturgy, the olfactory (sense of smell) system may be included. Specifically, the sensory aspects of the sacrament are the bishop's laying on the hand of the bishop, anointing with chrism, and the words: "Be sealed with the gift of the Holy Spirit." "The sign of peace (a handshake or other affirming gesture) that concludes the rite signifies and demonstrates ecclesial communion with the bishop and with all the faithful" (*CCC*, 1301).

Confirmation marks a stage of relative maturity as the confirmand chooses to accept the gift of the Spirit in commitment to living out their faith in an expanding social context. Proposing a psychoanalytic theory about the role of the brain in human development, Kernberg reflects on the development of the self. Neuropsychologically, as the self developmentally attains integration, the more mature, established self-concept incorporates autobiographical memory, projection to the future, personal use of language and unique thought patterns, and social connections.

The central neurobiological structure involved in this integration may be "the junction of the ventromedial prefrontal cortex and the anterior cingulate cortex. This area may carry a central function in the neurobiological integration of all the components of the self. (Kernberg, 2015, p. 400)

Eucharist: "At the heart of the Eucharistic celebration are the bread and wine that, by the words of Christ and the invocation of the Holy Spirit, become Christ's Body and Blood" (*CCC*, 1333). Physiological sensory systems involved are sight, language, hearing, touch, and gustation (taste), as well as perception, discernment, emotions, decision-making, and motor/behavioral. When incense is used liturgically, it is also olfaction. The priest celebrating the Mass recites the ancient Church-approved Canon with words of consecration from the Last Supper: "'This is my Body which is given for you. Do this in remembrance of Me.' And likewise, the cup after supper, saying, 'This cup which is poured out for you is the New Covenant in my Blood' (Lk 22:7-20, cf. Mt 26: 17-29; Mk 14:12-25; 1 Co 11:23-26) (*CCC*, 1339).

In the Eucharist, Catholics make physiological contact with the consecrated elements of the sacrament. Here, the *spiritual senses* are most real. In consuming the Eucharistic species, the faithful actually encounter Jesus himself, as he insisted: "My flesh is real food, and My blood is real drink" (Jn 6:55). They encounter the profound mystery of the personal divine-human person of Jesus who invites to union between himself and the individual member, unites all members in his own Body, and requires loving care for others. Interpersonal neurobiology derives from what Seigel (2006) calls the triangle of well-being: the brain, the mind, and relationships. "The mind and relationships regulate 'the flow of energy and information' (Siegel, p. 248)," the mind adjusting homeostasis and communication adjusting interpersonal conditions. A balanced mind demonstrates awareness, acceptance, and equanimity (Siegel, 2006, in Gambrel et al., 2016, p. 273).

According to Interpersonal Neurobiology Theory (IPNB), the mind that develops with support from appropriately responsive caregiving grows into self-acceptance and emotional self-regulation and in future, can relate well with significant others (Siegel, 2007) (Gambrel et al., 2016, p. 275). Healthy relationships derive from increasing coordination between the emotional limbic system and the rational prefrontal cortex, inclining the individual to emotional stability under stress (Siegel, 2007). The integrated, well-adjusted mind can show attunement, presence, acknowledgment, positive communication, and sensitive responsiveness (Gambrel, p. 274). Self-acceptance may promote emotional stability. Through attuned connection, "relationships shape our minds" (Siegel, 2023, Seeking consilience, para.6). Because of neuroplasticity, even if the individual did not develop under responsive formation by a loving and guiding caregiver, attunement with a good friend, partner, or therapist later in life can heal neural pathways that underlie maladjustment and can pursue a hopeful, optimistic future (Gambrel, p. 280). The Eucharist promotes healthy, positive relationships between the human person and Christ and among the faithful.

Reconciliation: "The sacrament of Penance consists in the penitent's "repentance, confession or disclosure of sins to the priest, and the intention to do works of reparation" (*CCC*, 1491) and the priest's absolution. The confessor proposes acts of *satisfaction* to repair the harm caused by sin and re-establish the virtues of a disciple of Christ (*CCC*, 1494). Physiologically, the sacrament involves language and hearing, as well as memory, discernment, and decision-making.

The sacrament of Reconciliation offers course correction for fallible humans who find that life effects the weakening or disruption of their resolve to pursue the path of virtue toward eternal life. There is a bidirectional exchange between the brain and the rest of the body. Visceral feedback enters the brain from the viscera, such as the intestines, lungs, and heart, and registers in the insula. *Interoception* is believed to be necessary for awareness of feelings. Inner perception of our bodily condition lets us know how we feel (Craig, 2009; Damasio, 1994) and may tell us how others are feeling (Fishbane, 2019, p. 52). Both conscious and unconscious systems are associated with memory. When we consciously recall facts and experiences, we access explicit memory through the hippocampus; when memories affect us without explicit recall, unconscious memory involves the amygdala and associated areas (Siegel, 2012, in Fishbane, p. 52).

As we saw with Baptism, empathy, feeling with another, and seeing through their eyes encompasses activation of the ventromedial and lateral prefrontal cortex, anterior cingulate cortex, anterior insula, and cerebellum. Assessment of self and interaction with others involve the ventromedial prefrontal cortex and anterior cingulate cortex. Assessment of others accesses the lateral prefrontal cortex. And the anterior insula has a principal role in comprehending social circumstances (Kernberg, 2015, p. 41). The cerebellum affects social cognition by its connection to the limbic system for emotion attribution (Hoche et al., 2016, p. 732). Emotions instigate self-other interactions, and when affective memory internalizes such interactions, internal working models incrementally form coordinated, habitual patterns of behavior that comprise character (Kernberg, p. 39).

The orbitofrontal cortex (OFC) and its executive functions have primary input on the evaluation of options for decision-making. "One current theory holds that the OFC maintains a cognitive map of relevant stimuli, their values, and potential outcomes" (Purves et al., 2019, p. 693). It operates like a switchboard, linking the environment with internal states and outcomes of potential choices. The OFC receives input from all the major sensory systems, although with few connections to motor networks, thus providing information to systems that select and execute behavior (p. 689). The neighboring ventromedial prefrontal cortex similarly uses a universal value "format" to which any proposed set may be compared (p. 692). The dorsolateral prefrontal cortex (DLPFC) is thought to orchestrate the most complex, flexible, and future-directed behaviors, using values and other factors to regulate input-output networks (p. 693). Values are also maintained and computed in the ventral striatum and dorsal anterior cingulate cortex. Studies suggest that the dorsal anterior cingulate cortex (dACC) plays an important role in the adjustment of actions after a mistake, including value-based decision contexts (Hochman, Vaidya, and Fellows, 2014, p. 10). Implicated in this research on a millisecond timescale were decision-making and action-monitoring processes involved in discontinuing an incorrect action to allow for a correct one. Further study of the executive-function regions of the brain might investigate the degree to which brain function affects slower, more deliberate human course correction as occurs in the sacrament of Penance.

Anointing of the Sick: "The sacrament of Anointing of the Sick is given to those who are seriously ill by anointing them of the forehead and hands with blessed oil, saying: 'Through this holy anointing may the Lord in his love and mercy help you with the grace of the Holy Spirit. May the Lord who frees you from sin save you and raise you'" (*CCC*, 1513). Sensory systems to which the brain is responsive include sight, language, hearing, and touch.

When individuals are seriously ill or in danger of death, Anointing of the Sick brings forgiveness and strength. A visit from a priest in the context of the Church's blessing can bring calm and peace to the sick person and their family and friends in attendance. Whether or not the sick person fully understands what is happening, they often sense being part of a ritual that has taken place for centuries and that brings relief in their hour of need. Chronic or serious stress can prompt prolonged release of cortisol, which can harm cells of the hippocampus with its numerous cortisol receptors. Reduction of cortisol can improve heart, brain, and immune function. A naturally occurring remedy is oxytocin, a hormone in the blood and neurotransmitter in the brain (Uvnas-Moberg, 2003). Activated by empathy and a gentle touch, oxytocin reduces cortisol and fosters feelings of wellbeing. Similar to oxytocin, vasopressin is found predominantly in males (Fishbane, 2019, p. 2).

Holy Orders: The sacrament of apostolic ministry includes three degrees: episcopate, presbyterate, and diaconate. The rite of the sacrament occurs within the Eucharistic liturgy, with a gathering of the faithful to witness the ordinand's assuming of a new role in the community. For all three degrees, the bishop imposes hands on the head of the ordinand and with the specific consecratory prayer asks God for the outpouring of the Holy Spirit and his gifts proper to the ministry to which the candidate is being ordained" (*Sacramentum Ordinis* [*SO*]: DS 3858) (*CCC*, 1573). For the bishop and priest, there is anointing with chrism and presentation to the bishop of the book of the Gospels, a ring, miter, and crosier. The priest is presented with a paten (a round shallow plate on which the Host [bread that is consecrated] rests during the Eucharistic liturgy) and chalice (a cup with a stem made of precious metal which contains Wine that is consecrated). The deacon is presented with the book of the Gospels. The physiological systems to which the brain is responsive include sight, language, hearing, touch, and olfactory. In preparation for the reception of the sacrament, systems for discernment, emotion, decision-making, and motor/behavioral networks are also activated.

The sacrament that ordains men in roles of service as bishops, priests, and deacons gives them the faculties to lead worship, teach, and build up the Body of Christ. Neurological networks that involve *action understanding* support the ministries of bishop, priest, and deacon. Action understanding has been found to be relational, occurring in "the context of interaction in which meaning and sense-making merge from an ongoing dialogic engagement" (Reddy and Uithol, 2016, p. 109). Studies of the mirror neuron system (MNS) have found evidence that it does not support a simplistic view of action understanding. Simply seeing another person act does not necessarily evoke imitation. Mirror neurons alone do not provide the observer with the meaning of the action, nor do they necessarily initiate its motor replication (Hickok, 2008; Reddy and Uithol, 2016).

On the other hand, mirror neurons support the capacity to understand others by replicating the perceptions and actions of others at the level of neurons. Social cognition develops through the mirror neuron system, as well as through interpersonal exchanges. According to the embodied simulation theory, mirror neurons in the motor system are "the neuronal basis of all social-cognitive processes" (Schmidt, Hass, Kirsch, and Mier, 2021, p. 1)—not the motor neuron system alone, but in an interpersonal context and relationally.

An fMRI study of 75 healthy adults had them complete three tasks: initiation, empathy, and theory of mind. Within participants and among tasks, investigators found "common activation in the frontal gyrus, inferior parietal cortex, fusiform gyrus, posterior superior temporal sulcus, and amygdala" (Schmidt, Hass, Kirsch, and Mier, 2021, p. 1). Such a shared neural network for varied social-cognitive processes indicates that "interpersonal understanding might occur by embodied simulation" (p. 1). The notion that the MNS underlies interpersonal understanding was supported (p. 16).

The sacrament of Holy Orders "confers an *indelible spiritual character* and cannot be repeated or conferred temporarily" (Council of Trent: DS 1767; *LG* 21, 28, 29; *Presbyterorum ordinis* [*PO*] 2; *CCC*, 1582). The sacrament enables the ordinand to serve as a representative of Christ for the Church in his office of priest, prophet, and king (CCC, 1581). "The character imprinted by ordination is forever. The vocation and mission received on the day of his ordination mark him permanently" (*CCC*, 1583). Since it is Christ who acts through the minister, if he is unworthy, as St. Augustine states, Christ's gift passing through him remains pure (*CCC*, 1584). The indelible character of the sacrament (of Baptism and Confirmation, as well as Holy Orders) means that an ontological change exists in the spiritual order of grace. It does not necessarily need to be captured by the perceptual apparatus of the brain. The formative instruction of the ordinand is intended to help him develop conviction about the sacred permanence of his ordination. This would register in the executive functions of the prefrontal cortex, maintaining values, discernment, and choice (See Penance, above, Purves et al., 2019, pp. 689-693). "Since it belongs to the supernatural order, grace escapes our experience and cannot be known except by faith. We cannot, therefore, rely on our feelings or our works to conclude that we are justified and saved (Council of Trent [1547]: DS 1533-1534). 'You will know them by their fruits' (Mt 7:20)" (*CCC*, 2005).

Matrimony: The sacrament of Matrimony confers grace on a male and female married couple resolved to commit to a lifelong relationship that is exclusive, stable, and lasting. By its nature, matrimony is "ordered toward the good of the spouses and the procreation and education of offspring" (*CCC*, 1601). "In the Latin rite, the celebration of marriage between two Catholic faithful normally takes place during Mass, because of the connection of all the sacraments with the Paschal mystery of Christ (cf., *SC* 61)" (*CCC*, 1621). "The spouses receive the Holy Spirit as the communion of love of Christ and the Church [cf., Eph 5:32]" (*CCC*, 1624). The baptized man and woman freely express their consent" (CCC, 1625), a 'human act by which the partners mutually give themselves to each other;' --'I take you to be my wife;' –'I take you to be my husband' (*GS* 48.1; *OCM* 45; cf. *CIC*, can. 1057.2)" (*CCC*, 1627). Although a ring is not essential, it is normally a sign of the bride and groom's promise of mutual fidelity. "The public character of the consent protects the 'I do' once given and helps the spouses remain faithful to it" (*CCC*, 1631).

The key to adult well-being is attachment, a sense of being able to rely on trusted others through the vicissitudes of life. Love is an attachment relationship (Hazan and Shaver, 1987; Johnson, 2004; Solomon and Tatkin, 2011). When attachment is secure, cognitive, affective, and social wellbeing at all ages is likely to follow. Insecure attachment (anxious or avoidant) is associated with distress. Throughout life, the need for comfort and soothing from others endures. Attachment involves giving as well as receiving care. Generosity and altruism activate reward systems in the brain (Moll et al., 2006, in Fishbane, 2019, p. 50).

The quality of marital relationships powerfully impacts health. Psycho-neuroimmunology studies the interactions among relationships, the brain, psychology, and the immune system. Better physical and mental health and increased longevity are associated with positive relationships, including marriage. The cycle of pursuit and distance in unhappy relationships may demonstrate the effects of anxious-avoidant insecure attachment. Conflicted relationships correlate with health problems and earlier mortality (Robles and Kiecolt-Glaser, 2003; Slatcher, 2010) (Fishbane, 2019, p. 53). It follows that the immune system is strengthened by social support (Kiecolt-Glaser, McGuire, Robles, and Glaser, 2002). The quality of one's relationships impacts one's ability to regulate emotions. Levels of the stress hormone cortisol diminish with communication of care and compassion. Not surprisingly, marriage affects health, for good or ill. Intimate partners' "commingled physiology" (Sbarra and Hazan, 2008) either fosters or impairs their health, contingent on the condition of their relationship (Fishbane, p. 54). "This love which God blesses is intended to be fruitful" (*CCC*, 1604).

Cognitive and sensory processes and the sacraments

We have considered some of the specific elements of the sacraments and how they might relate to various brain processes. However, it might be helpful to invert this discussion to see how specific brain processes might be related to the elements of sacraments. In this way, we focus more on the brain processes to see how they might provide a cognitive, emotional, and sensory foundation that supports human engagement in the sacraments. This discussion is not intended to imply localization of brain function to the exclusion of the extensive, intense interconnection among brain regions. This different perspective might contribute to neurotheology as helpful in understanding the relationship between the brain and the religious self.

Focusing and deciding

The frontal lobes are essential to higher-order executive functions of considering, planning, and deciding about behavioral responses to sensory or conceptual input. Frontal areas connect to cortical networks. These communicate with parietal-lobe attention and proprioception systems that perceive bodily position and movement and make visuomotor contact with the environment. Frontal areas also connect with temporal-lobe emotion and memory networks (Stucky et al., 2014). These areas secure data about the world and the body, integrate quick-moving contextual input, then evaluate alternatives, inhibit maladaptive options, allocate intellectual resources, and estimate the consequences of the choices an individual makes (Purves et al., 2019). Such interactions allow decision-making to manage perceptual, emotional, and action networks. In this way, and with the salience network, when we decide to engage in a sacrament, for example, Communion, it is our frontal lobes that help us to make that choice. In fact, it is the frontal lobes that help us plan our life's activities, such as going to church, praying, or walking up to receive Communion. One might ponder how challenging this process might be for those who have frontal lobe abnormalities, whether through damage or dementia. Such questions might have important practical applications in terms of helping them to engage in religious sacraments appropriately.

Attention needs to be volitionally directed to goals and cognitive demands in progress over time. The frontoparietal network supports 'top-down' interaction with volitional attention in setting behavioral priorities under conflicting demands. Frontal-lobe *alerting* involves the perception of incoming stimuli. *Orienting* denotes tuning of perception so that pertinent sensory data can be selected for processing. This orienting process might be essential for sacraments as these activities direct one toward God. Being oriented towards God or any other religious activity is necessary for a person to engage in that activity and derive the necessary experiences and attitudes that arise from that activity. *Executive attention* resolves discrepancies among thoughts, emotions, and behaviors. In this way, we can sift through various ideas and experiences to select the ones that are most consistent with our beliefs and goals. On one hand, this can be valuable for a deeply religious individual. However, when discrepancies become too great, our frontal lobes may not be able to fully resolve them, leading to psychological or spiritual struggle. Such situations may have important implications for helping people manage these struggles by suggesting approaches that support the person's frontal lobe processes and lead them to a more stable foundation of belief.

Sensory signals arriving at frontal and parietal cortices provide 'bottom-up' input about salient stimuli in the environment. Again, this might be important for recognizing visual imagery such as Jesus on the cross, the smell of incense, or the chords of the organ playing hymns. These salient stimuli identified as important are incorporated into a person's belief system. 'Top-down' input derives from the parietal lobe for visuomotor perspective and from the frontal lobe for working memory and goal setting. Focused attention is generally a combination of bottom-up and top-down processes. Top-down attention likely involves a dorsal frontoparietal network, while a more ventral frontoparietal network effects object recognition in the sensory background (Stucky et al., 2014, pp. 36-38).

Since we are considering meanings in the sacramental liturgy, it would be good to distinguish again between mind and brain (see Chapter Three). Mind is the power of the soul to reason. The soul is the substantial form of the body, comprised of intellect and will. The human person, with a spiritual soul, mysteriously united to the body, produces thoughts and choices. The brain may be considered a *complex neuroplastic responder* (Leaf, 2021, p. 2) to human intellect and decision-making to effect neurochemical, genetic, and electromagnetic changes. Thinking, feeling, and choosing drive structural changes in the brain unique to the person who has these particular experiences. Thoughts, feelings, and choices encode structural molecular changes in the brain's neuronal connections (Lewis, 2019, p. 2). Having acquired new meaning through the mind, the brain changes the way it perceives symbols and makes meaning of those symbols. The brain changes the way it perceives visual and other sensory inputs. Thus, our beliefs shape the way we see the world. And, of course, input from the world shapes beliefs as well. As we have seen, the relationship between the mind (soul) and the brain is best understood through (Thomistic) philosophy rather than neuroscience.

Vision and visualizing

Vision is important to religion since it helps us to see religious symbols, read sacred texts, and envision spiritual concepts, including God. Of course, blind persons can also have faith. One of our (ABN) earlier studies (Newberg and Waldman, 2009, p. 83f) asked people to draw how they visualized God. One category of drawings people made reflected anthropomorphic symbols, such as the *old man in the clouds,* which incidentally is not much different from what Michelangelo depicted on the Sistine Chapel ceiling. Another category of drawings pertained to natural objects such as stars, galaxies, rivers, and mountains. A third category of drawings portrayed God in a highly stylized manner with circles, swirls, and hearts. Finally, some people left the drawing blank, stating that God was undrawable. The important point here is that most people use some visual representation of God and many other religious concepts. Thus, the visual system allows us a window into religious beliefs.

The retina's photoreceptors—rods and cones—detect light. Retinal ganglion cells project to the optic nerve, then to the optic chiasm and the optic tracts. Most optic tract fibers terminate in the lateral geniculate nucleus (LGN) of the thalamus, which projects to the primary visual cortex in the occipital pole (Stucky et al., 2014, p. 28; Purves et al., 2019, p. 261). Fibers project to the parietal and frontal association cortex via the pulvinar nucleus of the thalamus. The visual cortex includes the striate cortex and the visual association cortex. Central visual structures include a structured map for the contralateral visual field, with increasingly specified perceptual selectivity, such as for dark-light edges, color, or direction of objects. The representation of vision in the cortex occurs through numerous distinct visual input paths that detect form, motion, and color (Purves et al., 2019). Thus, all types of visual imagery can be engaged during the celebration of the sacraments, taking advantage of different shapes and colors.

The visual association cortex diverges into two streams—ventral and dorsal. The ventral stream, terminating in the inferior temporal cortex, is dedicated to object perception. This pathway sends axons to the occipitotemporal association cortex and then to the anterior inferotemporal cortex. The ventral stream processes *structural and feature-based information* necessary for recognizing forms such as faces and objects (Stucky et al., 2014, p. 28). The 'dorsal' pathway, projecting to the parieto-occipital association cortex, processes mainly *spatial information* and is concerned with the observation of location, motion, visual attention, and eye-and- hand-movement control—visuomotor communication with the environment (Stucky et al., 2014, p. 28). Since the posterior parietal controls reach, grasp, and manipulation, it requires visual information regarding movement, location, and spatial position (Carlson, 2007, pp. 207-208). In general, the ventral stream perceives 'what,' while the dorsal stream is characterized mainly as answering 'where' (Purves et al., 2019, pp. 261-262).

These spatial relationships are important for religious beliefs as they provide us with a sense of where things are and how we relate to them. These relationships may also lie at the heart of sacred architecture so that the immensity of churches with their high arching ceilings literally gives people a sense of spaciousness that supports the beliefs that the sacraments express. Neuropsychologically, the notion of closeness to God comes from the brain's ability to perceive spatial, emotional, and theological closeness to God.

Hearing

If vision is important in the sacraments, hearing is equally or more so. "Faith comes through hearing" (Rm 10:17), writes St. Paul, and speech allows the person to respond in obedience to God. We *hear* the word of God, the hymns and prayers, and the sermon, and we hear and respond to the sacramental rites. These sounds provide important information upon which to develop our religious beliefs.

From the external and middle ear to the inner-ear cochlea, sound stimulates a traveling wave. When sounds are high-frequency, the traveling wave is widest at the base of the cochlea; when sounds are low-frequency, the traveling wave is widest at the cochlear apex. The basilar membrane's inner-hair-cell movements convert sound waves into electrical signals and send them to the brain. Cochlear signals pass via the auditory nerve to three primary sections of the cochlear nucleus. (1) The superior ciliary complex and lateral lemniscus nuclei process sound localization. (2) The inferior colliculus handles sound frequencies and localization in space. (3) The primary auditory cortex supports frequency perception and sound localization and is key for dealing with communication. Activity patterns of auditory cortex neurons are associated with the intelligibility of speech. Directly adjacent to the auditory cortex are principal speech comprehension areas (Purves et al., 2019, pp. 285-286).

The auditory organization is analytical in that it can discriminate among sounds with various timbres and generate distinct neural firing patterns. Left-right localization is achieved by analyzing differences in sound arrival time, intensity, and phase relations between the two ears (Carlson, 2007, p. 231). The auditory structure distinguishes the ever-varying activity patterns from the cochlear nerve axons to recognize the source of sound. Specific auditory-cortex neurons respond to stimuli such as descending or ascending tones. The auditory cortex, like the executive-function and visual systems, is arranged in two streams. The dorsal stream perceives the location, and the ventral stream analyzes the sound. Complex environmental sounds are perceived through activation of an area in the left posterior middle temporal gyrus (Carlson).

Music recognition requires discernment of note sequences and their relation to rules regarding pitch, rhythm, and harmony. These processes support the importance of hymns and how the sounds of the music induce various emotions and experiences. If we want to express the power of God, the organ might play loud, low sounds. And if we want to feel a sense of peace and bliss, we might sing light, melodic hymns. The superior temporal gyrus activates for simple tone recognition and an adjacent area for perception of melodies. Other specific brain regions perceive the beat of music and distinct rhythmic patterns. Musical training seems to enhance the primary auditory cortex in extent and sensitivity (Carlson, 2007, p. 231).

Speech, language, and symbolizing

It goes without saying that language is essential for understanding religion. We need to understand language to understand the Bible. We need language to recite prayers, sing hymns, and celebrate every sacrament. It is also through language and symbolization that we come to understand the meaning of the sacraments and incorporate that meaning into our beliefs, attitudes, and behaviors.

The left-hemisphere perisylvian cortices are central for language in most people (more than 95% of right-handers and more than 60-70% of left-handers [Blumenfeld, 2010]), and the right hemisphere gives language emotional tone. Cortical language representation is the same whether it is perceived or expressed—heard, spoken, seen, or gestured. The cerebral language areas are the primary elements of widely distributed regions that include symbols for objects, feelings, and concepts (Purves et al., 2019, p. 722). Broca's and Wernicke's areas are adjacent to the Sylvian fissure that distinguishes the frontal and temporal lobes. The temporoparietal cortex and inferior temporal cortices analyze phonological (sound-based) information. The left posterior inferior temporal cortex seems to involve the recognition of written words. The fusiform cortex analyzes word-form information (Carlson, 2007, p. 516).

Language processing begins with identifying and comprehending phonological sequences as words. Speech articulation of sounds and word and sentence production derive from various regions, such as the primary motor cortex face area. Receptive and expression language begins in Broca's area, with planning and initiating of speech sound sequences. Language repetition requires that phonological representations from Wernicke's area become motor-articulatory sounds in Broca's area. These two areas are connected by the arcuate fasciculus, a large white-matter structure that is larger in the left hemisphere (Stucky, 2014, p. 34).

These three perisylvian areas are essential to language abilities, but they function only through extensive projections to other cortical areas. There are multiple reciprocal communications with visual, auditory, and motor cortices that support meaning, comprehension, reading, enacting meaningful behaviors, choosing words, intending to communicate, and using language practically in daily life. Broca's area, for example, connects with the prefrontal, premotor, and supplementary motor areas. Interconnections among these regions seem essential to integrating syntax and grammar with language. Wernicke's area communicates with the parietal lobe for understanding language and writing and for associating sounds with meaning. Linking the language areas with visual areas in the inferior temporal lobe for word-form recognition is essential for converting graphemes to phonemes (words to sounds), which is key to reading ability. Connections through the corpus callosum enable the language-dominant hemisphere to participate in language processing with rhythm-and-pitch information to communicate emotional dimensions of speech (Stucky, 2014, pp. 35-36).

Touch, taste, and smell

Touch is important in mediating the perception of temperature, orientation, pressure, and interpersonal contact. Touch is involved in receiving the Eucharist, laying on of hands in Holy Orders, and anointing in Confirmation and Anointing of the Sick, as well as holding the Bible, shaking hands with a fellow congregant, or even feeling the back of the pew or the kneeler. These sensory stimuli that either affect the skin (mechanoreception) or that the body produces (proprioception) provide sensory data for processing in the somatosensory system. Several brain regions connected by ascending and descending neuronal pathways deal with somatosensory information. Mechanosensory sensory information sent to the brain from peripheral areas of the body originates in afferent (incoming) receptors. This information then travels through neurons in gray-matter (neural cell body) structures and white-matter (myelinated axon) tracts. This neuronal chain begins with first-order neurons: primary sensory neurons in the spinal cord's dorsal root and the cranial nerve ganglia. Ascending mechanosensory signals next pass through the brainstem nuclei. Finally, the route from the periphery to the cerebral cortex encounters the thalamus, which projects to the postcentral gyrus. Throughout the somatosensory system, these pathways are organized topographically. The quantity of cortical and subcortical space apportioned for different body parts is proportional to the concentration of peripheral receptors in the respective body parts. This complex intercommunication yields an integrated sense of the body in its environment (Purves et al., 2019, pp. 198-199).

Through manipulation and movement of objects, we gain information about their shape, texture, volume, and other physical qualities. With more tactile experience, the section of the somatosensory cortex dedicated to hands and fingers increases, for example, for practicing musicians. Precise, localized somatosensory information follows a periphery-to-brain route through nuclei of the dorsal spinal column and the medial lemniscus to the ventral posterior nuclei of the thalamus. Pain and temperature information ascends the spinal cord by way of the spinothalamic system. Sensations from inner organs reach the CNS through the axons of the autonomic nervous system. Various types of somatosensory receptors send their information to distinct regions of the somatosensory cortex (Carlson, 2007, pp. 245-246).

Taste is primarily involved with sacraments such as Communion, where the believer eats and drinks the consecrated Bread and Wine. Taste connects the faithful to the sacrament, associating physical sensation with spiritual experience. The taste of wine involves the brain in linking flavor to the action and its meaning. Taste is also part of many other ceremonies and holidays. Specific foods you eat associate you with a ritual that expresses and embellishes meaning.

The Church prescribes fasting as part of the ascetical practice of Lent, asking the faithful to fast to help "acquire mastery over our instincts and freedom of heart" (cc., *CIC* can. 1249-1251; *CCEO*, can. 882) (*CCC*, 2043).

Smell is also an essential sensory process. The sacraments are filled with smells, either directly or indirectly. You smell the church, the incense, the books, and the wine. Each of these smells, as with taste and touch, connects to the beliefs that support the sacraments and the rituals. Incense, a gift of the Magi at the birth of Jesus, has long been associated with worship rituals. Smells might be incidental in that a church building's scent may reflect its age and construction materials. Regardless, these smells, along with all the sensory processes, connect participants to the sacraments, making them spiritual and sensible for human nature.

Rituals: Effects on the brain

Top-down and bottom-up processing

What happens neurologically with rituals? There are top-down and bottom-up processes. Top-down routes begin with the cortex of the frontal and parietal lobes. For example, with prayer and meditation, then the limbic and autonomic nervous systems are activated, sending signals to the rest of the body (Newberg, 2018a, p. 173).

In the left inferior temporal lobe, top-down and bottom-up processing work together. Written words activate an area in the middle fusiform gyrus—the visual word form area (VWFA). The interactive account hypothesis (Price and Devlin, 2011) suggests that the VWFA requires interaction between top-down processing of symbolic meanings and bottom-up analysis of visual properties of stimuli (Song, Tian, and Liu, 2012, pp. 2, 14).

Since physiological evolution proceeds more slowly than environmental changes such as culture and ritual, the top-down/bottom-up interactive process is thought to demonstrate the neuronal recycling hypothesis (NR; Dehaene and Cohen, 2011). NR argues that "neural circuitry can be 'recycled' or converted to a different function than evolution originally required, one that is cultural. The original function of the circuitry is not entirely lost and constrains what the brain can learn. It is argued that the neural niche co-evolves with the environmental niche (Menary, 2014, p. 286).

Neuronal recycling retrains an ancient evolutionary function into one more appropriate to the current cultural context. The VWFA is thought to have, along with genetic constraints, learning-driven functional plasticity that can take advantage of environmental interaction with language and symbols in the service of cognitive development. "Our developmentally plastic brains exhibit learning plasticity when they are coupled to a scaffolded learning environment; the brain and we are cognitively transformed in a profound way" (Menary, 2014, p. 300).

Emotion, sacred symbols, and music

Anthropologists find traits such as "belief systems incorporating supernatural agents and counterintuitive concepts and having a communal ritual" in religion. The differentiating element of "religious ritual is found to be the conditioned association of emotion and abstract symbols evolved to extend social relations across time and space" (Alcorta and Sosis, 2005, p. 323).

Relevant here is the *costly signaling* theory (Sosis, 2000; Sosis and Bressler, 2003; Sosis and Ruffle, 2003, 2004). Costly signaling theory suggests that religious rituals can foster intragroup cooperation by sending credible symbols about preferred personal qualities and means of access to resources. Religious behaviors can represent costly signals that help to build social cohesion (Cronk, 1994a; Irons, 1996a, 2001; Sosis, 2003b). Religious ritual has been found to correlate significantly with heightened cooperation (Alcorta and Sosis, 2005, p. 324).

Communal ritual is fundamental to religion (Bloch, 1989; Durkheim, 1969; Eliade, 1958, 1959; Bourguignon, 1973, 1976; McCauley, 2001; Rappaport, 1999; Turner, 1967, 1969). Neurophysiologically, the constituents of ritual—attention, memory, and associational learning—prepare both the message sender and the receiver for follow-through (Rowe, 1999). The formality, repetition, and sequencing of rituals guarantee their costliness in energy and time expenditure. The time and energy, in turn, inclines the ritual message receiver or participant to endorse the purpose of the ritual (Alcorta and Sosis, 2005, p. 330).

Statues and images may serve as icons of religious rituals. Abstract religious symbols referencing intangible meaning, such as a road for a life path or identity development, also represent meaning and affect religious faith (Alcorta and Sosis, 2005). Through engagement in religious rituals, symbols, and practices are invested with affective quality. Ritual participation, symbols, and practices confer sacred meaning that inspires faith. "Neurologically, initial unconscious processing occurs in the brain's subcortical structures, including the basal ganglia, the amygdala, and the hypothalamus. This introductory processing seems to rate stimuli as either positive/approach or negative/withdrawal (Cacioppo et al., 2002)" (Alcorta and Sosis, 2005, pp. 332-333).

The dopaminergic reward system establishes an emotional process to motivate pursue- and-search behavior to approach and acquire rewarding objectives (Depue et al., 2002, p. 1071). This system originates in the ventral tegmental area of the midbrain and projects to the nucleus accumbens. Activation of this system releases dopamine (DA), a neuromodulator perceived to be rewarding (Davidson and Irwin, 2002) (Alcorta and Sosis, 2005, p. 333). Repeated potentiation of the reward system energizes DA transmission from incentive stimuli to the goal (DiChiara, 1995, p. 95). This results in linking positive affective quality to stimuli perceived while the organism is in a dopaminergically influenced reward state (DiChiara, 1995). Such 'incentive learning' creates associational neural networks that connect stimuli to behavioral motivators. Neutral stimuli are thus invested with positive, motivating qualities (Alcorta and Sosis, p. 334).

Ritual participants who meditate are found to show alterations in "brain wave patterns, heart and pulse rate, skin conductance, and other autonomic functions" (Austin, 1998; Davidson, 1976; Kasamatsu and Hirai; MacLean et al., 1997; Mandel, 1980; Newberg et al., 2001; Winkelman, 2000). "Meditation also alters neuroendocrine levels, including testosterone, growth hormone, and cortisol (MacLean et al., 1997)" (Alcorta and Sosis, 2005, p. 336).

Religious services are typically distinguished by music (Chaves et al., 1999; Bloch, 1989, p. 21). In Catholic worship, Gregorian chant, with its lack of rhythm, induces a contemplative tone. Music can generally be considered a *rhythmic driver* in accentuating the "formality, pattern, sequence, and repetition" characteristic of religious rituals (Alcorta and Sosis, 2005, p. 336). Neurophysiologically, music synchronizes biological oscillators, such as heartrate and breathing, to auditory rhythms (Scherer and Zentner, 2001, p. 372). Linking of "respiration and other body rhythms to these drivers affects a wide range of physiological processes, including brain wave patterns, pulse rate, and diastolic blood pressure (Gellhorn and Keily, 1972; Lex, 197; Mandel, 1980; Neher, 1962; Walter and Walter, 1949). Synchronized autonomic functions, including pulse rate, heart contractility, and skin conductance, are significantly associated with measures of empathy" (Alcorta and Sosis, 2005, p. 336). Music in religious rituals is found to foster empathy.

Religious rituals are generally classified as *doctrinal*—frequent, low-stimulation rituals that rely on semantic memory, or *imagistic*—infrequent, somewhat emotionally intense, and associated with episodic memory and social connection (Whitehouse, 2000; Deeley, 2004, p. 245). This distinction may not always apply. Repetitive, structured, doctrinal rituals predominate in religions that incorporate doctrinal statements, such as the Nicene Creed, that rely on semantic memory. The Catholic Mass might exemplify doctrinal ritual. Imagistic rituals that tend to be emotional and less frequent are characteristic of religions where personal witnesses are transmitted. Rituals in the Catholic charismatic movement, for example, might represent imagistic rituals (Whitehouse, 2000, p. 1; Deeley, 2004, p. 258).

Rituals can also coordinate intention, leading to social or political change (Bourgignon, 1973) (Alcorta and Sosis, 2005, p. 340). An example might be Pope St. John Paul II's 1959 Christmas Midnight Mass celebrated at Nowa Huta, Poland, in a field outside Krakow, under the threatening presence of armed Communists, that supported the solidarity movement, which eventually led to the fall of the iron curtain. This was, of course, a highly emotionally charged event.

Rituals, particularly when they are imagistic, communicate enhancement of meaning through sensory or semantic neural networks. Sensory processing of socio-emotional stimuli involves attention. Semantic neural systems involve right-hemisphere processing to attribute meanings in representations that are accepted as real although not fully understood (Deeley, 2004, p. 245). Religion and rituals are typically associated with Mystery that answers ultimate questions. Sensory and semantic rituals are not mutually exclusive. Both processes may stimulate cognitive-affective processing through the dopaminergic system, communicating a sense of ritual as significant and real. Through these neural, cognitive, and social processes, religious ideas become convictions (p. 245).

The brain as a dynamic, self-organizing system

Intelligence, personality, and character develop from a genetic blueprint, but the brain's fine-tuning comes through self-organization based on ongoing response to environmental interaction (Quartz and Sejnowski, 2002, p. 128; Strawn and Brown, 2013, p. 5). Through uninterrupted circumstances and social exchanges, neurons are affected by interaction with situations and other persons. The brain is a dynamical system retaining throughout life its initial potential to self-organize within genetic constraints in response to the current context (Strawn and Brown, pp. 5-6).

Through emotions, the brain constantly adjusts and attunes to its ongoing situation, particularly social circumstances. As we physiologically adjust to our physical and social circumstances, emotions provide conscious information about our relational position in the current situation (Strawn and Brown, 2013, p. 12).

Liturgical habit and spiritual transformation

Neuroscience finds that the brain is wired *for* and *by* habit. Repeated rewarding behaviors are embedded in neural circuits and shape connections to affect various aspects of life. In the sense that professor of philosophy and theology James Smith develops in *You Are What You Love: The Spiritual Power of Habit* (2016), we are formed by liturgical practices in part because we are "embodied with liturgical brains" (Dorman, 2021, p. 1). Our propensity to habitual behavior in the liturgical domain facilitates our following St. Paul's exhortation to "be transformed by the renewal of your mind" (Rm 12:32).

Habit formation happens through basal ganglia circuits. The basal ganglia are interconnected subcortical neuronal nuclei. Each nucleus consists of operationally associated neurons. The basal ganglia produce feedback loops to cortical neurons that then regulate behavior. Cortical neurons connect to basal ganglia neurons, make other contacts, and then loop back to influence the performance of other cortical neurons.

Looping through the basal ganglia are two neuronal routes that differentially affect cortical activity. One (excitatory) route activates cortical neurons associated with intentional or habitual behavior. The other (inhibitory) route inhibits cortical neurons that would oppose the desired outcome. Selective activation of excitatory and inhibitory cortical activity patterns regulates cortical activity to execute preferred or habitual behaviors. Alteration of the neuronal connections from the cortex to the basal ganglia and back demonstrates a type of neuroplasticity that can modify the connection potency of neurons and change accustomed behavior (Dorman, 2021, p. 2).

The basal ganglia function through either the associative or sensorimotor system. The associative structure aligns with goal-oriented behavior; the sensorimotor one regulates habitual activity. Many behaviors that are initially goal-directed eventually become habitual. The two systems cooperate in developing goal-directed skills, consolidating skills into habits, and undoing or replacing unwanted habits (Dorman, 2021, p. 2).

Religious culture safeguards the communication of valued learning. Central cortical association areas that combine numerous sensory signals and process abstract representations (O'Dougherty et al., 2001; Phelps et al., 2001) are the amygdala and orbitofrontal cortex. Representing sensory signals from the body and adding to sensations associated with emotional arousal are the insula and somatosensory cortices (Craig, 2004; Critchley et al., 2004; Damasio, 2000). Affective neuroscience has made progress in discriminating brain and body processes associated with generating emotional responses and connecting them to cognitive representations (Damasio, 1994, 2000; Rolls, 1999) (Deeley, 2004, pp. 254-255). Through religious rituals, beliefs with affective and compelling meaning are transmitted across time and to new places (Deeley, 2004, p. 245).

With colleagues, I (ABN) recently demonstrated that spiritual practices might lead to measurable brain changes (2017). Fourteen Christian participants in a seven-day Jesuit spiritual retreat were administered, before and after the retreat, positron-emission tomography (PET) brain scans that reflect enduring brain-signaling characteristics. All participants were found to have significant measurable alterations in the basal ganglia, a brain area associated with reward sensitivity and habit development. The study showed long-term, confirmed changes in brain activity related to the spiritual formation retreat. Measures of psychological health were also administered to the attendees. They all showed alterations in basal ganglia activity and improvement in wellbeing (Dorman, 2021, p. 2). Considering the small sample size, these were preliminary findings warranting further investigation.

Conclusion

Catholic sacramental theology emphasizes that images and symbols connect cognitive and emotional perception to religious meaning, uniting the individual and community to Trinitarian life and effecting human transformation in service of the Gospel. The spiritual sense can be a means of perceiving the Divine through effects like those communicated through sensory experiences. The Catholic sacramental system works through symbolic cognition and associative learning. The sacraments of initiation (Baptism, Confirmation, and Eucharist), of healing (Reconciliation and Anointing of the Sick), and at the service of communion (Holy Orders and Matrimony) can each be understood as both neurologically correlated with the brain and responsive to the soul (intellect and will). Rahner shows that with transcendental revelation, God takes the initiative in inviting the human person to communion through grace bestowed with creation, encouraging a response in faith, hope, and love. Sacramental liturgy can be seen as character formation that develops with liturgical mysticism. The sacraments are understood as responsive to cognitive and sensory processes of focusing and deciding, vision and visualizing, hearing, speech, language, and symbolizing, touch, taste, and smell. The brain, being a dynamical, self-organizing system, rituals affect both top-down and bottom-up neurological processing. Habitual liturgical participation leads through emotion, sacred symbols, and music to spiritual transformation.

Study Questions

1. How does Lonergan explain the Catholic sacraments?
2. How does Lonergan understand conversion?
3. What is meant by "spiritual senses"?
4. How does von Balthasar understand the senses, sensation, and imagination as mediating faith and grace?
5. What does Rahner mean in considering the human person a hylomorphic "spirit in the world" with a "pre-apprehension of the infinite"?
6. How does Rahner distinguish between *transcendental* and *categorical* revelation?
7. What does Rahner mean by the *supernatural existential*?
8. Might neurotheology explore the effects of spiritual experience on the brain? Explain your answer.
9. How do Catholics understand God as speaking through creation?
10. How does the Catholic sacramental system effect worship and holiness?
11. What four cognitive processes support the use of symbols?

12. What brain system affects salience and sense of realness?

13. Understanding that the right and left hemispheres are highly interconnected, how might they be distinguished regarding meaning-finding?

14. How do religious symbols use analogy?

15. How does baptism affect the neophyte (newly baptized)?

16. Why is careful adherence to the ritual formulae, as well as the right intention of the minister, important for the validity of the Catholic sacraments?

17. What do the ritual symbols (matter) and form of the sacrament of confirmation effect?

18. Why do Catholics consider the Eucharist—Liturgy and consecrated bread and wine—the source and summit of Christian spirituality?

19. What happens in the sacrament of reconciliation?

20. What are the elements of the sacrament of Anointing of the Sick and its graces?

21. What happens in the sacrament of Holy Orders, and what graces are conferred?

22. What are the essential aspects of Catholic marriage, and what does it symbolize?

23. In what ways can liturgy form character?

24. How can liturgy be called mystical?

25. What neurological functions would the sacrament of baptism likely engage?

26. Why would brain areas associated with the development of the self figure prominently in the ongoing grace of the sacrament of confirmation?

27. Why would brain structures and functions associated with IPNB dispose for and develop through the graces of the Eucharist?

28. Why would the sacrament of Penance activate brain areas associated with interoception, memory, empathy, self-assessment, social cognition, decision-making, and goal-setting?

29. What hormones are likely to affect the brain with the reception of the Anointing of the Sick? Explain.

30. How might neurological areas associated with action understanding and the mirror neuron system be activated with the practice of the sacrament of Holy Orders?

31. What is meant by the indelible character of baptism, confirmation, and Holy Orders?

32. Is grace experienced? Detected? Explain.

33. What would be the implications of your answer to the previous question (32) for brain scan studies? For neurotheology?

34. How do the psychological attachment system and physiological psychoneuroimmunological processes associated with the sacrament of Matrimony affect the brain?

35. How does relational quality in marriage affect the physical and mental health of the partners?

36. Which areas of the brain contribute to functions of focus and decision-making, for example, in the reception of the Eucharist?

37. What neural processes are associated with attention and prioritization?

38. Distinguish top-down from bottom-up processing.

39. How can the brain be seen as a *complex neuroplastic responder* to human intellect and will?

40. How neuropsychologically do our beliefs shape the way we see the world?

41. Why is Aristotelian-Thomistic hylomorphism, as well as neuroscience, needed to explain the soul-brain relationship?

42. Does vision itself elicit and support transcendent meaning, or does faith precede or follow perception?

43. How important are language and symbolizing in accepting, understanding, and expressing faith? Explain.

44. How do taste, touch, and smell in a person of faith support religious beliefs?

45. How does the "neuronal recycling hypothesis" help explain the learning of ritual language and symbols that change with culture over time?

46. How does "costly signaling theory" explain religious behaviors as a means of social cohesion?

47. What might be "costly" about costly signaling in religious practice?

48. How, neurologically, do rituals and symbols contribute to the meaning and communication of faith?

49. How, physiologically, does music support and enhance religious faith and practice?

50. How are religious rituals distinguished as doctrinal and imagistic?

51. What are neural, cognitive, and social processes that help to develop religious convictions?

52. How is the brain a dynamical, self-organizing system?

53. How, neurologically, are persons of faith "embodied with liturgical brains"?

54. How might the Catholic sacramental system affect spiritual transformation for persons of faith?

Chapter 8

The Neurophysiology of Catholic Practices

Church-directed prayer

Liturgy of the Hours

We saw in Chapter Seven that sacraments, through sensory, cognitive, and affective symbols, support human contact with God (Happel, 1989). In this chapter, we explore extensions of the sacraments in sacramentals and practices that incorporate more of human life into Catholic spirituality and their potential neurological correlates. Among forms of Church-directed prayer are the Liturgy of the Hours, Scripture and other spiritual reading, and meditation. We then consider how neurotheology and contemplative neuroscience might understand these aspects of Church-directed prayer.

Following the New Testament exhortation to "pray always" (1 Thes 5:16), the Catholic Church encourages communal and individual prayer daily, weekly, and yearly, as well as during liturgical seasons and feast days and on Sundays centered on the Eucharist. Daily prayer means morning and evening, with grace before and after meals, in the Liturgy of the Hours, and with the flow of the liturgical year (*CCC*, 2698). "The Church, in the course of the year, unfolds the whole mystery of Christ from his Incarnation and Nativity through the Ascension, to Pentecost and the blessed hope of the coming of the Lord" (*Sacrosanctum Concilium* [*SC*], *102*, no. 2, in *CCC*, 1194)."

The Liturgy of the Hours (or Divine Office), the official public prayer of the Church (*SC*, 8), prescribes periods of prayer around the clock (cf. *SC*, ch. IV, 83-101). The Roman Breviary was revised from 1965 to 1970, and its official English translation was published in 1975 in four volumes. The Breviary provides Bible readings and reflections from early Church leaders and saints for morning and evening prayers, midmorning, midday, and mid-afternoon, and night prayers (*SC*, 84, Eph 6:18). Clergy, religious, and laity who pray the Liturgy of the Hours "exercise the royal priesthood of the baptized. Celebrated in 'the form approved' by the Church" (*SC*, 84) (*CCC*, 1174), it is the prayer of Christ with his Body to the Father.

Rhythms of the liturgical year, the weekly cycle with Sunday focused on the Eucharist, and the daily Liturgy of the Hours has parallels in neurological circadian rhythms in the sleep-wake cycle and the process of aging. It is interesting that, like the Liturgy of the Hours spanning the day with set rhythms of prayer, neurological circadian (daily) rhythms follow a brain clock in the suprachiasmatic nucleus (SCN) of the hypothalamus. The SCN synchronizes peripheral oscillators in most cells and organ systems throughout the body. This keeps the body's time clock for all the organs, and when this normal rhythm is disrupted, negative physical and mental health effects are observed (Karatsoreos et al., 2011, p. 1657). Throughout their lifespan, individuals with depressive symptoms have been found to experience delayed sleep-wake cycles and activity patterns. In older age, this may bring additional disorganization of circadian rhythms. Mood disorders have been found to correlate with decreases in sleep consolidation, which is likely to affect sleep quantity and quality (Robillard, 2014, p. 7). The rhythms of prayer correspond to human physiological and psychological rhythms. When there is physiological disruption and dysregulation, psychological problems are likely to result. But since prayer involves communication with God, its restorative meaning leads to beneficial effects.

While no known studies have yet explored this, it seems reasonable that prayers throughout the day might help synchronize circadian rhythms. Such a possibility speaks to the potential power of prayer to help restore or maintain healthy rhythms throughout the day, year, and lifespan.

Narratives

Central to the Catholic faith is Scripture, the Hebrew Scriptures, and the New Testament. For Christians, the narratives of Scripture are all about Christ the Word, his Paschal Mystery—his passion, death, resurrection, ascension, and sending of the Holy Spirit—and of eternal life begun here in grace and lasting through eternity. " 'All Scripture is but one book, and that one book is Christ, because all divine Scripture speaks of Christ, and all divine Scripture is fulfilled in Christ' (Hugh of St. Victor, *De arca Noe* 2, 8)" (*CCC*, 134). The *Catechism of the Catholic Church* summarizes the high esteem in which Catholics hold Scripture and its usefulness:

> Such is the force and power of the Word of God that it can serve the Church as her support and vigor and the children of the Church as strength for their faith, food for the soul, and a pure and lasting font of spiritual life (*Dei Verbum* [*DV*], 21). (131)

Neuropsychologically, narratives help to integrate experience by affording meaning. When we endow specific meanings with significance by rehearsing them with some degree of emotional intensity, they likely connect across multiple neural systems as an indexing network that can affect how we respond. "Narratives call on our neural systems to integrate our feeling and thinking; our experience of having intense feeling and complexity of thinking is the essence of significance" (Walch, 2015, p. 154).

In the process of remembering experiences, the brain makes structural and functional changes. Contrary to intuition, memory is reconstructive. Neurons that fire together wire together in patterns more readily repeated (Siegel, 2012, p. 197). As we reinforce our memories, index them, and bolster their significance, they are more likely to move from short- to long-term storage. Long-term storage data become the substrate for a sense of self, ethical parameters, and choosing—the 'cognitive belief system' (Sousa, 2011, p. 52). Significant and coherent memories are formative" (Walch, 2015, p. 154-155). Narrative supports relational bonds, sharing understanding between the originator of the narrative and those who listen, and building associations among individuals, social groups, and cultures (Shaw, 1999, p. 34; Walch, 2015, p. 152). From the Catholic perspective, the use of narrative supports Jesus' method of communicating spiritual wisdom through telling parables and the Church's holding up the lives of the saints as stories of exemplary virtue. The principles of narrative validate the ancient practice of *lectio divina*—slow reflection on spiritual reading beginning with initial understanding and moving through penetration with the help of grace, to contemplative encounter and personal application. The current understanding of neuroscience supports this slow process of modifying our brains to support future behaviors and beliefs.

Meditation and spiritual development

While science, including contemplative neuroscience, uses the terms "meditation" and "contemplation" as equivalent, in Catholic spiritual theology, there is a difference. Meditation is a way of praying that involves active human striving to express union with the will of God through virtuous action. "Meditation is a prayerful quest engaging thought, imagination, emotion, and desire. Its goal is to make our own in faith the subject considered, by confronting it with the reality of our own life" (*CCC*, 2723). Contemplation is produced by the Holy Spirit. We cannot initiate, produce, or prolong the grace of contemplation, only dispose ourselves to receive it. We can carry out responsibilities while our inner faculties are drawn to God. The Spirit transforms the contemplative pray-er to a virtuous life (Carmelite Sisters, 2013). "Contemplative prayer is the simple expression of the mystery of prayer. It is a gaze of faith fixed on Jesus, an attentiveness to the Word of God, a silent love. It achieves real union with the prayer of Christ to the extent that it makes us share in his mystery" (CCC, 2724).

For Catholics, meditation is a reflective, discursive prayer practice that involves thought, feeling, imagination, and decision. Meditation intends to internalize the mysteries of Christ and to apply them personally to life (*CCC*, 2708). "Its goal is to make our own in faith the subject considered, by confronting it with the reality of our own life" (2723). It intends to strengthen faith convictions, foster conversion, and promote persevering choice to follow Christ.

In recent decades, meditation research has rapidly expanded to include over 4,000 scientific articles on the topic (U.S. National Library of Medicine) (Vieten et al., 2018, p. 2). The field of meditation research studies psychological, neuropsychological, and physiological changes connected with meditation practices, such as effects on perception, attention, intellect, and emotion. Physiological studies show the influence of such practices on body functions such as heart rate, blood pressure, the hormonal system, and the immune system.

Meditation has been found to promote both psychological and spiritual development by regulating attention, learning to observe rather than immediately reacting to stimuli, and choosing intentionally whether to respond. Practitioners develop a greater sense of context and autonomy in decision-making. They become less impulsive, reduce symptoms of depression and anxiety, improve relationships, and experience more connectedness and positive affect (Vieten et al., 2018). Mindfulness accesses intentional areas of the brain, such as the prefrontal cortex, self-referential regions like the parietal cortex, areas that integrate and connect, such as the anterior cingulate cortex, and feeling centers like the limbic system (Larrivée and Echarte, 2018, p. 952). The Catholic Congregation for the Doctrine of the Faith clarified the distinction between meditative forms. Some are derived from Eastern religions and are individualistic or simply therapeutic. Christian meditation is communitarian, a form of "prayer that is a personal, intimate, and profound dialogue between (the human person) and God" (Ratzinger, 1989)" (Larrivée and Echarte, p. 963). The three main prayer expressions of the Christian tradition are vocal prayer, meditation, and contemplative prayer (*CCC*, 2721). Contemplative prayer is a *gift*, a grace that can only be accepted with humility. It is a *communion* through which the Trinity conforms the human person made in God's image, to his likeness (2713).

Contemplative neuroscience

An emerging new field called contemplative neuroscience studies what happens in the brain with persistent meditation (Boccia, Piccardi, and Guariglia, 2015; Fox et al., 2014) and less persistent mindfulness exercises (Fox et al., 2017; Lazar et al., 2005; Holzel et al., 2011; Golink et al., 2016). Physiologically, meditation has been shown to affect "modulation of inflammation, cell-mediated immunity, self-relating processing, inhibitory control and protective factors in biological markers of aging" (Vietin et al., 2018, p. 2).

Dimensions of contemplative neuroscience include mindfulness, the assiduous desire to acquire more knowledge, and experiences of self-transcendence.[1] Mindfulness builds on metacognition, a process of becoming an *observing ego* that observes the stream of thoughts and feelings in the field of awareness as *blips on a radar* rather than reflections of the self. Decentering and cognitive re-perception promote disidentification of self from thinking and emotions, impulse control, and objectivity (Vietin et al., 2018).

The brain seems driven to pursue knowledge constantly and to use abstract conceptualization to interpret it. Taking in sensory data, the person tries to make sense of the world and find meaning. In prayer, the person interprets their religious experience, finding meaning for the experience in their belief system. Functional imaging of religious experiences suggests a combination of affective and cognitive elements. In religious individuals, religious experiences engage a frontal-parietal network consisting of the medial parietal and the dorsolateral and dorsomedial prefrontal cortices, areas that have been found to support reflexive evaluation of cognition (Azari et al., 2001, p. 1649, in Vietin et al., 2018). Contemplative practices may derive from experiences of self-transcendence. The individual emerges from a self-identity focused on body and ego to one where one contributes to broader world/universe perspectives (p. 4).

Contemplative neuroscience in a Christian context observes that mental health flows from a relational context and alignment with a universal objective philosophical order rather than from an exclusively individual context (Titus and Moncher, 2009). Since external reality, as well as the self causes both well-being and suffering, contemplative meditation promotes mental health through conversion to virtuous attitudes and behaviors (Larrivée and Echarte, 2018).

Spiritual transformation

Cognitive neuroscience supports theological, psychological, and psychoanalytic theories of the human person, which acknowledge that one cannot practice virtue consistently simply by wanting to. Unconscious personality dynamics may need to be addressed first. Catholics would say that keeping the moral law requires the grace of the Holy Spirit. St. Paul observed regarding the human condition: "I do not understand my actions. For I do not do what I want, but I do the very thing I hate" (Rm 7:15). Irrational unconscious thoughts, feelings, and object relations (Fairbairn, 1952; Guntrip, 1952) may need reform through more normative relationships in order to develop love and friendship (Hoffman and Strawn, 2009). Human relationships often tend to reflect one's relationship with God. Positive relationships between a person and others may parallel the person's relationship with God (Jordan, Niehus, and Feinstein, 2021).

Developmental neurobiology and psychology have found that lifespan development continues through adulthood. Piaget's levels of cognitive development, for example, continue after formal operations through postformal stages. In fact, currently, more than 100 models describe stages of psychological, moral, wisdom, spiritual, and other areas of adult development (Vieten et al., 2018). A meditative practice that requires the discipline of sustained attention and self-mastery, as well as cognitive, emotional, and ethical formation of mind and soul (Larrivée and Echarte, 2018), can lead to spiritual transformation.

Character strengths are exemplified in the natural virtues of prudence/practical reason, justice, courage, and temperance—the cardinal moral virtues. And, as we have seen, the life of supernatural grace is directed by theological virtues of faith, hope, and charity, as well as other virtues. Virtues support mental health, spiritual growth, and vocation (Titus and Moncher, 2009). For Catholics, the familiar refrain from St. Thomas Aquinas that "grace does not destroy nature, but fulfills it" (*ST* I, I, 8 ad 2) plays out in understanding virtue as building up and transforming rather than destroying natural proclivities and developmental progression. Grace is taken to be a supernatural gift, not a human attainment. Still, grace is necessary, as well as human cooperation, education, and therapy, to elevate human capacities for union with God and charity toward others (Titus and Moncher, 2009).

Spiritual transformation can take a lifetime or, for some individuals, can happen in seconds. Understanding spiritual transformation is challenging not only from a religious or theological perspective but also from a neuroscientific one. It makes more sense that transformations would occur over long periods. As mentioned, the brain can slowly modify its structure and function with repeated practice of prayer, meditation, or other tasks (e.g., learning mathematics). Over time, the neurons that support these processes become stronger, slowly transforming the person into a more spiritually virtuous person.

On the other hand, specific spiritual experiences can have a transformative effect rapidly and alter many facets of a person's life in a short time. Changes can include improvements in one's sense of spirituality or religiousness, decreased fear of death, increased well-being, and enhanced sense of meaning and purpose in life. It is not clear how such a transformation occurs. Is it possible that the brain rewires itself with neurons in minutes, breaking old connections and forming new ones? Or is it more likely that the brain already has various spiritual and virtuous elements that are *locked away* only to be *activated* during profound spiritual experiences? At present, the process is unclear. Future neurotheological investigations might find the mechanism by which spiritual transformation affects the brain, if not also the soul.

Brain correlates of Catholic practices

Network integrations

Religious practices engage brain regions that are organized into various neural networks, depending on whether the practices involve thoughts, emotions, or behaviors. Meditative concentration involves the frontal lobe; a liturgical procession activates the motor cortex. With each religious practice, many areas of the brain are integrated depending on the meaning and expression of each practice. Interestingly, a single brain structure can be implicated in many different functions at the same time, some directly associated with a given religious ritual and others supportive or indirectly involved. The anterior cingulate, for example, which is essential for spiritual exercises, operates in service of "learning, memory, focused attention, emotional regulation, motor coordination, heart rate, error detection, reward anticipation, conflict monitoring, moral evaluation, strategy planning, and empathy" (Newberg and Waldman, 2009, p. 42).

As we have seen, prayer and meditation have been found to affect neurological functioning and physical and mental health beneficially. Some practices increase activity in the frontal, parietal, limbic, and temporal regions of the brain, and others decrease activity in these regions (Newberg and Waldman, 2009, p. 63). Meditation has been found to activate frontal lobe areas associated with focused attention and working memory (Lazar et al., 2000, 2005; Lutz et al., 2004; Lou et al., 1999; Newberg et al., 2001). Meditation results in amplified activation in the prefrontal and orbital cortices, the anterior cingulate, and sensorimotor cortices (Newberg et al., 2001). Experienced meditators focusing on universal compassion have been found to generate high-amplitude gamma wave synchrony in frontoparietal regions. In addition, long-term practice was found to increase baseline brain activity for gamma band oscillation, suggesting that long-term meditation affects baseline brain activity (Davidson et al., 2003).

A study by Lazar et al. (2005) found that mindfulness meditators had significantly thicker prefrontal cortex regions, including the right middle and superior frontal sulci and the right anterior insula, areas associated with attention and sensory processing. Older subjects demonstrated the largest differences between groups, suggesting that "meditation may work to reverse age-related thinning of the prefrontal cortex" (Rossano, 2007, p. 51). The religious practice of charity involves the prefrontal cortex for its planning. The insula, which helps to interpret emotions since it is involved in prosocial behaviors, is associated with charity's empathic or compassionate feeling for others (Newberg, 2018a, p. 185).

Laterality for social/emotional relating and nonliteral meaning

The right hemisphere, according to psychiatrist Iain McGilchrist's theory, generally mediates social and emotional responsivity (Rosen, Allision, Schauer, et al., 2005; Perry, Rosen, Kramer, et al., 2001), self-awareness and inter-subjective processes such as empathy and identification with others (Decenty and Chaminade, 2003, in McGilchrist, 2021). Mirror neurons, central to our capacity for imitation, were considered localized to specific areas but are currently thought likely to characterize the functioning of the nervous system in general (McGilchrist, 2021, p. 201). Although both hemispheres have mirror neurons, considering their operation rather than the location in the brain, they are believed to be right-lateralized (Aziz-Zadeh, 2006). Instrumental action characterizes the left hemisphere; non-instrumental involves the right frontal and temporal areas (Benjamin-Ruben, Kesler, Jonas, et al., 2008, in McGilchrist, 2021, p. 202).

The left hemisphere may be generally proficient in grasping the *what* of motor actions, such as walking down a path; the right, particularly the right temporoparietal area, may better understand the *why*. However, since any action may have numerous interpretations, things are not that simple (Hamilton and Grafton, 2008). Understanding behavior requires the right hemisphere areas which do not "'simply function as part of a serial, unidirectional network' but are part of 'a highly dynamic process' (Ortigue, Thompson, Parasuraman, et al., 2009)" (McGilchrist, 2021, pp. 202-203).

At present, both hemispheres have been implicated in religious and spiritual practices and experiences, depending on the elements that they contain. Spirituality is usually expressed in music, image, ritual, and poetry by implicit contextual experiences that are more evocative than indicative (McGilchrist, 2021). It involves not just knowledge but loving knowledge that begins with a sense of being impressed with some aspect of reality that is other than and beyond our comprehension.

Meditation, depending on the type, may affect the brain in expectable ways. Gamma wave oscillations are likely to be affected. Gamma oscillations are rhythmic fluctuations that are noticeable across numerous brain areas, where they are thought to contribute to attentional selection and memory processing (Mably and Colgin, 2018). When meditation is visual, activity increases primarily in the right visual area; when meditation involves self-diminishment, activity decreases in spatial and self-orienting areas; with verbal/mantra meditation, activity increases predominantly in the left language area (Lehmann, Faber, Achermann, et al., 2001). Mindfulness meditators were found to show both state and trait changes with stronger gamma power in the right posterior cortex (Berkovitich-Ohama, Glickson, and Goldstein, 2012).

Mindfulness practitioners showed symmetric connectivity within hemispheres, higher in the right hemisphere (Berkovitch-Ohama, Glickson, and Goldstein, 2014). Anatomical changes include the thickening of the right insula and the right inferior parietal and somatosensory lobules (Lazar, Kerr, Wasserman, et al., 2005). Loving-kindness meditators have shown increased gray matter thickness in the hippocampus and right insula, areas associated with emotional regulation and intuitive bodily awareness (Holzel, Carmody, Vangel, Mayer et al., 2011; Holzel, Lazar, Gard, et al., 2011; Holzle, Ott, Hempel, et al., 2007; Luders, Kurth, Nan, et al., 2011). Meditators, in general, have shown increased right hippocampal volumes (Holzel, Carmody, Vangel, et al., 2011. With meditation, where self-other boundaries are diminished, a study found decreased right inferior parietal activity (Johnstone and Glass, 2008, in McGilchrist, 2021, p. 1358).

When the meditator experiences a delightful state, the left frontal pole typically activates. Colleagues and I (ABN) have found that excitation of the left frontal pole correlates with decreased activity in the left superior parietal region (Newberg, Alavi, Baime, et al., 2001; Newberg, Pourdehnad, Alavi, et al., 2003). Unsurprisingly, religious experience generally has been found to correlate primarily with the right hemisphere, particularly the right frontotemporal area (McNamara, 2009; Trimble and Freeman, 2006; Devinsky et al., 2008). Religious experiences commonly include the amygdala, the right anterior temporal, and the prefrontal cortices (Puri, Lekh, Nijran, et al., 2001). Usually, ordinary religion with regular beliefs and convictions correlates with frontal activation, while extraordinary religious experience has been found to localize to the temporal area (Devinsky and Lai, 2008). In one study, although generalization is arguable, aesthetic, religious experience was found to localize to the right hemisphere, and ritual religious experience to the left (Butler, McNamara, and Durso, 2011, in McGilchrist, 2021, p. 1358-1359).

Regarding social relating, important elements of religious practices—face-processing, eye-gaze perception, unconscious processing of emotional information in subcortical regions, and storing of unconscious emotional memories (Gainotti, 2012)—appear to relate more to the right hemisphere. In fact, a plethora of evidence verifies that the right hemisphere excels in "receiving, interpreting, recalling, and understanding all that pertains to emotion and social interaction" (Brancucci, Lucci, Mazzatenta et al., 2009). Within the right hemisphere, stronger lateralization was found for positive and more intense emotions (Bourne, 2010). Subjectivity in feelings, intentions, and beliefs as expressed in facial expression, intonation, and gesture (Velichkovsky et al., 2017) registers predominantly and more accurately in the right hemisphere (McGilchrist, 2021, p. 203-204, 214). It emphasizes fantasies, dreams, symbols, and imagination (Hoppe, 1977). Novel, unfamiliar expressions, particularly with metaphorical content, are right-lateralized. Irrespective of the important contribution of left-lateralized language, the right hemisphere better understands the broad picture, emotionally meaningful content, new links, and wide complexity of meaning (McGilchrist, 2021, p. 220).

An overview of more than 60 behavioral and brain scan studies observed that the right hemisphere is more involved when there are tasks with nonobvious or nonliteral meaning (Mashal, Faust, Hendler, et al., 2008). For example, right-hemisphere activity is involved with metaphor comprehension (Mashal, Faust, Hendler, et al., 2007, 2008, 2009; Schmidt, DeBuse, and Seger, 2007), particularly the right temporal lobe and right parietal lobe (Diaz, Barret, and Hogstrom, 2011; Bottini, Corcoran, Sterzi, et al., 1994; Pobric, Mashal, Faust, et al, 2008; Mashal and Faust, 2005; Mashal, Faust, and Hendler, 2007, 2008; Bambini, Gentilli, Ricciardi, et al., 2011; Ptat, Mason, and Just, 2012). In addition, metaphor comprehension also involves the right insula (Schmidt & Seger, 2009), the right parietal area (Cardillo, Watson, Schmidt, et al., 2012), and the right medial frontal and prefrontal cortices (Abrens, Lin, Lee, et al., 2007; Bottini, Corcoran, Sterzi, et al., 1994; Mashal, Faust, Hendler, et al., 2007, 2008; Lee and Dapretto, 2006; Schmidt and Seger, 2009; Stringaris, Medford, Ciora, et al., 2006). Clearly, understanding and making meaning of metaphors is widely distributed throughout structures of the right hemisphere (McGilchrist, 2021, p. 221).

The right anterior cingulate cortex is significant for connecting emotion with cognition. It is about 13% larger in the right as compared to the left hemisphere. Interconnected areas of the brain associated with social judgments and empathy include the anterior cingulate and the dorsolateral prefrontal frontoinsular cortices. Here, fast-conducting, spindle-shaped von Economo neurons are found exclusively. These specialized neurons are much more numerous in the right hemisphere (Allman, Tetreault, Hakeen, et al., 2010, 2011). Regarding intuition, the dorsolateral prefrontal cortex is key to maintaining nonverbal data in working memory (e.g., Rothmayr, Baumann, Endestad, et al., 2007; Nagel, Herting, Mawell et al., 2013; van der Ham, van Strien, Oleksiak, et al., 2010; Wager and Smith, 2003; van Dam, Decker, Durbin, et al., 2015). The right frontal cortex, which is central to emotional comprehension, is also key to the inhibition of emotional arousal (Kinsbourne and Bemporad, 1984, in McGilchrist 2021, 2021, p. 223).

Given all these findings, one can see how both the left and right hemispheres can contribute to religious and spiritual practices and experiences. The hemispheres appear to make their contributions both separately and, ultimately, together. When operating as an integrated whole, the brain seems capable of enabling highly complex and meaningful experiences.

Top-down and bottom-up processing

As mentioned in the preceding chapter on rituals, top-down and bottom-up processes are also important to consider regarding specific spiritual practices. Some religious practices begin with a top-down approach by paying cognitive attention to a belief or prayer, thus involving the frontal lobe. Through the limbic system, the person experiences a positive emotion like joy or love. A diminished sense of self with a connection to God, or a particular narrative, may be associated with a blockage of sensory input into the parietal lobe, a process called deafferentation. Autonomic activation (heartbeat, breathing) may follow with a response of awe or gratitude or a quiescent response with a sense of peace. There may be a paradoxical sense of simultaneous opposites, including a union of self and Other (Newberg, 2018, p. 173).

Bottom-up processes may typify spiritual practices that are highly ritualistic in which rhythms and bodily movements initiate autonomic nervous system changes in the body, then activate the limbic system and, subsequently, the cortical regions. It is important to observe these pathways and the directional flow of information not only to understand the neurological underpinnings of various practices but also to understand better how the practices achieve their spiritual effects.

Physiological correlates of spiritual development and practice

Comparative-religion scholars observe that humans persist throughout life in asking ultimate questions about the origin of the universe and the meaning of life, particularly about their purpose. Is there support for a "cognitive imperative" in the brain that does that? Early work by d'Aquili and me (ABN) explored the possibility of a cognitive imperative built into the brain that compels human beings to search for answers and solve problems. I (ABN) found perhaps the best neuroscientific evidence in the "default mode network"—structures that are active when the person is mind-wandering or daydreaming. The default mode network (DMN) activates structures, including the posterior cingulate and prefrontal cortices and specific areas of the temporoparietal and limbic networks, when the individual goes on automatic pilot. The DMN is always "on" and always thinking—about others, ourselves, the past, the future, and the world (Newberg and d'Aquili, 1999, pp. 169-170). When ultimate questions are not focal, they might be percolating in the DMN, just below the surface, more or less ready to emerge and assert themselves.

Humans are self-aware and see themselves as part of their environment and the larger picture. A brain region that seems particularly significant for pondering, rumination, and creativity is the posterior cingulate cortex (PCC). The PCC may be the brain's most metabolically active structure, which signals that it likely is doing something essential. It may regulate information about the self since the PCC is activated in retrieving data from autobiographical memory, projecting the self into the future, and thinking about others in relation to oneself. "These processes may involve complex representations of how the self relates to the broader environment, which includes the future and the roles of other people in it" (Purves et al., 2019, p. 700).

What about the subjective feelings that accompany emotional experiences? It may be that they arise as part of the general cognitive capacity for self-awareness. Feelings may derive from both conscious experience of implicit emotional regulation of neural connections between the amygdala and neocortex and explicit processing of semantic information in networks linking the hippocampus and neocortex. Feelings may arise from emotional working memory. When emotional associations become conscious, their substrate may include the prefrontal cortex, which guides our thoughts and behaviors (Purves et al., 2019, p. 677).

Christianity encourages believers to renounce the self in favor of God and to evaluate the self and events from God's point of view. MRI scans of self-referential processing compared non-religious and Christian participants performing tasks involving personal-trait evaluations for self and publicly known individuals. Investigators found activation of the ventral medial prefrontal cortex (VMPFC) for nonreligious participants and the dorsal medial prefrontal cortex (DMPFC) for Christians. Participants were also asked to rate the importance of Jesus' evaluation of one's personality. Rating scores were found to correlate positively with the activation of the DMPFC. The VMPFC engages in the representation of self-relevance of the stimulus, and the DMPFC with evaluation of self-referential stimuli. Christian beliefs showed diminished neural activation for self-relatedness of the stimulus in the VMPFC and increased neural activation for evaluation of self-related stimuli in the DMPFC (Han, Mao, Gu, Zhu, Ge, and Ma, 2008, p. 1).

If Christians need to consider a divergence between God's perspective and their own, the anterior cingulate cortex, which is near the DMPFC monitoring attention and conflict (Northoff and Bermpohl, 2004), will be activated. Christian beliefs and practices regarding self-denial and focus on self-evaluation from God's viewpoint lead to different social comportment and self-referential processing with different neural correlates (Han et al., 2008, p. 13). The Christian and nonreligious participants also differed in that Christians showed deactivation of the right inferior parietal cortex and the precuneus. The right inferior parietal cortex is involved in the distinction between self and other in self-recognition. The precuneus engages in attributing self-other perspectives and experiential self-reflection, possibly through mental imagery when episodic memories are retrieved. When believers are subliminally primed for God, the sense of self as the cause of action may be inhibited.

Neuroscience comparing Christian and nonreligious participants shows functional differences for social cognition in self-referential processing. These findings are concordant with Christianity's disclaiming the prominence and priority of the self while reinforcing how the person evaluates the self from the perspective (through the eyes) of God. This is a meta-cognitive level analysis of the person, presuming how God might view the person. Neurobiologically, this supports enhanced involvement of the DMPFC over the VMPFC in self-referential processing (Han et al., 2008, p. 13).

Catholic practices

Benediction and Forty Hours

Catholics believe that Jesus Christ is really substantially present—body, blood, soul, and divinity—in the Eucharist. Consecrated hosts are reserved as viaticum (provisions for the journey) to be carried to the sick who could not come to Mass. Since it is reserved, Catholics venerate the real presence in the Blessed Sacrament. The Eucharist, in the form of a large consecrated host, is placed in the luna, a circular glass or crystal plate that allows people to see the consecrated host itself. The luna is then inserted in a gold container called a monstrance that is placed on or near the main altar in a church. Originating in the 1400s was the devotion of Benediction. The church assembly sings hymns, prays special prayers, and the presider blesses the congregation with the Host. Catholics wanted the Eucharist displayed on special feasts such as Corpus Christi. In 1958, Benediction became an official liturgical devotion with Scripture readings, songs, prescribed vocal prayers, prayers, and a period of silent personal prayer.

In 1592, Pope Clement VIII proclaimed that Forty Hours Devotion, beginning with Mass and exposition of the Blessed Sacrament, should be held once a year in all churches of the Diocese of Rome. The devotion then spread to the rest of the world. Forty hours were prescribed because the body of Jesus was thought to have lain in the tomb for forty hours until he was raised on Easter. In 1973, the Vatican prescribed that once a year, a special period of devotion and prayer should be held in parish churches. The church assembly sings hymns and prays special prayers. Silent adoration is a prominent part of the devotion. The presider blesses the congregation with the Host. Recently, a simplified or shortened version of this devotion has been observed in some places (Eckstrom, 1982, pp. 110-111).

Benediction and the Forty Hours devotion combines ritual with communal Scripture reading/narrative, oral prayers, singing, the monstrance holding the Host, candles, incense, and individual periods of individual meditation. Neural correlates would include the visual, auditory, and olfactory sensory systems that enable a person to understand the narrative, say prayers, and connect the various stimuli with a coherent belief system. Scriptural narrative integrates meaning-making with the reinforcement of beliefs in a communal setting and strengthens relational bonds with Christ and the faith community. Meditation reinforces the activation of prefrontal and parietal cortices and the limbic system toward decentering and self-transcendent religious experience.

Sacramentals

Holy water, the crucifix, candles, a medal or scapular, the rosary, and a Bible are among the sacred symbols and objects that the Church blesses with a prayer and some sign such as laying on of hands, the sign of the cross, or sprinkling with holy water. These are sacramentals that bring human activities, various occasions in human life, and some Church ministries into the realm of the holy and encourage the participant to receive and cooperate with grace (*SC,* 60; *CCC,* 1667). Sacramentals can also respond to the culture and history of a particular region (*CCC,* 1668). Sacramentals are less productive than sacraments, but through the prayer of the Church for well-disposed faithful, sacramentals sanctify

> …almost every event of their lives with the divine grace that flows from the Paschal mystery of the passion, death, and resurrection of Christ. There is scarcely any proper use of material things which cannot be thus directed toward the sanctification of men and women and the praise of God. (*SC,* 61)

As the preceding chapter described in detail, each element of the sacraments can be associated with different sensory, emotional, and cognitive processes. Seeing the cross involves the visual system. It is the memory of the meaning of the cross that connects the visual symbol to Jesus' redemptive death on the cross. This is then conceptually linked to sin and the act of Jesus lovingly dying for sins to bring us forgiveness and grace as a fundamental tenet of the Catholic faith. The cross can evoke intense emotions such as love and gratitude. These feelings can lead to behaviors including worship, devotion, and charity flowing from the visual image of a cross.

The rosary

A Catholic prayer devotion dedicated to Mary, the mother of Jesus, the rosary is a ring of beads used to count five decades of the Hail Mary. A decade begins with the Our Father, includes 10 Hail Marys, and ends with the Glory Be. The rosary begins with the Apostles Creed, an Our Father, three Hail Marys, and a Glory Be. The rosary ends with the Hail, Holy Queen. The Christian origin of the rosary is thought to date to the early Middle Ages as a lay replacement for the

150 psalms of the Breviary. According to a fifteenth-century legend, St. Dominic (1170-1221) received the rosary in an apparition of the Blessed Virgin. Popes, over time, attached indulgences to the devotion, and in 1716, the feast of Our Lady of the Rosary was added to the Roman calendar (Eckstrom, 1982, pp. 221-222).

From ancient times, the mother of Jesus has been honored as the "mother of God" (since Jesus is God as well as Man) whose intercession the faithful seek in need. This devotion is not the same as the adoration accorded to God (*LG*, 66). Mary is *full of grace* but still just a human person. The rosary, with its joyful, sorrowful, glorious, and (recently added by Pope John Paul II) mysteries of light, can be called an "epitome of the whole Gospel" (cf. Paul VI, *MC*, 42; *SC*, 1063, 103; *CCC*, 971). The faithful are encouraged to meditate on the mysteries while praying the rosary or to meditate on the mysteries for a few moments, then focus on the words of the prayers. A benefit of the rosary is to help grow in virtue, particularly the supernatural virtues of faith, hope, and charity. Each decade offers practical examples of virtues to practice (Kelly, 2002).

Neurophysiologically, we again see processes that are connected by neural sensory, cognitive, and emotional processes. Holding and manipulating the beads require sensory and motor operation. Frontal lobe functions help with concentration on the rosary and regulate motor coordination. Areas of the brain involved in the sense of self and emotions are activated. Studies verify that saying the rosary can reduce anxiety and stress (Stockigt et al., 2021). This is unsurprising since frontal activation is known to reduce activity in the brain's emotional centers. The rosary, then, can contribute to emotional self-regulation. By eliciting virtuous acts of faith, hope, and charity, the rosary evokes beneficial cognitive and emotional dimensions of Catholic life.

Stations of the Cross

The Way of the Cross, or Stations, consists of individual pictures or symbols for the traditional fourteen steps of Jesus' passion and death. A 15th station for the resurrection has recently been added. The Stations are usually attached to the interior walls of Catholic churches. Stations may have originated with visits to Palestine and actual sites of Jesus' life and death. Stations likely became popular in the twelfth century, with Franciscans promoting the devotion in the fourteenth century. In 1731, Pope Clement XII set guidelines for the Stations (Eckstrom, 1982, p. 258).

The practice of following the Stations of the Cross incorporates the ritual activity of movement from one to the next. In following the Stations, one follows Jesus' path. The bodily movements, like the rituals described in the preceding chapter, are critical in associating the remembrance of Jesus dying on the cross for sins with some degree of experiential accompaniment. The actual bodily experience of the process, connecting body, mind, and soul.

Blessings and exorcism

Blessings are sacramentals that thank God for his gifts and invoke the name of Jesus, usually while making the sign of the cross. Blessings consist in prayers that persons, objects, meals, and places be sanctified as belonging to the domain of the holy. Some blessings perdure because they consecrate persons or set aside places and objects for liturgical use. Church buildings and altars are dedicated to blessings, as are holy oils, vestments, and other liturgical items (*CCC*, 1672). Neurophysiologically, blessings likely have a similar effect as that of prayer and other rituals. Blessings focus attention on gratitude and invoke the name of Jesus on a person or sacred object. Social connection, in this case with Jesus, has been shown to be important neurologically for religious expression. An MRI study by Kapogiannis et al. (2009), although limited by a small sample size, hypothesized that religious belief is associated with specific networks of neural activation. Results showed a strong correlation between a sense of relationship with God and measurement of the temporal lobe.

In the liturgical rite of exorcism, the Church publicly and authoritatively withdraws a person or object from the power of the Evil One. A simple exorcism is performed in the rite of baptism. A *major exorcism* can be performed only by a priest with the permission of the bishop. The priest must proceed with prudence, strictly observing the rules established by the Church. Exorcism seeks the expulsion of demons or to liberate them from satanic possession through the spiritual authority Jesus conferred on the Church. Before an exorcism is performed, it is important to distinguish whether the seeming presence of the Evil One might instead be a mental disorder that needs to be treated by psychological science (cf. *Codex Juris Canonici* [*CIC*], can. 1172).

From a neurological perspective, one might argue that an afflicted individual might suffer from a severe neurological or psychiatric disorder. Seizures or schizophrenia come to mind when considering patients with unusual, sometimes highly negative, intense religious beliefs or experiences. Exorcism interprets symptoms and behaviors spiritually. One might wonder what brain changes occur when an exorcism is successful. Does the procedure alter the brain of the person in some significant way that modifies the pathophysiological process? In other words, if a patient with schizophrenia improved as the result of an exorcism, might we find that the typical frontal and dopamine indications were modified? And if these changes occurred, was it because of the exorcism? Or could one argue that it works like electroconvulsive therapy? Perhaps this issue can be put another way: if an exorcism changes a seriously ill patient, does it change their neurophysiology, their soul, or both? To our knowledge, there are no studies of exorcism from a brain perspective, so future research will need to explore these questions.

Relics, scapular, medals, and incense

The word *relic* designates an object, particularly a part of the body or clothing, kept as a memento of a deceased saint. The Council of Trent (Session XXV) decreed that:

> The holy bodies of holy martyrs and others now living with Christ— which bodies were the living members of Christ and "the temple of the Holy Ghost" (1 Co 6:19) and which are by Him to be raised to eternal life and glorified are to be venerated by the faithful, for through these (relics) many benefits are bestowed by God on men. (Thurston, 1911)

The scapular is a large cloth over the shoulders extending nearly to the hem in front and back, part of a monastic habit for men and women religious. The small scapular consists of two quadrilateral pieces of woolen cloth connected by two strings or bands so that resting on the shoulders, the cloth pieces hang in front and back. Investment with a scapular approved by the Church may signal enrollment in a confraternity. The scapular is blessed and confers indulgences when the person wears it with devotion (Hilgers, 1912).

Medals are sacramentals made from metal with religious pictures or words. Catholics may wear medals on chains or carry them in pockets or purses. Ss. Peter and Paul were featured on medals from the second century. In the 1500s, Pope Pius V instituted an official blessing for sacred medals. In 1830, the Virgin Mary appeared to St. Catherine Labouré and asked to have a medal struck to promote prayer for her intercession on our behalf. Owing to numerous miracles attributed to its use, it is called the "miraculous medal." In 1910, Pope Pius promoted the scapular medallion, following an eleventh-century tradition from St. Peter Damian. The traditional scapular medal features the Sacred Heart of Jesus and an image of Mary (Eckstrom, 1982, pp. 170-171).

Artifacts such as medals or relics likely produce similar effects on the brain. Via visual or sometimes tactile stimulation, the person comes in direct contact with an object that relates to the primary tenets of Catholicism. As we mentioned in discussing the cross, such stimuli evoke visual responses that connect to cognitions and emotions. Studies have shown that visual stimuli serve as markers that can trigger neural networks associated with the amygdala to alert the brain about something important. A brief activation of the amygdala might trigger a sense of fear or fascination like what Rudolf Otto described (*Idea of the Holy*) as fundamental to religious experience. This is not to imply that awareness of reality may localize to a specific neural region or to misrepresent the complexity of brain function generally.

Incense is a sacramental made from plants and resins that is burned to produce a sweet-smelling white smoke. Ancient Israelites used incense for worship and to thank God for blessings (Ex 30:34f). Around 500 AD, incense was commonly used for funerals and to show respect for Church dignitaries. Later, liturgical incensing was used for the lectionary of Scripture readings, the altar, offertory gifts of bread and wine, the presider, and the congregation—all in some way representing the presence of Jesus (Eckstrom, 1982, p. 132). Incense is particularly prominent at Benediction of the Blessed Sacrament and for festive solemn Masses. Neurologically, the olfactory tract for a sense of smell connects to fibers in the middle section of the amygdala. This means that with a strong smell, the amygdala is activated. Ritual actions with the use of incense might be associated with amygdala stimulation, possibly augmenting sympathetic drive (Newberg, 2010, p. 163). As with the visual stimulus of a relic or medal, incense can produce intense feelings that connect the participant to tenets of the Catholic faith.

Pilgrimages and visits to shrines

Based on biblical texts, pilgrimages represent the "common condition of all Christians who have their true citizenship in heaven (Phil 3:20), groan and long for their heavenly dwelling (2 Co 5:2) and live as pilgrims and exiles (1 Pt 2:11)" (Lozano, in Stuhlmeuller, 1996, p. 737). Augustine referred to the whole Church as a pilgrim in a foreign land (*City of God*, 18, 51:2, in *LG*, 8). Vatican II referred to the "pilgrim Church" (*LG*, 50). Pilgrimage represents the inner itinerary of the faithful who journey toward union with God (Lozano, in Stuhlmeuller). Christians make pilgrimages either to a shrine of the Blessed Virgin or a saint or to a place where historical events are said to have occurred. Popular pilgrimage sites include the tombs of Ss. Peter and Paul in Rome, of St. James in Compostella, to Lourdes and Fatima where Mary appeared, and to the Holy Land. Pilgrimages have traditionally been penitential expressions of intention for conversion. They include immersion in a spiritual atmosphere and often donations for people experiencing poverty (Lozano, in Stuhlmeuller).

Pilgrimages involve the brain on many levels, from the planning to the journey to the arrival at the religious shrine or location. Along the way, the person requires neural processes for each step and with the experience itself. Being there, as with almost all practices and rituals, connects the individual to profound Catholic beliefs.

Discernment regarding practices

We have noted that sacramentals can also respond to the culture and history of a particular region (*CCC*, 1668). There are numerous other sacramentals and practices, some particular to specific cultures and geographical areas. The Church recognizes that at its core, the piety of the people is a storehouse of values that offers answers of Christian wisdom to the great questions of life. For the people, this wisdom is also a principle of discernment and an evangelical instinct through which they spontaneously sense when the Gospel is served in the Church" (CELAM, Third General Conference [Puebla, 1979], Final Document, 448; cf. Paul VI, *Evangelii nuntiandi* [*EN*], 48) (*CCC*, 1676).

Expressions of piety like sacramentals and practices expand the liturgical life of the Church. They do not replace the Liturgy but derive from and lead to it (*SC* 13.1; *CCC*, 1675).

Vatican II reminded the laity of their inherent baptismal dignity of sharing in Jesus' offices of priest, prophet, and king. The Council spoke of each Christian receiving from the Holy Spirit the gift of faith and particular charisms. Christians are called to participate in the *sensus fidelium* in communion with their leaders. Postconciliar reflection points to a growing sense, even a recent call by Pope Francis for the Church at every level to participate in synodality to allow a *consensus fidelium* to emerge.

The scope of the *sensus fidelium* includes the whole range of ecclesial questions. Yet the term has no commonly agreed meaning among theologians. Pastoral discernment through care and judgment of the bishops and norms of the Church is needed to ensure that practices of piety harmonize with liturgical seasons and foster understanding of the mystery of Christ. (*CCC*, 1676).

Conclusion

Catholic practices and sacramentals prepare the faithful to receive and cooperate with grace (*CCC*, 1670). They draw efficacy, as do the sacraments, from the death and resurrection of Christ and sanctify nearly every event of life. Blessings of persons, places, and objects praise God for his gifts and works and are directed to human sanctification (*CCC*, 1678). We have explored ways that neural correlates of Catholic practices and the use of sacramentals can promote spiritual transformation toward holiness and union with God. We next consider how psychology relates to Catholicism from a neurotheological perspective.

Study Questions

1. How are chronological rhythms for prayer marked by the liturgical and daily cycles and by the human brain?

2. What are some values of narrative, particularly Scripture, for neurological functioning as well as spiritual wellbeing?

3. What are some values and forms of meditation?

4. What are the physiological effects of persistent meditation?

5. What are some advantages of mindfulness and contemplative practice?

6. What is meant by "spiritual transformation," gradual or sudden?

7. What neural networks might be implicated in religious practice?

8. While the hemispheres are highly interconnected, what are right-left functional distinctions that McGilchrist observes for spiritual and religious experiences and practices?

9. How might spiritual practices engage top-down and bottom-up brain processes?

10. What difference regarding self-referential processing did Han et al. find between Christian and non-religious subjects? Explain.

11. What neural systems are associated with the Catholic practices of Benediction and Forty Hours devotion?

12. What are the spiritual benefits of using sacramentals?

13. What sensory, cognitive, and emotional processes are associated with sacramentals such as a cross?

14. What spiritual and neurophysiological benefits might attach to the rosary?

15. What are the spiritual and physical experiential aspects of the Stations of the Cross?

16. What is believed to occur spiritually with blessings and exorcism? What neurophysiological functions might be associated?

17. What are spiritual and neurophysiological associations with relics, scapulars, medals, and incense?

18. What are the spiritual meanings and neurophysiological correlates of pilgrimages and visits to shrines?

19. What is the objective of discernment regarding sacramentals and devotional practices?

Endnotes

[1] Psychology defines self-transcendence as the state where one can look beyond the self to concern for others. See www.dictionary.apa.org/self-transcendence.

Chapter 9

Psychology and Catholicism

The brain and psychological disorders

The relationship between psychology and religion, especially in the context of the brain, is quite complex. Originally, religion and psychology were distinct, with religion being more doctrinal and psychology pertaining primarily to human emotions. Over time, there was a growing shift in understanding religion from a psychological perspective. For example, German theologian Friedrich Schleiermacher (1768-1834) described religion as *a feeling of absolute dependence*. This has interesting psychological ramifications as it takes religion from being based purely on sacred texts to the experience a person may have.

American philosopher and psychologist William James (1842-1910), in his famous book *The Varieties of Religious Experience* (1902), took an expansive tour of different types of religious experiences, primarily from a psychological perspective (Goodman, 2021). His discussion of both beneficial and pathological experiences was also important in helping to understand the deeper relationship between psychology and religion. Through his descriptions, we can understand that there are experiences that improve a person's sense of health and well-being. Further, those individuals who have a *saintly* demeanor might be more likely to have positive religious beliefs and experiences. On the other hand, religion and psychology can sometimes turn negative. Pathological states related to cult behavior or other negative religious beliefs are important to understand.

German theologian Rudolf Otto (1869-1937), in his book *The Idea of the Holy* (1917), described religion as a complex mixture of fear and fascination (Sarbacker, 2016). These scholars explore religion from the experiential perspective, particularly emotions and feelings. The relationship between psychology and religion also matters from a neurotheological perspective since it enables us to identify various brain structures and functions that underlie religious emotions and experiences. We can explore where in the brain a feeling of fear or fascination may arise and use brain imaging studies to delineate these mechanisms further.

In the twentieth century, the relationship between psychology and religion soured with the work of Austrian neurologist and founder of psychoanalysis, Sigmund Freud (1856-1939). Freud saw religion as a kind of crutch derived from unresolved psychological problems from childhood. From this perspective, many in the field of psychology began to look at religion as a kind of confabulation to deal with neuroses or even a kind of delusion. Atheists like British evolutionary biologist Richard Dawkins write about this in books such as *The God Delusion* (2006).

A number of researchers have recently explored the positive relationship between religion and psychology. Benefits have been observed in terms of reduced anxiety and depression, reduced stress, and improved coping (Vieten et al., 2013). Further, psychologists like Lisa Miller and Brien Kelley have found that religion is frequently protective, even for adolescents, in terms of depression, suicide, and drug addiction (2005).

The brain and psychology

Whether one considers a positive or negative relationship between religion and psychology, neurotheology allows us to explore that relationship in terms of brain functions. While the literature is vast in terms of understanding the relationship between psychological problems and the brain, we can touch on several important points. For example, psychological problems are typically associated with abnormal brain processes. Emotional problems such as depression or anxiety typically alter functioning in the brain's emotional centers, the limbic system and insula, and in areas affected by the neurotransmitter dopamine. Brain scan studies frequently find abnormalities in these areas in patients with psychological problems. There are MRI studies showing differences in brain volume, but also fMRI and other studies showing different network activity underlying various psychological disorders. With effective treatment, symptoms are remediated. Abnormal frontal lobe function can lead to increased anxiety or depression. Similarly, improving frontal lobe function can help resolve psychological issues.

Whether treatment is by medication or therapy, both approaches tend to improve brain function as well as reduce psychological symptoms. It is the combination of medications and therapy that has the best results. Medications tend to have a *bottom-up* effect in that they affect central neural structures, such as the brain stem, before altering function in the frontal lobes or limbic system. Psychotherapy interventions tend to have a *top-down* effect in that they target higher cognitive areas, such as the frontal systems, eventually helping patients regulate their emotions.

Serious psychological problems such as schizophrenia or bipolar disorder are also rooted in abnormal brain function. Schizophrenia correlates with abnormalities in the frontal lobes, asymmetries between the brain hemispheres, functional network implications that manifest in positive and negative symptoms, and altered dopamine function. In fact, some original antipsychotic medications specifically targeted the dopamine areas of the brain to reduce symptoms.

Importantly, religious and spiritual practices and beliefs similarly affect the brain networks that are involved in psychological problems. As we have discussed, practices such as meditation and prayer help to enhance frontal lobe function. This enhances the entire frontal network that runs from the frontal lobes to the caudate nucleus of the basal ganglia to the thalamus, then down the spinal cord to the body. Meditation and prayer also affect emotional areas of the brain, like the limbic system and insula. In systematically affecting these brain areas, religious practices may bring psychological benefits.

The relationship between religiously oriented interventions and substance abuse may also potentially relate to brain processes. It is well known that addictions are associated with important neurotransmitter systems such as the dopamine and opiate systems. There is growing evidence that religious and spiritual practices may affect similar systems that involve the ventral frontal reward system of the brain. This may help to understand how the concept of a *higher power* invoked in programs such as Alcoholics Anonymous may correlate with the activation of brain areas involved in addictions to help people find a way to reach sobriety. This is not to imply that the notion of a higher power can be reduced to neural networks or neurotransmitter systems. It means that the human brain cognizant of a higher power may thereby register specific motivating effects to reduce symptoms of substance dependence.

Understanding the brain can also help us better explore what happens when religious beliefs go awry. People who join a cult or a terrorist organization or are overwhelmed by religious delusions or hallucinations clearly have unique changes in brain function. Trying to understand what happens in the brain during these negative associations between religion and psychology can help us not only understand why they occur but also find effective ways of managing them so that we can better redirect people to more positive beliefs and experiences.

Relationship between religious experience and the brain seen through pathology

Expanding our discussion about pathological processes and religion, it is important to note how many psychological disorders have been specifically associated with religious phenomena. We are all familiar with the stories of schizophrenic patients who believe that they are the Messiah, or more specifically, Jesus Christ. Others might become hyper-religious, deciding to pursue religious beliefs to the exclusion of all other daily-life activities. Since many schizophrenic patients hallucinate, they commonly report hearing voices, either from God or the devil/demons. It is not clear why they gravitate to religious content.

Another interesting disorder associated with religious experiences is temporal lobe epilepsy or seizures. Fewer than five percent of patients with temporal lobe seizures have unusual religious experiences (Devinsky and Lai, 2008). Individuals with temporal lobe seizures, particularly involving the insula, report unusual religious experiences, either during or between seizures (Picard, 2023). The temporal lobes accommodate processes for language, sound and vision, and emotions and may be associated with unusual religious experiences. Unusual religious experiences have been reported in patients with seizures also arising from other parts of the brain. We need to question whether there may be a direct relationship between seizures and religious experiences. Might a person have a genuine religious experience in the context of a neurological occurrence?

Several neurodegenerative diseases have been linked to changes in a person's religious or spiritual views. One interesting study of Parkinson's disease patients found that when they were affected on the left side, they were more likely to lose their sense of religious or spiritual beliefs (Butler et al., 2011). This is a fascinating result. Parkinson's disease primarily affects the dopamine system, which runs from the substantia nigra in the brain stem through higher cortical areas, so there could be many areas involved. Hence, one might expect there to be alterations in a person's religious beliefs as they develop Parkinson's. On the other hand, it is intriguing that it may be more related to dopamine areas on one side of the brain rather than another. Clearly, this needs to be explored further (cf. Redfern and Coles, 2015).

Patients with Alzheimer's disease may also experience changes in their spirituality. On one hand, as cognitive functions decline, they may lose their ability to think about abstract concepts from a religious perspective. On the other hand, there are many well-known cases of profoundly demented individuals who are still able to repeat certain prayers, such as the Lord's prayer, because it is so ingrained in them from an early age. Would these kinds of religious activities be beneficial for such patients in helping to support the brain processes that they still have preserved?

Yet another study explored brain-lesion effects on spirituality and found that when lesions such as tumors or strokes occur in the parietal lobes, they are more likely to be associated with an *increase* in feelings of self-transcendence (Crescentini et al., 2013; Miller et al., 2019) While self-transcendence is one dimension of spirituality and religious beliefs, it is interesting to note that such a finding is also consistent with the brain-scan studies of meditation and prayer. As we discussed, these brain scans show reduced parietal lobe activity with feelings of oneness or connectedness with the All. The insula regulates cognition and is associated with self-monitoring (Churchill, Hutchison, Graham, and Schweitzer, 2021). Finally, a recent brain-lesion study suggested that a small brain stem area called the periaqueductal gray may be involved in feelings of spirituality (Ferguson et al., 2022). More studies are needed to understand these associations.

Near-death experiences

Near-death experiences (NDEs) are another condition that is frequently associated with religious and spiritual elements. People who have an NDE often report an enhanced sense of spirituality after the experience, sometimes with lower levels of religiousness. Many people who have an NDE report the experience of having been in the presence of God, saints, or deceased individuals. Clearly, there is a substantial religious and spiritual component to near-death experiences. Since these experiences occur when people are physiologically near death, the idea that NDEs might portend some migration of the soul out of the body is intriguing. Similarly, some have argued that rather than the soul leaving the body, it may be our consciousness that can extend beyond the confines of the brain. In this regard, it is necessary to explore what goes on during these experiences, what happens in the brain, and how this relates to religious and spiritual experiences.

Discriminating normal from abnormal

The question of *normal* or *abnormal* religious experience is fundamentally important from a neurotheological perspective. First, we must address how we decide what is, in fact, normal or abnormal.[2] We must be careful not to define away a given experience as being abnormal. This means that if we define an abnormal experience as hearing any voice, then hearing the voice of God would be pathological. However, many people feel that they have heard the voice of God in one way or another without otherwise manifesting any other signs of schizophrenia or other mental disorders. So, are these abnormal or normal experiences?

How should we categorize people who give priority to their religious beliefs? On one hand, some might consider an individual who focuses on religion as central to their entire life, *abnormal*. But there are many people in every religious tradition—priests, nuns, rabbis, and imams—who do just that. They may be remarkably religious, but they are not psychologically abnormal. Of course, one might consider doing brain scans of people with religious or spiritual beliefs of varying intensity to see if comparisons among the scans show correlations with specific conditions or symptoms and whether they fall within the normal range. Such a study would be problematic since an exceptionally broad range of experiences and physiological parameters would need to be factored in. For example, if a brain scan study showed that religious people were more likely to have frontal-lobe function conducive to well-being, such findings would not necessarily apply to all religious people.

Furthermore, there would be atheists who had a similar frontal lobe function, perhaps suggesting a common denominator neurologically. Who would determine whether belief or disbelief in God's existence and activity falls within the normal range? If we consult religion, we might find that various faith traditions label certain religious experiences as abnormal. For example, some consider speaking in tongues deeply religious, while others are not sure or even attribute it to the devil.

Neurotheology would ask us to take a comprehensive and nuanced view of normal and abnormal religious experiences. We would need to understand that some *normal* people can have normal or abnormal religious experiences and that some *abnormal* people can also have normal or abnormal religious experiences. After all, persons with intellectual disabilities or autism, for example, can certainly practice faith and participate in religion. It is certainly possible that a person with schizophrenia has a perfectly normal religious experience or belief. Thus, trying to determine what is normal or not requires a complex approach that considers both religious and scientific perspectives.

Drug-induced spiritual experiences

An interesting example that gets to the heart of normal and abnormal experiences is drug-induced states. In the past ten years, there has been an explosion of research into how various psychedelic compounds can lead to profound experiences that are frequently referred to as spiritual. Several articles indicate that experiences under the influence of psychedelic drugs such as psilocybin or lysergic acid diethylamide (LSD) are rated by some as the most spiritual experiences in their life. In a survey of spiritual experiences that I (ABN) conducted with colleagues, we found a close concordance between those experiences that occurred under the influence of psychedelics versus those that occurred under "natural conditions" (Yaden et al., 2017b).

That psychedelic compounds might help induce spiritual experiences is also important from a neurotheological perspective. This is the case because we know specifically where these compounds go in the brain. The most common compounds affect the serotonin system, which is associated with powerful sensory phenomena as well as intense existential experiences. From a psychological perspective, it may be that spiritual experiences under the influence of psychedelics may have important therapeutic benefits. Initial studies find that LSD shows promising results in reducing depression and anxiety, and MDMA (3.4 Methylenedioxymethamphetamine) for patients with post-traumatic stress disorder (PTSD) symptoms (Peacock, 2022; De Gregorio et al., 2021).

While these effects are fascinating, there is the larger question as to whether a psychedelic-induced spiritual experience is real or not, *normal* or not. From our Western perspective, we tend to think of these as *artificial* experiences because they appear to be *produced* by the drug itself. However, shamanic cultures throughout the world have used these kinds of compounds—ayahuasca and peyote, for example—to induce spiritual states that are perceived to represent the spiritual realm. For these individuals, it is not a false experience but represents a real window into the spiritual world. Psychedelic experiences provide an intriguing area of research, although it is in its early days, with clinical studies ongoing. Psychedelics may help us understand the physiology behind spirituality and how real and normal these different experiences are. It will be important to define the meaning of *spirituality* (in Chapter Ten). As mentioned, Catholic theology would not recognize authentically *spiritual* experiences that are solely drug-induced.

Psychology from a Catholic perspective

The Catholic Church is generally in favor of psychology and psychological therapy for appropriate individuals.[3] *Gaudium et Spes,* The Constitution on the Church in the Modern World (1965) affirms the field of psychology for contributions that help to understand and impact human behavior: "(In) the culture of today . . . sciences which are called exact greatly develop critical judgment; recent psychological studies profoundly explain human activity" (54). "Advances in biology, psychology, and the social sciences not only bring the hope of improved self-knowledge; in conjunction with technical methods, they help exert direct influence on the life of social groups" (5). The Catholic Church encourages incorporating outcomes and practice of psychology:

> In pastoral care, sufficient use must be made not only of theological principles but also of the findings of the secular sciences, especially of psychology and sociology, so that the faithful may be brought to a more adequate and mature life of faith... May the faithful, therefore, live in very close union with (people) of their time, and may they strive to understand their way of thinking and judging perfectly, as expressed in their culture. Let them blend new sciences and theories and the understanding of the most recent discoveries with Christian morality and the teaching of Christian doctrine so that their religious culture and morality may keep pace with scientific knowledge and constantly progressing technology. (*GS*, 62)

Psychological operations that correlate with the aims and processes of science and religion are, predictably, associated with the structure and function of the brain. Humans appear to be wired to seek and ascribe causes, with neural networks that support causal comprehension, what d'Aquili and I (ABN) (1999) called the "causal operator." Neuronal structure and function seem to facilitate the pursuit of a Causal Agent behind a unified universe. We found in trained meditators alterations in the parietal lobe related to a diminished sense of self. The person had an enhanced awareness of oneness with Reality—a cognitive process we called the "holistic operator." Since cognitive science theory, as it associates with ultimate questions, is still in its infancy, "causal operator" and "holistic operator" are not found in neurological or neuropsychological literature. These invented terms attempt to name and categorize cognitive processes that underlie neural operations or networks activated by the pursuit of major philosophical questions. It may also be said, from a faith-based perspective, that the causal and holistic operators support human aptitudes for a relationship with God (Miner and Dowson, 2012, p 57).

According to Paul Vitz, author and professor who integrates psychology with the Catholic faith, now is an auspicious time to develop a Catholic perspective for the field of psychology.[4] There are several reasons for this. Research in physical and mental health shows the beneficial effects of religion/spirituality, particularly for intrinsically motivated practitioners. The number of Christian psychologists, therapists, and clients has grown, as have journals and resources on integrating Christianity with psychology and counseling. Contemporary psychological theories, i.e., positive psychology and virtue ethics, are not antithetical to the faith. Catholicism offers the advantages of a well-defined theology and distinct official morality to facilitate efforts to associate psychology with Catholic belief and practice (2011, p. 294).[5]

Vitz observed that most of the psychological theories originated from clinicians' work with troubled individuals in psychotherapeutic settings. The personality theories offer "applied philosophies of life" (2009, p. 43) based on limited views of the human person based on limited anthropologies and presuppositions. The main counseling and personality theories are secular. They either explicitly or implicitly omit God and ignore religious motivation (2009). Much psychological theory assumes that we can only know our subjective state; counseling aims to acknowledge and express our thoughts and feelings and to be accepting of others doing the same. *Truth* is thought to be primarily psychological. Feelings may be considered authentic, whatever they are, even though they change readily. Invariable moral basics for human thriving may generally be ignored—although that mistake is beginning to be rectified with orientation to virtues, as in positive psychology and virtue ethics (pp. 43-44).

Secular personality theories often tend to reduce values such as religious, moral, spiritual, or artistic ideals to lower motivations, such as sublimated instincts, and to consider consciousness to be driven by unconscious forces (Freud and Jung). Rather than breaking motivations down analytically, Christian theory synthesizes and constructs. Higher dimensions of personality seek the good, true, and beautiful, transforming lower impulses. By exception, a constructionist personality theory that is not explicitly Christian is Frankl's logotherapy (1993), which seeks existential meaning. Psychologist, Martin Seligman, and others with the positive psychology movement, also emphasize upbuilding in virtue and character strength (Vitz, 2009, p. 45).

Distinguishing Catholic from secular psychology

Secular psychology considers the individual primarily, with subjective, relative, individualistic morality that may weaken support for religious values, cf. American sociologist and educator Robert Bellah (1927-2013) and Canadian Catholic philosopher Charles Taylor. In *Habits of the Heart, Individualism and Commitment in American Life* (1985), Bellah, Madsen, Sullivan, Swindler, and Tipton observe that individualism has led to cultural ambivalence. They note that early American biblical religion and civic republicanism developed later into "utilitarian individualism of material self-aggrandizement and expressive individualism of emotive experience and self-exploration" (Hunter, 1986, p. 373). Self-enhancement takes center stage. Bellah and colleagues recommend reestablishing *communities of memory* from biblical religion and civic republicanism to foster a "public focus on commitment to the common good" (Yamane, 2007, p. 184).

In *A Secular Age* (2007), Taylor takes a historical approach to understand "why was it virtually impossible not to believe in God in, say, 1500 in our Western society, while in 2000 many of us find it not only easy but even inescapable?" (p. 25, in Kollar, 2011). Greatly over-simplifying Taylor's extensive study, we see that he traces the emergence of secularity from the Reformation to the Enlightenment to the current era of self-expression and personal choice to follow the gospel of individual freedom. Taylor chooses an optimistic stance in the face of the claim that, to many, science makes religion irrelevant: both science and religion pursue truth from different epistemological angles. He remarks that the expanding diversity of religions and cross-currents of spiritualities can be welcomed to help believers listen and mature in their faith. He recommends renewing meaning and hope by reconnecting with transcendence through exemplars in the saints (Shantz, 2010).

Catholicism endorses lasting moral principles based on revelation, including the Ten Commandments. Here, we are considering basic theoretical perspectives of secularity vs. Catholicism, not referring to the personal or collective moral behavior of either one. Catholicism clearly delineates morality, which is understood to promote human flourishing. To a large or small degree, mental pathologies may stem from disregarding moral law or possibly interfering with it.

Some current secular personality theories deny free will (i.e., Freud), at least implicitly, taking mind and behavior as determined by external and internal influences (Vitz, 2009, p. 44). Humanistic and existential psychologists highlight the significance of human agency and virtue. Eric Erikson (1902-1994) was a German-American developmental psychologist known for his theory of psychosocial developmental stages, which, for example, includes ego strengths (virtues). Abraham Maslow (1908-1970), an American psychologist known for his hierarchy of needs, refers to spiritual aspiration as central to the humanistic movement and promotes courage and optimism. Self-transcendence with peak experiences, flow, and self-actualization signal the positive psychology movement (Seligman and Csikszentmihalyi, 2000, in Brugger, 2009). Cognitive behavioral therapies (CBT) counter tendencies to downplay free will in favor of tendencies to regard the individual as largely determined by external and internal forces.[6] Catholic Christian representation of the person and personality emphasize freedom and the duty to choose the good and to acquire and practice virtue (Vitz, 2009, p. 46).

Secular personality theory is inclined to foster a healthy and mature, autonomous, individuated self. In fact, self-fulfillment is understood to be fundamental to the purpose of human life.[7] Christianity instead fosters interdependence. Christian fulfillment is understood to be self-giving love, freely caring for others, and ultimately attaining union with God (Vitz, 2009, pp. 45-46). Spirituality may develop following Erikson's model of psychosocial stages (1958, 1963), with essential achievements at each stage, beginning with trust achieved through hope and concluding with ego integrity attained through wisdom. James Fowler (1940-2015), an American theologian and professor of human development, proposed Christian-based stages of faith (1981) with insights into conversion and progression through advancing levels of faith commitment and expression. The stages begin with undifferentiated faith and move through to universalizing faith.[8] For development in prayer, Spanish Carmelite mystic and religious reformer St. Teresa of Avila (1515-1582) leads the reader through the mansions of *The Interior Castle* (1577). These religiously oriented perspectives can also be beneficial for helping people find paths toward psychological health and well-being. While secular approaches target psychological health and well-being, they do not have the added emphasis on fundamental principles found in religious traditions such as Catholicism.

Catholic Christian anthropology

As mentioned above, psychology deals with aspects of the individual, such as cognition, emotion, perception, behavior, and personality. The overall conception of the human person underlying these dimensions makes a difference. Various psychological theories presuppose an explicit or implicit philosophical anthropology of the person. For Catholic Christians, sources of philosophical reasoning include the Aristotelian/Thomistic tradition and Judeo-Christian revelation. Personalism, among other Catholic philosophies, has an adequate anthropology (cf. Burgos, 2021; Vincelette, 2020).[9] A Christian anthropology attempts to be systematic and coherent, rational, and faith-based, although it will largely be acceptable also to non-Christians. Christian anthropology can provide support for psychological assessment, diagnosis, theory, ethics, treatment, and training of psychologists (Brugger, 2009, p. 15).

Philosophical and theological sources in the Catholic intellectual tradition support anthropology with eight discrete, interrelated elements of the human person:

Humans are (a) bodily, (b) rational, (c) volitional, (d) interpersonally relational, (e) substantially one, (f) created by God in His image, (g) weakened personally and interpersonally because of sin, and (h) invited to become members of the body of Christ through faith and baptism. (Brugger, 2009, p. 5)

Elements (a) through (e) represent domains of the individual where limitations or distortions constitute mental disorders. Elements (f) through (h) are known through Christian revelation and redemption, clarifying metaphysical, teleological exigencies of the human person. Valid empirical findings of clinical science can be incorporated into each and all of the eight elements. Christian anthropology provides a means of organizing and interpreting clinical data in an effort to promote healing and human flourishing (Brugger, 2009).

Main secular personality theories, such as Freudian psychoanalysis, Rogerian person-centered therapy, and others, often rest on philosophical assumptions of implicit atheism since God is omitted. They conceptualize cases with a bent toward determinism, at least in theory, due to unconscious forces limiting free will. As we have seen, secular theories often gravitate toward moral relativism and subjectivism. In contrast, Catholic Christian dimensions of the person include "embodiment; interpersonal relationality over the lifespan; considerable free decision-making capacity; intelligence; and worth of the virtues" (Vitz, 2009, p. 420). These characteristics offer a lens for understanding and treating human pathology and for theological implications regarding the Trinity as the origin and end of human life.

The human person as a rational and free[10] embodied moral agent in relationship with the environment, other persons, and God has ramifications for human dignity and respect for life. Catholicism holds that from the beginning of life, the person is truly human. When underdeveloped and small, one is still truly human, just not fully grown. Those who are unconscious or unborn do not have less human worth or dignity, nor are they due less moral respect. "Human life must be respected and protected absolutely from the moment of conception. . . as having the rights of a person" (*CCC*, 2270). "Since it must be treated as a person, the embryo must be defended in its integrity, cared for, and healed, as far as possible, like any other human being" (*CCC*, 2274). Persons begin all at once when the living body begins. Otherwise, there would be a continuum for humanity, with some more human than others. "Those whose lives are diminished or weakened deserve special respect" (*CCC*, 2276).

Human persons maintain their identity as a determinant of continuity throughout their lifespan; from infant to elder, they are the same person, with one enduring soul. They also, through the body, grow and change physiologically with chronological development. This principle is validated in clinical psychology by the assumption that meaningful disturbance in self-perception over time is considered problematic (Brugger, 2009, p. 12). A person in a coma or sleeping, a fetus, or an older individual with Alzheimer's disease is always an embodied entity in a relationship, with potential for reason, will, and consciousness (Vitz, 2011, p. 303).

For Christians, revelation contributes substantially to anthropology, adding transcendent realities that natural reason could only dimly guess. Catholics find revelation in scripture and the Church's magisterium that humans are created, fallen, and redeemed. Contributing to Catholic understanding is the Church's tradition, including the lived experience of the faith by its saints, acts of charity, devotions, and the *sensus fidelium* that issues in dogmas like the Immaculate Conception. Humans being created in the image of God provides a basis for confidence in the fundamental goodness of human nature. Consideration of humans as the image of God supports the Rogerian unconditional positive regard that clinicians try to communicate to clients (Brugger, 2009).

The biblical doctrine of the Fall offers an epistemological foundation for understanding mental disorders as deficiencies in appropriate order within and among persons. Thus, from the Catholic perspective, even with psychotherapy's best efforts, healing is only partial improvement, and humans remain fallen. Freud has been variously quoted as promising through psychoanalysis to transform neurotic misery into normal human unhappiness

(*Studies in Hysteria* [1895]). However, this implies that the goal is not a sense of happiness or joy that is part of the Catholic psychological perspective.

Philosophical psychology

A Catholic model of psychology can point to the influence of Augustine, who is grounded in the Platonic tradition through Plotinus and noted for his psychological insight. Greek metaphysical categories were adopted, particularly by Aquinas, as helpful in developing and systematizing some Christian concepts. Aquinas' psychology follows Aristotelian ontology. This means that there is an objective order external to the human person that defines reality. Thomistic metaphysics, linked to revelation, names God as the Creator and Source of all that is. For Thomistic realistic metaphysics, human thoughts and feelings have their importance but are not of primary concern. Such realism puts a Thomistic model at odds with some modern psychological theory. A Catholic model of psychology assumes that human persons do not determine truth and value but need to adjust to the objective, already established, enduring order of God and creation, as it is presented in scripture and taught by the magisterium (Vitz, 2009, p. 44).

The human person, in a Catholic model of psychology, is a psychophysical unity with body and soul as a psychosomatic interaction. "Every psychosomatic interaction is a synthetic, inseparable act of a unified body-soul entity, that is, the act of a person" (Brugger, 2009, p. 11). Aquinas' way of analyzing the human psychosomatic unity was to move from observable effect to preexisting ability or potential. If the human person can see, there must be a power of sight grounded in the soul and actualized in the body in an organ or group of organs. Reason and will constitute executive powers, with intellect distinguished as speculative or practical and the will as an appetitive rational power (Butera, 2011).

The concept of person originated with historical efforts of philosophy and theology to work through the doctrine of the Trinity. Central to the discussion was the notion of dialogue. Revelation indicated that God 'communicated personally with Israel's prophets and with his Son Jesus. Through the dialogue among Persons of the Trinity, as recorded in Scripture, God was acknowledged to be a plurality of Persons. Genesis reveals that humans are made in God's image. In his *On the Trinity*, St. Augustine, using logic and psychology, saw in human memory, understanding, and will subsisting in one person an analogy for the Persons of the Trinity distinguished by their relationships in one God. History and experience show that we are interpersonal by nature. Humans are inclined to social interaction and, in fact, called to committed relationships in love with others and God as a means to attain full personhood (Vitz, 2009, p. 47).

As we have seen, a Christian anthropological model of the person—as bodily, rational, intentional, relational, substantially one, created, fallen, and redeemed—supports psychological healing and growth. This model can facilitate the integration of encouraging, hope-engendering aspects of the Christian faith, such as accompaniment and guidance of the person by a benevolent Creator and the redemptive value of otherwise seemingly senseless suffering through the vicissitudes of life. The model might lead Christians to a more mature faith, acceptance grounded in optimism, and spiritually oriented meaning.

A Catholic Christian representation of the person promotes natural virtues such as courage, justice, temperance, and wisdom for a naturally thriving life. It fosters theological virtues of faith, trust, and charity that unite the human person to God (Vitz, 2009). As we have seen, the Church recommends psychological theory and practice in pastoral care to promote growth in faith (*GS*, 1965, no. 62). Current psychological literature supports spirituality and religion as beneficial to health. A leading nonprofit organization, the National Alliance of Mental Illness (NAMI), recognizes the value of faith-based support by offering a website (www.nami.org/namifaithnet) to connect users to religious groups. The National Catholic Partnership on Disability (NCPD) has a Council on Mental Illness to provide webinars, workshops, and resources for persons with disabilities (Weaver, 2010, p. 15).

Catholic anthropology for clinical psychology

The philosophical and theological aspects of Christian anthropology, particularly the first four that the human person is bodily, *rational, volitional*, and *relational,* can provide a way to systematize and interpret information about symptomatology, disorder, and healing. The theologically based dimensions *created, fallen, and redeemed* can offer grounds for hope in assisting people in optimizing opportunities for growth and human flourishing since Catholic theology understands sin and disorder as a privation of the good, disorders in any anthropological domain of the person, whether cognitive, physiological, behavioral, or relational, is a privation at some level that needs repair.

Aquinas did not develop an analysis of emotional disorders. Still, he has been credited with anticipating the theoretical framework and the main principles and methods of cognitive behavior therapy (CBT) through his philosophical psychology (Aaron Beck, 1967). CBT demonstrates that humans are more than the sum of their material parts, in this case, the physiological structure of their brains and causal functional cerebral interactions. CBT holds that ideas have consequences, influencing the choices we make and the lives we lead through our bodies (Butera, 2011). Beck reflects that CBT:

changes man's perspective on himself and his problems. Rather than viewing himself as the helpless creature of his biochemical reactions, blind impulses, or automatic reflexes, he can regard himself as prone to learning erroneous, self-defeating notions and capable of unlearning or correcting them as well. By pinpointing the fallacies in his thinking and correcting them, he can create a more self-fulfilling life for himself (*Cognitive Therapy and Emotional Disorders*, 1976, p. 4). (Butera, 2011b, p.363)

Facilitating health through clinical psychology means enhancing occasions for healing, health, and happiness, optimizing opportunities for clients to reach their potential and purpose. When weakened intellect, will, or emotions are healed, transformed, and returned to friendship with God by grace, the person can grow in holiness (1 Pt 1:14-16) (Brugger, 2009).

Relationality and Catholic psychology

"Relationships are essential for basic human existence and development" (cf. Siegel, 1999). For infants, neurological development depends on caregiver interactions in order to build emotional regulation that fosters healthy relationships (Klemm, 2019). Social cognition seems to develop through brain areas that process faces, particularly a structure called the fusiform gyrus in the temporal lobe. This is the area that subserves facial recognition in the left hemisphere; damage there causes prosopagnosia. Social cognition also depends on structures such as the amygdala and orbitofrontal cortex, along with frontal executive function areas that judge contexts with shifting attention. Face-to-face conversation involves complex engagement of multiple circuits (Wildman and Brothers, 2002, p. 376). Language learning, too, proceeds developmentally from the primitive *we think* to the consciousness of one's thought processes forming, *I think*. Vygotsky concluded, "An interpersonal process is transformed into an intrapersonal process (1978, p. 57, in Vitz, 2009, p. 48).

The innate propensity for imitation, called social contagion, is seen in infants soon after birth, for example, in the nursery phenomenon of *contagious crying*. This may be due to *mirror neurons*[11] that fire both when one performs an action and when the action is observed in another (Berger and Luckmann, 1966). The attention of the frontal cortex is found to support both symbol acquisition (Deacon, 1997) and the development of the memory network for cognition in general (Wildman and Brothers, 2002).

The new field of interpersonal neurobiology points to multifaceted interaction between the body, the mind, and the brain, including its genetic endowment, the environment, and particularly close relationships. Psychotherapy builds on a therapeutic relationship of primary importance for explicit and implicit learning to develop an understanding of one's behavior and healthy relation to the self, others, and God (Clinton and Sibcy, 2012).

Psychology and theology integration

Attempts to integrate psychology with theology meet with difficulties we have referred to in Chapter Three on epistemology. Essentially, as we have seen, psychology, or the study of the soul, focuses on the human person—intellect, will, mind, emotions, and behavior, with neuropsychology investigating the brain—and may fruitfully follow a model of Christian anthropology. Catholic theology entails a wide ontological scope, with a realist metaphysics that begins with God, assumes that there is an objective order of being, and builds on revelation with faith-seeking understanding and application to life. Significant in relating to self, others, and God, for both psychology and theology, is spiritual experience. "Perceived relationship with God is a psychospiritual experience that requires a relational explanation" (Miner and Dowson, 2012, p. 55).

How can the human relationship with God be explained? A purely physicalist neuroscience will be inadequate. Metaphysics must be included. Beginning from an anthropological perspective on the spiritual dimension of the human person, reason and volition are spiritual faculties of the soul. In classical and Christian philosophy, the soul comprised of intellect and will is the immaterial animating principle. For Aristotle and Aquinas, as we have seen, the soul is the *form* of the psychosomatic human person. The soul is believed to enliven the bodily organs to perform their proper operations (Brugger, 2009). A theological explanation derives from the Trinity, showing God to be both transcendent and immanent. Human persons can respond to God's initiative, inviting attachment to the Persons of the Trinity. Psychological evidence points to humans being neurologically adapted or "hard-wired" for their relationship with God (Klemm, 2019, p. 6). Research has shown that God himself can be, for human persons, a legitimate attachment figure (Cherniak, Mikulincer, Shaver, and Granqvist, 2021).

One of the best-known theorists of spiritual and faith development, as mentioned, is theologian James Fowler, who wrote the book *Stages of Faith* (1981). His Christian-oriented work might provide a framework for the neurotheological investigation of the impact of developmental changes on an individual's spiritual perspective-taking and religious practice (Newberg and Halpern, 2018, pp. 248-249). The stages are: (0) primal faith, (1) intuitive-projective, (2) mythic-literal, (3) synthetic-conventional, (5) individuative-reflective, (6) conjunctive, and (7) universalizing faith (Milstein and Manierre, 2012, pp. 14-15). These, in turn, can be associated with stages of brain development throughout the lifespan (Newberg and Newberg, 2008; Werk, Steinhorn, and Newberg, 2021).

An interesting study by Milstein and Manierre (2012) considers Fowler's stages of faith as a measure for counselors to assess clients' spiritual/religious development to integrate spirituality into treatment. The process of *culture ontogeny* understands that abstract notions of religion and culture incorporate biologically with the neurophysiology of the developing brain. Counselors are encouraged to elicit the meaning of religion for clients in their emotional self-structure, considering both the *image of God* (personally internalized emotional resonance) and the *concept of God* (cognitive, doctrinal notions) and the degree of consonance between the two. In Fowler's model,

> With each developmental stage, there is the possibility of an increasingly complex and relational sense of God. As we grow older, the lifespan development of our organic, initially unreflective personal quest for meaning may then expand in self-reflective complexity (Fowler, 1981). A reason for these stepped stages is found in neurodevelopmental anatomy. (Milstein and Manierre, 2012, p. 12)

Neuroscience can be integrated with religion and mental health to help rationally explore matters such as selfhood, autonomy, consciousness, free will, morality, and emotions, and how to live with meaning and purpose. Neuroscience can clarify dimensions of beliefs, attitudes, decision-making, biases, and behaviors related to religion and can assist in pursuing spiritual goals and a flourishing life (Klemm, 2019, pp. 8-9).

Religious experience can be either mediated or unmediated by God. Ordinary interpersonal experiences occur through objects, persons, and interactions with the world. When God is believed to communicate *symbolically*, mediated religious experiences are involved, with meaning found in elements or patterns of events in the world (Peacocke, 2002, p. 243). *Signals* from God are reducible to the natural or human sciences. Religious meaning can be found through faith. The subject of mediated religious experiences typically has certain sensations, usually indescribable, when they are conscious of God or spiritual or eternal reality. The subject identifies religious experience through personal perceptions unique to the subject (Swinburne, 1979, p. 251).

Although God ordinarily communicates through elements of the world and using the structure and functions of the human brain, God as Creator certainly can communicate otherwise. God can also communicate directly and subtly without human conscious awareness. Divine conferral of actual and sanctifying capacity for union and transformation can be and is frequently communicated without human awareness, for example, in the baptism of infants or the dark night of spiritual growth.

Unmediated religious experiences, whatever their revelatory impact, are not entirely unmediated. They "arise in the context of a particular cultural and social background, a particular personal developmental history and the memories arising from it, and a particular set of conceptualizations about the nature and will of God" (Watts, 2002, p. 345). Divine action usually appears effective when the person has faith to acknowledge and reply to God's communication consciously. "Disbelief, however, does not take (one) outside the orbit of divine providence" (p. 327). A wide variety of experiences can be understood in terms of divine action.

Capacity for relationship with God and its effects

Human persons, with our capacity for relationships, can both relate appropriately to God and misunderstand what God may be trying to communicate (Watts, 2002). Communication by the Holy Spirit is known mainly through individual and collective human experience. Action undertaken allegedly under the direction of the Spirit will manifest in fruits of the Spirit: "love, joy, peace, patience, kindness, goodness, trustfulness, gentleness, and self-control" (Gal 5:22).

Since God does interact with people, they need to be open. The indwelling of God with believers implies their receptivity. People can be tuned to or resonant with God to varying degrees. Attunement suggests a divine interactive style that is generally gentle and peaceful, allowing the person to either respond or follow their plans. General providence ordinarily coincides with a credible sense of God's guiding of human thinking. However, rather than God inserting specific thoughts in people's minds, it is more likely that "people allow themselves to be drawn into a way of thinking that is in accordance with the mind of God" (Watts, 2002, p. 346). Once resonance is achieved, possibilities for empowerment occur that would otherwise not have been considered (Watts, 2002, p. 343).

Religious or ultimacy experiences generally relativize human assumptions and offer a glimpse of some kind into reality not ordinarily accessible in day-to-day life. Theological reflection expects psychological and behavioral effects, and often, such experiences become sources of a lasting transformation of character (Wildman and Brothers, 2002, p. 411). Recipients of religious experience who have been assured of the veracity of their faith, for example, often acquire a marked peacefulness. The effects of religious experience on disposition and life play a role in individual and communal discernment about the authenticity of the experience (p. 354).

In the end, psychology and Catholicism can engage in a rich interaction that ultimately supports the well-being of individuals in their daily lives as well as in the ways they engage their religious beliefs. The added dimension of neurotheology provides a neurological framework for deepening our understanding of psychology and Catholicism. Neurotheology would provide a potential for research by exploring psychological disorders and treatments from a Catholic perspective. Such research should be able, practically, to find effective ways of integrating Catholicism and psychology to promote human well-being, spiritual development, and growth in grace.

Study Questions

1. What are examples of the relationship between psychology and religion?

2. What are examples of psychological disorders rooted in abnormal brain structure or function?

3. How can spiritual and religious practice alter brain function or structure for good or ill? Explain with examples.

4. What are examples of disease conditions that point to an association between religious experience and the brain?

5. What do NDEs suggest regarding spiritual and religious experience?

6. What are some challenges in distinguishing what is abnormal?

7. What may be said about the drug-induced spiritual experience?

8. What are some Catholic perspectives regarding psychology?

9. From a Catholic viewpoint, what are the limitations and benefits of psychological theories and treatment models? Explain.

10. What do Bellah et al. see as problematic in the current subjective, individualistic Western culture? What do they recommend?

11. Do you agree with Taylor that science makes religion irrelevant?

12. Why and how might we reconnect with transcendence? Explain.

13. What are examples of psychological models / counseling theories, such as humanistic, existential, positive psychology, and CBT, that approach Catholic values of freedom, moral parameters, and emphasis on virtue?

14. What are the distinctions between secular personality theories and Catholic developmental principles?

15. What are the elements of Catholic Christian anthropology?

16. How does Catholicism understand the human person? What are the implications?

17. What are some elements that distinguish a Catholic from a secular model of psychology?

18. What are the fundamental aspects of Catholic anthropology for clinical psychology?

19. How, with examples, does a Catholic perspective on psychology view relationality?

20. What are some forms of psychology-theology integration?

21. How may humans relate with God, and what are the effects of such a relationship?

Endnotes

[1] Psychology defines self-transcendence as the state where one can look beyond self to concern for others. www.dictionary.apa.org/self-transcendence.

[2] In psychology, normal and abnormal were originally mathematical/statistical terms, e.g., Full-Scale IQ is *normal* in the distribution of IQ scores between 85 and 115 and abnormal if the IQ score is more than two standard deviations above or below the mean of 100. People with high IQs are statistically *abnormal*, although in their case, being abnormal is not pejorative.

[3] During the first two-thirds of the twentieth century, Catholic thought was largely unfavorable toward psychology due to early deterministic and atheistic presuppositions of psychoanalysis. Today, psychological theory and practice are much broader and more humanistic, and the Church encourages psychology and other social sciences in pastoral care.

[4] For more detail, see Vitz, P. C., Titus, C. S., & Nordling, W. J. (Eds.). (2020). *A Catholic-Christian meta-model of the person: Integration with psychology and mental health practice.* Sterling, VA: Divine Mercy University Press.

[5] *Integratus: Journal of the Catholic Psychotherapy Association.*

[6] Psychodynamic theory is no longer a uniform system. The second generation has begun to diverge from Freud with object relations theory and self-psychology.

[7] Western individualism may stem from the Renaissance/Reformation era and Western capitalist society.

[8] Fowler, who was a United Methodist pastor, is cited here not for fully supporting Catholicism but for his valuable contribution to understanding universal stages of faith.

[9] Burgos, J. M. (2022). *Personalist anthropology: A philosophical guide to life.* Wilmington, DE: Vernon Art and Science. Vincelette, A. (2020). *Recent Catholic Philosophies: Twentieth Century* (2nd ed.). St. Louis, MO: Enroute Books and Media.

[10] As we saw in Chapter Five, this position counters that of neuroscientists who argue against free will by drawing unwarranted implications from research, such as Libet's experiments.

[11] A corrective for those who would overemphasize the importance of mirror neurons is Hickok, G. (2014). *The myth of mirror neurons: The real neuroscience of communication and cognition.* New York: W. W. Norton & Company.

Chapter 10

Spirituality from a

Neurotheological Perspective

Spirituality and the brain

When looking at spirituality from a neurotheological perspective, it is important to consider the variety of potential connections linking spirituality with the brain but also explore aspects that might go beyond our current neuroscientific understanding. On one hand, theories have been proposed to help understand how spirituality might be linked to brain functions. However, spirituality also arguably has nonmaterial aspects that extend beyond general brain functions. In this chapter, we will explore scientific perspectives, but we must emphasize that neurotheology requires us to look beyond the purely scientific.

Much early work with neuroimaging has focused on spiritual practices and experiences that we have referred to throughout this book. Brain scans of people engaged in prayer, meditation, and other spiritual practices have helped us to understand better many of the brain areas that might be involved (Sporns, 2016). We have indicated that spirituality often includes emotions, thoughts, experiences, and behaviors. Thus, many different brain areas are likely to be involved, depending on the specific aspects of spirituality being investigated.

Perhaps the most important point is that there seems to be something specific about spiritual experiences, and more generally spirituality, that differentiates this phenomenon from everyday beliefs and experiences. There is something that specifically distinguishes spirituality from other aspects of human thought and experience. What type of characteristic or brain process might help us understand the unique nature of spirituality? This has been a prominent question for scholars in diverse fields exploring the nature of spirituality.

From my (ABN) previous work with colleagues in neurotheology, we have tried to elucidate specific elements that people refer to when identifying spiritual phenomena. Specifically, these include feelings of intensity, clarity, unity, surrender, and transformation. Further, each of these elements can be considered in relation to brain processes. But these terms can be used for "normal" types of experiences as well. We can have an intense feeling of joy when we succeed at work, and we can have a feeling of clarity when we experience an "aha" moment in solving a problem. There seems to be something uniquely different about spiritual experiences as they take these qualities to their respective extremes. Still, there appears to be a continuum of experiences that are referred to as "spiritual." Some people might call being in church a spiritual experience, while others might think first of an experience that has mystical elements to some degree. Both are considered spiritual, yet they seem to fall on a continuum. Despite such a continuum, there appears to be some "quantum jump" from ordinary to spiritual experiences that distinguish them.

Somatic marker hypothesis

One suggested approach that has been suggested is called the *somatic marker hypothesis.* This theory proposed by well-known neuroscientist Antonio Damasio proposes that a degree of intensity identifies various feelings as more important than others. This is most likely characterized by increased activity in emotional centers such as the amygdala along with the ventromedial prefrontal cortex and their connections. In some sense, this is consistent with the *intensity* dimension that we have referred to as a core component of spiritual experiences. However, critiques of this theory ask how much emotions alone guide human thought and behavior. We would argue that such emotional responses may be critical to spirituality, although not the only factor. Saints, for example, often experienced dry periods where they felt nothing in response to their prayer, yet importantly, remained faithful. Albanian-Indian nun and founder of the Missionaries of Charity, St. Mother Teresa, even in long years of dryness, maintained her spirituality.

Remembering and interpreting spiritual experiences

The transformative element that we have previously referred to has something to do with how we interpret and remember spiritual experiences in a way that is markedly different from other experiences in our lives. Spirituality, and more specifically, spiritual experiences, appear to elicit strong memories that are related to ideas or concepts of ultimate concern, as German-American existentialist philosopher and theologian Paul Tillich (1886-1965) would state. Thus, spiritual experiences are interpreted as being unique and separate from our everyday reality experiences. Spiritual experiences are remembered intensely and can even be incorporated into everyday beliefs and behaviors. Highly spiritual individuals may consider every aspect of their life from a spiritual perspective. The profound memories and meaning of spirituality pervade every aspect of their thoughts, feelings, and behaviors.

Subcortical predominance

Some have argued that spirituality derives more from subcortical structures. This would include the emotional centers of the brain. The limbic system—the amygdala, hippocampus, and limbic cortex: the cingulate gyrus and parahippocampal gyrus, and core structures such as the hypothalamus and the periaqueductal gray—regulate many bodily processes. These structures also affect the autonomic nervous system, regulating arousal and quiescent functions of the body. Studying these structures and their functions, especially with their connections to the frontal and temporal regions, can certainly help us understand the intensity of spiritual experiences and the often powerful transformative effects people experience. Effects impact not just the mind but the body as well.

Whole-brain processes

Of course, as we have argued throughout this book, many different areas of the brain are likely involved in spirituality and spiritual experiences. The intricate networks of the brain enable a person to process the complexity of spiritual experiences: the intense emotions (except in periods of dryness), the powerful cognitive and memory aspects, and the transformation of one's entire being. But while it is helpful to think about the many different brain processes all working together as part of human spirituality, we again are begging the question as to what specifically differentiates spirituality from many other human endeavors that incorporate thoughts, feelings, and experiences.

Neurotransmitters and spirituality

In early models of spiritual practices and experiences, neuroscience hypothesized many different neurotransmitter systems to be involved. Neurotransmitters such as serotonin and dopamine are known to affect emotional responses. Intense serotonin activity is associated with psychedelic experiences, which are often described as spiritual. In fact, in a study of psilocybin-induced experiences, a large percentage of participants reported that the experience was one of the most spiritual they had ever felt. We have mentioned previously that this is a complicating factor when interpreting spiritual experiences since it becomes important to distinguish those that occur under the influence of psychedelic compounds from those that occur more "naturally."

Dopamine is part of the brain's reward system. Some studies have suggested a release of dopamine during intense meditation practices. Further, as we have previously described, my (ABN) study with colleagues of a spiritual retreat program produced significant changes in the brain's receptivity to dopamine. Since spiritual experiences are associated with many different areas of the brain communicating with each other in broad networks, neurotransmitters such as acetylcholine that are involved with global brain communication are likely to be involved as well. We have also suggested that GABA (gamma-aminobutyric acid), the primary inhibitory neurotransmitter in the brain, may be associated with the deafferentation of the parietal lobe and the subsequent experience of unity that is prominent in spiritual experiences.

Other neurotransmitters are also likely involved, depending on specific elements of the sense of spirituality. But once again, we must ponder why certain types of experiences are labeled spiritual when all experiences involve neurotransmitter systems.

Thought not localized to neurons

Although we may consider a wide array of brain processes that can help us understand spirituality, along with many different theological, philosophical, and scientific questions, we still cannot clearly identify where spiritual thoughts come from. We have mentioned different brain areas, neurons, neurotransmitters, blood flow, metabolism, and complex neural networks.

But where in all that do our thoughts arise?

Neuroscience is still very far from finding the answer to that question. By themselves, none of the aspects of neurophysiology define thought and subjective consciousness. For neuroscience, the fundamental matter remains unanswered. Yet somewhere in all those quadrillions of neural connections, consciousness, and thoughts occur. Philosophy and theology, too, with answers about the hylomorphic brain-soul connection, find an element of mystery, with clear understanding elusive.

From the neuroscientific perspective, in the field of consciousness studies, there is a profound question as to whether consciousness arises from neuronal processes or is distinct from cerebral physiology. Some have argued that consciousness emerges from the incredibly complex interactions of nerve cells working together. Emergent properties such as wetness, for example, arise from water molecules. One molecule of water is not wet, yet billions of water molecules are. One neuron is not conscious. Is it possible that when billions of neurons interact, the person is?

The bottom line is that we do not know how we can link the exterior observed processes of the brain with our interior subjective experiences. No current neuroscientific theory appears even close to helping us understand the mystery of consciousness. And if we cannot understand consciousness, spirituality would seem to be similarly beyond our grasp. Whether neurotheology will help us to identify the relationship between the material brain and immaterial consciousness that we all experience remains to be seen. Hopefully, neurotheology provides an opportunity.

Search for a unified field theory: Nature of religious experience

Throughout this book, we have discussed the differences as well as the similarities between science and religion. It is particularly regarding spirituality that we may begin to be able to explore some unified field theory that brings science and religion together more effectively. The idea that religious experience is not only a spiritual connection but biological or material as well lies at the center of such a theory.

Neurotheology has long argued that this approach may provide the highest likelihood of bringing religion and science together. Neurotheology asks whether there might be an integrated approach that incorporates the spiritual and the biological. While the exact nature of such a final relationship is unknown until it may or may not be determined, neurotheology asks us to be open to all perspectives.

Neurotheology also recognizes that concepts such as consciousness and mind may yield similar problematic challenges for neuroscience. In fact, it may be through the exploration of consciousness from a spiritual perspective that neuroscience may best try to uncover its mysteries.

Mind and meaning-making

It is important to realize that the mind and brain help us to make meaning about the world around us, as well as about who we are as human beings and how we relate to the world. As we discussed in Chapter Two (*Body, mind, and soul* section), *mind* is a term preferred by empirical science that arose with modern philosophy, with emphasis on consciousness.[1] Science provides important approaches to understanding the world that can help us develop disciplines such as physics, chemistry, and biology that have produced amazing technological breakthroughs into the twenty-first century. On the other hand, science often falls short of dealing with the human condition, particularly ways of alleviating human suffering and the many ways that human beings engage in destructive behaviors both for themselves as individuals and for humanity. For example, it is one thing for science to help us understand how we might affect the climate. Still, science does not give us a clear answer on how humans should effectively approach the problem of climate change, accounting for economic, social, and political aspects of human life.

Religion provides guidance and meaning to help humanity understand how best to manage individual and communal affairs. One problem is that there are many different religions with different perspectives for solving such matters. A broader concern is to integrate the meaning and purpose that religion can evoke with science and technology that can help effectively connect to the physical world.

Neurotheology encourages exploration of these issues to understand how meaning and purpose in life can be engaged theologically, philosophically, spiritually, and religiously, as well as scientifically. From a Catholic perspective, *science* as the exploration of the physical universe could be integrated in a valuable but limited way; s*cience* as a rationally organized approach to knowledge could contribute more comprehensively.

Bridge for theology and science

With these lofty goals in mind, neurotheology may be a bridge for theology and science dialogue. Neurotheology tries to understand how the human brain engages theological questions while helping us deal with a sense of self, meaning, and purpose. Theology can also help us understand how we might utilize science in ways that preserve the highest moral standing and lead to positive change for individuals and society. Neurotheology examines diverse issues to be *optimistically critical* in figuring out optimal ways of bringing together what both theology and science have to say regarding the use of our current individual and communal resources and moving into the future.

Spirituality and transcendence

Individual and communal transcendence

Individual awareness of transcendence or the "numen" has been well described by German Lutheran theologian Rudolph Otto (1869-1937). In his classic *Idea of the Holy* (1917/1958), Otto observes that the numen presents itself as *wholly Other* with a mystery that evokes a feeling of awe, humility, and bewilderment, but also fascination and a sense of contact with comforting, attractive goodness and spiritual joy (Spitzer, 2015). Major world religions attribute to a Higher Power qualities of love, beauty, familiarity, and happiness raised to perfection (Otto, pp. 36-39, 31, in Spitzer).

According to philosopher and "father of American psychology" William James (1942-1910), as well as Otto, nearly all major religions and cultures report experiences of the numen. Transcendence is not attained by human effort but initiated by the divine *wholly Other.* "When this happens, we are transformed— we no longer think that we are merely physical or material but that we are transcendent, having a soul that can only be satisfied by supreme goodness itself" (Spitzer, 2015, p. 36).

Since the experience of transcendence is mainly subjective and unmerited, it may not be possible to prove that it is objectively true. As transcendent, such an experience cannot be subjected to the scientific method, empirical testing, or deductive evidence in the way that material objects can be studied (Spitzer, 2015). Most of the world's population (84%, according to the PEW Research Center, 2012) belong to a religion, and many have had the experience of the divine presence. This means that either something inherent in human nature generates experience of transcendence, or a mysterious, holy Other exists, or both. Researchers like Otto find a relational quality in the presence of the numen, a feeling of being invited to answer, then with repeated encounters, a sense of deepening response (Spitzer, p. 49). The Transcendent operates interpersonally and engages in dialogue. Human conscience, in fact, can be understood as a form of dialogue between human interiority and a transcendent searcher of hearts. Conscience as intuited moral rightness can be understood as derived from values inherent in human nature (p. 94).

Scholar of the cross-cultural history of religions, Mircea Eliade (1907-1986), found that most people around the world and over the centuries experience the sacred. They express religious experience through culture in myths and rituals, symbols, and communities. These become vehicles of communal connection with the transcendent (Spitzer, 2015). Eliade supports and expands Otto's contention about the individual experience of the transcendent, showing that communal expression is associated with religion. Regarding Catholicism, we addressed rituals in Chapter Seven.

The desire for ultimate truth, goodness, and beauty

Human consciousness points to the Transcendent in that our search for truth, goodness, and beauty is never satisfied. There is always more to desire and seek. Some neuroscience researchers call this the "cognitive imperative" (Newberg and d'Aquili, 2008). As St. Augustine put it: "You have made us for yourself, and our hearts are restless until they rest in you" (*Confessions* I, 1). German Jesuit theologian Karl Rahner calls this a *transcendent horizon* against which we measure whatever we may attain of truth, goodness, or beauty. According to Rahner:

> The experience of self and the experience of God, first, constitute a unity. For when, as subject, we see ourselves as *transcendental,* this transcendental subject is absolutely different from (what) we mean when we speak of *God.* Even the most radical truth of self-experience recognizes that we are finite, even though, in its sheer transcendentality, (we contain) an absolute orientation toward the infinite and the incomprehensible (Rahner, 1975, *Theological Investigations* XIII, pp. 124-129, in Lehmann, Raffelt, and Egan, 2000, p. 222).

Canadian Jesuit philosopher Bernard Lonergan (1904-1984), like Rahner, observed that humans have an immeasurable desire to look for causation and to know everything about everything. Even a child asks Why? and expects a real, correct, intelligible answer. We have a sense of the overall intelligibility of reality. There is an implicit awareness that the whole of reality can be known. Lonergan started with contingency. There must be:

> an explanation that goes beyond anything and everything we can imagine or know by correctly understanding all the data of sense and consciousness. (There must be One) whose existence grounds the intelligibility of being (but who is not) tangible, visible, or measurable. He is the first agent and final cause, the Creator of heaven and earth, of all that is seen and unseen. (Hefling, 1988, pp. 134-135)

Humans seek not only perfect intelligibility at the level of truth and being, the ultimate cause of the whole of reality, but we also pursue transcendent goods like love, moral goodness or justice, and beauty. These, too, we find only imperfectly in life. From childhood to old age, we look for and seem to expect more love, goodness, and beauty than we find. It seems an obvious fact of experience that in striving and attaining even the highest achievement, it soon proves not to have been enough and does not last. Our desires, too, as Lonergan observes, point to an infinite horizon.

> The love of God actualizes the ultimate basis (of self-transcendence), the unlimited potential of our knowledge and love. The love of God that Christian Scripture describes (Mk 12:30, Rm 5:5) is God's own doing. Lonergan's testimony clearly is that God's love is the crux of human authenticity, the fullest flowering of human self-transcendence. It is the warmth and light poured forth into our hearts by the Holy Spirit, the Christian God, given to us and received by us. Self-transcendence and God's love structure Lonergan's discussion of religious experience. When we are in love with God, our constant going beyond has engaged with a worthy beloved. We can keep going beyond with God endlessly. There is always more light, life, and love to serve, admire, and desire. (Conn, 1988, p. 61, in Gregson, 1988)

Self-transcendent experiences

Spirituality is hard to define and is a multifaceted reality that touches on many areas of human life (Zinnbauer and Pargament, 2005). Spirituality may mean relating to the *sacred* as "a divine being, divine object, Ultimate Reality, or Ultimate Truth as perceived by the individual (Hill et al., 2000, p. 66). The sacred "may also include persons, rituals, objects, narratives, texts, times, and spaces that are set apart as special, uniquely transcendent, and other than ordinary or profane" (Schults and Sandage, 2005, p. 161).

One way to understand spirituality is to examine self-transcendent experiences. These are temporary mental states characterized by a decrease in self-salience and an increase in relationality. "Self-transcendence can be regarded as a psychological state, personality trait, developmental process, value orientation, motivation, and worldview" (Wong, 2016). Austrian psychiatrist and founder of logotherapy Viktor Frankl (1905-1997) defines self-transcendence as emphasizing helping others rather than seeking one's potential fulfillment (1966). Self-transcendence can mean pursuing ultimate or situational meaning or one's vocation to a higher purpose (Kitson et al., 2020, p. 2). Psychological theorists add to psychologist Abraham Maslow's (1908-1970) hierarchy of needs (1943), after self-actualization, a sixth need—self-transcendence—where the individual is free to expand beyond their own culture, group, or environment, and no longer depends on others' opinions. The self-transcendent person is characterized by compassion, gratitude, and awe—compassion to be open to the other in need, gratitude to acknowledge having received, and awe to enhance humility before some aspect of the transcendent (Kitson et al., p. 2).

Rahner, as we have seen, claims universally for human persons a transcendent openness to the mystery of God's self-communication, even if "unthematic" and implicit. Norwegian professor of theology Ingvild Rosok shows that Rahner's spirituality completes his transcendental theology and assures its basis in Christianity. Rahner follows St. Paul's exhortation in Phil 2: 5-11 stating that Christians need to have the kenotic, self-giving mind of Christ, to surrender by (Ignatian) indifference, readiness to do the will of God, and grace-enabled loving self-giving surrender whatever the cost (Rosok, 2011).

Experiences may be self-transcendent when they result in reduced self-importance and a sense of association with something beyond the self. Familiar occurrences that have a self-transcendent element include "mindfulness, flow, peak experiences, mystical-type experiences, and certain positive emotions, such as love and awe" (Yaden et al., 2017a, p. 1). In self-transcendent experiences, one can experience a sense of unity with others or the environment. The degree of intensity may vary from opening oneself to a beautiful concert or sunset to a feeling of oneness with the universe. On the other hand, there are negative, pathological experiences of self-loss that can be diagnosed as disorders such as depersonalization. Still, remarkably positive self-transcendent peak or mystical experiences can have notable affirming, enduring influence on well-being and promote selflessly generous behavior for prolonged periods (Griffiths et al., 2008; Yaden et al., 2017a). Self-transcendence is essential to spirituality.

Qualities and measures of self-transcendence

Spirituality is understood to be more elemental than religion and to be associated with a sense of connectedness to self, others, the world, and a Higher Power (i.e., Fisher, 1997; O'Murchu, 2008; Hay and Nye, 1998; Tracy, 2000, 2003; Bosacki, 2001; Elton-Chalcraft, 2002). Likely to motivate action for justice, spirituality incorporates a sense of wholeness relating the self to the universe and others seen in their wholeness (Zohar and Marshall, 2000; Priestley, 2002). Waldman and I (ABN), in our study of spiritual awakening, found four elemental components: a sense of unity, intensity, clarity, and surrender (2016). A study by Yaden et al. (2016) associated spiritual awakening with selflessness and relation to something transcendent (Newberg and Waldman, 2018). Persons who experience self-transcendence frequently report feelings of awe, oneness with the world, a reduction in self-importance, and a growing association with essential truth (Johnstone et al., 2016). In *The Varieties of Religious Experience* (1902), William James observed that spirituality prompts an expanded range of life and power with knowledge and insight into truth that help the individual deal with the difficulties of life (Hyde, 2004).

Measuring self-transcendence, as with most aspects of spirituality or religiousness, is challenging. The experience of self-transcendence is subjective and typically requires a self-report measure. This often entails either a direct question about self-transcendence or a figure showing the relationship between self and the world, separate on one side and completely unified on the other. Since this is purely subjective, there are no objective or observable measures, and scales of self-transcendence remain subjective. An inventory approaching objectivity could involve observer reports, but even these would still actually be subjective.

Measures of self-transcendence include the "Spiritual Transcendence Scale (Piedmont, 1999), the Self-Transcendence Scale (Reed, 1991), the Adult Self-Transcendence Scale (Levenson, Jennings, Aldwin, and Shiraiski, 2005), and Temperament and Character Inventory's (TCI) Self-Transcendence Scale (Cloninger, Pryzbeck, Svrakic, Dragan, and Wetzel, 1994)" (Johnstone, 2016, p. 291). Inclination to self-transcendence may be heritable. Genetic studies found that identical twins, even separated at birth and raised apart, rate higher than fraternal twins for spiritual transcendence (Bouchard, Lykken, McGue, Segal, and Tellegen, 1990, 1999; Bouchard and McGue, 2003; Kirk, Eaves, and Martin, 1999; Kirk and Martin, 1999). Specific genes might correlate with a proclivity to spiritual transcendence "(Comings, Gonzales, Saucier, Johnson, and MacMurray, 2000; Gillespie, Cloninger, Heath, and Martin, 2003; Hamer, 2004; Lorenzi et al., 2005)" (Johnstone, p. 291).

Transcendence and neurophysiology

Neuroscience and spirituality

Although measuring self-transcendence is purely subjective, once it has been established that someone at least expresses that feeling, measures of brain function and other physiological processes can be obtained. In this way, objective measures can be correlated with the subjective measures reported by the individual.

In *Varieties of Religious Experience* (1902), philosopher and psychologist William James held that spiritual or religious experience is not simply a form of reason but provides a unique capacity and range of power (1977, p. 64). Spiritual experience empowers the individual to problem-solve in the challenges of life. Mystical states offer insight into truth otherwise not fully comprehended and carry a sense of credibility for future application (Hyde, 2004).

There has been some effort to find a particular "God spot" in the brain. The Center for Brain Circuit Therapeutics at Brigham and Women's Hospital, Boston, recently developed a strategy for demonstrating cognitive neural systems: *lesion network mapping*. The technique uses brain imaging to illustrate the cerebral connectome (the system of neural pathways considered collectively) to find out how lesions or injuries in one brain area impact a circuit of functioning in other areas. Neuroscientist Michael Ferguson, who developed lesion network mapping, explains that "It is like a string of lights where one bulb is loosened, and the whole string goes out" (Yasinski, 2021, p. 1).

Ferguson and colleagues recently published research (*Biological Psychiatry*) showing that the periaqueductal gray (PAG) area in the brain stem, which regulates breathing and heart rate, balance, coordination, fear conditioning, and pain modulation, also appears to be associated with spirituality and religion. Their study involved 88 patients prepared to undergo brain tumor removal who were asked about their religion and spirituality. Patients whose tumors involved the PAG reported either an increase or decrease in religion or spirituality. This was a novel insight supporting the conjecture that specific areas of the brain may be associated with spirituality and religion (Yasinski, 2021, p. 4).

Neuroimaging has shown that our spiritual and religious experiences, as well as all we experience, are tied to our neural networks (Jeeves and Ludwig, 2018). However, neuroimaging also reveals religious and spiritual perceptions and behavioral responses to be complex and multifaceted, involving the PAG but also many other brain networks working together. Since the body is closely connected to the brain, and mental states encompass a mysterious dimension beyond neurons, it would seem more accurate to say that the whole human person is spiritual or religious (Newberg, 2018b, p. 238).

The interinfluence of brain and body is bidirectional: our physical actions and behaviors have reciprocal effects on our thoughts, feelings, and convictions. With concurrent action, for example, by participating in the Eucharist, thought and belief are likely to be reinforced and to express more than is said in the rite (Jeeves and Ludwig, 2018).

Clinical applications of spirituality

Spirituality and religion have been found to have a neuroprotective effect against depression possibly. Psychiatrist and epidemiologist Myrna Weissman began in 1982 a study of 220 patients diagnosed with major depressive disorder. She administered to patients and matched controls regular surveys about activities likely to avert depression or relapse, including giving high importance to religion. Over several decades, she recruited the patients' descendants into the study. The researchers in the 2010s looked for differences in the brains of those who did or did not accord importance to religion. They conducted MRI scans of 106 of the children and grandchildren of the original cohort. Participants who considered religion important were found to have less cortical neuronal thinning in areas of the brain, which would indicate a risk of depression. Results showed a correlation between ascribing importance to religion and a lower incidence of depression (Yaskinski, 2021, p. 4).

According to studies in the U.S., 50-90% of possible subjects have experienced events capable of resulting in posttraumatic stress disorder (PTSD), while only about 8% of the population develops PTSD. It is not the stressors by themselves that lead to traumatic symptoms (Peres et al., 2007, p. 344). Clinical findings suggest that persons who develop PTSD have difficulty integrating the traumatic experience into a coherent narrative. PTSD treatment involves working through symptoms by synthesizing sensorial fragments in a cognitive account. Spirituality helps to promote resilience in survivors (Peres et al., p. 343).

Neuroscience suggests that the brain stores sensory fragments or information rather than full memories. When an event is retrieved, the event may not be fully factual, but each time the event is recalled, the event may be cognitively or emotionally altered. Brain scans of PTSD patients show reduced hippocampal volume and reduced left-hemisphere activation. Low activation was also found in the medial prefrontal cortex, anterior cingulate, prefrontal, dorsolateral cortex, and Broca's area. Increased activation was found in the emotional centers of the brain, such as the amygdala, consistent with a strongly negative emotional response (Bremmer, 2002; Hull, 2002, in Peres et al., 2007, p. 345).

It is thought that the hippocampus makes a cognitive map to categorize information associated with other autobiographical data to play a meaningful role in learning, integrating, and assessing information (Peres et al., 2007). Reduced hippocampal volume and activation may account for PTSD dissociation and problems with labeling memories and even new experiences with strong negative emotions (Gilbertson et al., 2002). PTSD models show increased amygdala activation that results in heightened fear (Hull, 2002). The prefrontal and anterior cingulate cortices provide cognitive integration and project to the amygdala for emotional memory and to the thalamus and temporal structures for long-term memory (Barbas, 2000). Reduced prefrontal cortical activation may inhibit cognitive integration and normal obstruction of negative amygdala signals. This would result in diminished fear and emotion regulation, as seen in PTSD symptoms (Nutt and Malizia, 2004, in Peres et al., 2007, p. 345).

Closely related to adequately functioning cognitive integration in the frontal cortices is the *sense of coherence* (SOC) (Antonovsky, 1987). SOC is in place when its three dimensions are active: (1) comprehensibility that life and its incidents together make rational sense; (2) meaningfulness, that life makes sense emotionally so that difficulties can be understood as surmountable challenges; (3) manageability: that one has resources to address the trials of life. SOC was found to correlate strongly with the perception of better physical and mental health (Eriksson and Lindstrom, 2006). Victims of trauma who develop resilience in perceiving and processing the experience typically find it easier to address PTSD symptoms (Peres et al., 2007). Trauma victims improve through recalling experiences where they demonstrated resilience, survived the event, and profited in some way from having passed through adversity (p. 346).

Spirituality and religion are based on personal responses to a search for understanding ultimate questions of life and meaning. Developing reasonable narratives that involve cognitive reprocessing based on a big-picture, ultimate questions, and spiritual or religious perspectives may help to integrate sensory fragments and reduce traumatic symptoms effectively (Peres et al., 2007, p. 343). Spiritual practices and experiences involve many of the brain structures mentioned above regions associated with PTSD. Thus, neuroscience further supports the benefits of spiritual and religious approaches.

Interpersonal neurobiology

Interpersonal neurobiology (IPNB), a relatively new interdisciplinary domain named by clinical professor of psychiatry Daniel Siegel, looks at ways that relationships across the lifespan shape the structure and function of the human brain. Central to IPNB is a focus on the reciprocal association of attachment patterns and neural systems. "The brain is a dynamic interpersonal system: just as neurons are constituted by their ongoing synaptic connections with other neurons, so too are brains continually being formed and reformed through ongoing interactions with other brains" (Hollingsworth, 2008, p. 841).

Specific brain structures and networks, specifically the prefrontal cortex and limbic system, are key to the interactions that involve neurobiology, relationships, and personality. While psychologist Louis Cozolino (*Neuroscience of Human Relationships*, 2006) concentrates on social connections among brains, Siegel emphasizes that the human mind is "a process that regulates the flow of energy and information" (2007, p. 5) both neurobiologically within the body and interpersonally (2006, p. 248). "The mind is said to emerge at the dynamic interface of embodied and relational processes, placing relationships at the heart of the human experience of reality" (Hollingsworth, 2008, p. 842).

Social relationships rely on important brain structures. External sensory and internal emotional data are synthesized through the orbital medial prefrontal cortex (OMPFC) to impact perception and interaction by connecting outside information with motivation and reward networks. The hypothalamus associates conscious experience with processes like hunger, thirst, and aggression. The hippocampus organizes emotional and spatial sequential memory and learning. Fear responses are mediated by the amygdala, which quickly evaluates and reacts to threats or dangers. The limbic system's cingulate cortex facilitates empathy, social cooperation, and longstanding emotional bonds. The anterior cingulate is associated with consciousness of bodily states and consideration of affective experiences. These key brain structures connected with the sensory, motor, and emotional networks, as well as additional cortical and subcortical areas, comprise the social brain (Cozolino, 2006, pp. 51-57, in Hollingsworth, 2008, p. 843).

Internal working attachment models are shaped by early caregiver experience. IPNB focuses on attachment patterns that may be secure or insecure. A secure relational style is likely to evidence empathy, optimistic expectations, emotional and behavioral self-regulation, and a facility for coherent life narratives. Insecure styles manifest in difficulties with emotional regulation, problems with long-term goal attainment, brief and inconsistent life narratives, challenges with memory and planning, feelings of internalized shame, and struggles with empathic perspective-taking.

The amygdala quickly and powerfully evaluates internal and external circumstances and activates autonomic hyperarousal long before consciousness comes online. Fear responses take their cue, generalize from past learning, and initiate anxiety based on inner and outer triggers. In social situations, the amygdala inhibits social contact with unfamiliar others until a sense of safety has been verified. Unless some intervention occurs, early-life attachment patterns are likely to endure throughout the lifespan. However, the prefrontal cortex can interact with insecure automatic reactivity, reprogramming through neuroplasticity biases from early life experience in favor of affiliation over fearful wariness. Supportive, resonant relationships at some point in life and deliberate effort to develop attentional skills can alter dysfunctional attachment in a healthier direction (Hollingsworth, 2008, p. 845).

According to IPNB, conscious attentional control through processes such as mindfulness and nonjudgmental self-reflective downregulation of automatic reactivity may contribute to neural integration. Deliberate attunement in a relaxed state to various aspects of the self may allow the generation of new synaptic linkages (synaptogenesis) and the emergence of new brain cells (neurogenesis). Interestingly, the mindfulness process that can open to attuned self-reflection is remarkably like empathic attunement to another person. "The same areas of the prefrontal cortex appear to be strengthened whether one is experiencing empathic connection with oneself or with another human being" (Wiegel, 2007; Lazar et al., 2005). For developing compassion and empathy, it appears that both intra- and interpersonal neurological resonance promote well-being (Hollingsworth, 2008, p. 846).

Neurobiological empathy and spirituality

Empathic awareness of the experience of others is a fully personal conscious activity that extends beyond biology to the spiritual dimension of the person. *Double-minded* attention is needed: minding at the same time both one's thoughts and the other's (Baron-Cohen, 2011). This double-minded attention involves two complementary dimensions—recognition of what another is thinking and feeling and an appropriate response. This process happens smoothly in the empathic person. Our personal, social, and professional relationships depend on our ability to understand and respond empathically.

Italian neuroscientist Giacomo Rizzolati and colleagues discovered mirror neurons in macaque monkeys in the 1990s. Mirror neurons in human frontal and parietal cortical areas (Cozolino, 2006) are located at the junction of emotional, visual, and motor sections. At base, mirror neurons are involved in action detection. Do they also hold the key to the empathic perception of the intentions of others? Is there a *mirror neuron system* that is essential to experiencing what others feel and responding with compassion? And do they allow us to predict what another person is likely to do, acting as virtual simulations of others' intentions?

At first, social science inferred that this was the case, that mirror neurons were key to empathy and social interaction. In 2012, *Perspectives in Psychological Science* published the results of a Mirror Neuron Forum where authors "debated the role of mirror neurons in action understanding, speech, imitation, and autism" (Heyes and Catmur, 2022). This forum, along with subsequent research, including professor of cognitive science Gregory Hickok's *The Myth of Mirror Neurons* (2014), found that, in fact, the contribution of mirror neurons is much more modest. Mirror neuron brain areas are active during observation and execution of action. Fewer than 10% (de Pellegrino et al., 1992) of the neurons in brain areas where mirror neurons are found have mirror properties. These areas are in the ventral premotor cortex and inferior parietal lobule, the dorsal premotor cortex, superior parietal lobule, cerebellum (Molenberghs et al., 2012), supplementary motor area, and medial temporal lobe (Mukamel et al., 2010, in Heyes and Catmur, 2022, p. 155). It is not clear that such areas constitute a system. Mirror neurons contribute to the low-level processing of perceived actions and contribute to the copying of body movement (p. 161). Mirror neurons do not contribute to high-level interpretation and do not infer actors' intentions (p. 156). The "broken-mirror" theory of autism was not supported (p. 157).

Empathy opens individuals to sharing needs, experiences, and goals. Connectivity occurs through the insula to the limbic system, which is essential for emotional processing and behavior. The superior temporal cortex encodes a visual representation of a perceived action and relays this data to the posterior parietal cortex, which encodes the kinesthetic dimension of the movement. This information is sent to the inferior frontal mirror neurons. In this way, the visual description of the perceived action matches with the predicted consequences of the potential imitative action, and imitation can begin. The insula connects to the posterior parietal, inferior frontal, and superior temporal cortex, as well as to limbic areas, particularly the amygdala, for emotional input. "Empathic resonance occurs via the connection between action representation networks and limbic areas, provided by the insula" (Carr et al., 2003).

While mirror neurons are not as influential in understanding and interpreting others as once thought, relationality through interpersonal neurobiology plays an important role in spirituality. Resonance in interpersonal neurobiology occurs through synchrony between the right temporoparietal junctions of both participants, including subcortical structures such as the amygdala, insula, and anterior cingulate medial frontal cortex (Schore, 2021).

Spirituality usually touches on existential matters that may be expressed in coherent narratives. Prominent in sacred rites is storytelling, a central means of neural integration.

> Because narratives require the participation of multiple structures throughout the brain, they require us to combine, in conscious memory, our knowledge, sensations, feelings, and behaviors. In bringing together

multiple functions from diverse neural networks, narratives provide the brain with a tool for both emotional and neural integration. (Cozolino, 2006, p. 304, in Hollingsworth, 2008, p. 852)

Through the neural integration of IPNB, spirituality opens participants to themselves and the sacred. The empathy and compassion involved in IPNB are likely to occur in safe, trust-based relationships. Such an environment is typically characteristic of the expression and experience of spirituality.

Physiology of transformative experiences

Transformative spiritual awakening experiences include thoughts, feelings, and behaviors associated with brain areas that relate to emotions and a sense of self as closely connected to the universe or God (Newberg and Waldman, 2018). Recent research emphasizes that the brain works as a unified whole, with systems or networks contributing to perceptions, thoughts, and feelings (Ledoux, 1998). Cognitions involving memory, concepts, and awareness of causality implicate the frontal and temporal lobes. Sensory experiences engage the visual, auditory, tactile, and olfactory areas projecting to the thalamus somatosensory cortex and include memory regions (Newberg and Waldman, 2009). Emotional areas incorporate limbic structures like the hippocampus and amygdala, the insula, and larger cortical systems (Touroutoglou, Hollenbach, Dickerson, and Feldman Barrett, 2012; Feldman Barrett, 2017). Since spiritual experiences often extend throughout the body, the autonomic nervous system is involved in regulating heart rate, blood pressure, respiration, and other physiological functions (Newberg and Iversen, 2003; Newberg and Waldman, 2018, p. 120).

We have noted that spiritual experience, when it is self-transcendent, involves reduced self-salience, a loss of the sense of self. Since the sense of self as well as self-orientation in space registers, particularly in the right parietal lobe, spiritual transcendence is likely to involve reduced parietal activation, particularly in the right inferior parietal lobe (Johnstone, 2016). Such changes in the parietal lobe have been observed in neuroimaging studies of intense spiritual practices.

Interestingly, while transcendent experiences affect transformation to some degree, they may also paradoxically include an enhanced sense of self. Significant spiritual experiences almost uniformly lead to changes for the better. Research shows that most by far (95-97%) of people surveyed reported an overall improvement in relationships, their sense of calling, health, purpose and meaning in life, and sense of spiritual or religious beliefs (Newberg and Waldman, 2018, p 126). Only 3-5% of those surveyed indicated a worsening in relationships, in their work, or regarding their sense of spirituality or religion.

Neuropsychology explains scientifically how selflessness is processed in the brain during spiritual experiences. Religions emphasize the value of selflessness to relate to a higher power or to deepen understanding of the meaning of life. Faith traditions foster selflessness as necessary for salvation as well as being an admirable human quality (Johnstone, 2016).

Researchers offer at least one reason why spiritual experiences may be transformative. The cerebral emotional and memory centers are in the temporal lobes. Heightened temporal-lobe activity in the emotional limbic system links to the hippocampus, which is essential in recording experiences in memory. Zohar and Marshal hold that a spiritual experience, even one lasting only a few seconds, can intensely activate the hippocampus, registering a strong, enduring, possibly lifelong emotional impact. This may partially account for the sometimes life-transforming quality of spiritual experience (Hyde, 2004, p. 45).

When spiritual experiences are emotionally strong, the limbic structures encode them in long-term memory, assuring that they may be recalled intensely and clearly. While the limbic system facilitates the perception of emotions, the insula, a cortical structure, appears to help with the interpretation of emotions. Meditation and prayer have been found to activate the insular system (Newberg, 2018b, p. 100). Neurotransmitters that affect the emotional intensity of positive spiritual experiences include dopamine, which registers reward feelings in the basal ganglia as well as the limbic system. Dopamine is thought to be instrumental in short-term reward, and serotonin in the long-term aftermath of the experience (p. 101).

With heightened activation of the brain's emotional centers, the limbic system, basal ganglia, and the higher cortical cognitive centers reduce their activation. This may account for the difficulty in describing spiritual experiences and their seeming to transcend rationality. After the experience, the person may regain their cognitive acuity and try to understand what happened, likely according to their established beliefs (Newberg, 2018b, p. 102).

Theological dimensions of spirituality

Awareness of the presence of God

Canadian neuropsychologist Michael Persinger found that stimulating the temporal lobe could elicit a *sensed presence*. This was thought to demonstrate that religious experiences are only neurochemical biological phenomena (1987, p. 4). Some claimed that this meant that mental states are localized to the brain. A problem with this idea is that although activation of parts of the brain can evoke artificial perception, it is unclear how this relates to genuine feelings since mental states typically connect to the real world and to meaning

(Jastrzebski, 2018). Conflating artificial, exteriorly stimulated perception with mental states represents a category of confusion. Neurons that generate thoughts are in the brain; the thoughts themselves do not have a location or occupy space (Edwards, 1997 in Hyde, 2004, p. 47).

Research in neurotheology offers the advantage of demonstrating that spirituality is embodied in human biology. "Functional brain imaging is making it increasingly clear that our religious and spiritual experiences, like all our experiences, are grounded in neural networks within our brains" (Jeeves and Ludwig, 2018, p. 136). At the same time, they are not entirely equivalent to neural effects. Religious and spiritual experiences must incorporate mental states that, while connected to neural networks, include a dimension perceived to be independent of the brain.

Theologically, spirituality is understood as the conscious experience of the presence of God rather than focusing on an inner, private soul sequestered from the social, external world. Spirituality begins with the activity and communication of the person with the world in conjunction with the spirit of God (Brown and Strawn, 2017).

Christian self-transcendence

We have noted that spirituality emphasizes self-transcendence—diminishment of self-salience and connection with others, the universe, and God. The Fall of Adam and Eve showed humans created in the image of God to be fallible in attempting to be like God on their own. Theologically speaking, humans become like God by accepting in faithful obedience the free divine offer of spiritual incorporation into God's incarnate Son. "A Christian must become selfless, giving self wholly to Jesus without reservation. Here, selflessness represents divine, unconditional, voluntary, and self-sacrificing love. The core point is that in Christianity, one's self-abandonment is critical" (Johnstone et al., 2016, p. 295). Christians choose to imitate Christ's self-emptying: "who being in the form of God, did not count equality with God as something to be grasped. But he emptied himself" (Ph 2: 6-7).

Christian self-transcendence, as we have seen, also has a communal dimension. Regarding the personal religious encounter with the divine, while thinking impacts action, action reciprocally influences thinking. Participation in the Eucharist, for example, as well as in prayer, sacraments, sacramentals, and religious practices, engages the body in influencing "thoughts, feelings, beliefs, and future behavior" (Jeeves and Ludwig, 2018, p. 141). Belief and worship with concurrent activity are likely to be formative for both the individual and the Christian community (Brown and Strawn, 2012).

Application to Catholic spirituality

The Christian tradition has generally spoken about spirituality as the variety of ways Christians strive to live their faith more devotedly. Some choose to follow an established school of spirituality or ecclesial movement (Cunningham, 2006). Originally, the term *spiritual* associated spirituality with the Holy Spirit (Rupnik, 2000, pp. 8-9. Irenaeus notes that "Men are spiritual by participation in the Spirit" [*Adv. Haer.* 5.6.1]). "There is no situation and no place which could not be *spiritual* because the Holy Spirit creates, penetrates, maintains, and sanctifies everything" (Kohut, 2012, p. 157).

In his book *What Makes Us Catholic?* (2003), theology professor Thomas Groome contends that "Catholicism does not *have* spirituality. Rather, it *is* spirituality" (Fox, 2004). He points to central components such as Catholic optimism, an incarnational perspective centered on Jesus, a sense of awe, the sacredness of life, gratitude, and fundamentally God's unconditional love and forgiveness (Fox). Following St. Paul's admonition to "be transformed by the renewing of your minds, so that you may discern what is the will of God: what is good and acceptable and perfect" (Rm 12:2), Catholic spirituality is sacramental. Participation in the mystery of Jesus through the Holy Spirit leads to growth in grace and spiritual maturity (Kohut, 2012).

Originally, spirituality meant a specific lifestyle pursued by a group of Christians. Over the centuries, it has evolved into the pursuit of a perspective and mode of spiritual life often outlined by religious institutes (orders and congregations) or ecclesial movements that follow specific spiritualities. The lifestyles of religious institutes were designed to relive some aspect of Jesus' earthly life through a charism or specific grace of the Holy Spirit. The charism works with human collaboration in historical circumstances and is passed on to others.

Catholic secular clergy and laypeople may not belong to a clearly defined and structured school or movement of spirituality, but they nevertheless have a spirituality. Their spirituality might be considered a form of *popular piety*, authentic and fruitful. It is likely, as is all spirituality, to need regular, consistent renewal (Kohut, 2012, p. 161). Religious institutes of men and women today include lay associates who, without taking vows, share in the spirituality of the founding charism. Religious orders and congregations with apostolates in colleges and universities, such as the Holy Cross Associates and Jesuit Volunteers, train graduates to engage short-term in missionary work. An increase in scholarly interest in spirituality has led to college and university programs in spirituality, some with graduate-level programs to train retreat leaders and spiritual directors. The Society for the Study of Christian Spirituality, for example, maintains a *Spiritus* journal. Its book *Minding the Spirit* (2005) clarifies methodologies, boundaries, and issues in the field of spirituality (Cunningham, 2006, p. 15). Spirituality returns in this way to the search for meaning and coherence within the parameters of Catholic belief and life. Catholic spirituality extends fundamental practices of participation in Liturgy and adherence to the creed to a variety of other expressions of spiritual life.

Since Catholic spirituality derives from grace—the action of the Holy Spirit—to which the human person responds, spirituality would seem to emerge from the mysterious dimension of the soul (intellect and will) where God communicates with the person. Neurophysiologically, several regions of the brain would seem to play an active, subordinate role in receiving and responding to divine grace. Only a few applications are suggested here, but there could be many more.

Spirituality can refer to the pursuit of self-transcendence through developing a spiritual life. Self-transcendence as meaning-making and a sense of coherence are linked to neural integration through narrative. Foundational for Catholic spiritual life is the strengthening of faith through narrative in the form of revelation as found in Scripture. "Faith comes through hearing" (Hb 11:1). Neurobiologically, receptivity to spoken or written Scripture engages auditory and visual sensory systems and projections to frontal cortices for interpretation. Proclamation of the Word of God involves receptive and expressive language systems.

Catholic theology attributes all expression of spirituality to divine initiative: "Not that we loved God, but that he loved us" (1 Jn 4:10). "There are different kinds of spiritual gifts but the same Spirit; there are different forms of service but the same Lord; there are different workings but the same God who produces all of them in everyone" (1 Co 12:4-11). Spiritualities are understood to derive from grace. Either in a religious institute or a lay movement, the pursuit of Catholic spirituality, at least to some degree and with varying emphases, prefers poverty and simplicity of life to wealth, purity and singleheartedness to sensuality, and obedience to self-promotion.

Contemplative spiritualities lived in enclosed communities, such as the Carthusians, Carmelites, and branches of the Benedictines, Dominicans, Poor Clares, Missionaries of Charity, and other institutes, give primacy to prayer in Eucharist, Liturgy of the Hours, spiritual reading, and meditation. Most other religious institutes are active-contemplative or institutes of apostolic spirituality. They also give priority to prayer with required daily hours for the Eucharist, parts of the Liturgy of the Hours, particularly Morning and Evening Prayer, or other prescribed community prayers, spiritual reading, and meditation.

Apostolic institutes are charged by the Church with specific ministries that serve the needs of the Church and the world, according to their charisms—diversity of gifts of the Spirit.

Catholic spirituality grows and develops with appreciative acknowledgment of the mystery of Jesus, incarnate and "put to the test in the same way as ourselves, apart from sin" (Hb 4:15), himself once subject to human cerebral limitations. The doctrine of redemption gives space and meaning for moral failures to be healed and restored through the sacramental system founded in the Paschal Mystery of his death, resurrection, and ascension. The goal of Catholic spirituality, including its neurophysiological components, is "to mature to the full measure of the stature of Christ" (Eph 4:13).

Spirituality as theological discipline

Spirituality in Catholicism also refers to an independent theological discipline. Spiritual theology evolved from what was called the *mystical problem.* Controversy about theology around the issue resulted in gravitation to three schools based in religious institutes: Dominican, Jesuit, and Carmelite, and led to a new academic department: *ascetical and mystical theology.* The first theological department for this new field opened in Rome at the Jesuit *Gregoriana* University in 1919 and at the Dominican *Angelicum* in 1920. About twenty years later, the two branches merged into the discipline of *spiritual theology.* Spiritual theology, based on biblical revelation and authentic Christian experience, systematically explores human union with God in Christ effected through the Holy Spirit in Church and world history, involving human collaboration with its development and individuality (Kohut, 2012, p. 161). Spirituality as a field investigates spiritual life and lifestyle theologically.

Spirituality, as we saw, can refer to schools for living Catholic life more intensely, derived from established religious institutes such as Jesuit or Carmelite or engagement in movements such as the Legion of Mary. Here, interpersonal neurobiology is prominent. Brain regions associated with trust-based safe-space-making for spiritual development, expression, and communication involve the orbitofrontal prefrontal cortex, hypothalamus, cingulate cortex, anterior cingulate, insula, amygdala, and prefrontal cortex. The mirror neuron system may play an important role in spiritual community life and spiritual growth through virtue. Transcendent experiences are likely to engage cognitive and emotional brain centers, higher cortical areas, the limbic system, the insula, and the basal ganglia.

Catholic spiritualities

There are many schools of Catholic spirituality developed over more than 2,000 years; we can only cover highlights here. Arguably, the most significant schools of Catholic spirituality derived from established religious institutes are: "Basilian, Augustinian, Benedictine, Dominican, Franciscan, Carmelite, Jesuit, Oratorian, Salesian, Vincentian, Passionist, and Redemptorist" (Kohut, 2012, p.

160). Primary saints and spiritual leaders who represent the various schools of spirituality include:

Patristic (Ss. Athanasius, Augustine, Gregory of Nyssa, and Dionysius the Areopagite), Monastic (Ss. Benedict, Bernard of Clairvaux, Hildegaard of Bingen, and Cecile Bruyère), Mendicant (Ss. Dominic, Catherine of Siena, Francis of Assisi, Bonaventure, and Angela of Foligno), Spanish Mysticism (Ss. John of Avila, Ignatius of Loyola, Teresa of Avila, and John of the Cross), French School of Spirituality (Cardinal Bérulle, Ss. Louis de Montfort, Thérèse of Lisieux, and Elizabeth of the Trinity), and Contemporary from Middle and Eastern Europe (Ss. Faustina Kowalska, Teresa Benedicta of the Cross [Edith Stein], Maximilian Kolbe, Teresa of Calcutta, and Pope John Paul II). (Avila Institute)

Basilians: One of several monastic communities (Byzantine rites) that follow the Rule of St. Basil (330-379), the theologian and archbishop of Caesarea in Cappadocia (modern Turkey). Their motto is "Teach me goodness, discipline, and knowledge" (Psalm 119). Basilians live in a community under obedience with hours of liturgical prayer, manual and mental work, and care for the poor. The Congregation of St. Basil was founded in 1822 by ten secular priests in France, with St. Basil as patron. They live in the community and minister in Christian education, teaching, and evangelization.

Augustinians: In 1244, Pope Innocent IV united several communities of hermits in Italy and gave them the rule of St. Augustine. Their motto is "One heart and one soul in God." A mendicant order, they wear a black habit. Augustinian spirituality means essentially applying charity to daily living (Downey, 1993). Characteristics of the order include communal living of the Gospel and liturgy, search for God and interiority with a focus on the Trinity, the image of God, grace, Christ Mediator and Physician, apostolic activities according to the needs of the Church, and cultivation of intellectual life. Notable members are St. Augustine, Ruysbroeck, St. Rita of Cascia, Gregory of Rimini, Walter Hilton, and Luis de Leon.

Benedictines: Founded in 529 by St. Benedict of Nursia in Italy, their motto is "Pray and work." In a monastic order, they wear a black or white habit. The God of St. Benedict is sovereign, and the monk responds with reverence, humility, and obedience (Downey, 1993). Characteristics include prayer and daily manual work, community life, and obedience as discernment of God's will. Notable saints include St. Benedict, St. Scholastica, and St. Gregory the Great. Benedictines balance devotion to God and attending to the needs of self, community, and the world. The daily rhythm of prayer is the Liturgy of the Hours. Benedictines developed the monastic prayer tradition of *lectio divina* (*sacred reading*), including *lectio* (reading), *meditatio* (slow prayerful rereading), *oratio* (brief prayers), and *contemplatio* (presence and communication with God).

Cistercians: Founded in 1098 by St. Robert of Solesme, St. Alberic, and St. Stephen Harding as a stricter branch of the Benedictines. Their motto is "Prayer and work." Their spiritual father is St. Bernard of Clairvaux, who entered the community in 1112. In the seventeenth century, Abbot de Rancé of La Grande Trappe monastery in Normandy enacted reforms. Trappists and Trappistines came to the United States in the late eighteenth century. A monastic order, they wear a habit of white tunic, black scapular with cowl, and black leather belt. They follow the Rule of St. Benedict, balancing prayer, reading, and work with cloister, with emphasis on silence, poverty, and simplicity. There are two observances: strict O.C.S.O. (Trappists) and more moderate O.Cist., both having had a revival of literary work. Notable members are St. Bernard of Clairvaux, Bl. Maria Gabriella Sagheddu, and Thomas Merton.

Carthusians: Founded in 1084 by St. Bruno of Cologne, their motto is "The cross is steady while the world is turning." A monastic religious order, they wear a white habit. Characteristics are contemplation, solitude, and a mixture of solitary and community life. The Carthusian liturgy is characterized by simplicity and sobriety.

Dominicans: Founded in 1216 by St. Dominic de Guzman in France, their motto is "To praise, to bless, to preach." A mendicant religious order, they wear a white habit with a rosary that hangs from the belt and a black hood. Characteristics are a communal life of prayer, study, preaching, and teaching. Notable saints include St. Thomas Aquinas, St. Catherine of Siena, and St. Albert the Great.

Franciscans: Founded in 1209 by St. Francis of Assisi in Italy, their motto is "Peace and the good." A mendicant religious order, they wear a gray/black or brown habit. Branches are Friars Minor, Friars Minor Conventual, and Friars Minor Capuchin. Characteristics are living the Gospel, following Jesus Christ, poverty, and fraternity. Notable saints include St. Francis of Assisi, St. Anthony of Padua, St. Bonaventure, St. Clare of Assisi, St. Pia of Pietrelcina, and St. Maximilian Kolbe.

Poor Clares: Founded in 1212 by St. Clare of Assisi in Italy. The second of three Franciscan orders, they take a fourth vow of enclosure. They dedicate themselves to prayer, penance, contemplation, and manual work, with strict cloister, fasts, and austerities. With moderation of the rule in 1264 by Pope Urban IV, the Order of St. Clare (O.S.C.) differentiated from the original Primitives. In 1406, St. Colette, a Franciscan abbess in France, reformed the Poor Clares to the original severity of the rule. The Capuchin Sisters from

Naples of 1538 and the Alcantarines of 1631 are also Poor Clares of strict observance.

Carmelites: Beginning as a community of hermits on Mount Carmel in Palestine, inspired by the prophet Elijah. The Rule of St. Albert, with Mary and Elijah as models, was approved in 1247. Their motto is "With zeal, I have been zealous for the Lord God of hosts." A mendicant order, they wear a brown habit and white cloak. Characteristics include contemplation and prayer, fraternity, and service. Notable saints are St. Teresa of Avila, St. John of the Cross, St. Thérèse of Lisieux, and St. Edith Stein.

Jesuits: The Society of Jesus was founded in 1540 by St. Ignatius of Loyola in France. Their motto is "For the greater glory of God." An apostolic religious order, they currently do not wear a habit. Characteristics are based on the Ignatian *Spiritual Exercises*: finding God in everything, evangelization, service, spiritual discernment, and education. Notable saints include St. Ignatius of Loyola, St. Francis Xavier, St. Isaac Jogues, St. Alphonsus Rodriguez, and St. Aloysius Gonzaga.

Oratorians: The Institute of the Oratory was founded in 1575 by St. Philip Neri in Rome. Oratorians are independent communities of secular priests and brothers under obedience but not bound by vows dedicated to prayer, preaching, and the sacraments. Their habit is a black cassock with a white collar that folds over the collar. They are associated with the Brotherhood of the Little Oratory, a confraternity of priests and laymen. Notable members are St. Philip Neri, St. Francis de Sales, St. John Henry Cardinal Newman, and Frederick William Faber.

The Congregation of the Oratory of Jesus and Mary Immaculate are called the Berullians as well as Oratorians. This congregation has some rules from St. Philip but was founded distinctly by Cardinal Pierre de Berulle and approved in 1613. The Society of Saint Sulpice was founded in 1641 by Jean-Jacques Olier to train candidates for the priesthood. John Eudes was an Oratorian before establishing the congregation of Jesus and Mary.

Salesians: Founded in 1859 by St. John Bosco in Italy, their motto is "Give me souls; take away the rest." The clerical religious congregation does not wear a habit. Salesian Sisters of St. John Bosco wear a gray habit. Characteristics include pastoral charity, joy and optimism, work and temperance, pastoral care of young people, and an asceticism of goodness. Notable saints are St. John Bosco, St. Dominic Savio, and St. Mary Mazzarello.

Vincentians: The Congregation of the Mission was founded in 1633 by St. Vincent de Paul. He launched organized charities integrating evangelization and charity to meet material and spiritual needs. Their motto is "He sent Me to bring Good News to the poor" (Lk 4:18), and their focus is "Whatever you do for the least of Mine, you do for Me" (Mt. 25:40). Their habit is a black clerical shirt. Vincentian spirituality evangelizes and is evangelized by the poor with low incomes and relies on divine providence.

Vincent's collaborator in ministry, St. Louise de Marillac, founded the Daughters of Charity in 1633, the first community of non-cloistered sisters. In 1809, St. Elizabeth Ann Seton founded the Sisters of Charity and, in 1810, established the first free Catholic school staffed by women religious for girls in need. Their motto is "The charity of Christ urges us." (2 Co 5:14). Bl. Frederic Ozanam founded the St. Vincent DePaul Society in 1833 in France for service to the poor experiencing poverty. Notable members are St. Vincent de Paul, St. Louise de Marillac, Bl. Frederic Ozanam, and St. Catherine Labouré.

Passionists: Founded by St. Paul of the Cross in 1720. "We seek the unity of our lives and our apostolate in the Passion of Jesus." A clerical religious congregation, they wear a tunic with the emblem *Jesu XPI Passio* (Passion of Jesus Christ) and traditionally wear sandals rather than shoes. They take a vow to keep the Passion of Jesus alive and mainly preach missions and retreats, engage in spiritual direction and pastoral work, social welfare projects, and education in missions.

The Sisters of the Cross and Passion were founded in 1852 by Fr. Gaudentius Rossi. Notable saints are St. Paul of the Cross and St. Gabriel of Our Lady of Sorrows. St. Gemma Galgani and St. Maria Goretti are counted for having been guided by Passionists, although both died before they could become members.

Redemptorists: Founded by St. Alphonsus Liguori in 1696 in Italy. They see God in the ordinary, serve the poor and most spiritually abandoned, work in parishes and shrines and with immigrants, and evangelize through media. Their motto is "Imitate Jesus, especially preaching the word of God to the poor." They dedicate themselves to evangelizing about Bethlehem, Calvary, the Eucharist, and Our Lady of Perpetual Help. Notable members include St. Alphonsus Liguori, St. John Neumann, and Bl. Francis X. Seelos.

Missionaries of Charity: Founded in 1950 by St. Mother Teresa in India. Their motto is "I thirst," which summarizes Mother Teresa's religious experience that God thirsts for us. They take a fourth vow to serve the poorest of the poor. The religious women wear a white sari with a blue border. Characteristics include universal love, radiating Christ, and the mystery of Jesus in the needy. Other branches are the Missionaries of Charity priests, Missionaries of Charity brothers, and Contemplative brothers and sisters.

Sisters of Life: Founded in 1991 by Cardinal John O'Connor in New York, they promote the value of human life from conception to natural death and take a fourth vow "to protect and enhance the sacredness of every human life." They wear a white habit with blue scapular. Their ministries support pregnancy, help after abortion, and end-of-life concerns.

Sisters of Notre Dame: Founded in 1850 in Coesfeld, Germany, in the spirit and rule of St. Julie Billiart by Sisters Mary Aloysia Wolbring and Ignatia Kuhling. The congregation witnesses God's goodness and provident care. They serve in 20 countries in education, pastoral care, healthcare, hospice, counseling, with people with disabilities, youth ministry, communications, daycare for older people, and missions.

Marians of the Immaculate Conception: Founded in 1631 by St. Stanislaus Papcsyznski in Poland. A clerical institute that promotes the Divine Mercy staffs the National Shrine of Divine Mercy and publishes the *Diary of St. Faustina.* They engage in evangelization, works of mercy, and prayer for the souls in purgatory. Notable members include St. Stanislaus Papczynski and Bl. George Matulaitis.

Norbertines. Founded by St. Norbert of Xanten in 1121 in France, Canons Regular of Premontre (Premonstratensians). Their motto is "To teach by word and example" to animate faith with action. They follow the rule of St. Augustine and are modeled after the Cistercians. There are also Norbertine nuns, an enclosed religious order. In 1893, Rev. Bernard Pennings, O. Praem., founded St. Norbert Abbey in DePere, Wisconsin. They wear a white habit and engage in ministries of education, parish work, broadcasting, and a center for Norbertine spirituality. Notable members are St. Norbert of Xanten, St. Evermode of Ratzeburg, and Bl. Gertrude of Aldenburg.

Catholic lay ecclesial movements, sometimes including priests, particularly since Vatican Council II, are generally more recent ways of expressing faith and spiritual life. Baptized lay Catholics organize to collaborate in catechesis, mutual support, cultural ministries, or missionary work. There is continuous growth in the number of ecclesial associations, with the International Associations of the Faithful Directory (2006) listing 122 movements. Pope John Paul II referred to a "new era of group endeavors of the lay faithful," encouraging such movements for "ecclesial communion in diversity and complementarity of charisms" (www.laic.va/content). These include Focolare, the Legionaries of Christ, Regnum Christi, Work of Schonstatt, Legio Mariae, Cursillo de Cristiandad, Marriage Encounter, Catholic Charismatics, the Sant'Egidio Community, Opus Dei, L'Arche, Light-Life, Oasis, the Neocatechumenate Way, Communion and Liberation, and new forms of religious life of men and women (Kohut, 2012, p. 160; Cunningham, 2006, p. 12).

Lay movements do not directly take on the obligations of the religious vows but follow the spirit of the evangelical counsels. They work "in the world" to be a leaven, striving to transform their ordinary work and social interaction with the light of the Gospel. There are also various cultural expressions of Catholicism, broadly, for example, northern and southern European, Irish, and Italian Catholicism in the one Church (cf. McGoldrick, *Ethnicity and Family Therapy*, 2005).

Neurobiology of spiritualities

How might the rich diversity of Catholic spiritualities in religious orders, congregations, and ecclesial movements relate to neurotheology? Some aspects of neurophysiology that might be affected by Catholic spiritualities include the periaqueductal gray (PAG) area of the brain that appears to associate with spirituality and religion (Yasinski, 2021, p. 4) when networking with multiple other areas (Newberg, 2018b, p. 238). Spiritual practices and experiences that promote understanding of responses to ultimate questions of life and meaning may link to a *sense of coherence* (SOC) (Antonovsky, 1987) and cognitive functioning in the frontal cortices. Catholic theology finds in Scripture and Tradition, despite the tragedies and vagaries of life, a SOC of comprehensibility, meaningfulness, and manageability (Eriksson and Lindstrom, 2006).

For community life and multifaceted communications in ministries, interpersonal neurobiology is continually "formed and re-formed through interactions with other brains" (Hollingsworth, 2008, p. 841). Central to the neurobiology of relationships and personality are the prefrontal cortex and limbic system, the social brain regions: the orbital medial prefrontal cortex, hypothalamus, hippocampus, amygdala, cingulate cortex, and cortical and subcortical sensory, motor, and emotional networks (Cozolino, 2006, pp. 51-57; Hollingsworth, 2008, p. 843).

The mirror neuron system, as we have seen, attunes the brain to others' emotional states and promotes empathy, kindness, and altruism (Cozolino, 2006, p. 59). Double-minded attention keeps in mind both one's own, and another's likely thoughts and feelings (Baron-Cohen, 2011), supporting the emergence of spirituality (deSouza, 2014, p. 48).

Interpersonal neurobiology fosters coherent narratives that help to integrate "knowledge, sensations, feelings, and behaviors" (Cozolino, 2006, p. 304), using stories to make sense of life and promoting spiritual development. For Catholics, the Incarnation and Redemption achieved through the Second Person of the Trinity, particularly through his death, resurrection, ascension, and sending of the Spirit, are the central narratives that give coherence and meaning to otherwise incomprehensible dimensions of human life, such as suffering, evil, and death, showing that in the end Love wins.

Spiritualities, being self-transcendent with reduced self-salience, are likely to involve reduced right parietal-lobe activation (Johnstone et al., 2016). Yet paradoxically, enhanced selflessness strengthens the sense of self toward spiritual and human maturity (Newberg and Waldman, 2018, p. 126; Johnstone et al., 2016). Prayer and meditation are central to Catholic spiritualities and may foster enduring memories of spiritual experience through activation of the hippocampus, with reinforcing neurotransmitters dopamine and serotonin (Newberg, 2018, p. 101). Following the spiritual experience, whether through sacraments, interpersonal interaction, or otherwise, the person is likely to try to understand the experience according to their beliefs (Newberg, 2018, p. 102).

Some key theological tenets of Catholicism support the interaction of the mind with other minds and with the environment. Likely to affect Catholic perception, cognition, emotion, and behavior are:

- the constant presence of the omnipotent, omniscient God;

- the continually renewed creation of the universe;

- the eternal exchange of life and love among the Persons of the Trinity;

- the ongoing creation of the human person made in the image of God with physiological neurobiological apparatus plus mysterious spiritual capacities of intellect and will, identity, consciousness, and decision-making;

- God's providential attention to both the course of history and the smallest details of life;

- the redemptive self-offering of Christ in the Paschal Mystery;

- the divine Indwelling of Father, Son, and Spirit in the soul;

- divine initiative in conferring grace—participation in divine life sanctifying the person and providing moment-by-moment practical assistance;

- the efficacy of prayer to affect with divine power the course of human events;

- the work of the Spirit in bestowing charisms and working actively to bring human persons along with creation to an eternal heavenly kingdom of life and love.

Catholic spiritualities begin in the communication of the person with the world in conjunction with the Spirit of God (Brown and Strawn, 2017). The communication of the person component likely has a variety of neurophysiological correlates that can help understand how that communication is perceived and incorporated into a person's life. Further, we would expect unique neurophysiological patterns associated with the different spiritualities in

Catholicism—a potentially fascinating direction for future neurotheological scholarship.

Study Questions

1. What are some qualities of spiritual experience?
2. How might Damasio's semantic marker hypothesis apply to spiritual experience?
3. What is distinct about interpretation and memory of spiritual experience?
4. What do subcortical predominance and whole-brain processing have to do with spiritual experience?
5. Which neurotransmitters appear to be associated with spiritual experience?
6. How does Catholicism explain how human persons can think and decide, as well as experience sensation, imagination, and emotion?
7. What is meant by a unified field theory regarding religious experience?
8. What is meant by individual and communal experience of transcendence?
9. How do Rahner and Lonergan characterize the human search for transcendence?
10. What is meant by self-transcendent experiences?
11. What are some qualities and measures of transcendence?
12. What do lesion network mapping and the PAG contribute to the association of neuroscience with spirituality?
13. What have been the clinical applications of spirituality as it relates to depression and PTSD, particularly regarding SOC and ultimate-questions perspectives?
14. What does IPNB, including inner-working attachment models, contribute to understanding the connection between relationality and neuroscience?
15. How does neurobiological empathy, including mirror neurons to some degree, associate with spirituality?
16. What are the physiological characteristics of transformative spiritual experiences, particularly regarding sense of self and emotionality?
17. What is the problem with evoking spiritual experience by stimulating a brain region?
18. How does theology understand spirituality?

19. Why is self-transcendence, both individual and communal, essential to Christian spirituality?

20. What are the characteristics of Catholic spirituality?

21. What may be included in the theological discipline of spirituality?

22. What brain areas may be involved in the practice of spirituality?

23. What are some schools of Catholic spirituality associated with orders and congregations, their founder, motto or charism, work, and notable saints?

24. What are Catholic lay ecclesial movements, and what are some examples?

25. Attributing Catholic spiritualities to grace and divine initiative, what are characteristics found in all, with varying emphases?

26. Distinguish contemplative from apostolic institutes.

27. How is neurobiology associated with primary elements of Catholic spiritualities?

28. What are some key Catholic theological beliefs that affect Catholic spirituality regarding perception, emotions, and behavior?

Endnotes

[1] A Catholic perspective might prefer the metaphysically and theologically based term *soul*—intellect and will. *Mind* generally refers to a power of the soul. Science today typically refers more to the *mind* than the *soul* for topics such as meaning-making.

Chapter 11

Mysticism, Catholicism, and the Brain

Neuropsychology of experience

How does neuroscience relate to mysticism? We will begin with spiritual and religious experiences and then explore mystical experiences. First, it would be useful to explore what neuropsychology means by *experience*. This is an area not yet definitively addressed by neuroscience (Johnstone, Cohen, and Dennison, 2021), but several theories have been developed. To have an experience, one must start with a *self* who does the experience. We saw in Chapter Three that the modern era (sixteenth to eighteenth centuries) in the West constituted a "turn to the subject" where the prior metaphysical and theological order of being was replaced by a primary emphasis on the individual human mind (Zagzebski, 2021, p. 67). Empirical science and political focus on autonomous self-governing individuals fell in line, and the *self*, with its unique subjectivity, attained priority (p. 18).

Neuroscientist Antonio Damasio (2010) offers a neuropsychological model that explains that experience occurs through an integrative *self* with both (1) a core self that instinctively responds to sensory stimuli processed in the brainstem and (2) an autobiographical self that integrates sensory experiences with memories.

The microgenetic theory (2015) of Jason W. Brown, a neurologist at New York University Medical School, analyzes conscious experience through phenomenological introspection. He proposes that subjective experience begins with activation of the brainstem, organized through *mid-brain pattern generators* developed with limbic-system memory and emotional significance and enhanced with neocortical sensory and motor articulation (Tucker, 2013, p. 725). Brown considers experience to involve the integration of sensory signals, memory, emotion, interpretation, and language.

German professor of psychology Julius Kuhl and colleagues suggest a model to explain experience with (1) an *integrated self* that combines cognitive, emotional, motivational, and volitional processes and (2) a *conceptual self* that thinks analytically (Kuhl et al., 2015 p. 119; Koole, 2009; Koole and Kuhl, 2007; Kuhl and Quinn, 2011). The integrated self looks for existential purpose and meaning as Swiss psychiatrist and psychoanalyst Carl Jung (1985-1961) (1969) and Austrian psychiatrist Viktor Frankl (1905-1997) (2014) describe in their psychological theories: analytic psychology and logotherapy, respectively

(Johnstone, Cohen, and Dennison, 2021). German professor of psychology Markus Quirin and colleagues (2015) found that *implicit self*-lateralized to the right anterior cortex, a neuropsychological system implicated in affect regulation, is "necessary for self-determined and mindful goal selection" and decision-making (Quirin, Frohlich, and Kuhl, 2016, Implicit Self section, para. 3).

American professor of psychology Brick Johnstone and colleagues account for *experience* through a neuropsychological model where the right hemisphere association area integrates "sensations (i.e., sight, sound, touch, taste, smell, proprioception) and mental experiences (i.e., thoughts, emotions, cognition)" into a unified *sense of self* which accounts for subjective experience (Johnstone, Cohen, and Dennison, 2021, p. 2). The sense of self can be increased, decreased, or distorted. Positive enhancement of the sense of self can foster increased empathy (Cozolino, 2006; Shamay-Tsoory et al., 2004). A negative sense of self-enhancement can lead to embarrassment, resentment, or pride. Sense-of-self impairment is associated with disorders such as schizophrenia. Conditions such as autism or sociopathy may correlate with an exaggerated sense of self to the detriment of the other. Reduced functioning of the right association cortex through injury or spiritual or religious rituals such as centering prayer can reduce cerebral blood flow to the right inferior parietal lobe (Newberg and Iversen, 2003), which can enhance neuropsychological capacity for spiritual transcendence (Barnby et al., 2015). Reduced right association area functioning has also been found to promote character traits and virtues such as willingness to forgive by reducing rumination on perceived wrongs to the self (Li and Lu, 2017). Johnstone, Cohen, and Dennison see experience as grounded in a sense of self that derives from the right association cortex integrating sensory perceptions with mental contents—thoughts, emotions, and cognitive schemas—to form subjective experience.

To summarize, a *sense of self* may be generally understood as at least an implicit sense of identity, core of subjective consciousness, and capacities for affect regulation, goal choice, and decision-making.

Considering the neurophysiology of mystical states and consciousness, how can we tell whether mystical states are not just subjective occurrences? We will explore the meaning of mystical experiences from a Catholic perspective, with reflections from neuroscience. Essential to authentic mysticism are virtue and sanctity. How might one identify an experience of grace in oneself or someone else? What neuroscientific considerations would apply? We will consider the stages that lead to a mystical union and what it is like for the one who arrives there. We will ask about the epistemology of mystical knowing. Finally, we will consider virtue and sanctity as theologian Karl Rahner and philosopher Bernard Lonergan present the experience of grace and consider the contribution of neuroscience.

Spiritual and religious experiences

Spiritual experiences are generally connected with purpose or meaning in one's life (Hodge and McGrew, 2006), psychological growth (Hall, Dixon, and Mauzey, 2004), or a relationship with a higher power (Rose, Westefeld and Ansley, 2008). Religious experiences are ordinarily associated with specific rituals and a multifaceted system of traditions (Fukuyama and Sevig, 1999; Worthington, 1989). Many scholars categorize both spiritual and religious experiences as transcendent, sacred, or mystical (e.g., Andresen, 2001; Bulkeley, 2005; Park and McNamara, 2006; Roberts, 2006). I (ABN) observe (2014) that this situates such experiences outside the realm of scientific measurement (Dixon and Wilcox, 2016, p. 92).

Spiritual, religious, or mystical experiences were studied by the Religious Experience Research Unit (1966-1985) at Oxford, England's Manchester College. The team led by marine biologist Alister Hardy (1896-1995) collected more than 4,000 personal reports of transcendent experiences. Participants recounted having been conscious of a "benevolent non-physical power which appears to be partly or wholly beyond, and far greater than, the individual self." Many experiencers indicated that they sensed a numinous presence evoking *trust, awe, joy,* or *bliss* or perceived lights, voices, or a feeling of having been touched (Beauregard, 2008, pp. 198-199). Spiritual or religious experiences have been reported around the world and throughout history. "In the Christian tradition, the Absolute is typically experienced as a Transcendent Personality, full of love and compassion, with whom one 's personality becomes temporarily merged and transformed into a similar, though finite personality" (p. 203). Interestingly, accounts of mystical experiences show notable similarities between different languages and cultures.

Neurotheology acknowledges that spiritual and religious experiences are also psychological and have important neurobiological correlates. Since transcendent experiences are subjective, personal, and emotional, they are not easy to define or measure (Newberg et al., 2005). Neurotheology, connecting transcendence and science with human experience, might make meaningful discoveries (Dixon and Wilcox, 2016). One challenge for neurotheology is to study spiritual experience using the natural sciences without inventing new concepts within mainstream research methods and reporting (Beauregard, 2008).

The connection between the brain and spiritual and religious experiences can be clinically applicable. For several decades, counselors have been encouraged to consider their clients' lives holistically, including spiritual and religious dimensions. The inclusion of clients' spiritual worldviews belongs to ethical therapeutic practice, a dimension of multicultural competence (Fukuyama and Sevig, 1999; Moodley, 2007). Neurotheology can contribute to counseling by continued research into measurable neurobiological effects of beliefs on brain function (Beauregard and O'Leary, 2008; Nelson et al., 2011; Newberg, 2014). Counseling with clients who are religious or spiritual should include a focus on understanding how their beliefs impact their symptoms and coping (Dixon and Wilcox, 2016).

For Lonergan, religious experience occurs in levels of consciousness beyond experience that take in sensate data. He situates religious experience in human intentional consciousness, on the fourth level, the transcendent fulfillment of deliberative consciousness (Rixon, 2001, pp. 490, 495). In a 1968 letter, Lonergan, responding to a question, answers that:

> While we do not in this life experience God, we do not know him apart from experience, for it is our experience of this world and of its complete intelligibility that provides the premises whence we infer his existence. (p. 489)

For Lonergan, religious experience is a "being in love with God without limits or qualifications or conditions or reservations, the proper fulfillment of the human person's unrestricted capacity for self-transcendence" (1957, pp. 105-106) (p. 490).

In my recent work (ABN), based on a survey of spiritual experiences involving approximately 2,000 respondents (Yaden and Newberg, 2022), spiritual experiences were divided into nine categories. Three were in the numinous domain—numinous, revelatory, and synchronous; four in the mystical domain—unity, self-loss, aesthetic natural, and aesthetic artistic; and two in the paranormal domain—known or unknown. This categorization revealed that *spirituality* can encompass a wide range of experiences. They may be God-oriented, numinous, or mystical in the sense of being associated with something absolute in the universe—a discrete entity, but not necessarily. There may be a supernatural component, including paranormal experiences of ghosts, demons, spirits, and so on, or numinous connections with God. Each of these experiences was considered spiritual. The term is broadly inclusive.

Mysticism: Definition

Lonergan's description of religious experience seems to approach mysticism. How is such an elusive concept defined? English writer and mystic Evelyn Underhill (1875-1991), in her classic work *Mysticism* (1911), understands it to be "the process which involves the perfect consummation of the love of God: the achievement here and now of the immortal heritage of man: the art of establishing conscious relation with the Absolute" (p. 81). Underhill insists that for the mystic, an intense point, ground, or substance of the human spirit touches the Absolute divine life that upholds reality. This finds the mystic claim for the possibility of union with God (Beauregard and O'Leary, 2008, p. 206).

What does union with God mean, to participate in God's knowing, feeling, and will? For Catholicism, theological distinctions are needed.

> God's knowledge is far different from human knowledge. When God knows something, it comes into being. His knowing is creative, not responsive like ours. God is pure subjectivity, totally transcendent to us; God is 'no-thing,' as mystics might experience in the night. Our knowledge of God comes from the effects of God that we experience: his love, forgiveness, creation, and so on. (G. Bednar, personal communication, April 23, 2023)

For Catholicism, the person who grows in faith, hope, and love responds to the divine initiative. Christ becomes key to their being and activity. They live in humble service and await the call to eternal life (McGonigle, 1993).

The social scientific study of Christian mysticism rests on two main definitions. First, union with a personal God, and secondly, a state of altered consciousness with the dissolution of self and union with a cosmic reality that may or may not be a personal God (Hood and Chen, 2013, in Lamm [ed.], p. 577).

According to scholars favoring theistic traditions like Christianity, mysticism is a direct sense of divine proximity. For Catholic mysticism scholar Bernard McGinn, mystical experience is "a special consciousness of the presence of God that by definition exceeds description and results in the transformation of the one who receives it" (1998, p. 26; Alexander, 2018, p. 296). Lacking the desire for love, there is "no adoration, no self-spending, no reciprocity of feeling between knower and Known" (Beauregard and O'Leary, 2008, p. 184). For theistic traditions—where mystics strive for union with a personal God—motivation is more than intellectual and extends to love, participation, and union; for Catholicism, it understands the theological distinctions regarding union between the Divine and human.

The second definition points instead to consciousness in an altered state, with the dissolution of self and union with a cosmic reality that may or may not be a personal God (Hood and Chen, 2013, in Lamm [ed.], p. 577). Mystical experiences seem to represent intense spiritual and religious experiences with intrinsic and transformational characteristics (Newberg, 2018b, p. 261). I (ABN) was able to aggregate mystical-experience brain-scan findings into five core attributes: intensity, clarity, unity, surrender, and a transformational effect (p. 267).

Classifications

Mystical states can be classified according to various categories: extrovertive and introvertive, dualistic and monistic, apophatic, and kataphatic. British educator, philosopher, and epistemologist Walter Stace (1886-1967) (1960) distinguished *extrovertive* from *introvertive* mystical experiences (see also Otto, 1932, pp. 57-72). Extrovertive mystical experience includes sense perception, such as awareness of the unity of the world and nature or *cosmic consciousness*. The extrovertive experience incorporates subjective merging with all that is. Introvertive experience is awareness of God or *nothingness* beyond time and space with loss of self (Hood and Chen, 2013, in Lamm [ed.], p. 587). Introvertive experience does not include differentiated content or sense perception (Jones and Gellman, 2022, p. 4). There is experimental evidence that the two types of experience (Dunn et al., 1999) result in different neurological readings that suggest different states of consciousness (Hood, 1997; Jones, 2018, p. 997).

Mystical experience may be classified as *dualistic* or *monistic*. Dualistic experience demonstrates some distinction, even if weak, between the experiencer and what they perceive. Theistic individuals typically have dualistic experiences, maintaining an ontological dissimilarity between the mystic, as a person, and God. These are common in the monotheistic traditions in which there is some profound connection with God without becoming unified with God. Monistic experiencers claim a sense of ultimate unity dissolving all distinction (Merkur, 1999), either perceiving the metaphysical oneness of everything or moving into pure consciousness (Jones and Gellman, 2022, p. 4). These are more common in traditions such as Buddhism, Daoism, and Hinduism. The mystic becomes one with ultimate reality.

Mysticism may be *apophatic* or *kataphatic*. Apophatic mystics contend that what they experience is *ineffable*, totally indescribable, and that nothing positive can be said about it. One can only say, for instance, what God is not. Typical of the Christian *via negativa* is pseudo-Dionysius the Areopagite, a Greek Christian theologian and Neoplatonic philosopher of the late fifth and early sixth century who wrote *Mystical Theology* in the apophatic theological tradition. Pseudo-Dionysius influenced the anonymous late fourteenth-century author of *The Cloud of Unknowing*. Apophatic prayer emphasizes the dissimilarity between God and any created means of representing him who can be grasped only by love (ch. 4). The human person, as open to the transcendent, opens primarily to the incomprehensible God (Egan, 1993b).

Kataphatic experience attempts to describe God or the object of the experience in positive terms, what St. Augustine called *the footprints of God*. This approach may use religious symbolism or expound the names of God. Kataphatic prayer emphasizes the similarity between God and creation. The

Spiritual Exercises of St. Ignatius of Loyola use a kataphatic method to meditate on the life of Christ (Egan, 1993a). These two styles may designate two stages in mystical life, with the apophatic usually seen as more advanced (Jones and Gellman, 2022, p. 5).

Attributes of mysticism

Mysticism is characterized by its attributes, some of the most universal being *noetic, ineffable,* and *paradoxical.* Noetic mystical experiences offer knowledge of what the experiencer perceives (see James, 2017). "Noetic quality refers to a strong sense of gaining a genuine and unmediated insight, or of encountering ultimate reality; the mystical experience, by definition, is felt to be 'more real than real'" (Letheby, 2021, p. 25).

Mystics who maintain that their experience is *ineffable,* that nothing authentic can be expressed about it, do not typically, however, have nothing to say. According to William James (2017, pp. 292-293), indescribability is an essential element of mystical experience. Even analogies, art, and metaphors must finally be found lacking (Jones and Gellman, 2022, p. 5). Since God is infinite, creatures can neither comprehend God's intrinsic nature nor adequately describe it.

Sometimes associated with ineffability is the *paradoxical* nature of mysticism. Walter Stace (1960, p. 212) considers the intended logical contradiction in any description to be a common attribute of mystical experience (Jones and Gellman, 2022, p. 6). Mystics may try to express their perception of reality using phenomenal terms, then find that they must deny what they have said. The reality beyond language and symbol comes across as paradoxical.

Neurophysiology of mystical states: Neural substrate and consciousness

Physiological aspects of mystical experiences correlate with biology, chemistry, and physics. Non-physiological dimensions like consciousness, spirituality, and the divine are not directly measurable by natural sciences. However, as we have seen, due to the hylomorphic unity of body and soul, non-physiological aspects can have a neural substrate. The thalamus, limbic system, and memory regions are engaged. The neurotransmitter dopamine contributes to determining salience. Dopamine communicates information about what objects and entities one needs to connect with or avoid (Newberg, 2018, p. 260). The limbic system generates fearful and aggressive responses. Thoughts about God as critical or vengeful are likely to activate the amygdala and project onto God a distant, authoritarian image. The anterior cingulate, between the limbic system and prefrontal cortex, alternatively predisposes to empathy, suppresses anxiety and anger, and inclines the person to acceptance and tolerance, to see God as loving (Newberg and Waldman, 2009, pp. 110-111).

Brain areas found to activate with mystical experiences include "the frontal cortex (right medial orbitofrontal, left medial prefrontal), temporal cortex (right middle temporal) and parietal cortex (right inferior and superior, left inferior) among other cortical and subcortical areas" (Dixon and Wilcox, 2016, p. 94). Neurotransmitter molecules that bind to post-synaptic serotonin receptors are currently under study. Of particular interest are neurotransmitter molecules' graded release, uptake modulation, and the number of neurons they influence. Neurotransmitters have psychoactive properties and can affect visual changes and altered states of consciousness that might include transcendent experiences. The pharmaceutical industry builds on the effects of neurotransmitter molecules on brain circuitry and their potentially lasting consequences for mental states, as do rituals of ancient religions (Anderson, 2013, in Lamm [ed.], p. 598).

Studies using fMRI to find neural correlates of mystical experience have focused on subjects' claims to have experienced the presence of God. Comparing readings with those of subjects engaged in ordinary memory tasks, researchers found for experience and recall of mystical states, activation of several regions on both sides of the brain. There are challenges, of course, in accurately interpreting brain region activations. Researchers have drawn some tentative conclusions, including that the mystical condition in brain areas is associated with subjects' sense of contacting a spiritual reality (Beauregard and Paquette, 2006, pp. 186-190; Anderson, 2013, in Lamm [ed.], pp. 600-601).

Neuroscientific research into mystical and associated states finds that the brain contributes additional modular activity to achieve altered states of consciousness.

> There are certain stable and structured or default modes called "attractor states" within which the brain functions. Because of the nature of complex systems, "very small perturbations can cause large effects or no effects at all" (Buzsaki, 2006, p. 110). (Anderson, 2013, in Lamm [ed.], pp. 601-603)

Modulation of data from the five senses plus pain and temperature constantly oscillate between excitation and inhibition, which assures stability and prepares for immediate changes in awareness and behavior. From this "progressively and unimaginably complex matrix of sculpted neural circuits" (p. 603), the mystic's perception, discipline, and maturing emerge.

As we have seen in Chapter Three on epistemology, according to Lonergan's theory, the human mind consists of an organism, psyche, and spirit. Mystical experience would derive from the psyche and among the levels of consciousness.

Mystical experience is still always associated with some aspects of the organism's neural activity. Mystical experiences, like all human experiences, are associated with neurological biochemical processes in the brain (Jones, 2018, p. 993). "All human conscious activity, religious or otherwise, has an underlying counterpart in the brain" (Sloan, 2006, pp. 247, 249, in Jones, p. 993). Science can establish that certain neural configurations correlate with mystical states; however, it cannot conclude that mystical experiences are generated by the brain alone (see Jones, 2016, ch. 4).

When neuroscience attempts to investigate mystical experiences, it comes up against the hard problem of consciousness (Chalmers, 1995). Science might be able to distinguish areas of the brain that are affected by a mystical event; capturing the mystic experience itself is something else. The lived subjective experience of qualia (experiential properties of sensations, perceptions, and feelings)—the sense of unity, selflessness, and feeling of being beyond time and space—is qualitatively different from its co-occurring neural basis (Jones, 2018, p. 1000). Science can explain neither what consciousness is nor why it exists nor how conscious experience is tied to physiological brain mechanisms. Consciousness cannot be referred directly to neurophysiological or biochemical processes.

Neuroscience could conduct neuroimaging experiments to identify differences in brain activity between listening to white noise and listening to Mozart. Still, would activation of specific brain regions explain all there is to know about these experiences? (Sloan, 2006, p. 253). There does not appear to be any way to evaluate subjective experiences with absolute accuracy from objective, third-person reports. To say that neural activity correlates with a mental state or experience does not explain what is happening. Science may observe, for example, a change in brain alpha-wave frequency; that does not mean that we understand why it occurs (Stall, 1975, p. 109, in Jones, 2018). In the same way, neuroscience studies the cerebral substructures closely related to experience; it cannot explain consciousness itself (Shear and Jevning, 1999, p. 189). As we have seen, mental states belong to philosophy and psychology.

Catholicism, as we have seen regarding epistemology, does not agree with scientific speculation that consciousness emerges solely from the sensory interaction of the brain with the environment. If that were the case, with death, consciousness, including personal identity, intellect, and will, would dissolve. A purely materialistic scientific explanation is contradicted by the revelation that humans are made in the image of God (Gn 1:27) and destined for eternal life (2 Pt 3:13). When neuroscientists study biological correlates of perceptual occurrences, even mystical ones, they do not study mystical experiences (Jones, 1986). "Measuring the spiritual or religious significance that an experiencer sees in these experiences after they are over is not measuring the experiences themselves" (Jones, 2018, p. 1003).

Consciousness may arise in an altered form as mystical awareness through spiritual training and practice, for example, through meditation—a fact supported by fMRI imaging. Research shows that meditation practices "change the architecture of the brain and thereby change how one learns, processes memory, regulates emotion, appropriates information, and understands various perspectives. Meditation can change how one knows the world, oneself, and God" (Alexander, 2018, p. 258). The practice of prayer was found to correlate with long-term neurological and epistemic changes, including one's understanding of life and one's purpose (p. 244).

Research with individuals in meditative states found that even 12 minutes of daily meditation practice is associated with increased cerebral activation of the hippocampus and frontal lobes (Newberg and Waldman, 2009). This could potentially lead to the health benefits of slowing aging and cognitive decline. It can lead to improvement in positive outlook, enhanced emotional regulation, and increased attention span (Davis and Hayes, 2011; Newberg et al., 2002; Dixon and Wilcox, 2016, pp. 101-102). Interestingly, meditation using a spiritually oriented rather than secular mantra was found to be more effective in reducing physical pain (Newberg, 2014).

Limitations of neuroscientific study of mystical experience

As we have begun to see, neuroscience faces criticism and acknowledges limitations in its study of mystical experiences. First is the hard problem of consciousness and qualia (specific examples of subjective experience). Critics observe that the measurement of brain activity does not capture the subjective phenomenology of mystical experience. And since all human experience has neural correlates, finding neural correlates of spiritual experiences is unsurprising. Correlation is not an explanation. Brain activity is not all there is to it. Observing the physiological effects of mystical experience does not trivialize religion or reduce spiritual experience to biochemical processes. Defenders of experimentation with spiritual practice would answer that meditators are not seeking psychological or emotional benefit or trying to explore mental states. Meditation, for them, is just one element in a comprehensive spiritual life oriented toward Reality as identified by their religious tradition (Jones, 2018).

Some studies about the neurological effects of meditation are criticized for methodological problems. Questions about the validity of the results of such studies (e.g., Cahn and Polich, 1999; Azari, 2006; Ratcliffe, 2006) have been raised in previous chapters. For example, when experimental samples are small, such as a total of 11 subjects from two different religious traditions in a SPECT imaging experiment with no control group, how generalizable are the results? (Kelly and Grasso, 2006, p. 247) Does a minimal change in blood flow support the idea that there is such a thing as "pure consciousness" (d'Aquili and Newberg, 1999, p. 118)? As the experimenters note, it is not clear what percent of blood-flow change would constitute significant change—10% or 20%? (Newberg and Lee, 2005, p. 477) Since mental events are extraordinarily complex, say some critics, is there even much value in looking for correlations between brain activity and spiritual practices? (Uttal, 2001, in Jones, 2018, p. 997). Can neuroscience contribute anything to our understanding of the subjective content of meditative experiences? (p. 992). Supporters respond that experiments regarding cerebral correlates of spiritual experience, whether science can verify that the subjects contact Reality or not, at least contribute to neuroscientific knowledge about how the brain works (see Goleman and Thurman, 1991; Austin, 1998, in Howard-Jones, p. 1010).

One criticism of the neuroscientific study of religion is its omission of the moral dimension (moral feelings and ethical behavior), one of the most significant aspects of religion (Peters, 2001, p. 494). Peters suggests a neurobiological investigation of the limbic system and frontal lobe neuronal network that lends value to experience (pp. 56-57). Furthermore, moral qualities like fairness, justice, empathy, selfishness, a sense of responsibility, the distinction between good and evil, and free will could be studied for their neurobiological underpinnings (d'Aquili and Newberg, 1999, pp. 55, 83, 86-87, in Peters, 2001, p. 495).

Pure consciousness events and constructivism

Among possible limitations of the neuroscientific study of mystical occurrences is the question of *pure consciousness*. Is mystical experience an example of pure consciousness, or do cultural influences affect what the mystic perceives and reports? This issue comes to the fore, for instance, with neuroimaging of Buddhist and Christian subjects, which show the same brain structures affected for purportedly the same spiritual exercise. They claim very different experiences, each corresponding to their religious tradition. The constructivist approach (Katz, 1978) tries to explain this conundrum. Constructivism points to the epistemological assumption that "there are no pure (unmediated) experiences" (Jones, 2018, p. 1004). This means that all experiences pass through the experiencer's cultural milieu for either perception or interpretation or both. The *predictive processing* model in neuroscience notes that when the person encounters new data, the brain processes it according to previous experiences. The person interprets what it finds based on its current expectations and predictions. The brain also continually compares new input with its expectations and, when a match fails, adjusts (see Griffiths et al., 2008; Clark, 2013).

Non-constructivists ask whether it might be possible to empty the mind of content that would generate cultural predictions or expectations so that at least some mystical experiences (Forman, 1990) would be direct and unmediated "pure consciousness events." Might the mystical event be the same in diverse cultures, with subjects interpreting it afterward according to their specific traditions? In other words, "experience need not be socially constructed even though knowledge about it is" (Hood, 2002, p. 100, in Jones, 2018, p. 1004).

A major philosophical criticism or limitation of neuroscience in studying mysticism is one we have considered in Chapter Three on epistemology. This is an example of our cyclical approach to the topic. Similar themes continue to recur and are considered from various vantage points. Speaking for philosophy and theology, professor of philosophy Michael Dodds (2017, pp. 45-104) compares ontological premises of empirical science with Aristotelian-Thomistic metaphysics. Contemporary science and the scientific method appear to constrict and reduce causality and its range. Dodds quotes Bunge (1979, p. 206) in characterizing causality in science:

> (a) the restriction of causation to *natural* causation (naturalism); (b) the further restriction of all varieties of natural causes to *efficient* causation; (c) the endeavor to reduce efficient causes to *physical* ones (*mechanism*); the requirement of *testing* causal hypotheses by means of repeated observations and, wherever possible, through reproduction in controllable experiments; (e) an extreme *cautiousness* in the assignment of causes and ceaseless striving toward the minimization of the number of allegedly ultimate natural causes (parsimony); (f) the focusing on the search for *laws,* causal or not; (g) the *mathematical* translation of causal connections. (Dodds, 2017, p. 48; in Alexander, 2018, p. 114)

Important to consider regarding mystical experience is the question of pure consciousness versus constructivism. Does a mystic come in contact with an occurrence of pure consciousness, or do they construct it during or afterward from an interpretation based on their mystical, religious, or cultural tradition? (Jones and Gellman, 2022, p. 7). *Pure consciousness events* claim that the experiencer, while awake and aware, operates in a vacuum of consciousness devoid of sense images, thoughts, and concepts, at least during the mystical event. Is this even possible? Contextualists or *constructivists* claim that cultural influences, such as memories, expectations, and beliefs from the mystic's cultural tradition, shape their perception and interpretation of the event while it is occurring, as well as afterward. They maintain that "there is no way to separate mystical experiences from their interpretations since our conceptual apparatus shapes our every experience (see Jones, 1909, introduction; Katz, 1978 and 1983; for criticism, see Evans, 1989; Forman, 1990 and 1999; Stoeber, 1992)" (Jones and Gellman, p. 9). The mystical event, say constructivists, belongs to the experience since, even if a pure consciousness event occurred, the subject's emerging from the event and ascribing meaning to it belongs to the experience.

My (ABN) experiments with Dr. d'Aquili (1999) suggest the likelihood of pure consciousness events in our neurological finding that blood flow in the parietal lobe was reduced during the purported experience of self-loss and oneness with the All (see also Hood, 2006). Scholars conjecture that:

> It should be possible for a mystic who undergoes a pure consciousness event to recall immediately afterward the awareness that was present in the event. The pure consciousness event plus the insight would constitute a complex mystical experience (with) awareness of a state of affairs not otherwise accessible. (Jones and Gellman, 2022, p. 11)

Consideration of constructivism arises from the results of d'Aquili and my (ABN) experiments (1999). Neurological readings from both Catholic nuns and Buddhist monks were similar. The Christians experienced *union with God.* The Buddhists perceived being "endless and intimately interwoven with everyone and everything the mind senses" (Newberg et al., 2001, pp. 6-7). The externally similar spiritual practices of the two groups were radically different in meaning and intention. At the same time, both groups attained a sense of transcendent unity that had a similar physiological effect on brains of all: reduced activation of the posterior superior parietal lobes (Newberg et al., 2001, pp. 4-5)" (Jones, 2018, p. 998).

If there were differences between the two different mystical experiences, was the problem with SPECT technology that it is not fine-grained enough to detect subtle neurological variations? Or did the two groups have the same pure consciousness experience but interpret it afterward according to their own religious and cultural traditions? If the latter, constructivism would be supported.

Can the same neural configuration produce different mental events and states of consciousness? The philosophy of mind theory of *multiple realizability* claims that multiple mental events and states can arise from the same neural configuration (see Jones, 2013; Polger and Shapiro, 2016, pp. 38-39, 47-48). Although even two similar sense perceptions would not be the same neurologically, according to multiple realizations, different mental experiences or states could involve the same general neural network. "Each mental event would have a unique neural configuration unless it is multiply realizable"

(Jones, 2018, p. 999). Also, if the mental event or state (experience) were multiply realizable, it might be attainable by different neural configurations.

There is the question, then, of the inverse: can the same neural configuration support two different mental events (i.e., spiritual experiences), as would be the case of the Christian and Buddhist meditators? To complicate the matter, we investigate subjects' mental experiences through accounts that may have been filtered after the fact through cultural or religious interpretation, if not through third-person information. How would we know whether the same or similar accounts by different meditators are equivalent experiences? (Schmidt and Walach, 2014, p. 3) Brain patterns are exceedingly individualized. In addition, neuroimaging does not take a simple, straightforward picture of the physiological configuration corresponding to a mental event. Brain imaging must depend on statistical averaging. Does neuroimaging statistical averaging obscure the uniqueness of individual brain patterns? Even when it is a question of the same meditative technique, there is no consensus for verifying participants' meditative-state neural patterning (Jones, 2018, p. 999).

This, again, leads to the conclusion that specific neural configurations do not equate to specific mental states. Participants could use the same meditative technique and experience different altered states of consciousness or mystical experiences. Without a consistent one-to-one correlation between neural configurations and mental states (experiences), neuroscience will not be able to explain mystical experiences. It would always be possible to elicit a comparable experience with a different neural configuration (Jones, 2018, p. 999). We are back to the gap between neural patterns and consciousness (Chalmers, 1995, p. 205; Jones, 2013, pp 109-110). The subjective felt experiences of the mind cannot equate or consistently correspond with the brain's physiological conditions. The gap is conceptual and methodological, as well as ontological. "No analysis of matter suggests the presence of phenomena of a radically different nature or why it should appear" (Jones, 2018, p. 1000). We saw in Chapters Three and Four that an Aristotelian-Thomistic hylomorphic anthropological explanation includes the conjunction of a physiological substrate with a soul that comprises psychic and spiritual levels of consciousness.

Because of the gap between the subjectivity of experiences and neurobiology, plus the observation from meditation that the same neural substrate may ground multiple altered states of consciousness, an accurate and reliable neuroscientific account of mystical experience may not be possible. The questions of constructivism and whether mystics encounter and can report *pure consciousness* add to the limitations of neuroscience in investigating mystical experiences. Neuroscience can observe unique neural configurations for altered states of consciousness and can thereby verify that mystical reports are more than simply well-intentioned exaggerations of ordinary mental states.

Experimentation with the phenomenology of mental states will always pose challenges to understanding the subjective felt sense of mystical experience (Jones, 2018, p. 1008). Whether it will ever be possible to develop methods that might bridge this gap is something for future neurotheological investigation.

The veridicality of mystical experiences

Mystical experiences are increasingly taken to be specific types of mental phenomena that feel *real* rather than imaginary (Newberg et al., 2001, p. 7, 143). Enlightenment experiences, I (ABN) contend, "cause long-term changes that affect the emotional and cognitive centers of the brain" and "are real in that they are related to specific neurological events that can permanently change the structure and functioning of the brain" (Newberg and Waldman, 2016, pp. 42, 25). Mystics undergo neurological as well as spiritual transformation. When using the term *real*, neuroscientists mean that mystical experiences have genuine neurological occurrences that can be measured. Mystics typically assert that their experience is *more real* than everyday life, and it generally affects them long afterward. At present, science cannot say whether such experiences are authentic or delusional, whether they represent the true reality or are merely human constructions (e.g., Newberg et al., 2001, pp. 143, 178-179).

The basic philosophical question for neuroscience regarding mystical experiences is whether they are veridical, not only for the experience but do they have something to say about reality itself? If, during mystical experiences, activity decreases in the parietal lobe association and orientation areas that maintain the sense of a separate self, does that mean that the *self* ceases to exist, that it comes and goes with neural activity (Jones, 2018, p. 1011)? Or is it just the *experience* of the self that is disappearing? *Self* here (see above) refers not to self-centered egoism in an attitudinal or moral sense—the self that one must deny to follow Christ (Mt. 16:24-25)—but to unique individual identity, however implicit, subjective consciousness, goal choice, and decision-making ability. The self that Jesus expresses in "I lay down my life for my sheep" (Jn 10:17).

Verification of the genuineness of mystical experiences becomes problematic due to the absence of cross-checking procedures for experiences of God. There are no agreed-upon guidelines for evaluating whether the experience was in an appropriate bodily and psychological position to have a mystical experience. And, of course, if God is involved, God is free to either reveal God's self or not to this or that person (Jones and Gellman, 2022, p. 15).

The validity of a mystical experience is generally sought in the life of the experience. Do they become saintly? (Wainright, 1981, pp. 83-88) Are positive results manifest in one's life overall, having become more virtuous? (Jones and Gellman, 2022, p. 14) Teresa of Avila advised that the discernment of whether an experience came from God or the devil would be found in the fruits of the experience: subsequent actions, personality, vividness of memory of the mystical event, correspondence with scripture, and confirmation by Church officials (Jones and Gellman, p. 16).

American philosopher and psychologist William James asked whether mystical experience lends credibility to theological assertions and saintliness (1958, p. 415). This means, first, are mystical experiences genuine, evidential contacts with a higher Reality, worthwhile not only for the experience but for anyone? To answer this question, there are established ways of epistemically assessing the validity of mystical experiences, called *doxastic practice*. Secondly, should others who have not had mystical experiences consider them authentic and evidential in support of religious beliefs? Defense of a positive response can be found in the "argument from experience" (Jones and Gellman, 2022, p. 13).

Doxastic practice and argument from experience

Doxastic practice, or logical reasoning about beliefs, according to Anglican epistemologist and philosopher of religion William Alston (*Perceiving God: The Epistemology of Religious Experience*, 1991), observes that through doxastic practice, one can evaluate the authenticity of Christian mystical experience as contributing to belief (Steup, 1997). Traditionally, Christian doxastic practice includes an *overrider system*. The overrider system includes consistency with Scripture, established Christian doctrine, and guidelines based on discernment regarding historical, mystical occurrences (Jones and Gellman, 2022, p. 14). Verification of the genuineness of mystical experiences is understood to encompass more than simply the experiencer's perception of something. The experiencer's moral life should substantiate their claim to interaction with God (Shannon, 2017). Regarding the objection that neurophysiology might explain the mystical experience, Alston notes that:

> The proximate cause of sensory perceptions (is generally understood to be) neural processes caused by physical objects. Why, then, should the premise that neural processes proximately cause mystical perceptions be a good reason for supposing that they are not (in normal cases) caused by God? (p. 231f). (Steup, 1997, p. 411)

This is not to imply that God is comparable to a physical object but that God could cause neural processes.

The argument for experience observes that mystical experiences usually occur in the circumstances conducive to their occurrences (Underhill, 1911, pp. 90-94), such as sanctity, a life of moral virtue, fundamental selflessness, and a certain attunement to God. Other people might also choose to embark on a mystical path to verify the experiencer's assertions (see Bergson, 1977, p. 210) (Jones and Gellman, 2011).

Mystical experience: Meaning

What exactly is meant by mystical experience, and what are its characteristics? A technical definition including diverse faith and non-faith traditions is: "A purportedly non-sensory awareness or a non-structured sensory experience granting acquaintance of realities or states of affairs that are of a kind not accessible by way of ordinary sense-perception structured by mental conceptions, somatosensory modalities, or standard introspection" (Jones and Gellman, 2022, p. 2). Breaking that down, *mysticism* refers to things that have to do with mystical experiences—practices, texts, traditions, written or spoken communication—in all world religions.

There is a disinclination today to identify mysticism with phenomena like St. Teresa of Avila describes in the sixth mansion of *The Interior Castle*—visions, locutions, ecstasies, and so on. St. Therese of Lisieux did not describe mystical experiences (unless perhaps a smile of the Blessed Virgin in her youth), particularly not in the 18 months of her dark night and temptations against faith, yet she continued to practice virtue. She might exemplify Rahner's *everyday* or *wintry* mysticism that, without mystical experience, lives in faith. Rather than total consciousness of God's presence, genuine mysticism entails being "fully convinced that Christ lives within us and (acting) in accordance with that conviction" (Bouyer, *Mysterion*, p. 348) without necessarily feeling anything (Wiseman, 1993, p. 689). Mystical knowledge is nonconceptual, conferring contact with Reality as it is, perceiving its essential traits, including the impermanence of all things. The mystic is generally understood to be transformed through their spiritual practices to an enlightened state rather than simply undergoing disparate episodic mystical events (Jones and Gellman, 2022, p. 3).

For acclaimed mysticism authority Evelyn Underhill, mysticism is "that process which involves the perfect consummation of the love of God: the achievement here and now of the immortal heritage of man. It is the art of establishing a conscious relation with the Absolute" (1911, p. 81). In her monumental classic work *Mysticism: A Study of the Nature and Development of Man's Spiritual Consciousness* (1911), Underhill observes that in the Christian context, mystics have developed healthily and fruitfully. Most of the European contemplatives who have left enduring accounts of mystic experience have been Christian. "The greatest mystics have been Catholic saints" (p. 105).

It is important to distinguish the specifically mystical from the broader topic of religious experience. The latter may include the mystical, but also visions and voices, spiritual feelings, and a sense of awe in a religious context. The fundamental religious experience, according to Protestant philosopher and biblical scholar Fredrich Schleiermacher, consists of a sense of *absolute dependence* (1963). For Protestant theologian and comparative religionist Rudolph Otto, experiences are *numinous* (from Latin *numen,* for *divine* or *spirit)* when they are perceived as *wholly other* than the experiencer, eliciting fascination or dread in the face of incomprehensible mystery (2010). Technically, following classification distinctions, Otto's experience would be dualistic, perceiving a difference between the subject and the numinous Other rather than monistic. A typical *sense of God's presence* would be numinous. "It depends on how intense the *presence* is. It can become so overwhelming that the sense of differentiation is suspended" (S. Payne, personal communication, April 17, 2023). It is also possible for mysticism to be secular (Jones and Gellman, 2022, p. 3).

British philosopher and epistemologist Walter Stace (1886-1967) delineated mysticism's *common core* of eight basic phenomenological components. These were operationalized, except for *paradoxicality,* in the Mysticism (M) scale of American psychologist of religion Ralph Hood (1942-). The eight elements include:

> *Timelessness/Spacelessness,* a sense of being outside spatiotemporal limitations; *Unity,* a unifying vision of the world as one; *Inner Subjectivity,* a perception of inner awareness in all beings; *Positive Affect,* blissful feelings that accompany mystical experience; *Sacredness,* a sense of the holy; *Noetic Quality,* a cognitive advancement in understanding the world; and *Ineffability,* the alleged inexplicability of mystic experience. (Hood and Chen, 2013, in Lamm [ed.], p. 587)

This is not to imply that the views of scholars of mysticism, such as Schleiermacher, Otto, James, and Stace, are somehow complementary or cumulative. In fact, they sometimes disagree. We are simply pulling together elements that contribute to this study.

Attempts to objectively measure reports of mystical experiences by both the spiritually non-religious and the religiously dedicated yield characteristics that are generally similar. Among empirically minded social scientists, a common assumption is that any purportedly divine explanation for mystical experiences would be inadmissible (p. 579). Mystics lacking a faith tradition typically score lower regarding meaningful explanations for such experiences (Hood and Chen, 2013, in Lamm [ed.], p. 588). When meaning-making is involved in mystical experiences, it positively affects relationships (Hogue, 2014). Persons more spiritually oriented find meaning in difficult, painful occurrences and see challenging circumstances as transient (Kohls, Sauer, Offenbacher, and Giordano, 2011, in Dixon and Wilcox, 2016, p. 100).

A distinctive characteristic of Christian mysticism over any other transcendent practice is its momentum towards generous charity. Mysticism in other faith traditions may or may not claim salience for charity. Christianity points to its Source and End in a Trinity of Persons in eternal loving self-gift. Mystical love is a total and deep tendency of the soul toward its Origin, fuller and more effective than intellectual philosophic vision.

> For silence is not God, nor speaking is not God; fasting is not God, nor eating is not God; oneliness (sic) is not God, nor company is not God; nor yet any of all the other two such quantities. He is hid between them and may not be found by any work of thy soul but only by love of thine heart. He may not be known by reason, He may not be gotten by thought, nor concluded by understanding, but He may be loved and chosen with the true, lovely will of thine heart. Such a blind shot with the sharp dart of longing love may never fail of the prick, which is God. (Johnston, *The Cloud of Unknowing*, 1996, p. 108).

In my (ABN) work with Mark Waldman, described in *How Enlightenment Changes Your Brain*, 2015), we found, as mentioned, that an analysis of approximately 2,000 descriptions of the most intense mystical or enlightenment experiences suggested five core elements. Those elements included a sense of unity, like that described just above. There is also a sense of intensity, which can refer to experiential elements, emotional aspects, the feeling of awe, or other elements that are perceived to be more intense than everyday experiences and delineate the mystical as something unique. There is a sense of clarity that provides knowledge or wisdom to the individual in a way that they had not been aware of prior to the experience. This knowledge can lead to a change in beliefs and behaviors, such as moral or altruistic shifts. The mystical experience is associated with a sense of letting go or surrendering to the experience as it feels as if it is coming to the person rather than having them go to it. Finally, there is the transformational element that makes it feel as if everything has changed for the person. It should also be noted that these elements are all associated with changes in brain activity, as we have discussed.

Transformative for character and life

The term *born again*, used mainly by Protestant Christians from the 1960s, derives from the New Testament: "No one can see the kingdom of God unless he is born again" (Jn 3:3). Catholics generally speak instead of renewing baptismal faith. Whatever the terminology, charismatic renewals among both

Catholics and Protestants are likely to feature transformative, life-changing encounters with the Holy Spirit. Charismatic experiences are proliferating in developing countries (Beauregard and O'Leary, 2008, p. 184).

What is the difference between charismatic manifestations and mystical experiences? Vatican Council II in *Lumen Gentium* 12 reaffirms charisms that have always been found among the faithful. They are "graces of the Holy Spirit . . . ordered to building up (of the Church), to the good of men, and the needs of the world" (*CCC*, 799). Charisms come in a wide variety: gifts of expressing wisdom, knowledge, faith, healing, miracles, prophecy, distinguishing spirits . . . for the common good (1 Co 12:7). In 2 Co 12:2-4, St. Paul refers to a mystical experience he had, "caught up to the third heaven." He refrains from sharing the content and accepts it as an extraordinary personal grace to strengthen him to persevere in his mission. There can be an overlap between charisms and mystical experiences. Discernment with a spiritual guide may be needed to determine whether the gift is a charism to be shared for ministry to others or a personal mystical grace best kept private, though still ultimately for the upbuilding of all (Charism, 2021).

Research has shown how the brain adapts to experience, preparation, training, and education—the introductory phases of mystical consciousness. From a theological perspective, mysticism includes intense contact with God but also a life that is transformed. Beginning with asceticism, Scripture reading, initial degrees of prayer, and spiritual direction, mystical encounters develop into a new way of life (McGinn, 2006, p. 519). The brain's neural networks are progressively consolidated, revised, and sculpted by faithful Christian living and daily renewal of life. In the words of St. Paul: "be transformed by the renewal of your mind" (Rm 12:2) (Anderson, 2013, in Lamm [ed.], p. 604).

Regarding causality, God acts in all creatures insofar as they seek the goodness of their nature and participate in God's causality. In the context of Christian prayer, human creatures' participation in divine causality has the effect of altering the mystic's neural base as they gradually come to understand the world and self as God does (Alexander, 2018, p. 299). God is always already present to every person, inviting them from within to acknowledge that in God they "live and move and have their being" (cf. Acts 17:28). This is the *telos* or final orientation of mystical practice. "The more one comes to recognize this participative action, the more one wills to cooperate with it, and the closer one draws epistemically to the center where God and the soul already exist in union" (Alexander, 2018, p. 301). Mysticism in contexts other than Christian may have similar, although alternative, descriptions and explanations for mystical experiences.

Teresa of Avila describes the gradual progression of prayer and its transformative effects from beginnings to mystical union. In *The Book of Her*

Life, she describes progression in meditative prayer as Four Waters. She returns to the theme of degrees of prayer in her *Interior Castle (IC)*. The first degree is like drawing water from a well, laboriously. Strenuous ascetical efforts demonstrate to God the person's desire to pursue a path of holiness (*IC* V, 11, 15). This is an initial transformation of desire. The goal of beginning with discursive meditation—step-by-step rational consideration of religious content to facilitate the transformation of life, is "to reach the point of failure with the intellect and skill to carry on" (*IC* V, 15.11, 15.13). The second degree of prayer allows the intellect to rest at times when the will is bound to God by love (*IC* V, 14. 2, 4). Memory is troublesome at this stage in drawing attention back to attachments. Slowly, the person is transformed and gradually takes on the qualities of divine love (*IC*, V, 15.4). They begin to understand that God dwells within and cooperate with His transforming action (Alexander, 2018, pp. 204-205, 211-212).

When considering the transformation that results from the mystical experience, neurological effects of spiritual and religious experience have been introduced and will be addressed in the following sections. Further exploration of the neurophysiological effects of mystical experience would be a challenge for future neurotheological research. Theoretically, since a person experiences new beliefs and behaviors, there will be changes in various parts of the brain that support these changes. Current brain imaging data suggest that there are long-term changes in brain function that result from spiritual practices and experiences. Studies of prayer and meditation reveal that, even at rest, the brain appears different over time. Long-term practitioners of meditation and prayer have changes in their frontal lobes, insula, and thalamus, which are involved in executive, cognitive, and emotional processes.

Mystical union

Stages of transformation: Purgative, illuminative, unitive

Underhill describes the stages of transformation on the mystical path. Awakening of transcendental consciousness shifts awareness to higher levels. This is not simply religious conversion, a sudden acceptance of religious beliefs, but a shift of awareness that involves the whole person in the remaking of consciousness and a change in attitude toward the world (pp. 176-177). The awakening is characterized by a sense of victory and freedom, conviction about the proximity of God, and love toward God. The new perspective might be described as "a sudden, intense, and joyous perception of God immanent in the universe and a new life corresponding to this new dominant fact of existence" (p. 179).

The stage of purification is a perpetual completion of conversion by character adjustment, turning to Reality and Truth, away from self-interest, thoughtless distractions, and empty pursuits. Whether a slender thread or a rope binds a bird, says St. John of the Cross, it is bound and cannot fly (*Ascent of Mount Carmel*, I,1, in Underhill, 1911, p. 212).

When some degree of purification has reoriented the person to God with some stability in control of instinctive attachments, the *proficient"* has achieved solid standards of thought and conduct with confidence in relation to God (Underhill, 1911, p. 234). The person may find affective enlargement in a sense of the presence of God, enhanced meaning in created things and intuitions regarding symbols, and energy for the intangible may be greatly increased (p. 240).

The dark night of sense may appear prior to the illuminative way of proficients, and the dark night of spirit may occur after it. These transitional passages force the person to acknowledge facets of the self in need of further purification and virtues that need strengthening. On the first night, the person learns to love without recompense, detached from sensory and self-centered gratification. On the second night, there is a deeper purification. The person sees him or herself with real imperfections and weaknesses they had overlooked. They experience emptiness, dryness, and darkness, as well as difficulties and distress in life circumstances. This contributes to reducing self-satisfaction and replacing it with a deepening humility[1] (Underhill, 1911, pp. 391-393).

The unitive life simplifies the powers of the soul, now transformed in union with God. In Christianity, there is always a distinction between God and the soul. Still, now, the person experiences a stable participation of its powers in God's way of knowing, feeling, and acting. The mystic feels that they live in God as in their home, now identified with any part of it while retaining their personality (Underhill, 1911, p. 420).[2]

Epistemology of mystical knowing

With this study of mysticism and neuroscience, questions arise about what precisely happens in mystical experience from the perspectives of causality, epistemology, theology, and psychology. Other areas could be raised, but we will begin with a brief cursory reference to these.

From a Catholic point of view, ultimately, God is the cause of the existence of everything else. But God's existence is totally different. He is subsistent in himself, meaning that his existence is the same as his essence (*ST* I, q. 3, a. 4, res.). Since created things cannot exist apart from God, Aquinas explains that created entities participate in God's existence (*ST* I, q. 104, A. 1 res.). "The causality of all created things is best understood as a participation in the ultimate causality of God" (Alexander, 2018, pp. 89-90).

God, then, acts in creatures, sustaining them in being and conferring the power by which they act. From the creatures' point of view, they participate in God's existence, which is to say, God's Being. It is God who confers participative beings on creatures and directs them to their end, to act according to the ultimate goodness of their natures. Some participation in God's being and agency can be found in all created things. "God is the final cause who both creates and draws forth the formal, material, and efficient causes" (Alexander, 2018, p. 101). This means that, ultimately, God is the *telos* of all causes. Whatever exists, by virtue of its creation, begins and ends in God. For the Christian mystic, this includes their knowing experientially that "God it is in whom we live and move and have our being" (Acts 17:28).

Mystical knowing can be understood as an epistemic capacity that gradually transforms neurological structures through prayer and meditation to attain an abiding awareness of the presence of God, who lives and acts in the human person. Neurological studies have shown that the practice of prayer, particularly meditation over time, can improve self-regulation, attention, impulse control, and mental flexibility (Newberg, 2013; Congleton, Holzel, and Lazar, 2015). Physical neurobiological transformations alter the way one regulates emotion, learns, remembers, assimilates information about the self, and engages in perspective-taking. With regular practice of meditative prayer or contemplation where God's action predominates, the subject can more readily develop capacities that extend their human potentialities and enhance their ability to think, feel, and act virtuously. The mystic can foster transformation in view of participative union with God.

In the process of mystical union with God, the person's spiritual knowing is transformed, amazingly, into the pattern of the Trinity. According to John of the Cross, the mystic does not simply know humanly about God. They attain a perfection of both human and divine knowing. "The soul's structure becomes included in the structure of God's self-knowing through mystical transformation into the Trinity" (Howells, 2002, pp. 33-34). While Aquinas holds that there are two human spiritual faculties, intellect and will, John of the Cross follows Augustine in considering three faculties: memory, intellect, and will (Bord, 976, pp. 75-80, in Howells, 2002, p. 16).

Since the human soul is already made in the image of God, mystical transformation brings the person's essential relationship with God to perfection. The person gradually deepens in accommodating to the presence of God within and in a union. At first, the person had only known God through creatures, as the Artist is somehow reflected in the artwork he produces. In union, God himself is known before creatures (Howells, 2002, p. 59). The natural cognitive structure of the soul knows natural images and forms of things; spiritual knowing uses 'general, indistinct' 'spiritual forms' that do not depend on natural forms (p. 39). Spiritual knowing occurs supernaturally through the theological virtues and capacities bestowed at baptism to relate to God in faith, hope, and love. God contacts us directly, spiritually, through theological virtues because the senses cannot perceive God. Natural and supernatural knowing are united in a single center in union, where the Trinity perfects and transforms natural human knowing (p. 39).

The process of mystical transformation consists of a continual movement between one spiritual state and another, between natural and supernatural organizations (Morel,1960, 2:26; de Longchamp, 1997, pp. 36-39, 86-87). John of the Cross observes that God visits the soul in the spiritual, not the sensory part.

> When these favors are bestowed . . . (only in the spirit, as we said), a person is usually aware without knowing how that the superior and spiritual part of his soul is withdrawn and alienated from the lower and sensory part. This withdrawal makes him conscious of two parts so distinct that one seemingly has no relation to the other and is far removed from it. And indeed, this is in a way true, for in the then-entirely spiritual activity, there is no communication with the sensory part. (*DN*, 23:14)

The soul does not stand still but constantly moves from one spiritual state to another (John of the Cross, *DN* 18:3-4). For John, "the soul lives where it loves" (*SC*, 8:3), defined mainly by its attachments. The self identifies its orientation not by what it knows but by what it desires and pursues. In mystical experience, the natural vitality toward objects in the world meets the orientation of the Trinity, and there is a deepening of the person's spiritual capacities. Two cognitive systems—one tending toward natural objectives and the other supernaturally directed toward union with God—are distinguished at superficial, then gradually more profound levels of unified relationality (Howells, 2002, p. 41). Corresponding to the distinction of sense and spirit, the soul has two corresponding directions and capabilities, interrelated in a single union. Once spiritual knowing has been realized, the sensory system is still functional. Still, the person is able, *at the first movement* of sensory perception, to raise their attention and cooperate with God (p. 34).

By grace, the person receives the capacity to relate to God within their ontological creatureliness, as he sees and loves himself (Maritain, 1932, p. 394). In virtue of its immediate relation to God, the person sees and loves through God, in union with and participating in God, though always ontologically distinct, as the creature to the Creator (Howells, 2002, p. 43). The natural dynamism of developing concepts through sensory information does not conflict with supernatural cognitive activity because, from the Catholic perspective, spiritual knowing derives not from the senses but from spiritual, supernatural capacities. "To be human is to be spirit, i.e., to live life while reaching ceaselessly for the absolute, in openness toward God" (Rahner, 1941/1994, p. 53).

For the person in union with God, mystical experience does not perdure as intellectual vision, which is unsustainable in this life. Moments of vision may occur at times, but as virtuous action (Howells, 2002, p. 128). The transformed intellect, memory, and will are oriented to serving God and putting his will into action, freely and deliberately (*LF* 3:77; 1:9). The human person's relationship with God is reciprocal, each voluntarily surrendering to the other. "The soul cannot practice or acquire the virtues without the help of God, nor does God affect them alone in the soul without her help. God and the soul work together" (*SC* 30:6) (Howells, pp. 37-38).

From the neuroscience perspective, one can ponder how the brain processes concepts such as soul, grace, and spiritual knowing. While the Catholic perspective is decidedly supernatural, neuroscience can elucidate the neurobiological correlates. The implication is that any supernatural process would necessarily have to intersect with something happening in the brain. Thus, if it is possible to ascertain the brain changes associated with these experiences and determine how such brain changes relate to changes in beliefs and behaviors, it might be possible to understand more fully how these interactions occur more fully.

Virtue, connaturality, and sanctity

Experience of grace and Spirit

According to Thomistic teleology, "every agent acts on account of an end" (*Cont.gent.* 3.2), and "every action is for the sake of a good" (3.4). This means that humans orient their consciousness toward being/reality as true and good. When conscience is well-formed, humans are habitually attuned to virtue; there is a natural epistemological connaturality (Ryan, 2014, p. 8). Theology adds that by grace, humans become "partakers in the divine nature" (2 Pt 1:4) and develop a supernatural aptitude for participating in God's life. Through the gifts of the Holy Spirit (wisdom, understanding counsel, knowledge fortitude, piety, and fear of the Lord [Is 11:2]), the human person attunes their cognitive, affective, and volitional capacities to the Spirit of God. Contributing to the process are the theological and moral virtues infused at baptism (faith, hope, charity, prudence, justice, fortitude, and temperance). Also foundational to growth in connaturality is the practice of the beatitudes (Blessed are the poor in spirit, the meek, they who mourn, they who hunger and thirst after justice, the merciful, the clean of heart, the peacemakers, they that suffer persecution for justice' sake [Mt 5:3-10]). The fruits of the Spirit (charity, joy, peace, patience, kindness, goodness, trustfulness, gentleness, and self-control [Gal 5:22-23]) verify the presence of grace and the Spirit of God. Together, this makes the graced human person experience a supernatural epistemological connaturality with God (Ryan, p. 9).

Andrew Pinsent suggests that the moral transformation of consciousness from natural to supernatural occurs, as Aquinas observes from Augustine, through God "working virtue in us, without us" (*De Grat. et Lib. Arb. xvii*). Essential to this process are the virtues, gifts, beatitudes, and fruits of the Spirit (VGBF). Pinsent observes that recent studies of triadic joint attention, where two persons direct their attention to a common point of reference to develop coordinated social cognition, apply well to Aquinas' understanding of the virtues, gifts, beatitudes, and fruits of the Spirit. The human person gradually shares a common perspective and attitude, attuning to the Spirit of God until a supernatural epistemological resonance occurs. Built on Buber's *I-thou* understanding of interpersonal dynamics oriented to friendship, second-personal joint attention fosters cooperative endeavor in love and eventually union (Riordan, 2015). The *sharing of minds* that happens in friendship reflects the interaction and instinct for virtue between the human person and God in a graced relationship (Ryan, 2014).

According to Catholicism, any person, including the agnostic or atheist, who "seeks the truth and does the will of God in accordance with their understanding of it, can be saved" (*CCC*, 1260). Reception of grace and the VGBF system that aligns the human person in friendship with God is at work in their lives, although they may be unaware of it. Such a non-believer would have a non-conscious knowledge of God (Ryan, 2014, p. 130). According to Rahner, the saints live by pure spirit:

> It is the reason for their strange way of life, their poverty, their desire for humility, their longing for death, their willingness to suffer, and their secret longing for martyrdom. They know that the human being is supposed to live as spirit in concrete human existence, not merely in speculative thought but truly at the border between God and world, time and eternity. (2010, pp. 186-187)

The saints and mystics experience grace, the movement of the Holy Spirit in their lives. There are likely degrees of the experience of grace, some of which are accessible to anyone. Rahner describes the experience of grace:

> Have we ever remained silent even though we wished to defend ourselves, even though we had been treated unjustly? Have we ever forgiven, even though we did not get rewarded for it, and the quiet act

of forgiveness was taken for granted? Have we ever been obedient, not because we had to and wanted to avoid negative consequences, but purely on account of the mysterious, silent, incomprehensible one we call God and his will?. . Have we ever been utterly alone? Have we ever made a decision based solely on the deepest voice of our conscience, the place where one cannot talk to anyone, cannot make things clear to anyone, where one is totally alone and knows one is making a decision that will not be accepted by a single person. . . Have we ever tried to love God when . . . we felt as if we were calling out to a void and to utter unresponsiveness, . . . when everything seemed elusive and meaningless? Have we ever been good to someone and received no word of gratitude, no acknowledgment, not even the reward of being recognized as having acted selflessly, fairly, or kindly?

When we find (such experiences), we will recognize we have experienced the spirit that we are talking about. The experience of eternity, . . . the experience that the purpose of being human does not rise and fall with the meaning and happiness of this world, the experience of courage and of a faith that risks a leap, a faith not supported by reason or derived from the world's principles or success. (Rahner, 2010, p. 186)

Lonergan, as we have seen, emphasizes human consciousness, showing systematically how spirituality can integrate mind and heart. Uniting the four levels of consciousness as delineated in his model—experiencing, understanding, judging, and deciding—is desire, the impetus for their movement. For Lonergan, as for Augustine, desire motivates spirituality, which transforms consciousness (Moloney, 2004, p. 124). He understands spirituality as the desire for value, the movement for self-transcendence, and ultimately, reaching for God, whether one recognizes it or not. "This orientation of our conscious intentionality gives our best definition of God: God is the reality which fulfills that fundamental orientation (1972, p. 341, in Moloney, 2004, p. 127).

Lonergan sees the transcendental notions of experience, understanding, judgment, and decision as a call to self-transcendence that can be transformed and completed by the supernatural gift of God's grace, leading the human person to a mystical horizon (Rixon, 2001). More than a philosopher, Lonergan is a theologian of grace, showing that recognition of God as a definitive Mystery emerges from human consciousness that pursues the ultimate in value. A young Jesuit on a retreat preached by Lonergan in 1941 remembered his emphasis: "Le métier de l'homme est de se passer." (The task of man is to transcend himself.) (Rixon, pp. 482-483). Self-transcendence finally means surpassing self in authentic love (Moloney, 2004).

Michael McCarthy (*Authenticity as Self-Transcendence: The Enduring Insights of Bernard Lonergan*, 2015) observes that Lonergan, following Canadian Catholic philosopher Charles Taylor, questioned the sufficiency of an exclusive humanism that would be content with the levels of consciousness and not pursue their ultimate orientation. Taylor refers to an *immanent frame*, the common intellectual and moral background of "description, explanation, choice, and action" shared by believers and unbelievers alike "that can be understood without reference to the supernatural or the transcendent" (McCarthy, 2015, p. 185, in Byrne, 2016, p. 7). Taylor's critique of this stance is that it is satisfied in scientific research with intelligible answers without asking why the universe *is* intelligible. "Can the universe be intelligible without an intelligent ground?" (Lonergan, 1972, p. 101, in Byrne, 2016, p. 9).

Lonergan's transcendental precepts or levels of consciousness illustrate the dynamics of human interiority and support all domains of human endeavor and authenticities in culture as well as religion (Byrne, 2016). His philosophy of mind and God point to a self-transcendent call to holiness. For Lonergan, this meant an other-worldly falling in love with God, a complete and permanent self-surrender, the pattern for a person's spirituality and subsequent life (Lonergan, 1972, p. 240). According to Christian theology, such a falling in love depends not on the human person but on God's initiative. "The love of God has been poured into our hearts by the Holy Spirit who has been given to us" (Rm 5:5).

After God's initiating descending movement, conversion requires an ascending human response as successive levels of human consciousness correspond with God's gift and manifest the fruits of the Spirit (charity, joy, peace, and so on [Rm 5:22-23]). For Lonergan, as for Catholic mystical theology generally, the grace of charity is key to religious experience. It is the loving person of faith who perceives that the universe is filled with love and meaning (1972, p. 290) (Moloney, 2004, p. 130). Lonergan concluded that theological reflection and loving service flow from a mysticism of transforming union (Rixon, 2001, p. 479).

The uncreated grace of the indwelling Trinity, as well as sanctifying and actual graces, assimilate the human person in the process of transforming union to participation in the grace of Christ. Grace produces in human persons a participation in the enlightening of understanding and alignment of will that characterized the humanity of Christ (Doran, 1990, Lonergan Folder 18, 2, in Rixon, 2001, p 485). In discussing the Ignatian *Spiritual Exercises,* Lonergan reflects on Ignatius' assumption that God acts directly in the human person and prioritizes union as the source from which service flows (*Spiritual Exercises,* annotation, 15) (Rixon, p. 487). Lonergan, following Augustin Poulain, S.J. (1836-1919), author of the classic *Graces of Interior Prayer* (1901), described mystical prayer in transforming union as permanent "transformation of the conscious intellect and will" (Folder 19, in Doran 1990) (Rixon, 2001, p. 486). With God operating supernaturally in intellect and will, one might expect to find that "a person's conscious knowing and willing through unitive prayer anticipate and stimulate a corresponding transformation and reintegration of his or her spontaneous biological and psychic sensibilities" (see Doran, 1990, in Rixon, p. 486). According to Lonergan, being in love does not replace human desires for unlimited knowledge and goodness that motivate authentic cultural improvement but assimilates them to a supernatural level driven by love attuned to the desires of God (Byrne, 2016, p. 13).

Again, the purpose of neurotheology in this context would be to examine concepts such as virtue, connaturality, and sanctity from a brain-related perspective. How does the brain comprehend and engage virtues? First, we can consider what virtue means, how we are able to delineate specific virtues cognitively, and how they are differentiated from sin and vice. Are virtues determined by behaviors, emotions, cognitions, or some combination of all of these? And depending on how that question is answered, we can explore what brain areas might be involved. As with all the neuroscience discussions thus far, there is an added richness to the theological discussion about these concepts that now goes beyond sacred texts or what is written by theologians to include what science might have to say about these important ideas in Catholicism.

Study Questions

1. For neuropsychology and neuroscientific theory, what is experience?
2. How does Kuhl distinguish the conceptual from the integrated self? Explain.
3. According to Johnstone, what happens when the sense of self that accounts for subjective experience is increased, decreased, or distorted?
4. What is meant by the "sense of self"?
5. How may spiritual experience be distinguished from religious experience? What do they have in common?
6. How are spiritual, religious, or mystical experiences characterized generally and by Christians?
7. Lonergan locates religious experience in transcendent intentional consciousness (see Chapter Three, epistemology). Explain.
8. How were spiritual experiences categorized in a recent study as numinous, mystical, or paranormal? Explain.
9. How does Underhill define mysticism?

10. What does Catholicism mean by union with God? Mystical experience?

11. What are the two definitions of mysticism for social scientific studies?

12. What are the five attributes of mystical experience from brain-scan studies?

13. What are the three main dual classifications of mysticism, and what do they mean?

14. What is meant by attributing to mysticism qualities of being noetic, ineffable, and paradoxical?

15. What brain regions or chemical processes are found to correlate to some extent with dimensions of perceived transcendence?

16. Does the correlation of mystical states with brain structure of function mean that physiological processes cause religious experience? Explain.

17. Do findings of association between neural processes and mystical experiences mean that they somehow must derive from the brain? Explain.

18. What is meant by qualia?

19. Where does science stand regarding consciousness at present?

20. Why does it seem to be impossible for neuroscience to evaluate subjective experiences of consciousness objectively?

21. Why does Catholicism, from philosophical and theological perspectives, not accept a materialistic or emergence theory regarding consciousness and religious experience?

22. Consciousness, itself seemingly inexplicable, can be modified through spiritual training and practice. Explain.

23. What are the limitations of the neuroscientific study of mystical experience?

24. How, according to Peters, might an alleged omission of neuroscientific study of the moral dimension of religion be rectified?

25. How does constructivism respond to the question of pure consciousness in the neuroscientific study of mystical experience?

26. What does it mean to say that no experience is unmediated?

27. What do you think about the contention of non-constructivists that experience need not be socially constructed?

28. What does Dodds, quoting Bunge, mean by saying that science appears to constrict causality and its range?

29. Do you think that pure consciousness events are possible, or are they always constructed? Explain.

30. What do multiple realizations contribute to the question of pure consciousness and mystical experience?

31. What problems for accuracy in brain imaging arise from statistical averaging?

32. How does hylomorphism explain the lack of a consistent correlation between neural patterns and consciousness?

33. Do the limitations in measuring mystical occurrences support the conclusion that mystical experiences are illusory? Explain.

34. What is meant by the realness of mystical experience?

35. How generally can veridicality of mystical experiences be verified?

36. How can the genuineness of Christian mystical experience be evaluated through doxastic practice, including an over-rider system?

37. Is the claim that neurophysiology might account for mystical experiences a valid objection? Explain.

38. What does it mean that the argument for experience can authenticate mystical experience?

39. What is meant by mystical experience?

40. How did St. Thérèse of Lisieux differ from St. Teresa of Avila regarding mysticism?

41. How is mystical distinguished from religious experience?

42. According to Stace, what are the eight basic elements of mystical experience?

43. Why might mystical experiences that include meaning-making impact relationships positively?

44. Why does the Christian mystical experience give precedence to generous charity?

45. How are charisms distinguished from mystical experiences?

46. When mystical experience is transformative, what happens theologically and neurophysiologically?

47. What is the *telos* of Christian mystical experience?

48. How does Teresa of Avila explain prayer progression and the transformation it effects?

49. How does Underhill characterize the awakening of transcendental consciousness?

50. What occurs in the spiritual stage of purification?

51. How may the illuminative stage of proficiency be characterized?

52. What happens in the transitional nights of sense and spirit?

53. How may the transformed person in the unitive life be described?

54. What is meant by saying that God is the *telos* of all causes?

55. What is meant by calling mystical knowing an epistemic capacity?

56. How does mystical knowing transform the faculties of the human soul?

57. How do the theological virtues transform human knowing?

58. Why does mystical transformation involve continual movement among spiritual states, natural and supernatural?

59. What determines self-orientation? Explain.

60. How in mystical transformation do the person and God work together?

61. What might neurotheology contribute to understanding transformation through mystical experience?

62. How do the theological and moral virtues, gifts of the Spirit, beatitudes, and fruits of the Spirit (VGBF) contribute to connaturality with God in a graced human life?

63. How might Pinsent's notion of triadic joint attention help explain human supernatural resonance with God?

64. Any person sincerely following their conscience, living by grace, and the VGBF system is in God's friendship. Explain.

65. How does Rahner describe the experience of grace?

66. What, according to Lonergan, is the orientation of the four transcendental precepts: experience, understanding, judgment, and decision?

67. According to Lonergan, why is supernatural charity key to religious experience?

68. How do Lonergan and Poulain describe the effects of mystical prayer in transforming union?

69. What might be concepts related to higher stages of spiritual life for neurotheology to explore?

Endnotes

[1] St. John of the Cross distinguishes between active and passive nights of sense and spirit. The passive nights are particularly purifying since they are not under our control (S. Payne, personal communication, April 16, 2023).

[2] Underhill modifies the traditional "purgative, illuminative, unitive" schema for her explanatory purposes to (1) Awakening, (2) Purgative, (3) Illuminative, (4) Dark Night of the Soul, and (5) Unitive stages.

Chapter 12

Catholic Theological Implications

Neurotheology encourages dialogue between neuroscience and theology. What are the implications for Catholic theology of its conversation with neuroscience? First, we need to define *theology*. Theology might mean a discipline oriented to revelation, faith, and philosophy that is usually restricted to Christianity but with themes that may also include other religions, such as Judaism (cf. Theilicke and Louthe, 2022). This chapter will consider how theology builds on divine revelation; ways that neuroscience and cognitive science of religion relate to theology; a Catholic understanding of the soul, again, this time from a theological perspective; and neuroscientific-theological reflections on the social-relational person. We will offer some reflections on Catholic neurobiological ethics, including moral reasoning, exemplars, narrative, embodied cognition, and end-of-life bioethics. The reader is invited to discern for themself how theology could engage in dialogue with neuroscience and perhaps offer additional suggestions.

Divine self-revelation

How do humans contact God or the divine Being? Or perhaps the question should be: How does God contact humans? Throughout the world and history, people have come to know the transcendent in multiple and varied ways. We cannot cover all possible ways that humans receive divine revelation, and certainly not in-depth; we will briefly refer to Judaism and Christianity.

A first human means of coming to know the transcendent is biblical: God's self-revelation to men and women (Delio, 2003). The Hebrew and Christian Bible reports God's speaking to individuals, as to Moses from the burning bush (Ex. 3) or to the prophets in dreams or otherwise.

Within the neurotheology framework, God's self-revelation in Judaism and Christianity is perceived through the senses. The human visual and auditory systems, for example, perceived the parting of the Red Sea or the small-town carpenter Jesus announcing, "I am the Way, the Truth, and the Life" (Jn 14:6).[1]

Before delving into the mysterious faith-based domain of theology, we come up against a problem that neurobiology cannot explain. Neuroscience focuses on physiological aspects of the encounter between the nervous system and the world, including abstract and spiritual dimensions, a complex and intricate process. Basic neurology registers only immediate perceptions and responds physiologically to sensory stimuli. One of the major continuing questions in neuroscience is the *neural binding problem* (NBP)—how elements that specific brain circuits encode can coalesce for perception, decision, and action for integrated, continuous conscious engagement with the environment and other minds.[2] The NBP, like the *mind-body problem,* remains an important challenge because neuroscience cannot currently explain how neural binding happens. And perhaps it never will.

It is interesting to note that the brain reacts similarly when we imagine something as when we perceive an actual object. "It would be difficult if not impossible to use brain imaging to prove which experiences of the world are real and which are not." Brain imaging, for example, could not determine whether Moses saw a burning bush or only imagined it (Newberg, 2018, pp. 323-324). Higher-level cognition interprets for purpose and meaning and does not do well with leaving perceptions anomalous. Encountering a bush burning but not consumed or listening to a seemingly ordinary man who works astounding miracles, the brain will look for and likely come up with an explanation.

Judaism and Christianity insist that revelation does not derive from human thinking and expression. The perceiver with faith receives and accepts a religious meaning of the event seen as divine self-revelation. The religious tradition discerns the authenticity of revelation and shapes its influence on human persons (Newberg, 2018, p. 325). Catholics hold that God has gradually revealed to humans his mystery through actions and words (*CCC,* 69). Catholicism affirms that God has lovingly communicated himself, providing the answers to questions humans raise about the purpose and meaning of life (*CCC,* 68).

Besides revelation accepted by faith, a second human way of coming to know the transcendent observes that God can be found through creation. As St. Paul asserts: "Since the creation of the world, God's invisible qualities—his eternal power and divine nature—have been clearly seen, being understood from what has been made" (Rm 1:20). St. Augustine remarks:

> Question the beauty of the earth, the sea, the air distending and diffusing itself, question the beauty of the sky. . . Question all these realities. All respond: 'See, we are beautiful.' Their beauty is a profession. These beauties are subject to change. Who made them if not the Beautiful One, who is not subject to change? (*Sermo* 241, 2; Migne, *Patrologia Latina* 38, 1134). (*CCC,* 32)

St. Ignatius of Loyola's (Jesuit) spirituality looks to find God in all things.

Thirdly, humans can come to know the transcendent through natural reason. God, "the first principle and last end of all things, can be known with certainty from the created world" (Vatican Council I, *Dei Filius* 2) (CCC 36). The Catholic Church is confident that all humans can know God, an assumption that supports "dialogue with other religions, philosophy, and science, as well as with unbelievers and atheists" (*CCC,* 39). Through divine revelation, religious and moral truths knowable by natural reason can be "known by all men with ease, with firm certainty, and with no admixture of error" (*Humani Generis,* 561) (*CCC,* 38).

Neurotheology wonders *how* God communicates with humans. Does God alter the firing of neurons? Does the human brain have a way of perceiving the supernatural? Science cannot answer this question (Clarke, 2015, p. 223). It belongs to a different order, out of reach for scientific inquiry. But while the answers to such questions may not be forthcoming, analyzing how the brain contributes to human spiritual and religious phenomena still has important implications both philosophically and clinically.

Neuroscience and theology

Theology, building on divine revelation, may find itself challenged by natural sciences such as neuroscience and the cognitive science of religion. When practitioners in these fields work within a materialistic framework, they may ignore or deny the spiritual dimension of human life or the existence of the Creator, whose traces can be found in creation. The Christian who comes upon their research findings may need to discern whether the scientific results need sorting through to reconcile them with faith. As we observed, the truth that science uncovers will not, in fact, contradict the truth of faith, although it might not be immediately evident that this is so. We will consider neurotheology as an attempt to engage both science and faith harmoniously, to see how neurobiology associates with spirituality, and to consider how the cognitive science of religion might relate to the Christian faith.

Neurotheology and revelation

Neurotheology studies "how the brain functions in terms of humankind's relation to God or ultimate reality" (d'Aquili and Newberg, 1999, in Burns, 2005, p. 177). From the viewpoint of neurotheology, revelation is more religiously than neurologically oriented in addressing ways that human beings understand that God exists and make known his intentions and will. Still, human beings can only understand in a limited way what God wants to communicate. Humans will only perceive and understand God within the scope of our neurophysiological apparatus, including a spiritual capacity, which is also always limited. And original sin that gives rise to personal sin obscures our intellect. Since religious beliefs, rituals, and behaviors impact brain processes, neurobiology may come into play. Given the complexity of religions, virtually every brain area is engaged with an expression of religious experience, belief, and practice (Newberg, 2018, p. 315).

Neuroscience might ask whether specific genes, neurotransmitters, or brain processes enhance the facility for receiving revelation. Geneticist Dean Hamer, working at the National Institutes of Health (NIH), suggests (*The God Gene*, 2005) that a gene called vesicular monoamine transporter 2 (VMAT2), the polymorphism A33050 variant on chromosome 10, may carry a C (cytosine) or *spiritual allele*. Hamer found a distinct association between the C on the VMAT2 polymorphism and a predisposition to spirituality, measured by the Cloninger Self-Transcendence Scale (Muller, 2008). Higher levels of self-transcendence have also been found to correlate with a dopaminergic or serotonergic increase. Neurotheology invites exploration of ways that spiritual and religious experiences correlate with brain processes (Newberg, 2018, p. 327).

Neurobiology and spirituality

Neuroscience has been called one of the most forward-driving current fields, impacting numerous other areas of study. Using the scientific method, neuroscience generally follows a materialistic model. Directly or indirectly, it is likely to ask: What is the human person? (Horvat, 2017, p. 1). Among the theoretical answers, materialistic epiphenomenalism claims that mental states arise from neural firing and nothing more (Burns, 2005). This reduces the mind to neurochemistry and denies the existence of a spiritual soul that informs the body and endures beyond death. As a result, neuroscientific research may often disregard spiritual-soul-based intellect-and-will dimensions of the human person. Neuroscientists have found areas of the brain tied to physical sensation, emotional responsivity, and executive functioning. Still, no brain area has been found that causes the person to make choices and decisions. If decisions were caused by brain functioning, they would not be free. "Humans clearly have a mental capacity that in some sense operates extra-neurologically" (Jewett and Shuster, 1996, in Burns, 2005, p. 185).

Neuroscience focuses on the human brain and central nervous system, often through a materialistic lens. Some neuroscientists find an in-built proclivity to spirituality in the human make-up; others may ignore or deny the spiritual dimension of the human person. A Catholic perspective, to recall, sees the person as a body-and-soul unity following Aristotelian-Thomistic hylomorphism. Catholicism integrates philosophy and theology with the natural sciences (Horvat, 2017, p. 1)

Cognitive science of religion and Christian faith

Another relatively recent field, the cognitive science of religion, may also be problematic to Christians who see it as *explaining away* their faith-based understanding of the way things are.

Cognitive science of religion (CSR) is an interdisciplinary field of study that centers on minds and how they work, rather than the brain and nervous system, as is the case with neuroscience. CSR may overlap with the fields of neuroscience, psychology, anthropology, linguistics, philosophy, and computer science (Barrett, 2017, p. 4).

The cognitive science of religion might explain religion as a by-product of human cognitive predispositions (White, 2017, p. 44). CSR scholars look for cultural constraints and predispositions, such as content and context biases, that could provide a perfectly natural explanation for individuals, communities, and societies adopting faith-based beliefs and practices. CSR might observe that human minds are naturally inclined to account for mysteries with invisible, superhuman, minded, intentional entities operating to favor or thwart human endeavors (Guthrie, 1993; Bering, 2011). Human minds are naturally disposed to attribute to supernatural beings with pertinent information about humans, orchestration of salvation or suffering. Human ideas, beliefs, and behaviors might derive from context, from other people in the environment. The notions of such persons are accepted based on social cues such as age, skill, prestige, or credibility-enhancing displays (CREDs) (Gervais et al., 2011, p. 6). Humans are also inclined to accept what the majority in their environment believe and to emulate models that are successful, older, and perceived to be credible (Ruczaj, 2022, p. 8).

CSR may tend to emphasize the observable and use empiricism, leaving out the immaterial, mainly because CSR works through the scientific method. In addition, the physical and concrete are both important and accessible. This does not mean that CSR scholars necessarily reject nonmaterial realities such as divinity or human souls (Barrett, 2017).

Christians generally regard God as communicating with men and women through ordinary revelation in the natural world and through extraordinary revelation, specifically through scripture. God, as we saw above, might reveal his character and attributes through the beauty and wonder of nature and human reason and reflection on life. General revelation might also encompass cultural expressions, rituals, myths, moral codes, search for purpose, and appreciation of values. CSR's highlighting of these aspects of the human experience does not necessarily lead to the conclusion that natural explanations of various aspects of human life exclude the dimension of spirituality or faith.

Belief is understood to mean cognitive (so brain-related) acceptance of a specific proposition as true (Nola, 2018, p. 75). Faith may be more than a cognitive activity, but it is at least that (Plantinga, 2000, p. 247). Christian theologians traditionally acknowledge that God can be known through nature and the created world (cf. Rm 1:20). However, they contend that the core content of Christian faith cannot be accepted without the grace of faith. Counterintuitive beliefs specific to Christianity, such as that God is triune, Jesus is God and man, Jesus died and rose for human redemption, can only be accepted by means of the grace of faith. "When St. Peter confessed that Jesus is the Christ, the Son of the living God, Jesus declared to him that this revelation did not come 'from flesh and blood,' but from 'my Father who is in heaven'" (Mt 16:17). Theology understands that the ultimate explanation for acceptance of Christian beliefs is the grace of faith.

A problem comes in with the CSR explanation that humans do not need grace. They—by context bias—naturally go along with natural human proclivities to accept what the culture accepts. CSR would say that cognitive learning mechanisms and cultural inclinations supplant any need for divine intervention, and religion appears irrelevant. God's role is reduced to simply supplying the content of faith in the teachings of Jesus. Theology's response to CSR would be that God is the ultimate originator of natural mechanisms that conduce to faith and that God transforms natural instruments by grace. Human proclivity could be grace that religion institutionalizes [S. Payne, personal communication, April 16, 2023]. In addition, there are numerous cases of individuals, including St. Paul, who were converted without any opportunity for context bias. CSR does not convincingly explain the formation of Christian beliefs (Ruczak, 2022, pp. 12-13).

Catholicism is clear about the human capacity to accept doctrines that could not be known from observation of the natural world.

> *Faith is a gift of God, a supernatural virtue infused by him.* 'Before faith can be exercised, man must have the grace of God to move and assist him; he must have the interior helps of the Holy Spirit, who moves the heart and converts it to God, who opens the eyes of the mind and makes it easy for all to accept and believe the truth' (*Dei Verbum* 5). (*CCC*, 153)

Neurotheology describes the mystery of God or ultimate reality as closely associated with the human brain. For Judaism, Islam, Christianity, and other religions, God is far more than the circuits and networks of the brain. Christian theology describes God in absolute, transcendental terms until words convey meanings too big to grasp—incomprehensible, omnipotent, limitless. Neuroscience correctly observes that if God is to be known by human persons, the brain will be the physical means through which perception of the divine occurs. Still, theology extends far beyond reason to the all-encompassing trinitarian personal Mystery, Source, and End. For theology, a correlation between an electrochemical neural event and a sense of oneness with all that is would be an interesting, informative discovery. However, changes in human brain networks would not lead to the conclusion that God is readily accessible to the human mind (Delio, 2003, p. 583).

Catholic view of the soul

As we mentioned in Chapter One, some basic challenging-to-define terms such as *mind, soul,* and *consciousness* recur again and again in these chapters. Each time, we try to provide a definition appropriate to the topic we are discussing. In a later chapter, the same term recurs, but now with additional nuances to consider. And, of course, we probably do not cover all possibilities; readers may contribute additional reflections. This cyclical approach applies to the *soul.*

In Chapter Two, we discussed the *soul* as distinguished from the *mind,* with historical background, the basic philosophical understanding of body-soul interaction, how the *soul* associates with the brain, a Catholic stance toward the soul, and the meaning of consciousness. In Chapter Three, we considered the *soul* from the perspective of epistemology, dimensions of consciousness or mind for Lonergan, and the meaning of the rational-volitional soul. In Chapter Four, we considered the *soul* as an organizing form. Chapter Five focused on the free will dimension of the *soul.* Now, in Chapter Twelve, we turn to the theological implications of a Catholic understanding of the *soul* as it is associated with neuroscience.

Soul: Distinctions between scientific and theological perspectives

Distinguishing the concept of the soul from theological as well as scientific perspectives has been challenging, especially since such a concept is generally foreign to scientific investigation. For example, Theologian Ilia Delio wonders:

> Why do we experience transcendence? Why are human beings, in their biological composition, not self-sufficient, self-contained, and completely fulfilled entities? What makes us humans *spiritual* beings? What impels us to seek relationship with another outside and beyond ourselves? That is, why do we need or desire to meditate or pray at all? These are fundamental questions that cannot be entirely answered or entertained by the discipline of neuroscience alone. (2003, p. 580)

Pope John Paul II, greeting a conference (1996) of the Center for Theology and Natural Sciences (CTNS) and Vatican Observatory (1996), confirmed the Church's pursuit of science-and-religion intellectual inquiry.[3] The Pope stressed the importance of considering revelation and including philosophy and theology in discussions that otherwise might result in materialist and reductionist theories. He emphasized that the human person is created in the image of God, the person is of intrinsic value, and persons are made for communion with others and with God. The Pope clarified that while the human body is formed from living matter, the soul is spiritual, created directly by God. The mind does not emerge from matter, nor is it epiphenomenal (inadvertently arising from physiological processes). The human person is ontologically different from the rest of natural creation. Scientific methods cannot measure the spiritual. Philosophy must explain human attributes like self-consciousness, freedom, and moral conscience. Then, theology looks for its final meaning. Revelation in the Bible calls humanity to acknowledge the living God and the human destiny of eternal life (John Paul II, 1996).

Contemporary neuroscience commonly maintains that there is no soul and that human mental activity is solely the by-product of the brain's electro-chemical activity. Early Christian thinkers like Justin Martyr (ca 100-165 CE) disputed the Platonic notion of the soul as being life in favor of the Christian insistence that the soul only partakes of life because "God wills it to live. . . for it is not the property of the soul to have life in itself" (Wolfson, 1993, p. 305, in Burns, 2005, p. 190). In medieval times, as we have seen, with Aquinas' incorporating Aristotelian metaphysics into theology, Christian thought considered the *soul* as the spiritual, enlivening form of the body, actualizing the human person's potential for thinking and loving. The soul accounts for both the biological life and the spiritual dimension of the body, making it a person. Christianity traditionally considers the soul to designate the personal dimension that survives death since it is not subject to dissolution. *Soul* in theology sometimes refers only to the spiritual dimension of the person. In a hylomorphic sense, the soul means the form of the body-and-soul human being. The spiritual soul after death, not fully a body-and-soul human being, expects reunification with a body (G. Bednar, personal communication, April 25, 2023). The soul is the principle of the person that is responsible for their decision-making and capable of union with God (Burns, 2005, p. 181).

Neuroscience generally tries to explain human thought and behavior as derived not from an immaterial soul but from brain processes. Canadian neuropsychologist Michael Persinger, for example, found that electrical stimulation of the temporal lobe can induce a *sensed presence*. He concluded that, therefore, the religious experience of God could be reduced to neurochemistry (1987, p. 4). Replication of Persinger's experiment with subjects donning a sham "God helmet" (with no electric current) suggested that factors such as anomaly-proneness, tendency to paranormal belief, sensory deprivation, and placebo effect influenced subjects' reporting of sensed presence of God (Simmonds-Moore, Rice, O'Gwin, and Hopkins, 2019).

A problem with reducing religious experience to neurophysiology is that religious experiences, notoriously difficult to define, include mental states. Mental states do register biologically but are not located entirely in the brain. Intellect exists in matter only because it belongs to the soul, which is the form of the body (*ST* Ia, q. 76, a. 1 ad 1). Neurons are in the brain, but the thoughts they generate do not occupy space or have a location (Edwards, 1977). In fact, for the rational soul to act, Aquinas held that it did not need a material organ (*ST* Ia, q. 78, a. 1 co). Intellectual power is different from, say, the capability of vision, which depends on the eye.

"The soul is not intelligence, but it is a principle of intellectual knowledge" (Gilson, 2002, p. 231). This might be the essential association between neuroscientific research and hylomorphism—that the soul's rationality does not depend entirely on neurophysiology and that intellectual ability is continually changing with the dynamics of neuroplasticity. Neural connections in the living cerebral organ are always forming and being pruned as the person's education and life experience adapt to the environment and relationships (Battro et al., 2013, p. 233). The capacity of reason is realized through the biological basis of neuroplasticity. There is an interdependence between the neural substrate and the human ability to think and to love, ever-changing throughout the lifespan.

This leads to the consideration of formal and final causes. Empirical science emphasizes material and efficient causes but normally does not pay attention to formal or final causes. To recall, Aristotle names the *material* cause *out of which* an object is made; the *efficient* cause is its principle of change or continuity; the *formal* cause is what the object is; and the *final* cause is its goal or purpose. A table, for instance, is made of wood (material cause), structured with a plane and four legs (formal cause), through carpentry (efficient cause), for dining (final cause).

Aquinas observed that since "nature does not fail in necessary things" (*ST* Ia, q. 78, a. 4 co), the human brain is harmonized with the capacities of the soul in assuring the unity of the human person. The rational soul, guiding human cognitive and volitional abilities, both animates the brain and affects its functioning, spirit acting on matter (Lejeune, 1992, p. 24). Aquinas does not see a problem in the powers of the soul impinging upon physicality (*ST* Ia, q. 76, a. 1 and 4) (Horvat, 2017, p. 20). Regarding formal and final causes, "nature has shaped the human brain (to be) harmonized with the powers of the soul assuring the unity" of the human person (Horvat, p. 20).

Neuroscientists can describe neurons and their connections (material cause) and how neuronal processes work (efficient cause) but cannot say *what overall purpose they serve* (final cause) (Northoff, 2014, p. xi). For Aquinas and Catholicism, the final cause of the human person is beatitude, "with its connotations of meaning, fulfillment, and openness to infinite and transcendental being (Larrivée and Gini, 2014, p. 3)" (Horvat, 2017, pp. 21-22).

Understanding personal identity raises questions that call for distinguishing scientific from theological perspectives. Does human identity depend on the continuity of memory? Brain networks, including the hippocampus, are responsible for learning and memory. Physical correlates of identity are derived from the memory of formative experiences and personal stories/narratives. If there is no spiritual dimension of the person, no soul, death is the end of identity. A materialistic neuroscientific viewpoint makes the question of consciousness and the existence of the mind more challenging to explain than it would be if the Mind (God) were posited as the *ground of being* (Tillich). The Origin of the Universe (Clarke, 2015, p. 223) A mechanical way of thinking is far from that of the biblical writers, early Church fathers, and medieval through contemporary Catholic philosophers (p. 219).

With neuroimaging, we can observe the activation of areas of our brain when we think or pray, expressing soul capacities. With the engagement of the soul, we have a sense of self. Soul communicates that humans are transcendent and that the spiritual dimension is real. According to the Catholic tradition, the spiritual dimension of the person endowed with intellect and will survives death. The Church, from both scripture and tradition, designates this element with the word "soul" (Sacred Congregation for the Doctrine of the Faith, *Letter on Certain Questions Concerning Eschatology*) (Horvat, 2017, p. 7). Tied to morality, the soul is what most authentically represents the person, the site of divine action within the individual, where Wisdom makes humans "friends of God and prophets" (Ws 7:27). More than consciousness or the self, the soul may be considered the locus of relationship (Burns, 2005, p. 193).

The social, relational person

Individual human minds become persons through relationships with others and with God. German Reformed theologian Jürgen Moltmann notes that the person emerges in the "resonance-field of relationships of I-you-we" and through the call of God (Brown et al., 1998, p. 225) (Burns, 2005, p. 192). Christian theology points to the Trinity as the communion of persons in whose image humans are made. Rather than an individualist view of the person, Christian theologians typically refer to the relational person with connotations of intersubjective meaning, thought, and experience (Laidlaw, 2007). In fact, social interactions essentially contribute to cognitive development, language, and the shaping of human behavior (Jeeves and Brown, 2009).

Jesus calls the individual into the relationship: "If anyone is thirsty, let him come to me and drink. Whoever believes in me, . . . streams of living water will flow from within him" (Jn 7:37-38). St. Paul, naming Christ the "image of the invisible God" (Col 1:15), emphasizes the importance of the individual believer relating to Christ—being "in Christ" (Rm 8:1; 1 Thes 4:16), "with Christ" (Phil 1:23), in the "body of Christ" (Rm 12: 4-5, 1 Co 12:27) (Wall, 2015, p. 48). From the Christian theological perspective, Jesus rooted his identity in God's narrative. Walking with the Emmaus disciples, he explained from Scripture all that pertained to himself (Lk 24:27). Christians, made sharers in the body of Christ and members of the household of God (Eph 2:19), see themselves as belonging to the narrative of God, with a destiny for eternal life with God and the redeemed human family.

The soul may also be understood as the openness of human beings to the world. Aristotle observed that "the soul is in a way all existing things" (1991, p. 431b, 21). Being "all existing things" here means the possibility of relating to and taking in, knowing, all that surrounds one. In this dynamic relationship, the human person and their environment mutually impact each other through the soul that animates and unites all parts of the individual. Joseph Ratzinger (the late Pope Benedict XVI) observes that openness in relating to the world, others, and God "constitutes what is deepest in (human) beings. It is nothing other than what we call 'soul'" (*Eschatology: Death and Eternal Life*, 1988, p. 155). "The more open we are, the more are we. . . The man who makes himself open to all being, in its wholeness and its Ground, and becomes thereby a 'self,' is truly a person (p. 155)" (Horvat, 2017, p. 18).

> Our openness to the world is what we call *soul* in its spiritual sense, and the more open we are, the more we become a person. This means that becoming a person is a task, as is becoming human. This way of using the *soul* derives from the soul being the form of the body as both a physical and spiritual form. (G. Bednar, personal communication, April 25, 2023)

Catholic neurobiological ethics: Moral reasoning

In Chapter Five on free will, we began to consider morality from a neuroscientific perspective and the ways that it is associated with Catholic moral theology. Here, we will revisit the theme from the perspective of moral theological implications when neuroscience contributes to understanding human morality, character, and virtue.

For research on self-referential, autobiographical processes at the neural level, neuroimaging studies point to the default mode network (DMN) (Immordino-Yang et al., 2012). The DMN is the brain at rest. Interestingly and counterintuitively, the brain is more active at rest than when cognitively driven toward a goal. Four DMN regions go into motion: the medial prefrontal cortex

(MPFC), inferior parietal lobule (IPL), posterior cingulate cortex (PCC), and insula. These areas are thought to correlate with introspective self-oriented psychological operations (Han, 2016, p. 209). Admiration of another person's moral virtue was found to activate areas in the DMN, the PCC, and the precuneus (Immordino-Yang et al., 2009; Englander et al., 2012). Other DMN regions, the ventromedial prefrontal cortex (VMPFC) and orbitofrontal cortex (OFC), were found to correlate significantly with moral cognition and with prosocial and moral emotion (Moll et al., 2007; Moll and de Oliveira-Souza, 2007; Reniers et al., 2012; Han et al., 2014, 2016; Sevinc and Spreng, 2014). The DMN is thought to be central to the moral self, of interest in character psychology. This means that neuroscience, amazingly, by measuring the strength of functional connectivity between DMN regions and areas correlated with moral qualities such as compassion and indignation, will be able to quantify at the neuronal level individuals' level of moral virtue (Han, 2016, p. 209).

What about virtue as a habit rather than an individual act? Would there be an observable neural difference between brain imaging of a single, one-off virtuous act and that of a person who relatively consistently behaves virtuously? Italian professor of human sciences Claudia Navarini reflects on the finding that virtues affect brain structure. Acquired virtuous expected behavior called *hypotheses of action* (*HA*s) confirm predictable behavioral patterns with likeliness, though not certainty or necessity, of virtuous response. "Neural traces of virtues can be interpreted as major indicators of *HA*s" (Navarini, 2020, p. 309).

Neuroscience can measure gray matter thickness in specific regions using high-resolution structural imaging to measure pathological or developmental alterations (Fischl and Dale, 2000). The microstructure of the human brain can also be quantified through an approach called diffusion-tensor imaging. This method measures anisotropy (the random motion of water molecules in magnetic fields to reflect their mobility in tissues) effects in nerve fiber tracts in the white matter (the axon connectors between neurons in the brain) (Assaf and Pasternak, 2008). There are several conditions in which the fiber tracts between nerve cells are affected that help understand why the brain does not function properly, such as from head injury or neurodegenerative diseases (Muller et al., 2021). Furthermore, there is some initial evidence that various spiritual practices, such as meditation, might affect these white matter tracts with the implication of being beneficial from a clinical perspective (Laneri et al., 2016).

Cortical thickness measurement of the Ventral Frontotemporal Network (VFTN) was found to correlate with spiritual experience, altruism, and love of neighbor, to be thinner with a diagnosis of major depression, and when thicker to show the neuroanatomical improbability of depressive symptoms (Miller et al., 2021, p. 1). The VFTN comprises the caudal-middle-frontal, entorhinal, fusiform, inferior-temporal, medial-orbitofrontal, pars-opercularis, rostral-middle-frontal, superior-temporal, and insula cortices (Desikan et al., 2006, in Miller et al., 2021, p. 3).

Interestingly, since the brain is a living organ, amplification or reduction in character qualities registers in brain structure and can also be quantified by neural measurement. *Phronesis* (practical wisdom), for example, derives from more than intellectual aspects of morality; it also involves motivation, emotion, and behavior (Stovall, 2011; Kristjansson, 2014; Han, 2016, p. 211).

Neuroscientific research finds that emotion plays a part in moral reasoning and choice. Numerous studies have found that individuals with intact cerebral functioning, except for damage to regions associated with emotion, demonstrated significant deficits in practical reasoning, social discernment, and interpersonal relating (Tranel, Hathaway-Nepple, and Anderson, 2007, pp. 319-332). Spezio found that complex cerebral interconnections include emotional signals inextricably mingled with circuits for judgment and action when these pertain to self and others (2011, p. 352).

From a Christian theological perspective, activation of various brain systems is hypothesized to reflect a neurotheological view of the experience of God. Psychotherapy with a spiritual/religious dimension identifies psychological systems of seeking, attachment, and theory of mind (understanding other people by ascribing mental states to them), each of which can be identified neurobiologically. Spiritual thirst may relate to the seeking system that reflects spiritual longing, restlessness, and an object-seeking relationship with God. Experience of a relationship with God may be associated with the attachment system of emotional, interpersonal connectedness with God. The theory-of-mind system may reflect persons' attributions about God or spiritual faith around the scriptural presentation of the life, teachings, and person of Jesus (Fayard, Pereau, and Clovica, 2009, p. 167, 169). The relationship with God clearly involves cognitive, emotional, decisional, evaluative, and behavioral aspects of the brain and mind.

Exemplars, narrative, and embodied cognition

Virtue ethics typically emphasizes the importance of the moral development of exemplars or role models. Contemporary Catholic theologian Linda Zagzebski focuses on the exceptionally good, exemplary person whose example demonstrates and promotes goodness and virtue (2009, pp. 41-57). Moral goodness is known when it is seen in the authentic witness of good persons (cf. *CCC*, 2030). In *Veritatis Splendor*, John Paul II points to Jesus as an ultimate exemplar and norm for Christians. Encounter with Jesus occurs both as he is presented in the Gospels and encounters with the living Christ (Melina, 2001).

Recent studies in neuroscience and psychology also point to the importance of exemplars (Peterson, 2012) and to ways that individuals in community settings learn virtuous behavior and pass it on (Keimer, 2009; Vogt, 2016). Neuroimaging, as we have seen, can even measure the width of neural connections in moral exemplars who actualize virtue in their lives. Physiological indices in the neural structure of exemplars who have acquired moral virtue can be compared with that of ordinary controls (Han, 2016, p. 208). Researchers find that moral exemplars integrate virtue into their sense of self. This means that functional connectivity among their ventral frontal-temporal network (VFTN) brain regions differs significantly from those of persons within normal limits (p. 110). When multiple experiments on virtue and character have been conducted, meta-analyses of results can yield valid and reliable findings regarding neuronal-level measurement of character and virtue (p. 212).

In an interesting study combining mirror-neuronal activation with response to moral dilemmas, researchers found that subjects who demonstrate greater empathy and perspective-taking also were more likely to solve moral dilemmas in the direction of harm-rejection affective (deontological [intrinsic rightness or duty]) response tendencies. This contrasted with outcome-maximization cognitive (utilitarian [ends justify the means]) response tendencies. Subjects who showed increased neural resonance or mirror-neuron activation of sensorimotor areas, including the posterior inferior frontal cortex (pIFC) while witnessing a video of inflicting minor pain on another correlated with higher genuine other-centered concern in solving challenging moral dilemmas (Christov-Moore, Conway, and Iacoboni, 2017).

American-Danish emeritus professor in the history of religions Armin Geertz proposes a *biocultural theory* of religion (2010), noting that research in the cognitive study of religion must observe that cognition is "embodied, encultured, extended, and distributed" (p. 304, in Turner, 2020, p. 223). Or, as we noted in Chapter Three, the brain is *embodied, embedded, enactive, and extended.* Considering either the brain or the social environment, the person is impacted relationally by their social, physical, and cultural context, including religion. Since religion is a powerful cultural institution, neuroscience considers not just the neurobiology of the individual brain but also its embodied condition and the formative impact of culture in human circumstances (Geertz, 2010, p. 317). The Church shapes belief, practice, and character toward moral virtue, as we have seen in Chapters Seven and Eight, through resources including narrative (Scripture, writings of the saints, and descriptions of their exemplary lives); the sanctoral cycle (commemoration of saints throughout the liturgical year); the Liturgy, particularly the Eucharist; sacraments and sacramentals, and Magisterial teaching.

Catholic bioethics: Brain death and resurrection

For a reductionist/materialist notion of the body-mind problem, the death of the individual is particularly concerning. If human identity, mind, consciousness, intellect, and decision-making derive exclusively from the brain, death and dissolution of the body are clearly the end of the person. Survival of the person beyond death would be out of the question. In clear contrast, Christianity and other world religions strongly believe in life after death for an aspect of the human person traditionally called the *soul*. While the popular mentality might think of the *soul* dualistically, a more philosophically accurate understanding could just as well be accepted.

The Christian definition of death has traditionally been the separation of the soul from the body. Both Pope Pius XII and John Paul II have referred to the determination of specific criteria for ascertaining death not to the Church but to medical science.[5] The customary criteria for determining the moment of death has been cardio-pulmonary, i.e., when heartbeat and breathing cease. Today, however, technological means may be used to maintain heartbeat and breathing after the brain has ceased to function. Medical professionals currently, with the approval of the Church, determine death through neurological criteria. These consist of "three basic signs: deep coma or unarousable unresponsiveness, absence of cerebral and brain stem reflexes, and apnea" (National Catholic Bioethics Center [NCBC], 2020).

The use of neurological criteria persists in being controversial because artificial means of maintaining a heartbeat can cause the subject to appear alive to sight and touch. In contrast, confirmation of neurological signs shows cessation of organismic integration. At death, "neurological activity throughout the entire brain, including the cerebrum, cerebellum, and brain stem" (NCBC) will have ceased. Opponents argue that:

> (1) brain death does not disrupt the somatic integrative unity and coordinated biological functioning of a living organism, and (2) guidelines for determining brain death lack sufficient power ... to detect elements of the brain that may retain the potential for recovery (with) optimal medical care. (Verheijde and Potts, 2010, p. 246)

Medical ethicists may continue to discuss the matter of brain death. Still, a Catholic may receive an organ from a donor declared deceased by neurological criteria when these are rigorously and consistently applied. Brain-death criteria do not cause the death of the subject; they only assess that death has already happened. "When all brain function is completely and irreversibly lost, this may be taken as a reasonable indicator that the immortal, immaterial, and rational soul is no longer present" (NCBC).

For clinicians who try to assess whether a patient is in a vegetative state lacking the possibility to recover consciousness and identity vs. those in a transitional condition with minimal consciousness or a locked-in state, fMRI imaging could be crucial. But it needs to be used cautiously. Clinicians need to discriminate whether signs of neuronal activity indicate unspecific, generic brain activation or voluntary responsiveness with awareness. The protection of human life and dignity is at stake (Vicini, 2012, pp. 183-184).

Christianity distinguishes itself by belief in the resurrection of Jesus from death. His rising represents the same perspective condition for all human persons at their deaths. Jesus' teachings about the world to come and the Kingdom of God point to an ethical, relational reality (Burns, 2005). As we have seen, human dignity derives from creation in the image of God, and God is a Trinity of persons. The human person, then, is also constitutively relational. The person's immortal soul is a gift from God, preserved beyond death, both as a sustained conscious identity of the person one has become and as "the cumulative effects of one's life on the cultural and communal memory" (p. 193).

While the New Testament shows firm belief in the resurrection of the body, the intervening state where the dead-and-not-yet-resurrected wait in union with Christ is not clearly described. Scripture indicates that humans, in their core personhood, maintain their existence beyond death without earthly bodies (Burns, 2005, p. 189). Jesus' resurrection and ascension point not to a separable soul-complete-without-a-body but to a transformed whole person— body informed and animated by the soul. The Church summarizes what we know about the elusive, mysterious afterlife:

> By death, the soul is separated from the body, but in the resurrection, God will give incorruptible life to our body, transformed by reunion with our soul. Just as Christ is risen and lives forever, so all of us will rise on the last day. (*CCC*, 1016)

Study Questions

1. How is theology defined?
2. What is meant for Judaism and Christianity by divine self-revelation?
3. In neurobiology, what is meant by the neural binding problem (NBP)?
4. Would brain scanning distinguish between an imagined and an actual perception? Why might this matter in brain-scanning religious experience?

5. When humans come upon a perplexing occurrence, what are they likely to attempt? Why would this make a difference in religious studies?

6. What are three ways humans can come to know that God exists and what God is like?

7. What are some human limitations in understanding and responding to revelation?

8. What are indications that genetics may predispose some persons to spirituality?

9. What is the contention of epiphenomenalism regarding the human soul?

10. Why does human decision-making pose a conundrum for materialistic neuroscience?

11. What is the Catholic view of the human person?

12. How might CSR, when it is materialistic and empirical, tend to explain away religious beliefs?

13. Why might natural explanations of human life still conduce to faith?

14. How do Christians understand the human ability to accept true propositions that are counterintuitive and not empirically verifiable?

15. How would theology answer CSR's attempts to reduce Christian beliefs to a human sociological, cultural, or psychological level?

16. How does Catholicism understand faith?

17. Why, from a Catholic perspective, would neural correlation with divine-human interaction not communicate much about God, the human person, or their relationship?

18. Would it make a difference if theology were incorporated with neuroscience in the interpretive dialogue?

19. How does theology understand the human soul?

20. Are thoughts, mental occurrences, and religious experiences that include mental states to be found in the brain's neural networks? Explain.

21. What are Aristotle's four types of causality? Explain with examples.

22. With which causes does neuroscience generally deal? Theology?

23. How does Catholicism understand the human soul?

24. How theologically are persons social, relational, and open to the world?

25. Why is the DMN central to the moral self?

26. How may hypotheses of action (HAs) be considered neural traces of virtues?

27. How can neural measurement of the VFTN show character qualities registered in brain structure?

28. How has neuroscience ascertained that emotion contributes to moral reasoning and decision-making?

29. How does Christian theology see the experience of God reflected in neurobiologically identifiable psychological systems?

30. How can neuroimaging measure virtue in moral exemplars?

31. How is the neurobiological measurement of empathy in neuronal sensorimotor areas shown to correlate with other-centered concerns in solving moral dilemmas?

32. How may Geertz's bicultural theory of religion apply to the Church?

33. What are the neurological criteria's three signs that the Church uses to ascertain death?

34. What does Catholicism believe about the immortality of the soul, survival of personal identity beyond death, and a final transformed body-soul person?

Endnotes

[1] There is considerable debate among Christian theologians about the meaning of divine self-revelation, both as process and content (cf. Wahlberg, 2020). Augustine "emphasized that Christian belief is produced by God working internally in the believer through grace." "Aquinas affirms both the supernatural, grace-induced character of Christian belief and its rational warrant" (Traditional Views section, para. 4-5). The *Catechism of the Catholic Church* notes that "'even though they contain matters imperfect and provisional' (*Dei Verbum* [*DV*] 15), the books of the Old Testament bear witness to the whole divine pedagogy of God's saving love" (122).

> The writings of the New Testament (*DV* 17, Rm 1:16) . . . hand on the ultimate truth of God's Revelation. Their central object is Jesus Christ, God's incarnate Son: his acts, teachings, Passion, and glorification, and his Church's beginnings under the Spirit's guidance (cf. *DV* 20). (*CCC*, 124)

[2] Multimodal integration of sensory nodes (groups of cells working together) may occur through biochemical oscillations coordinated by the thalamus and corticothalamic connections. Sensory frameworks may fit into a synchronous global oscillatory framework that may underlie human experience (Jerath and Beveridge, 2019).

[3] A resource for dialogue between Catholicism and science since 1990 has been the Center for Theology and Natural Sciences (CTNS) multi-year collaboration with the Vatican Observatory, based in the Graduate Theological Union in

Berkeley, California. Out of its 1996 conference emerged the volume of presentations: *Neuroscience and the Person* (1999).

[4] This might be a category mistake, comparable to saying that because stimulating the area of the brain that has to do with numbers, mathematics must be reducible to neurochemistry (S. Payne, personal communication, April 22, 2023).

[5] John Paul II. (2000). Address of the Holy Father John Paul II to the Eighteenth International Congress of the Transplantation Society. http://www.vatican.va/content/john-paul-ii/en/speeches/2000/jul-sep/documents/hf_jp-ii_spe_20 000829_transplants.html.

Chapter 13

Holiness, Grace, Soul, and the Brain

Call to holiness: Consciousness, spirituality, and grace

Jesuit theologian Karl Rahner, as we have seen in Chapter Eleven, rethought the meaning of consciousness. He observed that consciousness and knowledge can be seen from different angles. Thinking about it, we realize that we do not necessarily either know a thing or not. We may both know and not know something at the same time. In dense style, Rahner summarizes the various ways we can be aware. It is worth slowing down, perhaps rereading, what it means to distinguish separate levels of our unique capacity for consciousness:

> Human consciousness is an infinite, multidimensional sphere: there is reflex[1] consciousness (automatic, nonintentional awareness) and things to which we attend explicitly;
>
> - there is conceptual[2] consciousness of objects to which we attend explicitly;
> - there is conceptual consciousness of objects and a transcendental, unreflected[3] knowledge attached to the subjective pole of consciousness;
> - there is attunement[4] (resonating with the internal state of another person) and propositional knowledge[5] (knowing that or about a thing, person, or event), permitted and suppressed knowledge;
> - there are spiritual events in consciousness and their reflex (automatic) interpretation;
> - there is nonobjectified knowledge of a formal horizon;
> - and finally, there is the knowledge about this object itself. (*Dogmatic Reflections on the Knowledge and Self-awareness of Christ [KSC]*, in Kelly, 1992, p. 187)

Consciousness, with its various dimensions, derives from the fundamental human condition of being spiritual, self-understanding, transcendence, and freedom. Rahner describes an all-pervading basic state present even in persons who have never noticed it; it is always there, whether one is conscious of it or not. Whenever persons look away from themselves and engage intentionally with external realities, they do so from a position of simple self-awareness, an "apparently colorless, basic condition of a spiritual being, . . . an inescapable state of being lit up to oneself, in which reality and one's consciousness of reality are still unseparated from each other, (an awareness) . . . attained only very inadequately and never completely," although one may claim they have already always known it as the ground of all their knowledge (*KSC*, in Kelly, 1992, pp. 194-195). Rahner understands human knowing to implicitly comprehend being in total as an *enabling horizon* whenever it grasps individual things (Coolman, 2009, p. 793).

Lonergan makes a similar observation:

> Since through human consciousness, a psychological subject attains themselves not on the side of the object under the formality of the definable or of the true and of being but only the side of the subject and under the formality of the experienced, it follows that human consciousness is not a knowledge that is complete in itself but from its very formality and nature is a preliminary unstructured awareness that must be structured and completed by intellectual inquiry. (2002, p. 269)

Rahner reflects theologically that in every human person, "there is something like an anonymous, unthematic, perhaps repressed, basic experience of being oriented to God . . . which cannot (be) destroyed" (Egan, 2013, p. 44). Just as we often fail to notice our breathing, heartbeat, or self-awareness, we often fail to notice the horizon, or *objectless awareness* of God and of grace, our foundational spiritual condition, dimly perceived and taken for granted because it is closer to us than we are to ourselves. We often overlook or may deny this ever-extant presence of God (p. 45).

How is it that some persons, sometimes, can perceive and name the presence of God? Or if they do not actually perceive it, can they discern that God is operative? Catholic theology attributes this capacity to *faith* and calls God's intervention *grace*.

What is *grace?* Theologian of grace Rahner defines grace as essentially God's self-communication, addressed to all human persons.

> Therefore, all truly human activity is a free, positive or negative, response to God's offer of self—the grace at the heart of human existence. Because God offers nothing less than God's very own self to everyone, the human person is . . . mystical. This relationship stamps all personal experiences with at least an implicit, primordial experience of God. (Egan, 2013, pp. 43-44)

"Rahner is referring here to *uncreated grace*, that is, God's self-gift. Theologians often distinguish this from *created grace*, the effect of that self-communication in us" (S. Payne, personal communication, April 24, 2023).

According to Rahner, everyone experiences God, at least in a hidden way, constantly, not intermittently.

> People . . . have an implicit but true knowledge of God—perhaps not reflected upon and not verbalized, or better expressed, they have a genuine experience of God ultimately rooted in their spiritual existence, in their transcendentality, in their personality. (Egan, 2013, p. 45)

The experience of grace grounds the life of any person living according to their conscience (p. 44). In Chapter Ten, we have seen observations on spirituality by Lonergan. Philosophers, theologians, and saints across the centuries have observed that human persons are inveterate seekers, always desiring more, always seeing what we strive for against an infinite horizon. Rahner calls this an at-least-implicit experience of God.

Rahner understood the natural human openness to represent the mind implicitly seeking God in all thought and action. Ontologically, the human being is transcendentally disposed to be addressed by God. Rahner called this an *obediential potency,* the human creature's "attitude of listening to an eventual revelation" from God (*Hearer of the Word,* p. 16). The human person is ordinarily, in regular daily ways, interacting with ordinary things, naturally oriented toward God, toward an infinite horizon (Coolman, 2009, p. 794).

We have seen that psychology attempts to measure various dimensions of an individual's self-transcendence, and neuroscience looks for neurophysiological and electrochemical traces of spirituality and transcendence. Neuroscience can contribute to the dialogue with Catholic theology and, in fact, is a necessary conversation partner today as neuroscience advances. It offers the potential advantage of clarifying and supporting the faith for believers.

Neurobiology and transcendence

In the Catholic view, the human person experiences their spiritual nature in consciousness and mental life. Even at the cellular level, the rational mind is physiologically tied to the body. Although the physical powerfully impacts the mental, consciousness and soul afford the person the capacity, within the constraints of ignorance and the limits of physics, to make free choices that transcend the pull of the body (Materialistic neuroscientists would dispute these assumptions. See our explanation of the Catholic position in Chapter Three on epistemology).

> Scientists today often recognize the need to maintain a distinction between the mind and the brain or between the person acting with free will and the biological factors that sustain his intellect and capacity to learn. In this distinction, which need not be a separation, we can see the

foundation of that spiritual dimension proper to the human person, which biblical revelation explains as a special relationship with God the Creator (cf. Gen 2:7) in whose image and likeness every man and woman is made (cf. Gen 1:26-27). (Pope John Paul II, 2003, p. 2)

From the Catholic perspective, the human spiritual consciousness pursues, appreciates, and delights in goodness, truth, and beauty and considers itself obliged to promote the goods of life creatively. The Catholic tradition holds that the human person, in a material world with a physiology that includes the brain, is called to bring the spiritual domains of truth, goodness, and beauty into the material world. By this vocation, the human person glorifies God, the Creator of the material and spiritual orders (McGoldrick, 2012, p. 498).

Scientists themselves perceive in the study of the human mind the mystery of a spiritual dimension that transcends cerebral physiology and appears to direct all our activities as free and autonomous beings, capable of responsibility and love and marked with dignity. This is seen by the fact that you (members of the Pontifical Academy of Sciences) have decided to expand your research to include aspects of learning and education, which are specifically human activities. Your considerations focus not just on the biological life common to all living creatures but also include the interpretive and evaluative work of the human mind. (Pope John Paul II, 2003, p. 2)

This Catholic tradition of a *vocation to holiness* encourages us to be engaged both in self-actualization and in being an instrument for promoting positive, uplifting values in the world. Vatican II, the most recent Catholic ecumenical council, emphasized this:

When a man gives himself to the various disciplines of philosophy, history, and mathematical and natural science, and when he cultivates the arts, he can do very much to elevate the human family to a more sublime understanding of truth, goodness, and beauty, and to the formation of considered opinions which have universal value. Mankind may be more clearly enlightened by that marvelous Wisdom which was with God from all eternity, composing all things with him, rejoicing in the earth, delighting in the sons of men. (*Gaudium et spes*, 1965, par 57)

To summarize the Catholic position on the soul, the spiritual dimension of the person, the soul is the core of rational and moral body/soul existence. The human person is a hylomorphic unity and, after death, lives on as a separated soul. After the Second Coming of Christ, at the end of time, the human person lives on with a resurrected, transformed body. The inner life of consciousness is the site of the sense of self where one finds intimacy with God, who holds the soul, the person, in existence from one moment to the next. In the Catholic view, humans are made for God and will not find full goodness, truth, or beauty except in God.

> Consciousness is the image of the divine in human beings, and neurons are tools of a particular kind of spiritual life that is united to a body and constitutes the human person. As neuroscience attempts to unlock the many facets of human consciousness in concert with the wider world, it will continuously encounter the presence of the spiritual dimension of conscious rational life and its formative part in the person in all her idiosyncratic complexities. (McGoldrick, 2012, p. 499).

Grace enabling response to the divine Word

As we come to the topic of holiness and grace and their interaction with human neurobiology, we can only offer tentative reflections that will need more thorough, comprehensive consideration and distinctions proper to philosophy and theology. It is important to keep in mind that as soon as we enter the domain of divine revelation, theology, and faith, we are in the realm of mystery. The Revealer is the ultimate Mystery, and the human revelation receiver made in the image of God is grounded in mystery.

The Catholic Church holds that there is a universal call to holiness, that all people are called to be holy. "Be perfect, as your heavenly Father is perfect" (Mt 5:48). In Genesis, God tells Abraham, "Walk before me, and be blameless" (Gn 17:1). "The Lord has chosen each one of us 'to be holy and blameless before him in love' (Eph 1:4). Christians particularly, are called to holiness, to be saints" (Pope Francis, *Gaudete et exsultate* [*GE*] 1-2). "All Christians in any state or walk of life are called to the fullness of Christian life and the perfection of charity (*Lumen gentium* [*LG*] 40.2)" (*CCC*, 2013).

Grace means "*favor*, the *free and undeserved help* that God gives us to respond to his call to become children of God, adoptive sons and daughters, partakers of the divine nature and of eternal life (cf. Jn 1:12-18; 17:3; Rm 8:14-17; 2 Pt 1:3-4)" (*CCC*, 1996). "Grace is a *participation in the life of God*" (*CCC*, 1997). "This vocation to eternal life is *supernatural*. It depends entirely on God's gratuitous initiative, for he alone can reveal and give himself. It surpasses the power of human intellect and will, as that of every other creature (1 Co 2:7-9)" (*CCC*, 1998).

As we have noted, "since it belongs to the supernatural order, grace escapes our experience and cannot be known except by faith" (*CCC*, 2005). Rahner grounds our experience of grace in the transcendentality of human nature:

> God is both a given or reality and an experience of the knowing subject: a given of reality insofar as he constitutes the situation of anything we encounter and an experience insofar as he is non-thematically present

as the orientation of human transcendence toward coherence. (Buckley, 1980, p. 39)

According to Rahner, "God is always already giving Godself, and every human being must therefore be engaged with this mystery" (Shae, 2021, p. 652), at least implicitly or unconsciously. Neurotheological studies generally refer to *mystical experience* and its neural correlates, particularly involving a conscious sense of oneness with all that is, with a corresponding deafferentation of the parietal lobe. A Catholic understanding of the meaning of the *mystical* might accept neuroscientific findings but would also look for theological meaning.

> Spiritual progress tends toward union with Christ. This union is called *mystical* because it participates in the mystery of Christ through the sacraments—*the holy mysteries*—and in him, in the mystery of the Holy Trinity. God calls us all to this intimate union with him, even if the special graces or extraordinary signs of this mystical life are granted only to some for the sake of manifesting the gratuitous gift given to all. (*CCC*, 2014)

For theology, *mystical* refers to the sacraments and the effects of their specific graces. In Chapter Eleven, we defined and described mysticism from the perspective of spiritual striving toward union with God. Here, we return to it from the perspective of grace and holiness. The term *mystical* has evolved. In the New Testament, St. Paul referred to the apostles as "servants of the mysteries of Christ" (1 Co 4:1). The Church fathers (e.g., Origen) referred to a *mystical* interpretation of Scripture and to Christ's being hidden in the Eucharistic bread and wine. St. Bernard (twelfth century), by *mystical* meant a consciousness beyond ordinary experience through union with God. St. Teresa of Avila (fifteenth century) pointed to psychological criteria for discerning stages of the mystical journey. By mysticism, Thomas Merton (twentieth century) meant awareness of being transformed in Christ, and Rahner emphasized "every day" transcendence by grace to the boundless mystery of God (Wiseman, 1993, pp. 682-689). "The divine initiative in the work of grace precedes, prepares, and elicits the free response of man. Grace responds to the deepest yearnings of human freedom, calls freedom to cooperate with it, and perfects freedom" (*CCC*, 2022).

Rahner explains created (sanctifying and actual) grace[7] as God's self-communication to the transcendent human spirit, ordering the human person to the direct presence of God, whether consciously perceived or not. Grace transforms the transcendent dimension of the person so that the man or woman of faith is given a share in God's holiness and can attain God himself. In fact, uncreated grace—the Divine Indwelling—*is* God himself, the ground and goal of acts oriented to him. "No particular, categorical object of consciousness is assigned to this grace, which is present rather in transcendent experience" (Rahner, 1979, pp. 40-41).

Growth in grace and holiness: Transformative consciousness

Foremost Catholic scholar of the Western mystical tradition, Bernard McGinn, considers the mystical dimension of Christianity to be its beliefs and practices that lead to consciousness of the direct presence of God (Egan, 2013, p. 540). The mystic, he contends, becomes immediately conscious of new ways of knowing and loving through God's having become the direct, transformative center of one's life (p. 550).

Rahner understands consciousness as making us present to ourselves and God. "Whatever is known or loved as finite and particular ('categorical') is known and loved against the 'transcendental horizon' of holy Mystery, like a distant ship viewed against the sky" (Egan, 2013, p. 550). Rahner holds that we see specific knowledge against an implicit, obscure spiritual awareness of mysterious absolute Being—spirit, freedom, and God.

Regarding the freedom of a finite creature, Rahner observes that a certain degree of ignorance—the challenge of not knowing the outcome, of being unclear about the consequences—co-occurs with self-realization in human decision-making (Rahner, *KSC*, p. 189). Christian faith points to the eternal Word incarnate in Jesus as Alpha and Omega. God became human, so that to see him is to see the Father (Jn 14:9). He is the source and summit of the Christian Catholic faith, the exemplar for all virtue and holiness. The incomprehensible mystery is that and how Jesus, who became Man, has remained a creature. "He is *now* and for all eternity the *permanent openness* of our finite being to the living God of infinite eternal life. One always sees the Father only through Jesus" (Rahner, 1974, p. 44).

Christ is the exemplar of virtue and holiness—in whom dwells all the fullness of the Godhead bodily (Col 2:9). In Christ, two natures with two consciousnesses are unmixed and unchanged in one subject, one divine person aware of both his consciousnesses (Lonergan, 2002, p. 245). German philosopher and theologian Romano Guardini (1885-1968) concludes regarding Jesus that "the mind must never allow itself to be misled into seeming 'comprehension.' The whole problem—of his person and consciousness—is a mystery, the sacred mystery of the relationship of the triune God to his incarnate Son" (1954, p. 27).

We are considering human virtue and holiness, the call of every human person to strive to perfect the image of God that they ontologically are. Catholics understand the human virtues to be grounded in "the theological virtues, which adapt (human) faculties for participation in the divine nature (cf. 2 Pt 1:4)" since they relate directly to God. The theological virtues of faith, hope, and charity "dispose Christians to live in a relationship with the Holy Trinity. They have the One and Triune God for their origin, motivation, and object." (*CCC*, 1812)

> The theological virtues of faith, hope, and charity are the foundation of Christian moral activity. God infuses them into the souls of the faithful to make them capable of acting as his children and of meriting eternal life. They are the pledge and presence and action of the Holy Spirit in the faculties of the human being. (*CCC*, 1813)

Experience of grace

According to Rahner, "mysticism as the experience of grace grounds not only the ordinary Christian's life of faith, hope, and love but also that of anyone living according to his or her conscience" (Egan, 2013, p. 44). Rahner addresses not just exceptional, notable occurrences of mystical oneness with the All but a *masked mysticism* of the masses, in its most profound form, the unreserved love for another. "Accepting the depths of one's humanity, the depths of life and thus Mystery itself—fostered either with or without explicit Christian faith, hope, and charity—is the salient feature in Rahner's mysticism of everyday life" (p. 46).

In Chapter Eleven on mysticism, we considered Rahner's description of grace. He sees its evidence less in spiritual elation than in fidelity to God when he seems absent, in selfless generosity or fidelity to duty in ordinary life when no gratitude is forthcoming, or in commitment to onerous obligation without a sense of having done a noble deed (Theology of the Spiritual Life, in *Theological Investigations, 3*, 1974, pp. 87-88). He attempts to discern the subtle point at which the natural becomes supernatural when the Holy Spirit transforms the human receiver of grace through an act of faith to recognize and respond to divine revelation and invitation. Where human rationality and inclination would not venture, supernatural virtue steps in.

> Once we experience the spirit in this way, we (at least, we as Christians who live in faith) have also already, in fact, experienced the *supernatural*. It is not merely the Spirit but the Holy Spirit who is at work in us. Then is the hour of his grace. Then the seemingly uncanny, bottomless depth of our existence as experienced by us is the bottomless depth of God communicating himself to us, the dawning of his approaching infinity, which no longer has any set paths, which is tasted like nothing because it is infinity. (Rahner, 1974, p. 89)

Grace, as we have seen, differs ontologically from natural cognition, emotion, attitude, and behavior and does not necessarily register in human consciousness. From Scripture, Church teaching, and the lives of the saints, we can say that grace is operative when the human person defers to the divine. The radically deferential, obediential attitude that governs relations among the Persons of the Trinity also characterizes the image-of-God human person in their thinking, feeling, and acting.

> When we have let ourselves go and no longer belong to ourselves, when we have denied ourselves and no longer have the disposing of ourselves, when everything (including ourselves) has moved away from us as if into an infinite distance, then we begin to live in the world of God himself, the world of the God of grace and eternal life. (1974, p. 89)

God's self-communication to humanity, to the individual human person, is central to Rahner's understanding of divine kenosis. God has created human persons with the capacity to receive God in their inmost being (*Foundations of Christian Faith [FCF]*, 1976, p. 223) (Rosok, 2017, p. 52). Rahner sees the human person as necessarily *transcending* self and all other objectives toward an infinite horizon (God). The transcending human person called by the self-communicating God reaches toward this *mystery*, whether consciously or not (*FCF,* p. 210). The human person hopes for unity with the One toward whom their transcending is directed (*FCF,* p. 208). This hope is a consequence of God's grace and the human person's response to grace, even if implicit and non-conscious (Rosok, 2017, p. 53).

In *Hearer of the Word* (1941), Rahner focuses on the transcendental nature of the person implicitly listening for a word of revelation. He describes human *engracement* as "a *supernatural existential* that elevates, illuminates, and orients human transcendence toward its end in God" (Coolman, 2009, p. 794). Rahner holds that the human person finds themselves transcendentally attuned to divine self-communication. "Interestingly, this description of human nature seems to be confirmed by recent studies in neuroscience suggesting that attunement is, as it were, genetically 'hard-wired.' (See Newberg, d'Aquili, and Rause, 2001)" (p. 796).

We may or may not be aware of grace. Jesuit professor of theology Henry Shae notes that Rahner's transcendentality seeking verification in philosophy and theology for God's universal salvific will (1 Tim 2:4), where every human being is uninterruptedly in touch with nonthematic experience of an infinite horizon and hearer, at least implicitly, of God's self-giving revelation, runs into internal difficulties that may be called "transcendental overextension" (2021, p. 661).[10] We may not yet be able to resolve the question of how one could implicitly experience the transcendent when it does not register in human consciousness.

Connaturality and conditions for spiritual attunement

As we have seen, Rahner considers all humans as transcendental, spiritual creatures who are directly present to God as the ground and horizon of their existence, against which their dealings with daily life take place (*Theological Investigations* [*TI*], 5, p. 209). In Jesus, this intrinsic spiritual condition is the result of a hypostatic[8] assumption by the Logos of a complete human nature. Throughout his human development, Jesus was always "completely attuned to his Father's inspiriting love" (Kelly, 1992, p. 186). Jesus' hypostatic union is unique to him but analogous to the transcendental, spiritual condition of all human persons. Rahner describes this *direct presence-to-God* relationship as an *attunement* (*Gestimmtheit*) that serves as the foundation and horizon of consciousness, the "framework in which cognition and volition occur" (Coolman, 2009, p. 793). On an ethical level, attunement may refer to resonance or connaturality. Through repeated acts of virtuous knowing and loving, the person becomes connaturally attuned to the good (p. 798). The essential connection between nature and grace, for Rahner, can be found in their harmony or attunement (p. 799).

According to Aquinas, "charity makes us 'connatural' with God, uniting us to God' (*ST* II-II, q.45, a.2)" in a way that makes God directly present to us. Through connaturality with God, we intuitively understand the divine realities that we know through faith, but otherwise, we would be without charity (Garrigou-Lagrange, 1937, p. 315). Charity, Aquinas says, "adheres to God immediately" (*ST* II-II, q. 27, a. 4, sed contra). By the Holy Spirit's gift of wisdom, we perceive God as higher and more excellent than human knowledge can grasp, that "more lies hidden in things of faith than faith itself reveals" (John of St. Thomas, in Maritain, 1959, p. 262, in Duke, 2018, pp. 14-16).

Second-person perspective and Divine Indwelling

To understand *connaturality* or *attunement,* physicist and Catholic priest Andrew Pinsent, Research Director at the Oxford University Centre for Science and Religion, points to the experience of *joint attention,* or second-personal relatedness. This is *thinking with* an attuned resonance between persons that involves joint attention to a third entity. This human experience begins in infancy with a baby following the mother's gaze and lasts through life in the shared attention of friends looking out on the world. A subjective experience, joint attention is triadic: person-person-object. The *meeting of minds* (Elian et al., 2005) involves (1) awareness of the other person, (2) cognitive coordination with the other, (3) an inclination to approve their synchronization, and (4) a joint understanding and purposeful attitude toward the object (Pinsent, 2015a, p. 1610). From a theological perspective, second-personal relating translates to a supernatural level. Belief in a personal and loving God who can infuse spiritual capacities into human persons sees that God empowers humans to relate to God second-personally as *I* to *you* or *I-thou* (Buber, 1923). The experience in time can culminate in attuned divine-human friendship (Pinsent, 2015a, p. 1607).

Experimental psychology finds that joint attention in an infant with their caregiver contributes to the child's social-neurobiological development. "Full joint attention requires that a person 'share an awareness of the sharing of the focus that often entails sharing an attitude toward the thing or event in question'" (Hobson and Bishop, 2003, p. 185, in Pinsent, 2015b, p. 43).

The divinely bestowed supernatural gift of sanctifying and actual grace inclines the human person to friendship and cooperation with God, to a developing connaturality and attunement. With baptism, the human person becomes a dwelling for the Persons of the Trinity, a recipient of the uncreated grace of the Divine Indwelling.

> The ultimate end of the whole divine economy is the entry of God's creatures into the perfect unity of the Blessed Trinity (cf. Jn 17:21-23). But even now, we are called to be a dwelling for the Most Holy Trinity. "If a man loves me," says the Lord, "he will keep my word, and my Father will love him, and we will come to him, and make our home with him" (Jn 14:23). (*CCC*, 260)

Western virtue ethics, based on the Aristotelean principle of *eudaimonia— happiness, flourishing* was expanded by Thomas Aquinas' introduction of the *infused* virtues (Pinsent, 2015a, p. 1603). The infused virtues differ from the ordinary understanding of virtue as habituation to an attitude or behavior through repeated practice. Infused virtues are more like dispositions or capacities that incline a person to a kind of joint attention relationship with God. The recipient of divinely infused virtues develops attitudes to a variety of subjects that, without the relationship, they would not have (p. 1606). The infused theological virtues might be thought of as intended to reverse a kind of spiritual *autism* caused by the Fall. God's asking Adam, "Where are you?" (Gn 3:9) manifested a rupture in attuned divine-human relations (pp. 1606-1607).

Aquinas explains that the infused virtues differ from typical attitudinal/ behavioral habituation in that failure in the form of a single serious, deliberate moral offense can cut off the person's relationship with God and deprive subsequent acts of their merit. The state of divine friendship and harmonious second-person relationship can terminate with even one grave offense. It would be like a husband-wife relationship where one partner is unfaithful. The offender may continue to help with chores around the house and pretend that nothing has changed, but unless the fundamental infidelity is resolved, the relationship is seriously damaged. When it is resolved by forgiveness and reconciliation, harmonious second-person relating can be restored (Pinsent, 2015a, p. 1607).

Interpersonal neurobiology and holiness

We have seen how Catholic theology might understand holiness from a developmental, relational psychological perspective as human connaturality or attunement with God or as a second-person relating to the Indwelling Trinity. How might neuroscience contribute to understanding the second-person perspective as it relates to holiness? A recent brain-scan study showed that in facing moral dilemmas, Catholics, in contrast to non-believers, use perspective-taking, factoring in the viewpoint and attitudes of another Person.

Roman Catholic beliefs have been found to demonstrate specific neural reactions to moral quandaries. A brain-scan study investigated whether religious beliefs influenced neural and behavioral responses to moral problems (Christensen et al., 2014). Forty-eight moral dilemmas were presented to 11 Catholic and 13 atheist women. Results showed a differential activation between the two groups of the precuneus and in the prefrontal, frontal, and temporal regions. For deontological (although only morally good) actions, Catholics recruited the precuneus and tempo-parietal junction, and for utilitarian moral judgments, the dorsolateral prefrontal cortex (DLPFC) and temporal poles. Atheists did not show differentiation in area; they recruited only the superior parietal gyrus for both deontological and utilitarian judgment. Both groups were then tested regarding personal and impersonal moral problems. For utilitarian responses to impersonal moral dilemmas, Catholics showed increased activation in the DLPFC and posterior cingulate cortex (PCC). For deontological moral judgments for personal problems, Catholics showed nuanced responses in the anterior cingulate cortex (ACC) and superior temporal sulcus. A limitation of this study was its small, ungeneralizable sample size. Thus, much more research in this direction is needed.

Results show that norms acquired through religious doctrine and practice do influence moral judgment. Dilemmas included a confrontation between two incommensurable prohibitions of Catholic belief (in this case, to care and help vs. not to kill). Catholics' cognitive wrestling with challenging moral propositions was evident in neural imaging of their moral reasoning process (Christensen et al., 2014, p. 240). The findings suggest that Catholics engaged in perspective-taking, considering what their faith indicated that God would approve or, according to the popular Christian saying, "What would Jesus do?" This would seem to suggest a second-person perspective not seen in individuals who self-identify with atheism.

Relationality appears to prevail when it comes to holiness. The human person relates with the Trinity and promotes the well-being of other human persons. Interpersonal neurobiology (IPNB), intersecting with spirituality, offers insights and therapeutic suggestions for human psychological and spiritual growth conducive to holiness.

Spirituality is one of the terms in our cyclical approach to the main themes of this study that recurs again and again, each time with meaning from a new angle. Spirituality may be considered "an important, abiding, multilevel-multidimensional aspect of human experience that touches on manifold dimensions of life, including the sociocultural, intellectual, emotional, behavioral, neurobiological, and existential" (Zinnbauer and Pargament, 2005) or more simply, "a way to relate to the sacred" (Hollingsworth, 2008, p. 839). Interpersonal neurobiology is uniquely positioned to promote a concomitant awareness of self and others that fosters empathy. Here, reciprocal sharing does not mean boundaryless fusion but includes appropriate self-differentiation (maintaining identity and autonomy while relating meaningfully with another).

The *brain* may be considered an open system. The person continually interacts with other persons and the environment, developing and revising itself across the lifespan. Clinical professor of psychiatry Daniel Siegel sees the human *mind* as interpersonal as well as neurobiological, "a process that regulates the flow of energy and information" (2007, p. 5). *Mind* may be thought of as emerging "at the dynamic interface of embodied and relational processes" (Hollingsworth, 2008, p. 842).

IPNB as a theory and working model emphasizes particularly the brain regions, such as the prefrontal cortex and limbic system, that involve the interaction of neurobiology with relationships and personality formation. The right limbic brain regions are central to self-regulation and socioemotional processing (Schore, 2003a), as well as empathy. The middle prefrontal cortex is key to the "functional flow of states of mind across time" (Siegel, 1999, p. 8), the coordinating process of neural integration. With improved neural integration, the person is better able to be self-aware, regulate emotion, modulate response to stress, develop biographical narratives, respond empathically, and build satisfying relationships (Hollingsworth, 2008).

Cozolino highlights areas critical to the social brain. Long-term emotional connections, empathy, and cooperation with others are linked to the *cingulate cortex*. For directing perceptions, behaviors, and interactions and integrating external sensory and internal emotional data with motivation and reward networks, there is the *orbital medial prefrontal cortex* (OMPFC). To connect consciousness with physical processes like hunger and thirst, sexual behavior, and aggression, the *hypothalamus* is activated. For awareness of physical states and consideration of affective experiences, the *anterior cingulate* is operative, and to negotiate a wide range of emotions, the *insula cortex*. The *hippocampus* helps with organizing affective, spatial, and sequential learning and memory. The *amygdala* speedily detects danger and responds to threats with a fight-or-flight reaction. In addition, the cortical and subcortical sensory, affective, and motor networks and regulatory systems constitute the social brain (2006, pp. 51-57, in Hollingsworth, 2008, p. 843).

Neurobiologists find that attunement—interpersonal and intrapersonal— contributes significantly to human well-being. Trusting and loving interpersonal relationships like friendship, marriage, psychotherapy, or any meaningful interpersonal bonding can engage neuroplastic processes. These can heal psychological wounds and repair neural dysfunction. The intrapersonal process of mindfulness—nonjudgmental attention to one's internal thoughts and feelings with centering in the present moment—can facilitate brain integration as well as emotional regulation and impulse control.

The mirror neuron system at the junction of visual, emotional, and motor neural centers in the frontal and parietal lobes helps attune to the mental and emotional states of others. Humans who *feel felt* in experiencing affective attunement to another attentive person are likely to develop and express empathy and respond with effective compassion while sustaining a secure state of self-awareness. From a spiritual perspective, secure intra- and interpersonal attunement and resonance with others can foster a sense of transcendence in contact with the sacred. Interpersonal neurobiology and spirituality together can foster secure, trusting relationships. These facilitate neuroplasticity toward higher levels of neural integration, leading to empathy and compassion toward others and spiritual receptivity to the sacred (Hollingsworth, 2008, p. 852).

"Holiness is the most attractive face of the Church," Pope Francis reflected. "But (also) outside the Catholic Church and in very different contexts, the Holy Spirit raises 'signs of his presence'" (*GE*, 2018, no. 9). The Catholic Church uses processes of beatification and canonization (official recognition of a deceased person as a saint) to verify signs of heroic virtue such as martyrdom or a self-sacrificial life. The saint is proclaimed to be worthy of veneration by the faithful as exemplary in imitating Christ. But not only the beatified or canonized are among the saints. Also saintly are ordinary men and women on whom the Holy Spirit bestows grace to be holy (*GE*, nos. 5-6).

> Very often, holiness is found in our next-door neighbors, those who, living in our midst, reflect God's presence. In those parents who raise their children with immense love, in those men and women who work hard to support their families, in the sick, in elderly religious who never lose their smile. Each saint is a mission planned by the Father to reflect

and embody, at a specific moment in history, a certain aspect of the Gospel. (*GE*, nos. 7, 19)

Psychological health and growth in holiness

How might neuroscience or its concomitant psychological contributors, such as interpersonal neurobiology and spirituality, help to promote holiness? We keep in mind that holiness derives from grace rather than from human effort, but human cooperation is indispensable.

An fMRI study involving 17 children with high-functioning autism spectrum disorder (ASD) found that intranasal administration of oxytocin (OT) significantly increased brain activity around judgments regarding socially meaningful (eyes) pictures, in contrast with socially non-meaningful (vehicles) ones. Affected by OT were the striatum, middle frontal gyrus, medial prefrontal cortex, right orbitofrontal cortex, and the left superior temporal sulcus. In addition, social judgments were associated with increased salivary OT concentrations along with increased right amygdala and orbitofrontal cortex activation. Thus, oxytocin was found to selectively affect children with ASD regarding how they process socially meaningful stimuli and foster their social attunement. (Gordon et al., 2013, p. 20953). It would be interesting to follow up this study with larger ones, as well as studies designed to see whether oxytocin might facilitate second-personal relationships.

Research on religious coping finds that an individual's stress resilience is positively associated with attachment to God, "a relatively stable emotional bond that forms through continuous communication and requires interaction, pleasure, and relaxation" (Sharifi, 2018). A 2018 cross-sectional study in Iran included 300 elderly patients with chronic low back pain. They were administered a demographic form, a religious coping survey, and questionnaires on attachment to God and perceived pain intensity. Significant correlations were found between pain intensity and degree of attachment to God and religious coping (Hatefi et al., 2019, p. 465). Secure attachment, as opposed to insecure, anxious, or avoidant styles, is associated with better psychological health. Those securely attached to God who valued their relationship with God were found to have better mental health (Leman et al., 2018, in Hatefi et al., p. 466).

A study exploring attachment to God, interpersonal attachment, religiosity, and moral disengagement involved 30 offenders in Italian jails. Subjects were administered a semi-structured interview for demographic, medical, social, and legal data and scales on attachment to God, general attachment style, and intrinsic/extrinsic religiosity. Results found that extrinsic religiosity predicts moral disengagement and is associated with avoidant attachment to God (D'Urso, 2019, p. 1). Attachment to God is a construct supported by a study conducted by Kirkpatrick and Shaver (1992). It shows that as a child relates to their caregiver with a secure, ambivalent, or avoidant attachment style, God can serve as an attachment figure. He can serve as a secure base that reassures, protects, and allows exploration because he is available in stressful situations. God can represent a safe place to store hopes, desires, anxieties, and problems with a sense of belonging and of being listened to and supported (Kirkpatrick and Shaver, 1992; Pace, Cacioppo, and Schimmenti, 2011).[9] Cassiba, Granqvist, Costontini, and Gatto (2008) found that a personal relationship with God can be considered attachment even though nobody apart from the sacramental presence of Christ normally appears to the believer (D'Urso et al., 2019, p. 2).

Intrinsic religiosity values faith, is motivating, promotes self-transcendence, and implies sacrifice and commitment. Faith involves acceptance of a set of beliefs that people internalize and decide to pursue; it becomes a major reason for living (Fizzotti, 2008). Attachment to God with intrinsic religiosity links to prosocial and altruistic thinking (D'Urso, 2019, p. 8).

Saintliness

What is the end of the journey to holiness? What for Catholic theology is the *unio mystica* that neuroscience correlates with neural deafferentation of the parietal lobe? We might ask foremost Catholic mystics Teresa of Avila and John of the Cross about the goals of the mystical life. Like Augustine, they affirm that through the soul, the human person made in the image of God is already from the moment of creation in an intersubjective, trinitarian relationship with God (Howells, 2002, p. 125). With a mystical or transforming union, the deepened self moves outside the bounds of its natural life and into God. The self is included in the life of the Trinity to the degree that all the person does is in relation to the Trinitarian God. "In union, the mystical self knows both God and itself at once without going through creatures as in natural knowing" (p. 126). In heaven, the person will enjoy the beautiful vision of God. Here, having attained permanent union with God, the person goes out to do the work of Christ in the world with greater strength (Teresa of Avila, 7 M 4:4-10) (Howells, p. 128). Teresa concluded, "Do you know what it means to be truly spiritual? It means becoming the slaves[11] of God. Spiritual persons can be sold by him as slaves of everyone, as he was" (7 M, 4:8).

The spiritual process of arriving at a transforming union involves a heightened consciousness of God where loving awareness of the divine presence becomes habitual. The human person, having "cleared the mind of created forms and having removed all inordinate desires . . . becomes one spirit with God, not substantially, but consciously" (Granville, 1991, p. 186). The person becomes aware of the eternal mystery and is responsive to grace in good works: "For we, beholding the glory of the Lord with unveiled (open) face, are transformed into the same image from glory to glory as by the Spirit of the Lord" (2 Co 3:18) (p. 186).

Pope Francis, reflecting on beatified and canonized saints, observes that they are not "sourpusses" but men and women with joyful hearts, open to hope. Grounded in a "daily existence of family ties, study, and work, social, economic, and political life, they constantly strive to carry out God's will." The saints, "always alive and timely, provide a fascinating commentary on the Gospel." (Causes of Saints, 2022). The pope recommends a prayer he has prayed daily for 40 years by St. Thomas More:

> Grant me, O Lord, good digestion and also something to digest. Grant me a healthy body and the necessary good humor to maintain it. Grant me a simple soul that knows to treasure all that is good, and that doesn't frighten easily at the sight of evil but rather finds the means to put things back in their place. Give me a soul that knows not boredom, grumbling, sighs, and laments, nor excess of stress because of that obstructing thing called 'I.' Grant me, O Lord, a sense of good humor. Allow me the grace to be able to take a joke to discover a bit of joy in life and to be able to share it with others. (*GE*, 2018, fn 101)

Catholic view of the Word as full Truth

Catholicism is encouragingly supportive of science. "Those who teach theology in seminaries and universities collaborate with those versed in sciences, sharing their resources and points of view (Pope Paul VI, *Gaudium et spes*, 62 [1965]). There is a fundamental Catholic principle of non-contradiction. "The same God who establishes the intelligibility of the natural order reveals himself as the Father of the eternal Word; in him is 'the full truth'" (cf. Jn 1:14-16) (John Paul II, *Fides et ratio.*, [1998]).

Pope John Paul II explains how the Church pursuing natural and faith-based truth concludes that the definitive truth sought by both science and faith can be found in the Word, the second Person of the Trinity, incarnate in Christ:

> The unity of truth is a fundamental premise of human reasoning, as the principle of non-contradiction makes clear. Revelation renders this unity certain, showing that the God of creation is also the God of salvation history. It is the same God who establishes and guarantees the intelligibility and reasonableness of the natural order of things upon which scientists confidently depend and who reveals himself as the Father of our Lord Jesus Christ. This unity of truth, natural and revealed, is embodied in a living and personal way in Christ, as the Apostle reminds us: "Truth is in Jesus" (Eph 4:21; Col 1:15-20). He is the eternal Word in whom all things were created, and he is the incarnate

Word who in his entire person reveals the Father (cf. Jn 1:14, 18). What human reason seeks "without knowing it" (cf. Acts 17:23) can be found only through Christ: what is revealed in him is "the full truth" (cf. Jn 1:14-16) of everything which was created in him and through him and which therefore in him finds its fulfillment (cf. Col 1:1). (Pope John Paul II, 1998, *Fides et ratio*, par. 34)

Ultimately, mystery

We recall that this chapter deals with the realm of mystery. When God communicates with the human person by grace, God's presence and operation might register on the physiological level so that a brain scan could pick it up. It also might not. God could work on the purely spiritual level of intellect and will, and his presence might not be observable or measurable. There were saints such as St. Paul of the Cross and St. Mother Teresa of Calcutta who spent long years practicing faith, hope, and charity to a heroic degree and were conscious more of the absence than the presence of God. They were known by their fruits (cf. Mt. 7:16). We can appreciate the saints and find them exceptional exemplars. Along with neuroscientific exploration, a Catholic perspective would respect the mystery of the human soul and person made in the image of God and the mystery of God's interaction with his saints.

Implications of theology-neuroscience dialogue

In Chapters Twelve and Thirteen, we considered various dimensions of the dialogue between theology and neuroscience from a Catholic perspective and reflected on implications for growth in grace and holiness. Bringing forward some highlights from our explorations might help us to reflect on possible benefits for conversation in view of a potential new field of neurotheology. These suggestions are not exhaustive; revisions or additional ideas are most welcome. We start with suggestions from the Church in support of dialogue between faith and science.

As we have seen, the Pastoral Constitution on the Church in the Modern World, *Gaudium et spes* (1965) acknowledges that:

Although the Church has contributed much to the development of culture, experience shows that . . . it is sometimes difficult to harmonize culture with Christian teaching. These difficulties do not necessarily harm the life of faith. Rather, they can stimulate the mind to a deeper and more accurate understanding of the faith. The recent studies and findings of science, history, and philosophy raise new questions that affect life and demand new theological investigations. Furthermore, theologians, within the requirements and methods proper to theology, are invited to seek continually more suitable ways of communicating doctrine to the men of their times, for the deposit of Faith or the truths are one thing, and the manner in which they are enunciated, in the same meaning and understanding, is another. In pastoral care, sufficient use must be made not only of theological principles but also of the findings of the secular sciences, especially of psychology and sociology, so that the faithful may be brought to a more adequate and mature life of faith.

Catholic theology endorses Aquinas' Aristotelian hylomorphic model of the soul as a form of the body and the unity of the human person. When a believer lives out their faith using cognition, emotion, attitude, and behavior, physiological effects register in the brain. While the cognitive science of religion tends to interpret religious practice on an empirical, natural level, Christians instead understand religious practice in terms of the grace of faith. Theology knows God as the absolute transcendent Mystery and divine revelation as originating in God. Neuroscience studies the neural apparatus through which, from a Catholic perspective, the human person graced with faith perceives and apprehends divine self-communication in a limited human way. Interdisciplinary neurotheology might explore ways that the human person could internalize revelation and live out its message.

From a Catholic perspective, dimensions of the human soul, such as identity, intellect, consciousness, and decision-making, derive from spiritual capacities endowed by the Creator who infuses the soul at conception. Being made in the image of God is the source of ineradicable human dignity for every person. Neuroscience can observe, to some degree, but not measure or control, spiritual aspects of the human soul. Still, since the spiritual, psychological, and physiological are closely interwoven, neuroscience can make a valuable contribution to understanding the neural bases of human functioning.

Christianity holds that humans reflect the social nature of the Trinity—interdependent relationality—in view of human personal development and the social pursuit of the common good. In openness to the world and others, human persons strive for Truth, Goodness, and Beauty. Theology has long recommended virtue for human flourishing. Neuroscience is beginning to demonstrate that it can show measurable evidence of the practice of virtue in specific neural regions. The neuroscientific theory also expands the understanding of the brain as embodied, embedded, enacted, and extended. Neuroscience might continue to explore the promise of virtue in its neural dimensions for human social and spiritual flourishing.

Catholic theology holds that the neurophysiological dimension of the human person was assumed with body-and-soul corporality by the incarnate Word. Catholicism holds that the soul survives beyond death and will be reunited with the body at the final general resurrection. Jesus is immortal, and by virtue of their souls, so are all human beings, ultimately to be reunited with our bodies, transformed beyond death to live forever. Neuroscience might make a valuable contribution by continuing to explore end-of-life issues from a Catholic perspective.

Catholic pastoral practice can benefit from the neuroscientific study of consciousness informed by Rahner's theology of transcendence, with appropriate theological understanding, and by other theologians endorsed by the Church. Respect for God's self-gift to all human persons and the presence of grace, even if implicit, where persons act with goodwill, can promote appreciative regard for every other, however diverse or disadvantaged, with an open attitude to persons of every or no faith tradition. Connaturality or attunement, second-personal relating, and interpersonal neurobiology associate theology and neuroscience in describing from a Catholic perspective the dynamics of social interaction, grace developing into union with God, appreciation of grace and the Divine Indwelling, and holiness.

Study Questions

1. What meanings or levels of consciousness does Rahner suggest?

2. How does Lonergan understand human consciousness?

3. Why, according to Rahner, do we often fail to notice the horizon of our awareness?

4. For Catholic theology, what is *grace*?

5. What does Rahner mean in saying that everyone receives God's uncreated grace?

6. What does *obediential potency* mean?

7. How might dialogue with neuroscience benefit Catholic theology?

8. According to Pope John Paul II, what are indications that scientists perceive a spiritual dimension of the human mind?

9. What, in summary, is the Catholic position on the soul?

10. What does Catholicism mean by the universal call to holiness enabled by grace?

11. How, for Catholic theology, has the meaning of *mystical* evolved?

12. How, regarding mystical experience, might Catholic understanding interpret neuroscientific findings of conscious oneness with all that is, corresponding to parietal-lobe deafferentation?

13. What dimensions of a Catholic understanding of mystical experience might research in the emerging field of neurotheology explore next?

14. What is meant by transformative consciousness?

15. How does Rahner understand the experience of grace?

16. What does Rahner mean by the *supernatural existential*?

17. Are grace and mystical union always perceived or experienced by the mystic or others? Explain.

18. What is meant by attunement, resonance, or connaturality with God?

19. How does Pinsent describe connaturality as joint attention?

20. How might the Thomistic understanding of infused virtues facilitate the attunement of the human person with God?

21. What preliminary findings did neuroscientific research into moral judgment show regarding perspective-taking by religious individuals?

22. Why might the study of IPNB contribute to understanding the fundamentals of holiness?

23. How is psychological health related to growth in holiness?

24. What happens in a saintly transforming union regarding attitude, consciousness, and behavior?

25. How does the Catholic principle of non-contradiction apply to the dialogue between science and faith?

26. Is grace necessarily brain-scannable? Explain.

27. What are some implications of a neuroscience dialogue with theology?

Endnotes

[1] Reflex refers to an involuntary, automatic, nonconscious response to a stimulus.

[2] Conceptual is based on mental concepts.

[3] Not reflected on or considered

[4] Attunement refers to resonance or being in harmony with the internal world of another.

[5] Propositional knowledge is knowledge that or about.

[6] Philosophy: underlying reality or substance

[7] "Sanctifying grace is a habitual gift, a stable and supernatural disposition that perfects the soul itself to enable it to live with God, to act by his love. *Habitual grace,* the permanent disposition to live and act in keeping with God's call, is distinguished from *actual graces,* which refer to God's interventions, whether at the beginning of conversion or in the course of the work of sanctification" (*CCC,* 2000).

[8] "We confess that one and the same Christ, Lord, and only-begotten Son, is to be acknowledged in two natures, without confusion, change, division, or separation. The distinction between the natures was never abolished by their union, but rather the characteristics proper to each of the two natures, was preserved as they came together in one person and one hypostasis" (Council of Chalcedon [451 AD]: DS 302; *CCC,* 467).

[9] Of course, this psychological meaning of God as an attachment figure must include understanding God as he is, not simply a personal projection that may be distorted.

[10] Rahner himself, in a lecture for his eightieth birthday just prior to his death, acknowledged, "Naturally, I know there is perhaps very much in my theology that does not clearly and unambiguously fit together." He requested "from both supporters and opponents that they approach his theology with gracious goodwill," considering more his approach and questions than "results" that can "never really be conclusive" (Shae, 2021, pp. 637-638). "The symbolic, phantasmic, linguistic, and historical dimensions of experience . . . of our participation in the divine self-communication, . . . a reciprocally constitutive role for the concrete is simply never transposed into Rahner's theology of transcendentality" (p. 660).

[11] "Slaves" here is taken to mean an attitude of humble, willing service of others for the sake of God, who is humbly, willingly serving us. It is not intended to justify involuntary servitude or dehumanization.

Chapter 14

Critique, Clarifications, and Future Directions

Catholic support for study of neuroscience and theology

We have reflected, through the chapters of this book, on the interrelationships between neuroscience and Catholic theology in the emerging potential field of neurotheology. Critiques have emerged of the field as a whole and of various topics. We would like here to recap principal reflections and models of neurotheology, review critiques, and offer some clarifications from a Catholic perspective. Of course, we will not cover all there is, but we hope to stimulate future dialogue, investigation, and scholarship.

First, does Catholicism endorse the study of neuroscience and theology and the ways they interrelate? Recent Popes unequivocally support investigation and progress in the biological sciences and dialogue of scientists with the philosophical and theological community. Pope John II writes:

> I am more and more convinced that scientific truth . . . can help philosophy and theology to understand ever more fully the human person and God's revelation about man. . . For this important mutual enrichment in the search for the truth and the benefit of mankind, I am, with the whole Church, profoundly grateful. . . . Neuroscience . . . through the study of chemical and biological processes in the brain, contribute(s) greatly to an understanding of its workings. But the study of the human mind involves more than the observable data proper to the neurological sciences. . . . Scientists themselves perceive in the study of the human mind the mystery of a spiritual dimension that transcends cerebral physiology and appears to direct all our activities as free and autonomous beings, capable of responsibility and love, and marked with dignity. . . . Thus your considerations focus not just on the biological life . . . but also include the interpretive and evaluative work of the human mind. . . . In (the) distinction (between the mind and the brain), we can see the foundation of that spiritual dimension proper to the human person, which biblical Revelation explains as a special relationship with God the Creator (cf. Gen 2:7) in whose image and likeness every man and woman is made (cf. Gen. 1:26-27). (November 10, 2003).

Pope Benedict XVI writes:

> An interdisciplinary approach to complexity shows that the sciences are
> not intellectual worlds disconnected from reality but rather that they are
> interconnected and directed to a unified, intelligible, and harmonious
> reality . . . originating in God's creative Word. . . . I am convinced of the
> urgent need for continued dialogue and cooperation between the
> worlds of science and faith in the building of a culture of respect . . . and
> for the long-term sustainable development of our planet. Without this
> necessary interplay, the great questions of humanity leave the domain
> of reason and truth . . . with great damage to humanity, to world peace,
> and our ultimate destiny. (2012)

Pope Francis writes:

> Neurosciences offer ever-increasing information about the functioning
> of the human brain. Fundamental realities of Christian anthropology,
> such as the soul, self-awareness, and freedom, now appear in an
> unprecedented light and can even be seriously called into question by
> some. . . . As I wished to affirm in the Encyclical *Laudato Si'*: 'We urgently
> need a humanism capable of bringing together the different fields of
> knowledge . . . in the service of a more integral and integrating vision' (n.
> 141), to overcome the tragic division between the 'two cultures'—the
> humanistic-literary-theological culture and the scientific one. . . . to
> encourage a greater dialogue among the Church, the community of
> believers, and the scientific community. (November 18, 2017)

The Vatican Observatory, as we have seen, has been in collaboration with the
Center for Theology and Natural Sciences (CTNS) in Berkeley, California, since
1990. Their joint publication, *Neuroscience and the Person* (1999), supports
neurotheology as a mutual collaboration between theology and neuroscience.
Neuroscience, with its recent advances, can elucidate physiological aspects of
the human being, and theology can broaden and enrich awareness of
dimensions of the person beyond the physical (Gaitan, 2017).

Models of neurotheology: A multidisciplinary discipline

British writer and philosopher Aldous Huxley (1894-1963) introduced the term
neurotheology (*The Island*, 1962, p. 112) with the idea that it might become a
frontier science developing knowledge built on the assumption that human
cognition in the human person is potentially inexhaustible. We have seen that
neurotheology is multidisciplinary, incorporating fields such as cognitive
science, neurobiology, medicine, genetics, physics, psychology, anthropology,
and sociology, as well as neuroscience, theology, and religious studies.
Neurotheology, focused on religious experience and practice, strives to develop

a shared discourse based on research from a wide range of disciplines, covering levels from the neurological to the theological-mystical (Gaitan, 2017). "Religion is undoubtedly the most complex manifestation of the most complex phenomenon known to science, the human mind (2006)" (2017, p. 11).

Neurotheology has been a potential field developing over approximately 40 years. As with any new area of study, there are aspects still to be worked out. For example, I (ABN) was never fully satisfied with the word *neurotheology*. It was the term that caught on for the field that studies the intersection between neuroscience and religion (2010 in Gaitan, 2017, p. 5). My reason for developing neurotheology as an independent field of research is that it might be able: (1) to answer important questions, such as issues regarding subjective experience, the mind, and the soul; (2) to offer new angles in neuroscience and theology; and (3) to enrich some of the cross-disciplinary contributing fields (2010) (du Toit, 2015, pp. 15-16).

Some critics object that neurotheology ought not to be an autonomous field; it would more appropriately be a subdivision of either neurology or theology. If neurotheology were subordinate to neuroscience, neuroscientists could object that the sciences are not intended to meet religious needs; they focus on building a fund of empirical knowledge about the universe (Capra et al., 1992, p. 139). If neurotheology were subordinate to theology, each religion would have its neurotheology addressing neurological dimensions of religious/ mystical/spiritual (RMS) experiences (du Toit, 2015, p. 114). *In Theological Neuroethics: Christian Ethics Meets the Science of the Human Brain* (2017), British Reformed Protestant theologian Neil Messer engages in a debate between theology and science. He holds that theology, as broader, should be given the dominant voice (Alexander, 2020). He observes that Christian theology "will often require standard neuroethical (and we could say, neurotheological) questions be reconceived and reframed in new ways, enabling creative, illuminating, and sometimes unexpected responses" (Nairn, 2017). The research findings of neurotheology as a separate field are intended to benefit both neurology theology and religious studies.

Correlating RMS experience with the brain

Gaitan and Castresana (2021) find that since the 1980s, neurotheology has followed one of two models. The first and most prevalent model has been to seek correlations between religious/mystical/spiritual (RMS) experiences and brain structures and functions (Runehov, 2007). This model follows two tracks: it is causally agnostic and methodologically reductionistic. One approach to finding neural correlates for RMS experiences offers supplementary information to contributing fields such as psychology, anthropology, or religious studies. The researchers avoid speculating about what ontologically is happening and describe their subjects' causal explanations (Asprem and Taves, 2018; Beauregard and Paquette, 2006; in Gaitan and Castresana, 2021, p. 2).

A second approach follows scientistic assumptions in describing religious experiences in exclusively neuroscientific terms (Shukla et al. 2013). Canadian neuroscientist Michael Persinger (1983) and Indian-American neuroscientist V. S. Ramachandran (1998) follow this trend. It comes down to ontological reductionism, with God as a product of the brain (Gaitan and Castresana, 2021, p. 2). The naturalistic, reductive causal theory is thought to prevail in recent years due to its seemingly rigorous theory and method. Since science cannot comment on God as causal, this approach may be more ideology than neuroscience (pp. 2-3).

A dialogic model

My (ABN) alternative model may be called dialogic, a balanced epistemological interaction between neuroscience and theology. Both fields of knowledge contribute to the mutual enrichment of each (*Principles of Neurotheology*, 2010). The object is "to facilitate a sharing of ideas and concepts across the boundary between science and religion. Such a dialogue can be considered a constructive approach that informs both perspectives by enriching the understanding of both science and religion" (2010, p. 2, in Gaitan and Castresana, 2021, p. 3). Since the brain is central to the human person, *theological*—in the sense of religious—events are likely to register neurologically. This makes neurotheology an extensive field of investigation. Theology could engage in considerable debate about the range and specifics of topics neuroscience might address.[1] I (ABN) acknowledge that not all theological topics will be explored to the same degree. Neurotheology might contribute minimally to some topics and more completely to others (pp. 3-4).

Integrative neurotheology

A model called integrative neurotheology focuses on religious experiences and related phenomena, incorporating a wide range of disciplines with the intention of articulating an interdisciplinary knowledge base. Swedish theologian Anne Runehov indicates that if I (ABN) enhanced my model "by adding to it the expertise of, for example, sociologists, theologians, philosophers of religion, and psychologists, I would have an exploratory model that even if it adopts methodological reduction, will avoid hasty reductive conclusions" (Gaitan and Castresana, 2021, p. 4).

It has always been my (ABN) hope that a truly integrative model for neurotheology might be feasible. It most likely requires an initial approach that is more dialogical in order to find common ground and develop approaches that would be open to both scientific and theological investigations. I hope that this book is the beginning of such a model that integrates religious ideas with scientific ones and incorporates personal spiritual discovery along with scientific discovery.

Critiques and clarifications

Neurotheology, as noted, is an emerging discipline open to dialogue and adjustment. There are some gaps and inaccuracies, some omissions regarding philosophy and theological anthropology that need to be worked through, at least for dialogue with issues raised by Christianity and Catholicism. Some critiques involve what some Catholics and others consider philosophical lacunae or epistemological concerns (some of which were addressed in Chapter Three), and some issues are methodological (some of which were addressed in Chapter Four). We will try to recap some of the principal critiques here. Although the term *neurotheology* includes *theology*, which typically connotes Christianity, the field is open to all religions, including non-theistic ones. Since this book looks at neurotheology through a Catholic lens, some critiques are raised by Catholic respondents. We will attempt to offer clarifications regarding concerns. Some critiques should be taken into consideration; others may represent some degree of misunderstanding; some of the issues raised may need more thought and dialogue. In some cases, the ongoing neuroscience-theology dialogue may consider an adjustment in neurotheology's initial conceptions.

Relativist ontology and subjectivist epistemology

A basic objection to neurotheology is what seems to be a relativist ontology and subjectivist epistemology, perhaps reflecting the Kantian position that the world can only be grasped through operations of the human brain and mind (du Toit, 2015, p. 15-16). A priori, because the brain produces a *second-hand* or *pre-processed* view of reality, whatever can be thought about reality is an assumption (Newberg, 2010, p. 69; cf. d'Aquili et al., 1999, pp. 170-171). "We can never know for certain whether the thoughts we harbor . . . are commensurate with the reality that exists in the world" (Newberg, 2010, p. 249). A Thomistic Catholic perspective would agree that perceptual bias or preconception can distort human judgment; still, the human mind can know the real world as it is (Critchley, 2013, p. 171).

Associated with a relativist assumption is the principle that neurotheology does not privilege either neuroscience or theology (Newberg, 2010, p. 145). "No ontological priority should be given to either the material universe or to God. Neuroscientific and theological perspectives must be considered comparable contributors to neurotheological investigations (Newberg, 2010, p. 54)" (du

Toit, 2015, pp. 12, 23). Corollary to a subjectivist epistemology is neurotheology's description of the relationships among brain, mind, and God: "God cannot exist as a concept or as reality anyplace else but in your mind. (T)he mind is mystical by default" (Newberg, d'Aquili, and Rause, 2002, p. 37). Since the theologian's *a priori* assumption is that God exists and is personally concerned with creation, equalizing fundamental faith in God with human-reasonable science presents a problem for theology. A Catholic theologian would hold that, although science could be found to support established doctrines, religious doctrine rests on revelation rather than on scientific theory (du Toit, 2015, p. 87).

> Faith and science address different types of realities that call for different methods. Science deals with things, while faith deals with the mystery of God as "no thing." Science investigates the operation of things (their various physical causes and relationships), and faith investigates the meaning of things (their source and goal together with their implications for human conduct). Faith, therefore, looks for different propositions than science does" (Bednar, 2023, personal communication).

A way forward for neurotheology would reaffirm its already-established principle of respect for the convictions of both theology and science, leading to a fruitful dialogue beneficial to both fields.

Neurotheology aspires to become a meta- and mega-theology (Newberg, 2010, pp. 64-65; Barrett, 2011, p. 133; Jeftic, 2013, p. 274; du Toit, 2015, pp. 3, 53, 115-116). Some analysts conclude that this aims to ultimately characterize all religious-mystical-spiritual (RMS) experiences, including absolute unitary being (d'Aquili and Newberg, 1999, p. 195f), by their neurological substrate. Neurotheology would then show the world's religions their underlying neurological foundations. Neurotheology is thought to pursue a paradigm shift from either neuroscience or theology, or both, in explaining reality (du Toit, 2015, pp. 53-54). A problem with either neuroscience or theology predominating would be that science cannot answer ultimate questions that fall outside its experimental purview, and theology cannot depend for its verification on scientific falsifiability (Jeftic, 2013, p. 276). Grace manifesting in prayer, for example, could be authenticated not by a PET scan but by fruits of the Spirit (Gal 5:22) in one's life (du Toit, 2015, p. 115).

Anticipating a paradigm shift would keep neuroscience and theology in creative tension. As I (ABN) noted in Chapter Two (section *Goals of Neurotheology*), although neither neuroscience nor theology would take precedence, this is not to imply that theology would be subsumed under neuroscience. If future research proves that, in fact, some religious experience cannot be traced neurologically, I (ABN) would find that interesting to study

(*Principles of Neurotheology*, 2010, p. 120). We will need to think outside the box to find a theory and methodology appropriate to the potential new field of neurotheology.

Naturalistic or open to the spiritual/supernatural

A recurring question in the field of neurotheology is whether it is reductive/materialistic or open to the spiritual and supernatural. We have seen that some neuroscientists in the field hold the first position, others hold the second, and some, at times, nuance into one or the other. Reductionistic naturalists claim that religious experiences derive from activation of networks in the frontal and temporal lobes and the limbic system, with subsequent parietal cortex deactivation (Boyer, 2003; d'Aquili and Newberg, 1993; Ramachandran, 1998; Persinger, 1983). Naturalists claim that since electromagnetic stimulation of specific brain areas can evoke religious experiences, they must be natural, not sacred or mystical. A naturalist position points to the co-occurrence of religious experiences with disorders such as schizophrenia, epilepsy, or bipolar disorder (Persinger, 1997). Naturalists observe that religious experience can be induced pharmacologically with drugs such as amphetamines, LSD, mescaline (the active ingredient in peyote), and ayahuasca (Roberts, 2006). Some naturalists conclude that religious experiences may be traced to residual cerebral activity due to insufficient activation of specific brain structures (Dawes and MacLaurin, 2013; Boyer, 2003; Atran, 2002; in Gaitan, 2017, pp. 14-15).

Neuroscientists engaged in neurotheological themes that hold a position alternative to materialism observe that many brain areas, approximately 12 neural systems, contribute to religious experiences, according to Beauregard and Paquette (2006). No brain regions have been found to date that serve only religious experiences; each network also activates for non-religious contexts. Subjects in studies with brain scanning during religious activities did not present with psychopathology either during or prior to the experiments (Beauregard and Paquette, 2006). And there are neuroimaging findings that appear to verify mental causation for neurobiological results (Gaitan, 2017, p. 15). Religious experiences have shown a positive top-down causal impact on mental and physical health (Fingelkurts and Fingelkurts, 2009; Ellis, 2009; Beauregard, 2007; in Gaitan, 2017, p. 15).

On the other hand, some scholars are open to the prospect that there are possible supernatural aspects related to spiritual experiences. This can come in two main forms—a supernatural deity that intervenes to cause all or part of a spiritual experience or a model of human consciousness that is *non-local* and can affect and be affected by things at a distance. Exploring these two possibilities in more detail, the former is more obvious from the religious perspective. It makes sense that if God exists and interacts with human beings, then God is causing some communication or spiritual experience within a given individual. Some of the most common types of spiritual experiences are numinous ones that can include revelatory experiences as well. In such experiences, a person comes into more direct contact with God. Some studies have suggested that practices such as intercessory prayer might be able to affect biological outcomes (Baesler and Ladd, 2009). If there is a belief in the existence of God, that experience is real and associated with the actual interaction with a supernatural being.

The second type, involving non-local consciousness, has to do with the notion that consciousness can extend beyond the brain or might even have its origin outside the brain. Some scientists have found evidence that consciousness can extend beyond the brain by using mental processes to move or change physical objects, a hypothetical paranormal phenomenon. To date, experimental findings have been inconclusive. If one assumes that consciousness itself is the primary stuff of the universe, then human consciousness and experience derive from a more universal, non-material consciousness. While this type of theory is more commonly associated with Eastern traditions such as Buddhism or Hinduism, the creation story in the Bible suggests that the physical world derives from God's consciousness. In this way, the physical world is derived from the non-material, and hence, our experiences can also derive from non-material origins.

Neurotheology based in experience

Neurotheology is criticized for supporting a *neurotheological hermeneutic* based on *experientialism* (Newberg, 2010, p. 87), the understanding that all thoughts, ideas, and feelings flow from human experience (du Toit, 2015, pp. 15-16). Neurotheology was preceded by significant scientists such as "William James (1842-1910), Rudolph Otto (1869-1937), Sigmund Freud (1856-1939), and James Leuba (1867-1946)" (Gaitan, 2017, p. 13), all of whom studied religious experience within the discipline of psychology. Religious experience, and particularly mystical experience, is extremely subjective. "Neurotheology moves in a field of experiences that are difficult to define in exact terms due to the large number of nuances with which they can be presented" (pp. 12-13).

Critics of neurotheology assert that it is difficult to say how fundamental religious experience or mysticism is to the practice of religion. Religion is individual and collective, varied and multilevel, situated in cultural, social, and linguistic contexts. Religion cannot be said to be based fundamentally on experience and cannot be fully explained by neurological processes. The nine cognitive operators presented in *The Mystical Mind* (d'Aquili and Newberg, 1999), particularly the causal and holistic operators, since they are not standard terms in neuroscience, should be taken with caution (Russell et al., 1999).

Psychologist and Anglican minister Fraser Watts observes that it is not clear that highly speculative neurotheological theory can apply well to revelation-and-faith-based theological concerns (Burns, 2005, p. 179).

Neurotheology is criticized for its basis in the religious experience of subjects engaged in an intentionally generated religious behavior, such as reciting Psalm 23 or centering prayer. Religious experience generally happens spontaneously and is unpredictable, as when Thomas Aquinas, toward the end of his life, stopped writing the *Summa Theologiae* because, in comparison with what had been revealed to him, his work was so much "straw." It would be impossible to prove that religious experience is consistently accompanied by a change in neurological blood flow (Burns, 2005, p. 179). Experiences of oneness with the Divine Being might range along a continuum from a slight sense of unity watching a sunset or attending a church liturgy to the extraordinary sense of connection to something beyond oneself in a mystical experience (Newberg, 2010, p. 164, in Gaitan, 2017, p. 12).

Critics of neurotheology note that it is also not entirely clear that a sense of the unity of being is central to religious life or the underlying state of all religious experience. Other features of religious experience include (a) consciousness of an all-inclusive Presence, (b) awareness of a divine plan for one's life, (c) having prayers answered, (d) a sense of divine guidance and help, (e) absence of a sense of time and space, (f) feelings of peace, joy, and love, (g) positive sense of the present moment (Fingelkurts and Fingelkurts, 2009), (h) feelings of physical and mental wellness, (i) ineffability of the experience, (j) changes in attitude and behavior in a positive direction (Rubia, 2009, in Gaitan, 2017). We would agree with these critiques but also emphasize that neurotheology, as we conceive it, can address many of these questions and should not be limited only to specific types of religious experiences or practices. By expanding the realm of neurotheology to embrace all aspects pertaining to religious and spiritual traditions, neurotheology has the potential to be a vibrant field of exploration.

Brain scanning images with fMRI during experimental subjects' report of religious experience show neurological patterns, but critics of neurotheology contend that brain scans cannot be considered "a photograph of God" (d'Aquili, Newberg, and Rause, 2002; d'Aquili and Newberg, 1999). Anne Runehov observes that:

> The blue-red or yellow spots that the neuroscientists see on the screen of the SPECT when scanning the brain of a meditator experiencing AUB or eating apple pie are pictures of neurochemistry and not pictures of God or pie (2007, in Brandt et al., 2010, p. 307)

Again, I (ABN) would agree that brain scans show only neurological effects: they do not record the objects of the subject's perception. At present, brain scans cannot distinguish whether they are showing the brain initiating an experience or the brain responding to one (du Toit, 2015, p. 26). However, as studies proceed, it might be possible to ascertain better what the brain is doing during a variety of states and experiences related to perceptions of the external world.

As we saw, grace may or may not register neurologically. Mystical experiences can be transformative without being consciously perceptible. Consider apophatic mysticism or the night of faith (cf. Mother Teresa), where heroic virtue continues to manifest over decades while the subject reports an absence of religious experience. Religious practice involves a wide range of experiences with complex interaction (Jeftic, 2013, p. 272), which means neurologically, locating specific brain areas for religious experience is likely to be impossible.

Critics of neurotheology observe that, at times, God may seem to be conflated with the brain or with the brain's Absolute Unitary Being (AUB) and to be other and higher than that experience (Newberg, d'Aquili and Rause, 2002, pp. 140, 172). Identification of AUB with God is unlikely to come from neuroscience but would be a faith claim (Delio, 2003, p. 577). One might also conclude either that religious experience is only one of the multiple brain states or that there is no real distinction between the brain and God. Neurological data do not tell anything specific about God's existence or operation. Critics wonder about the claim of neurotheology that when the experimental subject encounters a "really real" AUB that feels more real than external reality or subjective consciousness of self, "the self and the world must be contained within, and perhaps created by the reality of Absolute Unitary Being" (Newberg et al., 2001, p. 155). For theology, conclusions derive from revelation; they do not follow from empirical observations or subjective experiences (Burns, 2005, p. 179). It would not be clear to theologians that neuroscientific interpretation of AUB should lead to the conceptual revision of theology (cf. d'Aquili and Newberg, 1999, in Jeftic, 2013, p. 263).

I (ABN) would agree with the merit of these critiques but also emphasize that neurotheology can address many of these questions. It should not be limited only to specific types of religious experiences or practices. By expanding the realm of neurotheology to embrace all aspects pertaining to religious and spiritual traditions, neurotheology has the potential to be a vibrant field of exploration.

Reductionist or religionist

Neurotheology, as we have seen, may be understood as either reductionist or religionist. Reductive neuroscience of religion attempts to show that religion may be replaced with "non-mysterious neurological functions (or malfunctions)"

(Brandt, Clément, and Manning, 2010, p. 306). D'Aquili and I (ABN), in our experiments with meditating Buddhist monks and Franciscan nuns, followed a religionist understanding of the neuroscience of religion, showing the authenticity of religious awareness (1999). Our brain scan images demonstrated the incidence of reported religious or mystical experiences. Critics of our approach surmise that neurotheology intends to replace unscientific theology with the new scientifically verifiable discipline of neurotheology (Brandt, Clément, and Manning, 2010, p. 306). In fact, we intend to respect the discipline of theology and engage in a mutually beneficial dialogue between neuroscience and theology. A dialogic interpretation of neurotheology (recall Barbour's model of science-theology interaction: conflict, independence, dialogue, and integration) would benefit both neuroscience and theology.

Admittedly, the notion of nine cognitive operators introduces non-standard terms in the field of neuroscience. The operators are seen as hypothetical ways to aggregate theoretical combinations of neural networks oriented in common directions. The *cognitive operators* (d'Aquili and Newberg, 1999), particularly the *causal* and *holistic operators*, lead to theological conclusions about neurological correlates of religious experiences. The *causal operator,* located in the left hemisphere inferior parietal lobe and the primarily left frontal lobes' anterior convexity and their respective connections, confer a causal attribution on sense perceptions, even when causality seems uncertain. In religious experiences, the *holistic operator,* located in the nondominant hemisphere's posterior superior parietal lobule and surrounding areas, activates a state of *absolute unitary being* (AUB), which may be fundamental to all religious experiences. The quiescent (parasympathetic) and arousal (sympathetic) systems surge simultaneously, and there is a sense of being overwhelmed by both calming and arousal networks. There is a deafferentation of the orientation area, and the subjective sense of self is lost. The sense of boundaries is dissolved, and one is left without thoughts, words, or sensations (2002). I (ABN) acknowledge that the foregoing interpretation may not be valid and further research is needed.

Theologically oriented critics of neurotheology find objectionable the localizing of the principle of causation within the human brain rather than ascribing it to God. And they object to attributing to a sense of unity with all that is the fundamental basis of all religious experience. They find that for neurotheology, "theological concepts are not determinative; rather, they are derivative from prior mystical experience" (Brandt, Clément, and Manning, 2010, pp. 306-307). They object to the conclusion that new neuroscientific findings would lead to reconstruction of theology based on "a neurological knowledge of the mystical mind" (p. 307). As we saw, while theology is open to verifiable contributions from neuroscience, theology derives from revelation rather than scientific theory.

Constructivist

Critics of neurotheology claim that its objective is to find direct correlations between brain activity and subjective religious experiences when, as we have seen, brain and mind processes are as idiosyncratic as are fingerprints, and they depend on complex, multi-leveled, cultural-and-linguistic contextual interpretations. Constructivism observes that experiences are always culturally mediated. Mystical experiences are instantaneous and unpredictable, and they are impacted by the subject's constructive processes of expectations, memory, language, and culture. These dimensions affect the subject's spirituality and, therefore, their experience while the experience is taking place and their interpretation afterward. Spirituality, religion, religious experience, and mysticism are all extraordinarily complex (Gaitan, 2017, pp. 11-12). As we discussed in Chapter Four on neurotheology methodology, it is extremely challenging to operationalize the construct of *religious experience* and to rigorously apply the scientific method for accurate assessment and generalizable experimental findings across multiple subjects, each of whom is unique regarding religious experience.

From a theological/faith perspective, God is not a mental construct but a mysterious ultimate Reality. Biblically based theology holds God to be "the Lord of all creation, creator, and redeemer, transcendent, determining, self-limiting, immanent, creative participant in the cosmic narrative (Barbour, 1997, p. 329f)" (du Toit, 2015, p. 118). Faith does not derive from human knowledge; it is a gift and relationship with God. Revelation confers certitude about truths revealed; revealed truths are not irrational, although they are beyond human reason. Belief in God and religious experience are accompanied by intense conviction, giving purpose and motivation to the lives of many people across cultures and throughout history, particularly regarding life after death. This faith conviction entails a complex religious experience involving the whole person (Sanguineti, 2015).

Critics of neurotheology observe that there cannot be a neuro-equivalence of theology (Martinez-Selio, 2009) because theology is about God, his perfections and attributes, and human knowledge about God through reason or faith. The existence and qualities of God cannot epistemologically be the object of neuroscience (Gaitan, 2017, p. 5). On the other hand, from the perspective of neurotheology, *theology* could have a broader meaning, including transcendence, spirituality, religion, mysticism, and God, among other constructs (Acosta, 2015). Neurotheology might be understood as a discipline dealing with ways that "God becomes accessible to human experience" (Gaitan, 2017, p. 5).

From a theological perspective, critics contend that neurotheology cannot produce a meta- or mega-theology. Neurotheology would not be able to demonstrate that there is no real difference between "God is Trinity" and "God is not Trinity" (Jeftic, 2013, pp. 274-275). The result would be a universalist, neurologically oriented super-religious-studies project with theologies and practices of individual religions evened out (Graf, 2007, p. 260). Religion would lose its dimension of relational and personal commitment; it would be watered down to another reflective exercise (Jeftic, 2013).

Critics observe that neurotheology attempts to investigate what reality is but through a biological rather than philosophical or theological lens (Newberg, d'Aquili, and Rause, 2001, pp. 142-156). This approach explores religious experience and comes to theological conclusions about God based on neuroscientific brain-scanning data. It has sometimes not been clear whether neuroscientists subscribe to an ontological order that includes God or, following the modern scientific paradigm, begin and end with the human mind. "There's no other way for God to get into your head except through the brain's neural pathways. Correspondingly, God cannot exist as a concept or reality anyplace else but in your mind (p. 37)" (Delio, 2003, p. 576). This leaves the existence of God as an open question with no definitive metaphysical support.

> The realness of an Absolute Unitary Being is not conclusive proof that a higher God exists. Still, it makes a strong case that there is more to human existence than sheer material existence. As long as our brains are arranged the way they are, God, however we define that majestic, mysterious concept, will not go away. (Newberg, d'Aquili, and Rause, 2001, p. 172).

The scientific paradigm excluding God leaves only a persistent experiential inquiry from the human teleological search for ultimate truth, goodness, and beauty.

Is Absolute Unitary Being taken to be equivalent to God? Without philosophical and theological investigation, there is confusion:

> Either the objective external (material) world or our subjective awareness of that world and the sense of self (spiritual world) must be the primary, ultimate reality, the source of everything real. Subjective and objective reality cannot both be (ultimate). One must be the source of the other. (Newberg, d'Aquili, & Rause, 2001, p. 144, in Delio, 2003, p. 581)

This study of the encounter of Catholicism with an evolving, developing potential field of neurotheology provides a philosophical, epistemological analysis of a naturalistic (materialistic) vs. a transcendent (spiritual/ supernatural) perspective. Neuroscience, at times, coincides with a paradigmatically empirical scientific viewpoint that begins and ends with the human mind but may also fit into one that Catholicism stands on—metaphysically grounded in a realist philosophical order with God as the Originator and End of everything, including human reality. Neurotheology, as an emerging, developing field, is open to dialogue with its critics and to appropriate revisions of some of its original conjectures.

Philosophical hazards in neuroscientific study of religion

Scholar at Oxford's Center for Science and Religion Daniel de Haan observes that from a philosophical perspective, those who study religion neuroscientifically need to be aware of hazards or fallacies. These commonly occur in many neurotheology studies and cause confusion. Hopefully, they have been or will be addressed in my (ABN) studies. Some examples are:

(1) *The Mereological Fallacy:* The part is taken for the whole, sub-personal functions for human characteristics. Human persons are religious, not their brains. The brain can be the subject of psychological attributes only as a manner of speaking, not in reality (Bennet and Hacker, 2003, p. 3, in de Haan, 2020, p. 49, 56).

(2) *The Fallacy of the Disappearing Person:* This fallacy is like the first. It is persons who have beliefs, desires, and intentions, not their brains or their nervous system (de Haan, 2020, p. 58). Also, human persons do not lose their ontological identity by having dementia or neurological deficits, no matter how severe their psychological impairments (p. 59).

(3) *The Hazard of the Unreflective Conceptual Framework:* Neuroscientists need to be careful in operationalizing their definitions and interpreting their experimental results (p. 52). It is particularly important to distinguish conceptually between personal-level terminology and sub-personal-level mechanisms. Terms from common-sense psychology, like cognition, memory, and conscious emotions such as *fear,* ought not to be uncritically conflated with nonconscious mechanisms like *threat detection* (which confused LeDoux's experimental findings) (p. 52).

(4) *The Hazard of Causal Monism:* This is closely associated with the Hazard of Extreme Reductionism or the principle of parsimony. An obvious example of reducing a multiplicity of explanations for a complex reality with a single causal explanation is to attribute religious experience to neurobiological operations.

(5) *The Fallacy of Misplaced Contingency:* In this context, the reality of God depends on one's experience of God. "In order for God to exist, we must exist because humans give a conscious voice to the existence of God" (Delio, 2003, p. 578).

(6) *Hazards of Cognitive Science:* Alternative approaches to cognitive theory are unresolved and debatable. For example, the 4 Es of cognition, that it is embodied, embedded, enactive, and extended, are not necessarily accepted by all neuroscientists. These theories are theoretical and unproven in neuroscience.

(7) *The Hazard of Scientism:* This identifies the scientific method as the only true and reliable source of knowledge from empirical scientific investigation. This epistemological position is self-defeating because scientism itself cannot be verified empirically. And it rules out non-empirical disciplines, such as logic and mathematics, that are required for scientific experimentation (de Haan, 2020, pp. 64-65).

(8) *The Hazard of Numinous Neural Localization:* This represents the effort to use neuroscientific methods, particularly brain imaging, to locate areas of the brain that correlate with religious experience. As we have seen, both brain function and religious experience are extremely complex, involving multiple connections in various brain areas and numerous intersecting levels of interpretation. There is also the difficulty, if not impossibility, of isolating and replicating a duplicable religious experience for a large enough representative sample that findings might generalize to a population.

Some difficulties with neurotheology as a potential field are mentioned here, although this study from a Catholic perspective may have largely addressed them. A central concern is the issue (see Chapter Three) of neurotheology trying to exceed its epistemic limits by addressing ultimate philosophical and theological concerns within the limits of empirical science. Main problems include (1) the assertion that neurotheology can prove or deny the existence of God; (2) the claim to find the *God spot* in the human brain; (3) confusion about the mind-brain problem (mental and spiritual vs. physiological levels) and its impact on the interpretation of experimental findings; (4) the commitment of research neuroscientists to either religion or agnosticism or atheism, which may influence analysis of findings (Gaitan, 2017, pp. 13-14).

I (ABN) would argue that these are topics that can be carefully addressed within the context of neurotheology. If neurotheology is to be successful, care must be taken not to exceed its limits but also to utilize the opportunities to explore how the brain helps us to engage each of these concepts philosophically and theologically. In other words, neurotheology most likely won't prove or disprove God's existence, but it can tell us how and why the brain tries to address these questions and may suggest to some degree how and why we come to certain answers.

Neurotheology, say some critics, should be understood not as a separate field but as an aspect of neurology or theology. Neurotheology could be either a neuroscientific study of religious phenomena or a theological application of neuroscientific research findings (Jeftic, 2013, p. 262). Critics of neurotheology as a separate field recommend that (a) it function within either neuroscience or theology as supplementary and informing, not trying to transform them; (b) it not try to develop an impossible meta- or mega-theology; (c) it acknowledge that not all RMS experiences can be explained through experience; and (d) it promotes dialogue between neuroscience and theology, rather than trying to integrate the two fields in a fundamental way (du Toit, 2015, pp. 115-116). I (ABN) would argue that the new field of neurotheology might also want to test the limits to see how far it can go, keeping in mind its epistemological boundaries.

Future directions: Neurotheological expectations

As we have seen in Chapter Three on epistemology, the human soul is often regarded as the animating substantial form of the body and co-constituent with the body of the single human person. The *mind* is the rational power of the soul. The soul's operations, such as sensory perception, appetites and emotions, and consciousness, are essentially associated with neural structures that provide their necessary *material cause.* Since thoughts and voluntary actions are wholly spiritual and deal not only with physical objects but with ontological realities such as possibilities, metaphysical beings, and God, they depend for their operation on a brain and nervous system as the material cause but do not derive essentially from a physical organ (Sanguineti, 2013, pp. 1067). The powers of the human intellectual (mind) and volitional soul surpass the capabilities of the body. However, they require activation of the brain as necessary but not sufficient for their functioning. "Our mind goes far beyond the brain. It is open to the whole of reality, to the universe, and to God, both in knowledge (thought, self-consciousness) and in love, with the possibility of thought and free choice" (Sanguineti, p. 1067). There is a difference in level between mental or psychic operations and their corresponding neural basis (Sanguineti, 2007, 2014, 2015).

For studying the relationship between empirical neurosciences and theology and for research on matters such as religious experience and belief in God, philosophy plays a necessary clarifying role. Do neuroscientific studies evaluate the truth or authenticity of religious content? Are they consequential for philosophical interpretations of religion in a universal way? Can the study of the brain contribute to the assessment of spiritual activity? Professor of philosophy at Holy Cross Pontifical University, Rome, and Austral University, Argentina, Fr. Juan José Sanguineti answers in the negative. The domains and content of philosophy and theology operate on epistemic levels different from the sciences.

Neurotheological studies can make a valuable contribution to understanding the neural and psychological dimensions of religious activities. Neuroscience can support discernment regarding the authenticity of some religious experiences and symptoms of pseudo-religious disorders (Sanguineti, 2015). Neurotheology might also observe in some individuals a predispositional causality to specific aspects of religiosity (*ST* II-II, q. 155, a. 4, ad 2; q. 156, a. 1, ad 2), although the causality would be partial and material (Sanguineti, 2015).

A critique of neurotheology prior to this study is that the possibilities of its neuroscientific dimension would be "difficult to justify in epistemological and methodological terms. On the contrary, it does seem possible to study religious experiences, regardless of the cultural, social, geographical, and doctrinal framework in which they are experienced, appealing to different methods and approaches" (Gaitan and Castresana, 2021, p. 5).

A major challenge for neurotheology, as we have seen in Chapters Three and Four, is that it attempts to combine the natural sciences with the humanities— philosophy and theology (Sanguineti, 2018). Sociological studies suggest (Reiner, 2011; McCabe and Castel, 2008; Weisberg et al., 2008) that both the scientific community and popular opinion give preference to neuroscience over other disciplines (Gaitan and Castresana, 2021, p. 8).

The following future directions for neurotheology give only general suggestions for avenues to explore. None of them is worked out in detail with examples. Experts in these areas are invited to consider and investigate, criticize, adjust, or develop these ideas.

Coordinated pluralism

We have been discussing science as if it were derived from a self-understood scientific model that comes to sound, rational, empirically derived findings from rigorous hypothesis testing. However, some mid-twentieth-century philosophers of science have observed that science is quite complex in social practice. Efforts to solve global problems like climate change or healthcare concerns such as a pandemic and multidisciplinary, interdisciplinary, and transdisciplinary initiatives are complicating the picture. Philosophers of science have challenged the notion of a single universal scientific method (Feyerabend, 1975). A pluralist philosophy of science considers diverse theories, models, and explanations in scientific practice (Ludwig and Ruphy, 2021).

Biologist and philosopher Sandra Mitchell suggests that Huxley's (1962) view of neurotheology as a range of disciplines studying religious experience might develop with a non-reductionist model called integrative pluralism. She observes (2009) that a more pragmatic, pluralistic approach to scientific experimentation would need to acknowledge the complexity of combining different sciences and levels of explanation. Mitchell observes that an expanded epistemology for science will be needed to accommodate aspects of the human person and human problems that do not fit the classic scientific model. One obvious example is religious experience, with its subjectivity and extraordinary complexity. She indicates that an expanded epistemology would incorporate (a) epistemological pluralism, with multiple explanations and methods at various levels of analysis; (b) a kind of democratic pragmatism, acknowledging that reality encompasses numerous kinds of certainty and levels of conceptualization; and (c) an "evolutionary and dynamic dimension of knowledge" that demands innovative ways of analyzing nature and organizing knowledge (p. 13, in Gaitan and Castresana, 2021, pp. 8-9).

> Canadian professor of philosophy Jacqueline Anne Sullivan (2017) observes that pluralists in the philosophy of science have emphasized the importance of a plurality of theories, concepts/conceptual frameworks, perspectives, methods, models, and explanations (in psychology and neuroscience) to the advancement of scientific knowledge (see, e.g., Chang, 2012; Kellert, Longino, and Waters, 2006; Mitchell, 2003). (p. 141).

On the other hand, Sullivan cautions that unrestricted pluralism can block progress with a lack of taxonomic guidelines. She recommends instead *coordinated pluralism* through knowledge-building initiatives, such as Cognitive Atlas, Cog Po, and Experiment Factory. Coordination might be facilitated through online databases "(BrainMap, NeuroSynth), ontologies (Cognitive Atlas, CogPo), and open-source software (Experiment Factory)" (Sullivan, 2017, p. 141).

Mitchell notes that to understand the ways that psychological functions arise from the brain, diverse fields of science need to integrate their data, constructs, and explanations "(e.g., Bilder, Howe, and Saab, 2013; Cuthbert and Kozak, 2013; Piccinini and Craver, 2011; Poldrack et al., 2011; Sanislow et al., 2010; Stinson, 2016)." The integrative effort, however, is hindered by the lack of uniform terminology for hypothesized constructs for psychological operations "(e.g., Bilder, Hoew, and Saab, 2013; Poldrack et al., 2011; Poldrack and Yankoni, 2016; Sullivan, 2016a, 2016b, 2016c; Uttal, 2001)" (Sullivan, 2017, p. 129). *Coordinated pluralism* aims to harmonize scientists' "conceptual, investigative, taxonomic, and integrative practices in ways that strike an appropriate balance between pragmatic and realistic goals" (p. 130). She observes that since the human person is complex, aspects such as neurophysiology and religious experience need to be investigated through multiple perspectives. Neuroscience alone, for example, cannot handle spiritual, even supernatural dimensions.

"We need multiple layers of explanatory accounts because the human person is a physical, biological, psychological, and spiritual reality, and because these aspects of its reality, though interdependent, are not mutually reducible" (Clayton, 2004, p. 148, in Gaitan and Castresana, 2021, p. 9).

Transversal spaces

The transversal spaces theory of J. Wentzel van Huyssteen (1942-2022) suggests a model for a "non-reductive, non-assimilative dialogue between neuroscience and theology"[3] (Bennett, 2019b, p. 108). Van Huyssteen, the late Princeton theology and science professor and South African Dutch Reformed minister, uses philosopher Calvin Schrag's notion of *transversal rationality*. It can be illustrated by the mathematical metaphor of a line intersecting other lines to indicate the intersection of alternate communications. Van Huyssteen contends that dialogue or integration between science and religion, when each domain is varied, diverse, and lacking common terminology, needs an expanded view of rationality. The search is for a "cross-disciplinary conversation with full personal convictions yet open to criticism in a safe space for conversation" (Stone, 2000, p. 417). Van Huyssteen suggests trans-rationality, where each partner in the dialogue maintains their convictions while seeking areas of the intersection so that each discipline can make a worthwhile contribution. "Individuals submit their judgment for evaluation by their peers but do not necessarily accept it. We should seek a continual feedback relationship between communal assessment and individual judgment" (p. 419).

Essential to van Huyssteen's view is that dialogue need not lead to a compromise that dilutes or temporizes with inalienable faith convictions. There is openness to dialogue to find common ground and potential benefit for the common good, with humility to see that, however, grounded in truth, one's position includes some degree of fallible personal interpretation.

> Experience is never pure and immediate but always interpreted. There is never a direct access to truth. With the 'stories of our lives, or our traditions, our religious faiths, our sciences, and our theologies' (van Huyssteen, 1999, p. 212), epistemology and hermeneutics are always intertwined. (Stone, 2000, p. 421)

The natural sciences emphasize controlled and precise observation and experimentation. In philosophy, the focus is on the knower. The theologian stresses religious experience, story, and ritual. Religious explanations share with philosophical explanations answers to ultimate questions, "generality or depth and an emphasis on systematic coherence and meaningfulness" (van Huyssteen, 1999, p. 261, in Stone, 2000, p. 421-422). Theology offers a view complementary to science that can clarify elements of worldview and purpose. Theologian Walter Brueggeman called van Huyssteen's approach "a compelling invitation to rethink science and religion in a way that refuses to be adversarial" (2007, p. 30).

A transrationality perspective echoes the neurotheology principle that neither the assumptions of science nor those of theology are taken to be normative (Bennett, 2019b, p. 121). "Any material admitted to transversal-space dialogue must first be shown to be rationally defensible. No belief or materials, either scientific or theological, can claim a privileged status with respect to interrogation within such dialogue" (p. 122). Common interests or terms or research in different disciplines are identified, then shared problems are explored together. "Transversal spaces are dynamic places of interaction based on the shared tools of rational inquiry, which come into transient existence as part of specific transdisciplinary engagements" (van Huyssteen, 2006, p. 35). Transrationality offers optimism for authentic conversation across disciplines and for "overlaps and shared resources of rationality, even with differing standards of rationality in different contexts" (Stone, 2000, p. 416). Neuroscience could hold to an empirically based experimental standard of more-or-less rigorous hypothesis testing. Theology, grounded in revelation, builds on the rationality of hermeneutic discipline, in the case of Catholicism, with scripture, the Church's magisterium, and tradition as guarantors of the authenticity of its conclusions.

"The development of transversal outcomes receives impetus from an integral element of van Huyssteen's refiguring, viz., the pursuit of optimal understanding, and its realigning with improved problem-solving ability, rather than with correlation to 'absolute truth'" (Bennett, 2019b, p. 124). He warns against transferring theological principles as data into science (van Huyssteen, 2006, pp. 323-324). On themes such as the soul and identity, intentionality and free will, and responsibility and morality, neuroscience can contribute with experimental data that may challenge long-standing theological concepts. Both theology and neuroscience have valuable contributions to a fuller understanding of humanness (Bennett, 2019b, pp. 126-127). Van Huyssteen is recognized for opening possibilities for epistemological overlaps and a broadened comprehension of rationality (Stone, 2000, p. 416).

Theoretically, transversal spaces dialogue results in the contributing disciplines' return to their fields to "expand, clarify, or challenge their respective understandings of the area being explored" (van Huyssteen, 2006, p. 264), as well as possibly making discoveries at the limits where the contributing disciplines meet. The question remains, however, whether this process achieves its objectives. Theology, derived from revelation rather than reason, might soon find constricting the principle that the entire process rests on *rationality*, giving primacy to science. Bennett believes that van Huyssteen's transversal spaces can be further developed in favor of neurotheology (2019b, p. 122).

Developing future scholars in neurotheology

While the field of neurotheology (either explicit or implicit) has been growing over the past 30 years, there is always the sense that we are just "scratching the surface." Therefore, many future scholars are needed to explore and expand this field. We hope that there are several important avenues for developing future scholars. The current path is typically taken by people like myself (ABN) who have expertise in one aspect of neurotheology, in this case, the neuroscientific, and then develop a working understanding of the theological or religious side. By paradigm, there are many paths as people may enter the field of neurotheology from a diverse set of scientific and religiously oriented fields, including but not limited to:

- Physical or Health Sciences: Neuroscience, neurobiology, cognitive neuroscience, neuroimaging, psychiatry, psychology, neurology, medicine, consciousness studies
- Social Sciences: Sociology, anthropology, social work, social psychology
- Religious/Philosophical: Religious studies, theology, pastoral care, divinity studies, clergy, philosophy

Further, scholars may come from almost any religious or spiritual background, including major religions such as Christianity, Judaism, Islam, Buddhism, and Hinduism, as well as many other traditions including but not limited to Sikhism, Mormonism, Jainism, Yogism, Baha'i, along with many thousands of folk religions. Beyond these named traditions, there are various approaches that people may take when engaging in neurotheology, including monotheism, polytheism, henotheism, animism, totemism, atheism, agnosticism, pantheism, duotheism, and deism. In the end, there are literally thousands of approaches to neurotheology.

In addition to exploring neurotheology from various religious/spiritual systems, there is the challenge of developing more specific educational programs. There are certainly some programs that currently exist that combine science and religion in the context of the mind or brain.[3] However, future programs can hopefully be developed to offer advanced degrees in neurotheology, either Masters's or Doctorate programs. These programs would likely require coursework in both the sciences and religious or spiritual disciplines.

Perhaps the ideal scenario would be for people to engage in neurotheology with dual advanced degrees in a scientific discipline and a religious or spiritual discipline—for example, people who have an M.D. and have a Ph.D. in theology or people who have a Ph.D. in psychology as well as in religious studies. Or perhaps there could be clergy with scientific degrees, such as a rabbi who also has a degree in cognitive neuroscience or a nun who has a degree in psychology.

Importantly, for neurotheology to be a vibrant field, many different types of scholars are likely to be needed, which will support the interdisciplinary and integrative approach that future neurotheology should embrace.

Conclusion

Spanish professor of philosophy Leandro Gaitan concludes that "neurotheology, even with the gaps and inconsistencies typical of a still emerging science, meets the necessary conditions to be recognized as such" (2017, p. 24). Its focus, the complexities of religious experience, the difficulties unavoidable in its method, and the difficulty of staying within the research parameters make neurotheology a challenging discipline. In engaging the brain-religion relationship, neuroscientists need to be aware that they can only make a partial contribution. Science contributes to but cannot exhaust a topic that requires a more inclusive level of reflection (p. 24).

Professor of philosophy in Rome and Argentina, Rev. Juan José Sanguineti, concurs.

> The collaboration of philosophy and neuroscience implies the mutual enrichment of both disciplines. In some areas, if philosophy ignores neuroscience, it is in danger of being incomplete or vague. On the other hand, neuroscience without philosophy runs the risk of reductionism. (2013, p. 1068).

The human person, as we have seen, is extraordinarily complex, particularly the relationship between body and soul as one substantial unity. The Catholic Council of Vienna (1312) affirmed hylomorphism to explain human body-soul unity, and Aristotelians, including Aquinas, addressed reflections on which neuroscience could build in the Christian tradition. The levels of consciousness that transverse the domains of neurobiology, psychology, spirituality, and mysticism, from the physiological to the spiritual, including grace, virtue, and sanctity, are challenging to understand for their subtle interconnection, and even more so when the Spirit of God moves among them.

We have tried to explore the positive aspects and potential of neurotheology in understanding the brain from a perspective inspired by Catholic theology. As mentioned, we do not mean that a particular brain function makes one a Catholic believer. Rather, we have attempted to understand how the person engages from a neurological viewpoint in many diverse dimensions of the Catholic faith—from theology to prayer to rituals to behaviors to experience.

We hope that this neurotheological perspective helps Catholics find new ways of exploring their faith and those who are not Catholic to understand the power and beauty of the Christian tradition.

We leave with these important and encouraging words of Pope Francis:

> Dear friends, I am pleased that various universities throughout the world, Catholic and non-Catholic, are taking part in this event (Conference on Body, Mind, and Soul). I encourage you to undertake and pursue interdisciplinary research involving various centers of study for the sake of a better understanding of ourselves and our human nature, with all its limits and possibilities, while always keeping in mind the transcendent horizon to which our being tends. I ask God to bless your work, and I express my hope that you will always retain your enthusiasm, and indeed your wonderment, before the ever-deeper mystery of man. For as Saint Augustine, echoing the Bible, tells us in words that remain ever timely: 'Man is truly a vast abyss' (*Confessions* IV, 14, 22). Thank you. (2021)

Study Questions

1. What has been the attitude of the Church toward the study of neuroscience and theology together?
2. Should neurotheology be a subdivision of neurology or theology or an independent disciplinary field? Explain.
3. One model of neurotheology correlates RMS experiences with brain structure and function. What is meant by calling this model causally agnostic? Methodologically reductionistic?
4. What is meant by a dialogic model of neurotheology?
5. What problems for Catholic theology are posed by neurotheology's alleged relativist ontology and subjectivist epistemology? Explain.
6. What are the implications of reductionistic/materialistic neuroscience?
7. What are the implications of neuroscience open to the spiritual/supernatural?
8. What would be the problems with basing neurotheology on experience? Why can experience not be entirely explained by neurological processes?
9. Would using terms that are non-standard in neuroscience, like causal operators, be problematic for neurotheology or legitimately creative? Explain.
10. Do you agree with Watts that neurotheology might not apply well to theological concerns? Explain.

11. If neuroscience measures neurophysiological aspects of religious experience, to what degree can neurotheology comment on the whole experience? Explain with examples from criticisms in this direction.

12. What are some of the complex dimensions of religious experience?

13. Can neuroscience conclude that God is perceived in the "real" subjective experience of AUB? Explain.

14. Why would theology object to considering conclusions of neuroscientific findings derived from subjective human experience?

15. What objections to neurotheology do constructivists raise?

16. What are theological objections to neurotheology from the viewpoint of God and faith?

17. What do critics mean by objecting to a neuro-equivalent of theology?

18. How could neurotheology broaden the meaning of theology?

19. Why could there, or not, be a meta- or mega-neurotheology?

20. What is the problem with neurotheology investigating reality from a biological rather than philosophical or theological perspective?

21. What would be the problem with equating AUB with God?

22. What is the mereological fallacy?

23. What is the fallacy of the disappearing person?

24. What is the hazard of the unreflective conceptual framework?

25. What is the hazard of causal monism?

26. What is the fallacy of misplaced contingency?

27. What are the hazards of cognitive science?

28. What is the hazard of numinous neural localization?

29. What is meant by neurotheology's central concern: exceeding its epistemic limits by addressing philosophical and theological issues within the limits of science?

30. What do critics of neurotheology as a separate field recommend as alternatives? Explain.

31. How are body and mind, neural and mental, physical and spiritual distinguishable levels of the human soul and person?

32. What are epistemological differences among philosophy, theology, and the sciences?

33. Can the sciences evaluate religious content and philosophical interpretations of religion or spiritual activity? Explain.

34. According to Sanguineti, what might neurotheology contribute to religious activities?

35. Why would scientific and popular preference for neuroscience over other disciplines make neurotheological research problematic for theology?

36. What does Mitchell mean by *coordinated pluralism*?

37. Might van Huyssteen's *transversal spaces* model apply to the neuroscience-theology dialogue?

39. What are some suggestions for developing scholars in neurotheology, particularly from the Catholic or Christian perspective?

Endnotes

[1] For example, the provability of God's existence, God's nature, good and evil, freedom, sin, and virtue, revelation, God's relationship with human beings, the existence of a soul, and how salvation may be achieved (Newberg, 2010).

[2] *The Shaping of Rationality: Toward Interdisciplinarity in Science and Theology*, 1999, and *Alone in the World: Human Uniqueness in Science and Theology*, 2006.

[3] There are several programs available for those interested, including studies at Saybrook University; Fuller Theological Seminary; Columbia University Teachers College and the Spirituality Mind Body Institute; Duke University Center for Spirituality, Theology and Health; and the George Washington University Institute for Spirituality & Health (GWish).

References

Abbott, W. M. (Ed.). (1966). Documents of Vatican II. New York: Herder and Herder.

Abu, H. O., Ulbricht, C., Ding, E., Allison, J. J., Salmoirago-Blotcher, E., Goldberg, R. J., & Kiefer, C. I. (2018). Association of religiosity and spirituality with quality of life in patients with cardiovascular disease: A systematic review. *Quality of Life Research, 27(11)*, 2777-2797. doi: 10.1007/s11136-018-1906-4.

Acosta, M. (2015). Neuroteologia. Es hoy la nueva teologia natural? Naturaleza y Libertad : *Revista de estudios interdisciplinares*, 5, 11-51.

Adolphs, R., Glascher, J., & Tranel, D. (2018, January 16). Searching for the neural causes of behavior. *Proceedings of the National Academy of Sciences of the United States of America, 115*(3), 451-452. doi: 10.1073/pnas.1720442115.

Afford, P. (2020, September). Using neuroscience to map the whole person: Peter Afford guides us through the systems that influence emotions, behavior, and personality. *Therapy Today, 31*(7), 1-7.

Alcorta, C. S., & Sosis, R. (2005). Ritual, emotion, and sacred symbols: The evolution of religion as an adaptive complex. *Human Nature, 16*(4), 323-359. doi: 10.1007/s12110-005-1014-3.

Alexander, A. (2020). (Review). *Theological neuroethics: Christian ethics meets the science of the human brain* by Neil Messer. *Journal of Moral Theology, 9*(2), 209-211.

Alexander, A. R. (2018). *Mystical brain, divine consciousness: A theological appropriation of cognitive neuroscience.* (Unpublished doctoral dissertation. Fordham University, New York).

Allen, C., & Trestman. (2020, Winter). Animal consciousness. In E. N. Zalta (Ed.), *The Stanford encyclopedia of philosophy*. Retrieved from https://plato.stanford.edu/archives/win2020/entries/consciousness-animal.

Allen, J. A. (2016). Bernard Lonergan's critique of knowing as taking a look. *Heythrop Journal, 57*(3), 451-460. doi: 10.1111/heyj.12147.

Alston, W. (1991). *Perceiving God: The epistemology of religious experience.* Ithaca, NY: Cornell University Press.

Amen. W. (2023). *The Daniel plan.* Retrieved from https://www.danielplan.com/start

American Psychological Association. (2013). What role do religion and spirituality play in mental health? (Interview with K. I. Pargament). Retrieved from https://www.apa.org.

Ammon, K., & Gandevia, S. C. (1990). Transcranial magnetic stimulation can influence the selection of motor programs. *Journal of Neurology, Neurosurgery, and Psychiatry, 53* (8), 705-707.

Anderson, D. E. (2012). Neuroscience. In J. A. Lamm (ed.), *The Wiley-Blackwell Companion to Christian mysticism* (pp. 592-609). Hoboken, NJ: Wiley-Blackwell.

Anderson, E. (2013). Neuroscience. In J. A. Lemm (Ed.), *The Wiley-Blackwell companion to Christian mysticism* (pp. 592-609). West Sussex, U.K.: John Wiley & Sons.

Andresen, J. (2001). *Religion in mind: Cognitive perspectives on religious belief, ritual, and experience.* Cambridge, U.K: Cambridge University Press.

Anscombe, G. E. M. (1957/2000). *Intention* (2nd ed.). Cambridge, MS: Harvard University Press.

Antonovsky, A. (1987). *Unraveling the mystery of health: How people manage stress and stay well.* San Francisco: Jossey-Boss.

Aquinas, T. (1250s/2023). *On the principles of nature.* Retrieved from https://www3.nd. edu/~afreddos/papers/Aquinas

Aquinas, T. (1259/1952). *De veritate: On truth.* Washington, DC: Henry Regnery Publishing.

Aquinas, T. (1265/2019) *Summa contra gentiles. 4 vols.* (The Aquinas Institute, Ed.). Steubenville, OH: Emmaus Academic Publishing.

Aquinas, T. (1948). *Summa theologica.* (Vols. 1-3). (Fathers of the English Dominican Province, Trans.). New York: Benziger Brothers.

Aristotle, & McMahin, J. H. (1991). *The metaphysics.* Amherst, NY: Prometheus Publishing.

Aristotle, & Reeve, C. D. C. (350 BC/2017). *De anima.* Indianapolis, IN: Hackett Publishing.

Arraj, J. (1993) *Mysticism, metaphysics, and Maritain: On the road to the spiritual unconscious.* Chiloquin, OR: Inner Growth Books.

Ashbrook, J. B., & Albright, C. R. (1997). *The humanizing brain: Where religion and neuroscience meet.* Cleveland, OH: Pilgrim Press.

Aspren, E., & Taves, A. (2018). Explanation and the study of religion. In B. Stoddard (Ed.), *Method today: Redescribing approaches to the study of religion* (pp. 133-157). London, U.K.: Equinox.

Assaf, Y., & Pasternak, O. (2008). Diffusion tensor imaging (DTI)-based white matter mapping in brain research: A review. *Journal of Molecular Neuroscience, 34,* 51-61. doi:10.1007/s12031-007-0029-0.

Atran, S. (2002). *In gods we trust: The evolutionary landscape of religion.* Oxford, U.K.: Oxford University Press.

Augustine, St. (400/2012). *De Trinitate: On the Trinity.* New York: New City Press.

Austin, J. H. (1998). *Zen and the brain.* Cambridge, MA: MIT Press.

Avila Institute. (2023). Retrieved from Avila-institute.org/spiritual-formation

Azari, N. (2006). Neuroimaging studies of religious experience: A critical review. In P. McNamara (Ed), *Where God and science meet: How brain and evolutionary studies alter our understanding of religion, vol. 3: The psychology of religious experience* (pp. 33-54). Westport, CT: Greenwood Press.

Azari, N., Nickel, J., Niedeggen, M., Hefter, H., Tellman, L., Herzog, H., Seitz, R. J. (2001). Neural correlates of religious experience. *European Journal of Neuroscience, 13,* 1649-1652.

Baesler, E. J., & Ladd, K. (2009). Exploring prayer contexts and health outcomes: From the chair to the pew. *Journal of Communication and Religion, 32*(2),

347-384. Retrieved from https://digitalcommons.odu.edu/communication _fac_pubs

Baglow, C. T. (2020). Faith and science: The foundation of a Catholic approach to science. McGrath Institute for Church Life. Notre Dame University. In C. T. Baglow (Ed.), *Faith, science, and reason: Theology on the cutting edge* (2nd ed.). Downers Grove, IL: Midwest Theological Forum.

Barbour, I. (1990). *Religion in an age of science.* San Franciso, CA: HarperOne.

Barbour, I. (1997). *Religion and science: Historical and contemporary issues.* New York: HarperCollins.

Barbour, I. G. (2000). *Religion and science: Historical and contemporary issues.* New York: HarperCollins.

Barnby, J. M., Bailey, N. W., Chambers, R., & Fitzgerald, P. B. (2015, November). How similar are the changes in neural activity resulting from mindfulness practice in contrast to spiritual practice? *Consciousness and Cognition,* 36, 219-232.

Barrett, J. L. (2017). Cognitive science of religion and Christian faith: How may they be brought together? *Perspectives on Science and Christian Faith,* 69(1), 3-12.

Barrett, N. F. (2011). [Review of the book Principles of Neurotheology by Andrew Newberg]. Ars Disputandi, 11, 133-136. Retrieved from http://www.Ars Disputandi.org

Basilian Fathers: Our charism. (2023). Retrieved from https://basilian.org/en/

Basilian: Byzantine rite monasticism. (2023). Retrieved from https://basilian. org/en/about-us/our-charism

Battro, A. M., Dehaene, S., Sorondo, M. S., Singer, W. J. (Eds.). (2013). Neurosciences and the human person: New perspectives on human activities. Vatican, Rome: Pontifical Academy of Sciences.

Beauregard, J. (2019). *Philosophical neuroethics: A personalist approach. Vol. 1: Foundations.* Wilmington, DE: Vernon Press.

Beauregard, J. (2023). *Philosophical neuroethics: A personalist approach. Vol. 2. Practical neuroethics.* Wilmington, DE: Vernon Press.

Beauregard, M. (2007). Mind does really matter: Evidence from neuroimaging studies of emotional self-regulation, psychotherapy, and placebo effect. *Progress in Neurobiology,* 81, 218-236.

Beauregard, M., & O'Leary, D. (2008). *The spiritual brain: A neuroscientist's case for the existence of the soul.* Chapters 7-10. New York: HarperCollins.

Beauregard, M., & Paquette, V. (2006). Neural correlates of a mystical experience in Carmelite nuns. *Neuroscience Letters,* 405(3), 186-190.

Beck, A. T. (1979). *Cognitive therapy and emotional disorders.* New York: Plume. Penguin Books.

Beck, A. T., Rush, A. J., Shaw, B. F., & Emery, G. (1967/1987). *Cognitive therapy of depression.* New York: Guilford Press.

Bellah, R. N. (1986, February 21). Habits of the heart: Implications for religion. Lecture 5: St. Mark's Catholic Church, Isla Vista, California. Retrieved from http://www.robertbellah. com/lectures_5.htm

Benedict XVI, Pope. (2007). *Spes Salvi*. Encyclical Letter on Christian Hope. Retrieved from https://www.vatican.va/content/benedict-xvi/en/encyclicals/documents/hf_ben-xvi_enc_20071130_spe-salvi.html

Benedict XVI, Pope. (2012, November 8). Address of His Holiness Pope Benedict XVI to members of the Pontifical Academy of Sciences on the occasion of the plenary assembly. Retrieved from www.vatican.va/content/benedict-xvi/en/speeches/2012/november/documents/hf_ben-xvi_spe_20121108_academy-sciences.htm

Bennet, P. (2019a). "Landscape plotted and pieced": Exploring the contours of engagement between (neuro)science and theology. *Zygon: Journal of Religion and Science, 54*, 86-106.

Bennet, P. (2019b). "Things counter, original, spare, strange:" Developing a postfoundational transversal model for science/religion dialogue." *Zygon: Journal of Religion and Science, 54*, 107-128.

Bennet, P. (2019c). "All trades, their gear, and tackle and trim:" Theology, cognitive neuroscience, and psychoneuroimmunology in transversal dialogue. *Zygon: Journal of Religion and Science, 54*, 129-148.

Bennett, M. R., & Hacker, P. M. S. (2003). *Philosophical foundations of neuroscience* (1st ed.). Malden, MA: Blackwell.

Berger, P. L., & Luckmann, T. (1966/1975). *The social construction of reality*. London, U.K.: Penguin.

Bergman, R. (2008). Teaching justice after MacIntyre: Toward a Catholic philosophy of moral education. *Catholic Education: A Journal of Inquiry and Practice, 12*(1), 7-24.

Bering, J. (2011). *The belief instinct: The psychology of souls, destiny, and the meaning of life*. New York: W. W. Norton.

Bianchini, D. A. (2015, December 7). What are the differences between religious orders? Retrieved from www.religious-vocation.com.

Bilder, R. Howe, A., & Saab, F. (2013). Multilevel models from biology to psychology: Mission impossible? *Journal of Abnormal Psychology, 122*(3), 917-927.

Bingaman, K. A. (2013). The promise of neuroplasticity for pastoral care and counseling. *Pastoral Psychology, 62*(5), 549-560. doi: 10.1007/s11089-013-0513-0.

Black, D. S., & Slavich, G. M. (2016). Mindfulness meditation and the immune system: A systematized research of randomized controlled trials. *Annals of the New York Academy of Sciences, 1373*(1), 13-24. doi: 10.1111/nyas.12998.

Bloch. M. (1989). *Ritual, history, and power*. London, U.K.: Athlone Press.

Blommestijn, H., Huls, J., & Waaijman, K. (2000). *The footprints of love: John of the Cross as guide in the wilderness*. (Trans. J. Vriend). Leuven, Belgium: Peeters.

Boccia, M., Piccardi, L, & Guarriglia, P. (2015). The meditative mind: A comprehensive meta-analysis of MRI studies. *BioMed research international*, 2015.

Boston University Medical Center. (2021, April 21) Association versus causation. Module 1: Population health. Retrieved from https://sphweb.bumc.bu.edu/otlt/

MPH-Modules/PH717-QuantCore/PH717-Module1A-Populations/PH717 -Module1A-Populations6.html

Bourgignon, E. (Ed.). 1973). *Religion, altered states of consciousness, and social change.* Columbus, OH: Ohio State University Press.

Bourgignon, E. (Ed.). Possession. San Francisco, CA: Chandler and Sharpe.

Bouyer, P. (2003). Religious thought and behavior as by-products of brain function. *Trends in Cognitive Sciences, 7*(3), 119-124.

Brandt, P.-Y., Clément, F., & Manning, R. R. (2010). Neurotheology: Challenges and opportunities. *Schweitzer Archiv fur Neurologie und Psychiatrie, 161,* 305-309. Retrieved from http://www.sanp.ch

Brown, J. W. (2015). *Microgenetic theory and process thought.* Bedfordshire, U.K.: Andrews, U.K., Ltd.

Brown, W. S., Murphy, N., & Malony, H. N. (Eds.). (1998). *Whatever happened to the soul? Scientific and theological portraits of human nature.* Minneapolis, MN: Fortress.

Brueggemann, W. (2007, December 25). Wired to believe. [Review of the book *Alone in the world: Human uniqueness in science and theology,* by J. W. van Huyssteen]. *Christian Century, 26,* 28-30.

Brugger, C. (2009). Psychology and Christian anthropology. *Edification: Journal of the Christian Association of Psychology Studies, 3,* 5-18.

Buber, M. (1923). *I and thou.* Eastford, CT: Martino Publishing.

Buckley, M. J. (1980). Within the holy mystery. In L. O'Donovan (Ed.), *A world of grace* (pp. 31-49). New York: Seabury Press.

Bulkeley, K. (2005). *Soul, psyche, brain: New directions in the study of religion and brain-mind science.* New York: Palgrave Macmillan.

Bunge, M. (1979/2008). *Causality and modern science.* 4th ed. Philadelphia, PA: Routledge.

Burgos, J. M. (2021). *Personalist anthropology: A philosophical guide to life.* Wilmington, DE: Vernon Press.

Burkhart, J. J. "Sensus Fidelium." (2023, February 23). *New Catholic encyclopedia.* Retrieved from https://www.encyclopedia.com

Burns, C. P. E. (2005). Cognitive science and Christian theology. In K. Bulkeley (Ed.), *Soul, psyche, brain: New directions in the study of religion and brain-mind science.* New York: Springer.

Butera, G. (2011). Second Harvest: Further reflections on the promise of the Thomistic psychology. *Philosophy, Psychiatry, and Psychology, 17*(4), 317-346. doi: 10.1353/ppp.2010.0029.

Butera, G. (2011). Thomas Aquinas and cognitive therapy: An exploration of the promise of the Thomistic psychology. *Philosophy, Psychiatry, and Psychology, 17*(4), 347-366. doi: 10.1353/ppp.2010.0023.

Butler, P. M., McNamara, P., Ghofani, J., Durso, R. (2011). Disease-associated differences in religious cognition in patients with Parkinson's Disease. *Journal of Clinical and Experimental Neuropsychology, 33*(8), 917-928. doi: 10.10 80/13803395.2011.575768.

Buzsaki, G. (2006). *Rhythms of the brain.* New York: Oxford University Press.

Byrne, P. H. (2021). Notre Dame Philosophical Reviews. [Review of the book *Authenticity as self transcendence: The enduring insights of Bernard Lonergan* by M. H. McCarthy]. Retrieved from https://ndpr.ne.edu/reviews/authenticity-as-self-transcendence-the-enduring-insights-ofbernard-lonergan

Cacioppo, J. T., Gardner, W. L., & Berntson, G. G. (2002). The affect system has parallel and integrative processing components: Form follows function. In J. T. Cacioppo, G. G. Berntson, R. Adolphs, et al., (Eds.), *Foundations in Social Neuroscience* (pp. 493-522). Cambridge, MA: MIT Press.

Cahn, B. R., & Polich, J. (1999). Meditation states and traits: EEG, ERP, and neuroimaging studies. *Psychological Bulletin*, 132, 180-211.

Candelario, D. A. (2009). George Tyrrell and Karl Rahner: A dialogue on revelation. *Heythrop Journal, 50*(1), 44-57. doi: 10.1111/j.1468-2265.2008.00416.x.

Caponi, F. J. (2007). A speechless grace: Karl Rahner on religious language. *International Journal of Systematic Theology, 9*(2), 200-222. doi: 10.1111/j.1468-2400.2007.00253.x.

Cappas, N. M., Andres-Hymen, R., & Davidson, H. (2005). What psychotherapists can begin to learn from neuroscience: Seven principles of brain-based psychotherapy. *Psychotherapy: Theory, Research, Practice, Training, 42*, 374-383.

Capra, F., Steindl-Rast, D., & Matus, T. (1992). *Belonging to the universe: New Thinking about God and nature*. New York: Penguin Books.

Carlson, N. R. (2007). *Physiology of behavior*. (9th ed.). Boston, MA: Allyn and Bacon.

Carmelite Sisters of the Most Sacred Heart of Los Angeles. (2013, June 10). Meditation and contemplation—What is the difference? Retrieved from https://carmelitesistersocd.com/2013/meditation-contemplation/

Carr., L. Iacoboni, M., Dubeau-M.-C., & Lenzi, G. L. (2003, April 7). Neural mechanisms of empathy in humans: A relay from neural systems for imitation to limbic areas. *Biological Sciences, 100*(9), 5497-5502. Retrieved from https://loi.org/10.1073/pnas.0935845100.

Cassibba, R., Granqvist, P., Costantini, A., & Gatto, S. (2008). Attachment and God representations among lay Catholics, priests, and religious: A matched comparison study based on the adult attachment interview. *Developmental Psychology*, 44(6),1753–1763.

Catholic Church. (1995). *Catechism of the Catholic Church*. New York: Image, Doubleday.

Catholic Culture. (2023). *Fr. John Hardon's Modern Catholic dictionary*. Retrieved from www.catholicculture.org/culture/library/dictionary/index.cfm?id=36024

Chalmers, D. (1995). Facing up to the problem of consciousness. *Journal of Consciousness Studies,* 2(3), 200-219.

Chang, H. (2012). Is water H2O? Evidence, realism, and pluralism. Boston Studies in the Philosophy of Science, 293. Dordrecht: Springer Netherlands.

Charis Doctrinal Commission. (2021, July 28). What is the difference between mystical experiences and charismatic manifestations? Catholic Charismatic Renewal International Service. Retrieved from https://www.charis.international/

en/what-is-the-difference-between-mystical-experiences-and-charismatic-manifestations.

Chaves, M., Konieczny, M. E., Beyerlein, K., & Barman, E. (1999). The national congregations' study: Background, methods, and selected results. *Journal for the Scientific Study of Religion, 38,* 458-476.

Chen, Y., Kim, E. S., & VanderWeele, T. J. (2020, December). Religious-service attendance and subsequent health and well-being throughout adulthood: Evidence from three prospective cohorts. *International Journal of Epidemiology, 49*(6), 2030–2040. doi: 10.1093/ije/dyaa120.

Cherniak, Mikulincer, Shaver, & Grandqvist. (2021). Attachment theory and religion. Elsevier. Retrieved from www.sciencedirect.com/science/article/pii/S2352250X2030172X

Christensen, J., et al. (2014). Roman Catholic beliefs produce characteristic neural responses to moral dilemmas. *Social Cognitive and Affective Neuroscience, 9*(2), 240-249. doi: 10.1093/scan/nss121.

Christov-Moore, L., Conway, P., & Iacoboni, M. (2017). Deontological dilemma response tendencies and sensorimotor representations of harm to others. *Frontiers in Integrative Neuroscience, 11,* 1-9. doi: 10.3389/fnint.2017.00034.

Churchill, N.W., Hutchsion, M. G., Graham, S. J., & Schweitzer, T. A. (2021, May 21). Insular connectivity is associated with self-appraisal of cognitive function after a concussion. *Frontiers in Neurology, 12.* Retrieved from https://doi.org/10.3389/2021.653442.

Clark, A. & Chalmers, D. (1998). The extended mind. *Analysis, 58*(1), 7-19. Oxford, U.K.: Oxford University Press.

Clark, A. (2013). Whatever next? Predictive brains, situated agents, and the future of cognitive science. *Behavioral Brain Science, 36,* 181-204.

Clarke, P. (2015). *All in the mind? Does neuroscience challenge faith?* Oxford, U.K.: Lion Hudson.

Clayton, P. (2000). Neuroscience, the person, and God: An emergentist account. *Zygon: Journal of Religion and Science, 35*(3), 613-652. doi: 10.1111/0591-2385.00301.

Clayton, P. (2004). *Mind and emergence: From quantum to consciousness.* New York: Oxford University Press.

Clayton, T. (n.d.). Political philosophy of Alasdair MacIntyre. *Internet encyclopedia of philosophy: A peer-reviewed academic resource.* Retrieved from http://iep.utm.edu/p-mac

Clifford, A. M. (2004). Catholicism and Ian Barbour on theology and science. In R. J. Russell (Ed.), *Fifty years in science and religion: Ian G. Barbour and his legacy.* Hants, U.K.: Ashgate.

Clinton, T., & Sibcy, G. (2012). Christian counseling, interpersonal neurobiology, and the future. *Journal of Psychology and Theology, 40,* 141-145.

Coffee, D. (2004). The whole Rahner on the supernatural existential. *Theological Studies, 65,* 95-118.

Cohen, M. R., & Nagel, E. (2007). *An introduction to logic and scientific method.* NY: Harcourt, Brace, & World.

Comstock, G. W., & Patridge, K. B. (2008, October). Historical paper: Church attendance and health. *American Journal of Epidemiology, 168*(7), 819-826.

Congleton, C., Holzel, B. K., & Lazar, S. W. (2015). Mindfulness can literally change your brain. *Harvard Business Review.* Retrieved from https://hbr.org/2015/01/mindfulness-can-literally-change-your-brain

Congregation for Catholic Education. (2016). The Gift of Priestly Formation, *Ratio fundamentalis institutions sacerdotatis.* Retrieved from www.semscience. net.

Conn, W. E. (1988). The desire for authenticity: Conscience and moral conversion. In V. Gregson (Ed.), *The desires of the human heart: Introduction to the theology of Bernard Lonergan.* NY: Paulist Press.

Coolman, B. T. (2009). Gestimmtheit: Attunement as a description of the nature-grace relationship in Rahner's theology. *Theological Studies, 70,* 782-800.

Cortez, M. (2017, April). [Review of the book *Neuroscience and the soul: The human person in philosophy, science, and theology* by T. M. Crisp, S. L. Porter, and G. A. Ten Elshof (Eds.)]. *Science and Christian Belief, 30*(1), 78-79.

Cosgrove, M. (2018). *The brain, the mind, and the person within the enduring mystery of the soul.* Grand Rapids, MI: Kregel Academic.

Cozolino, L. (2006). *The neuroscience of human relationships: Attachment and the developing social brain.* New York: W. W. Norton and Company.

Craig, A. D. (2004). Human feelings: Why are some more aware than others? *Trends in Cognitive Sciences,* 8(6), 239-341.

Craig, A. D. (2009, January). How do you feel—now? The anterior insula and human awareness. *Nature Reviews Neuroscience,* 10(1), 59-70.

Crawford, S. (Ed.). (2011). General introduction. *Philosophy of mind: Critical concepts of philosophy.* (4 Vols.). London, U.K.: Routledge.

Crescentini, C., Aglioti, S. M., Fabbro, F., & Urgesi, C. (2013). P 140. Virtual lesions of the inferior parietal and prefrontal cortex alter implicit religiousness and spirituality in healthy individuals. *Clinical Neuropsychology, 124*(10). doi: 10.1016/j.clinph.2013. 04.217.

Critchley, H. D., Wiens, S., Rotshtein, P., Ohman, A., & Dolan, R. J. (2004). Neural systems supporting interoceptive awareness. *Nature Neuroscience,* 7, 189-195.

Critchley, P. (2013). Being and knowing: A Thomist reading of Immanuel Kant. Retrieved from https://mmu.academia.edu/PeterCritchley/Books.

Crowe, F. E., & Doran, R. M. (1988). *Collected works of Bernard Lonergan.* Toronto, Canada: University of Toronto Press.

Cunningham, L. S. (2006, February 24). Catholic spirituality: What does it mean today?" *Commonweal, 133*(4), 11-15.

Cunningham, P. (2011, Summer). Are religious experiences really localized within the brain? The promise, challenges, and prospects of neurotheology. *Journal of Mind and Behavior, 32*(3), 223-249.

Curtis, J. M., & Curtis, M. J. (2016). Factors related to susceptibility and recruitment by cults. *Psychological Reports, 73*(2). Retrieved from https://doi. org/10.2466/pro.1993.73.2.451.

D'Aquili, E., & Newberg, A. B. (1993). Mystical states and the experience of God: A model of the neuropsychological substrate. *Zygon,* 22, 177-200.

d'Aquili, E., & Newberg, A. B. (1999). *The mystical mind: Probing the biology of religious experience*. Minneapolis: Fortress Press.

D'Urso, G., Petruccelli, I, & Pace, U. (2019). Attachment style, attachment to God, religiosity, and moral disengagement: A study on offenders. *Mental Health, Religion, and Culture, 22*(1), 1-11. doi: 10.1080/13674676.2018.1562 429.

Dadosky, J. D. (2010). Is there a fourth stage of meaning? *Heythrop Journal, 51*(5), 768-780. doi: 10.1111/j.1468-2265.2009.00518.x.

dal Covolo, E. (March 17, 1999). The encounter of faith and reason in the Fathers of the Church. Vatican City, Europe: *L'Osservatore Romano*, 9-10.

Damasio, A. (1994/2005). *Descartes' error: Emotion, reason, and the human brain*. London, England: Penguin Books.

Damasio, A. (2000). T*he feeling of what happens: Body, emotion, and the making of consciousness*. London, U.K.: Vintage.

Damasio, A. (2010, November 9). *Self comes to mind: Constructing the conscious mind [electronic resources]*. Westminster, MD: Pantheon Books. Random House Digital.

Damasio, A. (2012). *Self comes to mind: Constructing the conscious mind*. New York: Pantheon Books.

Daniel, A. E, (2013). The immortality of the soul in the thought of Thomas Aquinas. Academia. Retrieved from https://academia.edu/29459315/

Darr, R. (2020). Virtues as qualities of character: Alasdair MacIntyre and the situationist critique of virtue ethics. *Journal of Religious Ethics, 48*(1), 7-25.

Davidson, B., & Irwin, W. (2002). The functional neuroanatomy of emotion and affective style. In J. T. Cacioppo, G. G. Berntson, R. Adolphs, et al., (Eds.), *Foundations in Social Neuroscience* (pp. 473-490). Cambridge, MA: MIT Press.

Davidson, J. R. (1976, Spring). The physiology of meditation and mystical states of consciousness. *Perspectives in Biology and Medicine*, 345-379.

Davis, D., & Hayes, J., A. (2011). What are the benefits of mindfulness? A practice review of psychotherapy-related research. *Psychotherapy, 48*(2), 198-208.

Dawes, G. W., & MacLaurin, J. (Eds.). (2013). *A new science of religion*. New York: Routledge.

Dawkins, R. (2008). *The God delusion*. Boston: HarperCollins.

De Gregorio, D., Aguilar-Valles, A., Preller, K. H., Heifets, B. D., Hibicke, M., Mitchell, J., & Gobbi, G. (2021, February 3). Hallucinogens in mental health: Preclinical and clinical studies on LSD, psilocybin, MDMA, and ketamine. *Journal of Neuroscience, 41*(5), 891-900. Retrieved from https://doi.org/10 .1523/INEUROSCI.1659-20.2020.

De Haan, D. D. (2018). Hylomorphism and the new mechanist philosophy in biology, neuroscience, and psychology. In W. Simpson, R. Koons, & N. The (Eds), *Neo-Aristotelian perspectives on contemporary science* (pp. 1-27). Oxfordshire, U.K.: Routledge.

De Haan, D. D. (2020). Philosophical hazards in the neuroscientific study of religion. In A. Coles & J. Colicutt (Eds.), *Neurology and religion* (pp. 48-70). Cambridge, U.K.: Cambridge University Press.

Deacon, T. W. (1997). *The symbolic species: The co-evolution of language and the brain*. Scranton, PA: W. W. Norton.

Deeley, P. Q. (2004, December). The religious brain: Turning ideas into convictions. *Anthropology & Medicine, 11*(3), 245-267. doi: 10.1080/136484 7042000296554.

Dehaene, S., & Changeux, J. P. (2000). Reward-dependent learning in neuronal networks for planning and decision making. *Progress in Brain Research, 126,* 217-229.

Dehaene, S., & Cohen, L. (2011, June). The unique role of the visual word form area in reading. *Trends in Cognitive Sciences, 15*(6). doi:10.1016/j.tics.2011. 04.003.

DeKlerk, B. J., & Kruger, F. P. (2016). Continuous formation of liturgy through social cognition, *Theological Studies, 72.* Retrieved from http://dx.doi.org/10. 4102/hts.v7213.3170.

Delio, I. (2003, September). Brain science and the biology of belief: A theological response. *Zygon: Journal of Religion and Science, 38*(3), 573-585. doi: 10.1111/1467-9744.00522.

Delio, I. (2013). Faith and the cosmos. *America.* In P. McCaffrey (Ed.). *Faith and Science.* Ipswitch, MA: EBSCO.

Depue, R. A., Luciana, M., Arbisi, R., Collins, P., & Leon, A. (2002). Dopamine and the structure of personality: Relation of agonist-induced dopamine activity to positive emotionality. In J. T. Cacioppo, G. G. Berntson, R. Adolphs, et al., (Eds.), *Foundations in Social Neuroscience* (pp. 1071-1092). Cambridge, MA: MIT Press.

Desikan, R. S., Ségonne, Fischl, B., Quinn, B. T., Dickerson, B. C., . & Killiany, R. J. (2006). An automated labeling system for subdividing the human cerebral cortex on MRI scans into gyral-based regions of interest. *Neuroimage, 31*(3), 968-980.

Devine, A. (1911/2023). Passionists. In *The Catholic encyclopedia.* New York: Robert Appleton. Retrieved from http://www.newadvent.org/cathen/1152 1d.htm

Devinsky, O., & Lai, G. (2008, May). Spirituality and religion in epilepsy. *Epilepsy and Behavior, 12*(4), 636-643. Retrieved from https://doi.org/10.1016/j. yebeh.2007.11.011.

Díaz, J.-L. (2000, September). Mind-body unity, dual aspect, and the emergence of consciousness. *Philosophical Psychology, 13*(3), 393-403. doi: 10.1080/09515080050128187.

DiChiara, G. (1995). The role of dopamine in drug abuse viewed from the perspective of its role in motivation. *Drug and Alcohol Dependence, 38,* 95-137.

Dillern, T. (2020). The act of knowing: Michael Polani meets contemporary natural science. *Foundations of Science, 25,* 573-585. Retrieved from https://doi.org/10.1007/s10699-019-09626-3.

DiPaolo, E., & De Jaegher, H. (2012). The interactive brain hypothesis. *Frontiers in Human Neuroscience, 6.* Article 163. Retrieved from https://doi.org/ 10.3389/fnhum.2012.00163.

Dixon, S., & Wilcox, G. (2016). The counseling implications of neurotheology: A critical review. *Journal of Spirituality in Mental Health, 18*(2), 98-107. doi: 10.1080/19349637. 2015.1064804.

Dodds, M. J. (2009). Hylomorphism and human wholeness: Perspectives on the mind-brain problem. *Theology and Science, 7*(2), 141-162. doi: 10.1080/14 746700902796759.

Dodds, M. J. (2014). *Philosophical anthropology.* (2nd ed.). Oakland, CA: Western Dominican Province.

Dodds, M. J. (2017). *Unlocking divine action: Contemporary science and Thomas Aquinas.* Washington DC: Catholic University of America Press.

Dodds, M. J. (2019, Summer). The reality of the soul in an age of neuroscience. *Nova et Vetera, 17*(3), 893-912. doi: 10.1353/nov.2019.0056.

Dorman, D. (2021). The liturgical brain: Neuroscience of habit. Retrieved from https://godandnature.asa3.org/dorman-liturgical-brain.html

Downey, M. (Ed). (1993). *New dictionary of Catholic spirituality.* Collegeville, MN: Liturgical Press.

du Toit, D. (2015). *What science? Whose theology? A reformed theological response to Andrew Newberg's neurotheological model.* (Unpublished master's dissertation). University of Stellenbosch, Cape Town, South Africa.

Duke, M. (2018). A loving kind of knowing: Connatural knowledge as a means of knowing God in Thomas Aquinas's Summa Theologica. *Lumen et Vita 8,* 12-18.

Dunn, B. R., Hartigan, J. A., & Mikulas, W. L. (1999). Concentration and mindfulness meditations: unique forms of consciousness? *Applied psychophysiology and biofeedback,* 24(3), 147–165. https://doi.org/10.10 23/a:1023498629385

Dunne, T. (2003). Generalized empirical method in ethics. Retrieved from https://www.academia.edu/32843646/Generalized_Empirical_Method_in_Ethics.

Durkheim, E. (1915/1969/2016). *Elementary forms of the religious life: A study in religious sociology.* Oxford, U.K.: Oxford University Press.

Edwards, K. J. (2015). When Word meets Flesh: A neuroscience perspective on embodied Spiritual Formation. *Journal of Psychology and Christianity 34,* 228-239.

Egan, H. D. (1993a). Affirmative way. In M. Downey (Ed.), *The new dictionary of Catholic spirituality* (pp. 14-17). Collegeville, MN: Liturgical Press.

Egan, H. D. (2013). The mystical theology of Karl Rahner. *The Way, 52,* 43-62.

Egan. H.D. (1993b). Negative way. In M. Downey. *The new dictionary of Catholic spirituality* (pp. 700-04). Collegeville, MN: Liturgical Press.

Ekstrom, R. R. (1982). *New concise Catholic dictionary.* Mystic, CN: Twenty-Third.

Eliade, M. (1958). *Rites and symbols of initiation: The mysteries of birth and rebirth.* Dallas, TX: Spring Publications.

Eliade, M. (1959). *The sacred and the profane: The nature of religion.* New York: Harcourt Brace Jovanovich.

Eliade, M. (1968). *Myth and reality.* Scranton, PA: HarperCollins.

Ellis, G. F. (2009). Top-down causation and the human brain. In N. Murphy, G. F. R Ellis, & T. O'Connor (Eds.), *A downward causation and the neurobiology of free will* (pp. 63-82). Berlin-Heidelberg: Springer-Verlag.

Ellis, R. D. (1999, Spring). Integrating neuroscience and phenomenology in the study of consciousness. *Journal of Phenomenological Psychology, 30*(1), 1-27. doi: 10.1163/156916299X00020.

Emmons, R. A., & McNamara, P. (2006). Sacred emotions and affective neuroscience: Gratitude, costly signaling, and the brain. In P. McNamara (Ed.), *Where God and science meet: How brain and evolutionary studies alter our understanding of religion* (pp. 11-30). Westport, CT: Praeger.

Encyclopedia Britannica. (2018). *Psychokinesis. Encyclopedia Britannica.* Retrieved from https://www.britannica.com/topic/psychokinesis

Encyclopedia Britannica. (2023). Basilian. Retrieved from http://basilian.org/en/about-us/our-charism/

Encyclopedia Britannica. (2023). Cistercian. Retrieved from http://www.britannica.com/topic/Cistercians

Encyclopedia Britannica. (2023). Epistemology. Retrieved from https://www.britannica.com/topics/epistemology

Encyclopedia Britannica. (2023). History of science. Retrieved from https://www. britannica.com

Encyclopedia Britannica. (2023). Oratorian. Retrieved from https://www.britannica.com/topic/Oratorians

Encyclopedia Britannica. (2023). Poor Clare Spirituality. Retrieved from https:// www. britannica.org

Englander, Z. A., Haidt, J., & Morris, J. P. (2012). Neural basis of moral elevation demonstrated through inter-subject synchronization of cortical activity during free-viewing. Plos One, 7, e39384. doi: 10.1371/journal.pone.0039384. Public Library of Science.

Evans, D. (1989). Can philosophers limit what mystics can do? A critique of Steven Katz. *Religious Studies*, 25(1). 53-60.

Exline, J. (2013). Religious and spiritual struggles. In K. I. Pargament (Ed.), *APA handbook of psychology, religion, and spirituality: Context, theory, and research* (pp. 459-475). Washington, DC: American Psychological Association.

Exline, J. J., & Geyer, A. L. (2004, April-June). Perceptions of humility: A preliminary study. *Self and Identity*, 3(2), 95-114.

Fagerberg, D. (2019). *Liturgical mysticism.* Steubenville, OH: Emmaus Academic.

Fakhri, O. (2021). The ineffability of God. *International Journal for Philosophy of Religion, 89,* 25-41.

Fayard, C., Pereau, M. J., and Ciovica, A. (2009). "Love the Lord with all your mind": Explorations on a possible neurobiology of the experience of God and some implications for the practice of psychotherapy. *Journal of Psychology and Christianity, 28,* 167-181.

Ferguson, M. A., Schaner, F. L. W. V. J., Cohen, A., Siddiqi, Sh., Merrill, S. M., Nielsen, J. A. .& Fox, M. A. (2022, February). A neural circuit for spirituality and religiosity derived from patients with brain lesions. *Biological Psychiatry,* 91(4), 380-388.

Ferguson, M. A., Schaper, F. L. W. V. J., Cohen, A., Siddiq, S., Merrill, S. M., Nielsen, J. A., Fox, M. D. (2022). A neural circuit for spirituality and religiosity derived from patients with brain lesions. *Biological Psychiatry, 91*(4), 380-388. doi: 10.1016/j.biopsych.2021. 06.016.

Fields, S. (1996, June). Balthasar and Rahner on the spiritual senses. *Theological Studies, 57*(2), 224-241. doi: 10.1177/004056399605700202.

Finglehurts, A., & Finglehurts, A. (2009). Is our brain hardwired to produce God, or is our brain hardwired to perceive God? A systematic review on the role of the brain in mediating religious experience. *Cognitive Process,* 10, 293-326.

Fishbane, M. D. (2019, December). Healing intergenerational wounds: An integrative relational-neurobiological approach. *Family Process, 58*(4). Retrieved from https://web-s-ebscohost-com.eresources.cuyahogalibrary.org/ehost/detail/detail?vid=56sid=25621a8b-8c17-41a8

Flippen, D. (2006, Spring). Was John Paul II a Thomist or a Phenomenologist? In *Faith and Reason* (pp. 65-106). Front Royal, VA: Christendom College. Retrieved from https://www.catholicculture.org/culture/library/*view.cfm?recnum-8105.*

Fontana, L. L. B. (2018). Human transcendence as a locus of revelation and foundation for theological work: Implications from Rahner's *Hearer of the Word. Teocomunicacao, 48*(1), 82-96. doi: 10.15448/1980-6736.2018.1.31907.

Forman, R. K. C. (1999). *Mysticism, mind, consciousness.* Albany, NY: State University of New York Press.

Fowler, J. W. (1981/1995). *Stages of faith: The psychology of human development and the quest for meaning.* San Francisco, CA: HarperOne.

Fowler, J. W. (1991). *Weaving the new creation: Stages of faith and the public church.* New York: HarperCollins.

Fox, K. C., Dixon, M.L., Nijeboer, S., Girn, M., Floman, J. L., Litshitz, M., et al., (2016). Functional neuroanatomy of meditation: A review and meta-analysis of 78 functional neuroimaging investigations. *Neuroscience & Biobehavioral Review,* 2016, 65, 208-228.

Fox, K. C., Nijeboer, S., Dixon, M. L., Floman, J. L., Ellamil, M., Rumak, S. P. et al. (2014). Is meditation associated with altered brain structure? A systematic review and meta-analysis of morphometric neuroimaging in meditation practitioners. *Neuroscience & Biobehavioral Reviews,* 2014, 43, 48-72.

Fox, T. C. (2004, February 27). Mapping the spirituality of Catholicism. [Review of the book *What makes us Catholic: Eight Gifts for Life* by T. H. Groome]. *National Catholic Reporter, 40*(17), 21.

Francis, Pope. (2013, November 24). *Evangelii Gaudium:* Apostolic exhortation on the proclamation of the Gospel in today's world. 242, 243. Retrieved from https://www. Vatican.va/content/francesco/en/apost_exhortations/documents/papa-francesco_ esortazione-ap_20131124_ evangelii-gaudium.html.

Francis, Pope. (2017, November 18). Address of His Holiness Pope Francis to participants in the plenary session of the Pontifical Council for Culture. Retrieved from www.vatican.va/content/franncesco/en/speeches/2017/november/documents/papa-francesco_20171118_plenaria-cultura.html

Francis, Pope. (2018). *Gaudete and Exsultate:* On the call to holiness in today's world. Retrieved from http://www.vatican.va/content/vatican/en/search.html?q=Gaudete+et+exsultate

Francis, Pope. (2021). Video message of His Holiness Pope Francis to participants in the Fifth International Conference entitled "Exploring the mind, body, and soul: How innovation and novel delivery systems improve human health." Retrieved from www.vatican.va/content/francesco/en/

messages/pont-messages/2021/documents/papa-francesco_20210508_
videomessaggio-mindbodysoul

Francis, Pope. (2022). Address of His Holiness Pope Francis to participants in
the symposium promoted by the Dicastery for the Causes of Saints. Retrieved
from https://www.vatican.va/content/francesco/en/speeches/20221006-
convegno-causedeisanti.html

Frankl, V. E. (1993). *Man's search for meaning: an introduction to logotherapy.*
Cutchogue, NY: Buccaneer Books.

Frankl, V. E. (2014). *The will to meaning: Foundations and applications of
logotherapy.* New York: Penguin USA.

Freud, S. (1895/2004). *Studies in hysteria.* London, U.K.: Penguin Classics.

Froese, T. (2015). Enactive neuroscience, the direct perception hypothesis, and
the socially extended mind. (Unpublished manuscript for *Behavior and Brain
Sciences*). Retrieved from https://www.academia.edu

Fukuyama, M. A., & Sevig, T. D. (1999). *Integrating spirituality into multicultural
counseling: Multicultural aspects of series 13.* Thousand Oaks, CA: Sage.

Gailliardetz, R. R., & Clifford, C. E. (2012). *Keys to the Council: Unlocking the
teaching of Vatican II.* Collegeville, MN: Liturgical Press.

Gaitan, L. M. (2017). *Neurotheology.* Retrieved from https://www.academia.edu.

Gaitan, L. M., & Castresana, J. S., & Zollner, H. (2021). Is an integrative model of
neurotheology possible? *Religions, 12*(4), 1-11. Retrieved from https://mdpi.
com/journal/religions. doi: 10.3390/rel12040277

Galanter, M., Hansen, H., & Potenza, M. N. (2021) The role of spirituality in
addiction medicine: A position statement from the spirituality interest group
of the International Society of Addiction Medicine. *Substance Abuse, 42*(3),
269-271, doi: 10.1080/08897077.2021. 1941514.

Gall, T. L. & Guirguis-Youngr, M. (2013). Religious and spiritual coping: Current
theory and research. In K. I. Pargament (Ed.), *APA handbook of psychology,
religion, and spirituality: Context, theory, and research* (pp. 349-364).
Washington, DC: American Psychological Association.

Gallagher, H. L., & Frith, C. (2003). Functional imaging of "theory of mind."
Trends in Cognitive Sciences, 7(2), 77-83.

Gambrel, L. E., Faas, C., Kaestle, C. E., & Savla, J. (2016, February 12).
Interpersonal neurobiology and couple relationship quality: A longitudinal
model. *Contemporary Family Therapy.* doi: 10.1007/s10591-061-9381-y.

Garcia-Valdecasas, M. (2005, September). Psychology and mind in Aquinas.
History of Psychiatry, 16, 291-310. doi: 10.1177/0957154X05051920.

Garrigou-Lagrange, R. (1937). *Christian perfection and contemplation.* Freiburg,
Germany: B. Herder.

Gay, V. P. (Ed.). (2009). *Neuroscience and religion: Brain, mind, self, and soul.*
Lanham, MD: Lexington.

Geertz, A. W. (2008). How *not* to do cognitive science of religion today. *Method
and Theory in the Study of Religion, 20,* 7-21.

Geertz, A. W. (2010). Brain, body, and culture: A biocultural theory of religion.
Method and Theory in the Study of Religion, 22(4), 304-321. doi: 10.1163/
157006810X531094.

Geertz, C. (1993/2017). *Religion as a cultural system. In The Interpretation of Cultures.* New York: Fontana Books.

Gellhorn, E., & Keily, W. F. (1972). Mystical states of consciousness: Neurophysiological and clinical aspects. *Journal of Nervous and Mental Disease,* 154, 399-405.

George, M. (2020). Neuroscience and the human soul [Audio recording]. The Thomistic Institute. Retrieved from https://www.soundcloud.com/thomistic institute/neuroscience-and-the-human-soul-prof-marie-george

Gervais, W., Willard, A., Norenzayan, A., & Henrich, J. (2011). The cultural transmission of faith: Why innate intuitions are necessary, but insufficient, to explain religious belief. *Religion,* 41, 6.

Gilson, E. (1932/1991). *The spirit of medieval philosophy.* South Bend, IN: Notre Dame University Press.

Goleman, D., & Thurman, R. A. F. (Eds.). (1991). *MindScience: An east-west dialogue.* Boston, MA: Wisdom Publications.

Golink, R. A., Meijboom, R., Vernooij, M. W., Smits, M., Hunink, M. M., (2016). Eight-week mindfulness-based stress reduction induces brain changes similar to traditional long-term meditation practice—A systematic review. *Brain and Cognition,* 108, 32-41. Retrieved from https://doi.org/10.1016/bandc.2016.07.001 PMID:27429096

Goodman, R. (2021, Spring). William James. In *The Stanford encyclopedia of philosophy. Retrieved from* https://plato.stanford.edu/archives/spr2022/entries/james

Gordon, I, Vander Wyk, B.C., Bennet, R. H., Cordeaux, C., Lucas, M. V., Eilbott, J. A., Pelphrey, K. A. (2013). Oxytocin enhances brain function in children with autism. *Proceedings of the National Academy of Sciences, 110*(52), 20953-20958. Retrieved from http://www.pnas.org/cgi/doi/10.1073/pnas.1312857110

Graf, F. W. (2007). God's brain: Some critical remarks on modern neurotheology. *European Review,* 15, 257-264.

Granfield, D. (1991). *Heightened consciousness: The mystical difference.* Mahwah, NY: Paulist.

Grassie, W. (2008). The new sciences of religion. *Zygon: Journal of Religion and Science, 43*(1), 127-158. doi: 10.1111/j.1467-9744.2008.00903.x.

Gregson, V. (Ed.). (1988). *The desires of the human heart: An introduction to the theology of Bernard Lonergan.* Mahwah, NJ: Paulist.

Grialou, Marie-Eugene. (1986). *I want to see God: A practical synthesis of Carmelite spirituality.* Westminster, MD: Christian Classics.

Griffiths, T. L., Kemp, C., and Tenenbaum, J. B. (2008). Bayesian models of cognition. In R. Sun (Ed.), *The Cambridge handbook of computational psychology* (pp. 59-100). Cambridge, U.K.: Cambridge University Press.

Grim, B.J., & Grim M. E. (2019). Belief, behavior, and belonging: How faith is indispensable in preventing and recovering from substance abuse. *Journal of Religion and Health, 58*(5), 1713-1750. doi: 10.1007/s10943-019-00876-w.

Guardini, R. (1954). *The Lord.* Chicago, IL: Henry Regnery.

Guntrip, H. (1952). The psychotherapist is a parent and exorcist. In J. Hazell (Ed.), *Personal relations therapy: The collected papers of H. J. S. Guntrip* (pp. 63-88). Northvale, NJ: Jason Aronson.

Guthrie, S. E. (1993). *Faces in the clouds: A new theory of religion.* Oxford, U.K.: Oxford University Press.

Haggerty, D. (2022. *Saint John of the Cross: Master of contemplation.* San Francisco: Ignatius.

Haidt, J. (2001). The emotional dog and its rational tail: A social intuitionist approach to moral judgment. *Psychological Review, 108*(4), 814-834. doi: 10.1037/0033-295X.108.4.814.

Hamer, D. (2005). *The God gene: How faith is hardwired into our genes.* New York: Anchor Knopf Doubleday.

Hampson, P. (2019). [Review of the book *The brain, the mind, and the person within: The enduring mystery of the Soul,* by M. Cosgrove]. *Science and Christian Belief, 31*(2), 217-218.

Han, H. (2016). How can neuroscience contribute to moral philosophy, psychology, and education based on Aristotelian virtue ethics? *International Journal of Ethics Education, 1,* 201-217.

Han, H., Chen, J., Jeong, C., & Glover, G. H. (2016). Influence of the cortical midline structures on moral emotion and motivation in moral decision-making. *Behavioral Brain Research, 302,* 237-251. doi:10.1016j.bbr.2016.01.001.

Han, H., Glover, G. H., & Jeong, C. (2014). Cultural influences on the neural correlate of moral decision-making processes. *Behavioral Brain Research, 259,* 215-228. doi.10.1016/j.bbr2013.11.012.

Han, S., Mao, L., Gu, X., Zhu, Y., Ge, J., & Ma, Y. (2008, March). Neural consequences of religious belief on self-referential processing. *Social Neuroscience, 3*(1), 1-15.

Han, S., Northoff, G., Vogeley, K., Wexler, B. E., Kitayama, S., & Varnum, M. E. W. (2013). A cultural neuroscience approach to the biosocial nature of the human brain. *Annual Review of Psychology, 64,* 333-359. doi: 10.1146/annurev-psych-071112-054629.

Happel, S. (1989). The sacraments: Symbols that redirect our desires. In V. Gregson (Ed.). *The desires of the human heart: An introduction to the theology of Bernard Lonergan* (pp. 237-254). Mahwah, NJ: Paulist.

Hardon J. A. (2001, Spring). The meaning of virtue in St. Thomas Aquinas. *Faith and Reason: The Journal of Christendom College, 26,* 1-6.

Hardon, J. A. (1980). *Modern Catholic dictionary.* Garden City, NY: Doubleday.

Hatefi, M., Tarjoman, A., & Borji, M. (2019). Do religious coping and attachment to God affect perceived pain? Study of the elderly with chronic back pain. *Journal of Religion and Health, 58*(2), 465-475. doi: 10.1007/s10943-018-00756-9.

Hazan, C., & Shaver, P. (1987). Romantic love conceptualized as an attachment process. *Journal of Personality and Social Psychology, 52,* 511-524.

Hefling, C. C. (1988). Philosophy, theology, and God. In V. Gregson (Ed.). *The desires of the human heart: An introduction to the theology of Bernard Lonergan.* New York: Paulist Press.

Heiden, P., Heinz, A., & Sieferth, N. R. (2017). Pathological gambling in Parkinson's disease: What are the risk factors, and what is the role of impulsivity? *European Journal of Neuroscience, 45*(1), 67-72. doi: 10.1111/ejn.13396.

Helminiak, D. (2010). "Theistic psychology and psychotherapy:" A theological and scientific critique. *Zygon, 45*(1), 47-74. doi: 10.1111/j.1467-9744.2010.01058.x.

Helminiak, D. A. (2006, March). The role of spirituality in formulating a theory of the psychology of religion. *Zygon, 1*(1), 191-224. doi: 10.1111/j.1467-9744.2006.00733.x

Helminiak, D. A. (2015). *Brain, consciousness, and God: A Lonerganian integration.* Albany, NY: University of New York Press.

Helminiak, D. A. (2021, April). A genuinely scientific psychology based on Lonergan's analysis of consciousness. *Clinical Psychiatry, 7,* 1-4. Retrieved from http://www.imedpub.com

Henson, D., Morrill, B., & Barina, R. (2023). Healing health care: Moving the sacramental tradition from the edges to the center of Catholic healthcare. Conference on Medicine and Religion. Retrieved from http://www.medicineandreligion.com

Hess, N. J., & Allen, P. L. (2008). *Catholicism and science.* Westport, CT: Greenwood.

Heyes, C., & Catmur, C. (2022). What happened to mirror neurons? *Perspectives on Psychological Science, 17*(1), 153-168. Retrieved from http://www.psychologicalscience. org/PPS doi: 10.1177/1745691621990638.

Hickok, G. (2008). Eight problems for the mirror neuron theory of action understanding in monkeys and humans. *Journal of Cognitive Neuroscience, 21*(7), 1229-1243. doi: 10.1162/jocn.2009.21189.

Hickok, G. (2014). *The myth of mirror neurons: The real neuroscience of communication and cognition.* New York: W. W. Norton & Company.

Highfield, R. (1995). The freedom to say "No"? Karl Rahner's doctrine of sin. *Theological Studies, 56*(3), 485-505. doi: 10.1177/004056399505600304.

Hilgers, J. (1912). Scapular. In *The Catholic encyclopedia.* New York: Robert Appleton. In *New Advent Catholic Encyclopedia.* Retrieved from https://www.newadvent.org/cathen/13508b

Hill, P. C., & Hood, R. W. (1999). *Measures of religiosity.* Birmingham, AL: Religious Education Press.

Hill, P. C., & Pargament, K. I. (2003, January). Advances in the conceptualization and measurement of religion and spirituality: Implications for physical and mental health research. *American Psychologist, 58*(1). pp. 64-74. doi: 10.1037/0003-066X.58.1.64.

Hobson, R. P., & Bishop, M. (2003) The pathogenesis of autism: Insights from congenital blindness. *Philosophical Transactions of the Royal Society B: Biological Sciences* 358, 335–344.

Hoche, F., Guell, X., Sherman, J. C., Vangel, M. G., & Schmahmann, J. D. (2016). Cerebellar contribution to social cognition. *Cerebellum, 15*(6), 732-743. doi: 10.1007/s12311-015-0746-9.

Hochman, E. Y., Vaidya, A. R., & Fellows, L. K. (2014). Evidence for a role for the dorsal anterior cingulate cortex in disengaging from an incorrect action. *Plos ONE, 9*(6), 1-11. doi: 10.1371/journal.pone.0101126.

Hoffman, L. W., & Strawn, B.D. (2009). Normative thoughts, normative feelings, normative actions: A Protestant, relational psychoanalytic reply to E. Christian Brugger and the faculty of IPS. *Journal of Psychology and Theology, 37*, 125-136.

Hoffman, T., & Michon, C. (2017, May). *Aquinas on free will and intellectual determinism.* Retrieved from http://www.philosophersimprint.org/017005

Hole, S. (2017). [Review of the book *Neuroscience and the soul: The human person in philosophy, science, and theology,* by T. M. Crisp, S. L. Porter, and G. A. Ten Elshof (Eds.)]. *Reviews in Religion and Theology, 24*(3), 460-462. doi: 10.1111/rirt.12974.

Hollingsworth, A. (2008). Neuroscience and spirituality: Implications of interpersonal neurobiology for a spirituality of compassion. *Zygon: Journal of Religion and Science, 43*, 837-860.

Hood, R. W. Jr. (2006). The common core thesis in the study of mysticism. In P. McNamara (Ed.), *Where God and science meet, Vol. 3: The psychology of religious experience* (pp. 119-138). Westport, CT: Praeger.

Hood, R. W., & Chen, Z. (2013). The social scientific study of Christian mysticism. In J. A. Lemm (Ed.), *The Wiley-Blackwell companion to Christian mysticism* (pp. 577-591). West Sussex, U.K.: John Wiley & Sons.

Hood, R. W., Jr. (2002). The mystical self: Lost and found. *International Journal for the Psychology of Religion, 12*(1), 1-14.

Horvat, S. (2017). Neuroscientific findings in the light of Aquinas' understanding of the human being. *Scientia et Fides, 5*, 1-27.

Houston, P. (2021). Expanding historical theological perspectives through transdisciplinary meta-methodological engagement. *Studia Historiae Ecclesiasticae, 47*, 1-14. Retrieved from http://dx.doi.org/10.25159/2412-4265/9150

Howard-Jones, P. (2010). *Introducing neuroeducational research: Neuroscience, education, and the brain from context to practice.* Philadelphia, PA: Routledge.

Howells, E. (2002). *John of the Cross and Teresa of Avila: Mystical knowing and selfhood.* New York: Crossroad.

Hugh of St. Victor. (1130/1992). The moral/mystical ark of Noah. In C. Mathuen & A. Spicer (Eds.), *Studies in Church history,* 28 (pp. 99-116). Cambridge, UK: University of Cambridge Press.

Hummer, R., Rogers, R., Nam, C., Ellison, C. G. (1999). Religious involvement and U.S. adult mortality. *Demography,* 36, 273-285.

Hunter, J. D. (1986, September). [Review of the book *Habits of the heart: Individualism and commitment in American life*]. *Journal for the Scientific Study of Religion, 25*(3), 373-374. doi: 10.2307/1386303.

Huxley, A. (1962/2009). *The island.* New York: Harper Perennial Modern Classics.

Hyde, B. (2004). The plausibility of spiritual intelligence: Spiritual experience, problem-solving, and neural sites. *International Journal of Children's Spirituality, 9*(1), 39-52. doi: 10.1080/1364436042000200816.

Immordino-Yang, M. H., McColl, A., Damasio, H., Damasio, A. (2009). Neural correlates of admiration and compassion. *Proceedings of the National Academy of Sciences, U.S.A.,* 106(19), 8021-8026.

James, W. (1902/1958/2017). *The varieties of religious experience: A study in human nature.* Edinburgh, Scotland: CrossReach Publications.

Jastrzebski, A. K. (2018). The neuroscience of spirituality: An attempt at critical analysis. *Pastoral Psychology, 67*(5), 515-524. doi: 10.1007/s11089-018-0840-2.

Jeeves, M. (2013). *Minds, brains, souls, and gods: A conversation on faith, psychology, and neuroscience.* Downers Grove, IL: InterVarsity Press.

Jeeves, M. A., & Ludwig, T. E. (2013). *Psychological science and Christian faith: Insights and enrichments from constructive dialogue.* W. Coshohocken, PA: Templeton.

Jeeves, M. A., & Ludwig, T. E. (2018). *Psychological science and Christian faith: Insights and enrichments from constructive dialogue.* West Coshohocken, PA: Templeton.

Jeeves, M., & Brown, W. S. (2009). *Neuroscience, psychology, and religion: Illusions, delusions, and realities about human nature.* West Conshohocken, PA: Templeton Foundation Press.

Jeftic, A. (2013). Andrew Newberg's model of neurotheology: A critical overview. *Philotheos, 13*, 261-278.

John of the Cross, St. (1591/1991). *The collected works of St. John of the Cross: the Ascent of Mount Carmel, the Dark Night, the Spiritual Canticle, the Living Flame of Love, Letters,* and *Minor Works.* Washington, DC: ICS Publications.

John Paul II, Pope. (1979). Apostolic Exhortation *Catechesi Tradendae.* Retrieved from https://www.vatican.va/content/john-paul-ii/en/apost_exhortations/documents/hf_jp-ii_exh_16101979_catechesi-tradendae.html

John Paul II, Pope. (1983). *Code of Canon Law.* Retrieved from https://www.vatican.va>cic-cann1364-1399_en

John Paul II, Pope. (1985, July 17). Church document: Scientists and God. Retrieved from http://www.semscience.net

John Paul II, Pope. (1988). Church document: Message to Rev. G. V. Coyne, S.J., Director of the Vatican Observatory. Retrieved from http://www.sem science.net

John Paul II, Pope. (1993). *Veritatis splendor* (The splendor of truth). Retrieved from https://www.vatican.va/content/john-paul-ii/en/encyclicals/documents/hf_jp-ii_enc_06081993_veritatis-splendor.html

John Paul II, Pope. (1994). *Crossing the threshold of hope.* New York: Alfred A. Knopf Publishing.

John Paul II, Pope. (1996). Message to the Vatican Observatory conference on evolutionary and molecular biology. Retrieved from http://www.ctns.org/research/past-research/sceintific-perspectives-divine-action/neuroscience-and-person

John Paul II, Pope. (1998). Encyclical letter: *Fides et ratio,* 29, 34. Retrieved from http://www.semscience.net

John Paul II, Pope. (2000). Address of the Holy Father John Paul II to the 18th International Congress of the Transplantation Society. Retrieved from http://www.vatican.va/content/john-paul-ii/en/speeches/2000/julsep/documents/hf_jpii_spe_20000829_transplants.html

John Paul II, Pope. (2001). *Novo millennioiInuente.* At the beginning of the third millennium. Retrieved from http://www.vatican.va/content/john-paul-ii/

en/apost_letters/2001/documents/hf_jp-ii_apl_20010106_novo-millennio-
ineunte.html

John Paul II, Pope. (2003). Address of John Paul II to the members of the
Pontifical Academy of Sciences (10 November). Retrieved from http://www.
vatican.va/content/john-paul-ii/en/speeches/2003/november/documents/
hf_jp-ii_spe_20031110_academy-sciences. html

Johnston, W. (Ed.). (1996). *The cloud of unknowing and the book of privy
counseling.* New York: Image Random House.

Johnston, W. H. (2011, September). Schools of spirituality: Drawing from the
wealth of the Catholic tradition. *Catechist.* Retrieved from http://www.
catechist.com

Johnstone, B., Cohen, D., & Dennison, A. (2021, August 200. The integration of
sensations and mental experiences into a unified experience: A neuropsychological
model for the "sense of self." *Neuropsychologia, 159,* 1-35. Retrieved from
https://www.sciencedirect.com/science/article/pii/SOO28393221001901

Johnstone, B., Cohen, D., Konopacki, K., & Ghan, C. (2016). Selflessness as a
foundation of spiritual transcendence: Perspectives from the neurosciences
and religious studies. *International Journal for the Psychology of Religion,
26*(4), 287-303. doi: 10.1080/10508619.2015.1118328.

Jones, M. K. (2015). The four transcendental imperatives of Bernard Lonergan.
Retrieved from https://equivalentexchange.blog/2015/12/09/the-four-
transcendental-imperatives-of-bernard-lonergan

Jones, R. H. (2018). Limitations on the scientific study of mystical experiences.
Zygon: Journal of Science and Religion, 53(4), 992-1017.

Jones, R. H. (2018, December). Limitations on the neuroscientific study of
mystical experiences. *Zygon: Journal of Religion and Science, 53*(4), 992-1017.

Jones, R., & Gellman, J. (2022, Fall). Mysticism. In E. N. Zalta (Ed.), *Stanford
Encyclopedia of Philosophy.* Retrieved from https://plato.stanford.edu/
archives/fall 2022/entres/mysticism.

Jordan, K. D., Niehus, K. L., & Feinstein, A. M. (2021). Insecure attachment to
God and interpersonal conflict. *Religions 12*(9), 1-12. Retrieved from https://
www.mdpi.com/journal/religions. doi: 10.3390/rel12090739.

Jordan, K. D., Niehus, K. L., & Feinstein, A. M. (2021, September). Insecure
attachment to God and interpersonal conflict. *Religions* 12(9), 739-739.

Jowett, B. (n.d.) Tripartite soul theory. Retrieved from http://www.tripartite-
soul-theory. com/platos-republic/chariot-allegory.html.

Jung, C. J. (1969). *On the nature of the psyche.* Princeton, NJ: Princeton
University Press.

Kant, I. (1787/2088). *Critique of pure reason.* (M. Weigelt, Ed.). London,
England: Penguin Classics.

Kapogiannis, D., Barbey, A. K., Su, M., Zamboni, G., Kreuger, F., & Grafman, J.
(2009). Cognitive and neural foundations of religious belief. *Proceedings of the
National Academy of Sciences, 106*(12), 4876-4881. doi: 10.1073/pnas.0811
717106.

Kapur, S. (2003). Psychosis as a state of aberrant salience: A framework linking
biology, phenomenology, and pharmacology in schizophrenia. *American
Journal of Psychiatry, 160*(1), 13-24.

Kapur, S. Mizrahi, R., & Ming, L. (2005). From dopamine to salience to psychosis—linking biology, pharmacology, and phenomenology of psychosis. *Schizophrenia Research, 79*, 59-68.

Karatsoreos, I. N., Bhagat, S., Bloss, E. B., Morrison, J. H., & McEwen, B. S. (2011). Disruption of circadian clocks has ramifications for metabolism, brain, and behavior. *Proceedings of the National Academy of Sciences, 108*(4), 1657-1662. doi: 10.1073/pnas.1018375108.

Karo, R., & Friedenthal, M. (2008). Kenosis, anamnesis, and our place in history: A neurophenomenological account. *Zygon, 43*(4), 823-836. doi: 10.1111/j.1467-9744.2008.00962.x.

Kasamatsu, A., & Hirai, T. (1966). An electroencephalographic study on Zen meditation. *Folio Psychiatrica & Neurologica Japonica, 20*, 315-336.

Katz, S. T. (1978). Language, epistemology, and mysticism. In S. T. Katz (Ed.), *Mysticism and philosophical analysis* (pp. 22-74). New York: Oxford University Press.

Katz, S. T. (Ed.). (1983). *Mysticism and religious traditions.* Oxford, U.K.: Oxford University Press.

Kavanaugh, K. & Lisi, C. (2010). Teresa of Avila. *The interior castle: Study edition.* Trans. K. Kavanaugh & O. Rodriguez. Washington, DC: Institute of Carmelite Studies.

Kavanaugh, K., & Rodriguez, O. (Trans.). (1991). *The collected works of St. John of the Cross.* Washington, DC: Institute of Carmelite Studies.

Kellert, S. H., Longino, H. E., & Waters, C. K. (Eds.). (2006). *Scientific pluralism. Minnesota Studies in the Philosophy of Science,* Minneapolis, MN: University of Minnesota Press.

Kelly, E. F., & Grosso, M. (2007). Mystical experience. In Kelly, E. F., Kelly E. W., Crabtree, A., Gauld, A., Grosso, M., & Greyson, B, *Irreducible mind: Toward a psychology for the 21st century* (pp. 495-575). Lanham, MD: Rowman & Littlefield.

Kelly, G. B. (Ed.). (1992). *Karl Rahner: Theologian of the graced search for meaning.* Minneapolis: Fortress Press.

Kernberg, O. (2015). Neurobiological correlates of object relations theory: The relationship between neurobiological and psychodynamic development. *International Forum of Psychoanalysis, 24*(1), 38–46, http://dx.doi.org/10.1080/0803706X. 2014.912352.

Kiecolt-Glaser, J. K., McGuire, L., Robles, T. F., & Glaser, R. (2002). Emotions, morbidity, and mortality: New perspectives for psychoneuroimmunology. *Annual Review of Psychology, 53*(1), 83-108.

Kirchoff, R. W., Tata, B., McHugh, J, Kingsley, T., Burton, M. C., Manning, D., Chaudhary, R. (2021, April). Spiritual care of inpatients focusing on outcomes and the role of chaplaincy services: A systematic review. *Journal of Religion and Health, 60*(2), 1406-1422. doi: 10.1007/s10943-021-01191-z.

Kirkpatrick, L. A., & Shaver, P. R. (1992). An attachment-theoretical approach to romantic love and religious belief. *Personality and Social Psychology Bulletin,* 18(3), 266–275.

Kirsch, K. M. (2023). How "Catholic" should a Catholic studies program aspire to be? *Logos Supplement, 26*(5), 32-37.

Kitson, A., Chirico, A., Gaggioli, A., & Reicke, B. (2020). A review of research and evaluation methods for investigating self-transcendence. *Frontiers in Psychology, 11*, 1-14. doi: 10.3389/fpsyg.2020.547687.

Klemm, W. R. (2019). Whither neurotheology? *Religions, 10*(11), 1-16. doi: 10.3390/rel10110634.

Knight, C. (1999). Sex and language as pretend play. In R. Dunbar, C. Knight, & C. Power (eds.), *The evolution of culture.* Edinburgh, Scotland: Edinburgh University Press.

Knuuttila, S. (2022, Fall). Medieval Theories of the Emotions, In E. N. Zalta (Ed.), *The Stanford Encyclopedia of Philosophy.* Retrieved from https://plato.stanford.edu/archives/fall2022/entries/medieval-emotions.

Koenig, H. G. (2001). Religion and medicine IV: Religion, physical health, and clinical implications. *International Journal of Psychiatry in Medicine, 31*(3), 321-336.

Koenig H. G. (2012). Religion, spirituality, and health: the research and clinical implications. *ISRN Psychiatry,* 2012, 278730.

Koenig, H. G., Hays, J. C., Larson, D. B., George, L. K., Cohen, H. J., McCullough, M. E., Meador, K. G., & Blazer, D. G. (1999). Does religious attendance prolong survival? A six-year follow-up study of 3,968 older adults. *The Journals of Gerontology. Series A, Biological Sciences and Medical Sciences,* 54(7), M370–M376.

Kohut, P. V. (2012). The offer of Catholic spirituality. *European Journal of Theology, 21*(2), 156-165.

Kok, B. E., Coffey, K. A., Cohn, M. A., Catalino, L. I., Vacharkulksemsuk, T., Algoe, S. B. . . . Frederickson, B. L. (2013, July). How positive emotions build physical health: Perceived position social connections account for the upward spiral between positive emotions and vagal tone. *Psychological Science, 24*(7), 1123-1132. doi: 10.1177/0956797612470827.

Kollar, R. (2011, May). [Review of the book *A secular age* by Charles Taylor. *Heythrop Journal, 52*(3), 535-536. doi: 10.1111/j.1468-2265.2011.00663_77.x.

Koole, S. L. (2009). The psychology of emotion regulation: An integrative review. *Cognition and Emotion,* 23, 4-41.

Koole, S. L., & Kuhl, J. (2007). Dealing with unwanted feelings: The role of affect regulation in volitional action control. In J. Shah & W. Gardner (Eds.), *Handbook of motivational science.* New York: Guilford.

Korup, A. K., Thygesen, L. C., Christiensen, R. D., Johansen, C. Sondergaard, J., & Hvidt, N. C. (2016). Association between sexually transmitted diseases and church membership: A retrospective cohort study of two Danish religious minorities. *Biomedical Journal,* 6. doi: 10.1136/bmjopen-2015-010128.

Korzybski, A. (1958). *Science and sanity: An introduction to non-Aristotelian systems and general semantics.* Lakeville, CT: International Non-Aristotelian Library Publishing.

Kotchoubey, B., Tretter, F., Braun, H. A., Buchheim, T., Draguhn, A., Fuchs, T., Tschacher, W. (2016). Methodological problems on the way to integrative human neuroscience. *Frontiers in Integrative Neuroscience, 10*, 1-19.

Krebs, V. J. (2016). [Review of the book *Soul machine: The invention of the modern mind*, by George Makari]. *Analytical Psychology,* 63, 538-542.

Retrieved from www.academia. edu/37294753/Review_of_George_Makaris _Soul_Machine.

Kreeft, P. (2011). *The God who loves you: Love divine, all loves excelling.* San Francisco: Ignatius Press.

Kroenke, C. H., Kubzanski, L.D., Schernhammer, E. S., Holmes, M. D., & Kawachi, I. (2006). Social networks, social supports, and survival after breast cancer diagnosis. *Journal of Clinical Oncology, 24*(7), 1105-1111.

Kuhl, J., & Quirin, M. (2011). *Seven steps to freedom and two ways to lose it.* Gottingen, Germany: Hogrefe Publishing.

Kuhl, J., Quirin, M., & Koole, S. (2015, March). Being someone: The integrated self as a neuropsychological system. *Social and Personality Psychology Compass, 9*(3), 115-132. Abstract retrieved from https://web-s-ebscohost-com.eresources.

Kuhn, T. S. (1962/2012). *The structure of scientific revolutions.* (3rd ed.). Chicago, IL: University of Chicago Press.

Laidlaw, J. (2007). A well-disposed social anthropologist's problems with the 'Cognitive Science of Religion.' In H. Whitehouse & J. Laidlaw (Eds.), *Religion, anthropology, and cognitive science,* (pp. 211-246). Durham, NC: Carolina Academic Press.

Laird, M. (2005). The "open country" whose name is prayer: Apophasis, deconstruction, and contemplative practice. *Modern Theology, 21*(1), 141-155. doi: 10.1111/j.1468-0025.2005.00279.x.

Laneri, D., Schuster, V., Dietsche, B., Jansen, A., Ott, U., & Sommer, J. (2016). Effects of Long-Term Mindfulness Meditation on Brain's White Matter Microstructure and its Aging. *Frontiers in Aging Neuroscience, 7,* 254. https://doi.org/10.3389/fnagi.2015.00254.

Larrivee, D., & Echarte, L. (2018). Contemplative meditation and neuroscience: Prospects for mental health. *Journal of Religion and Health, 57*(3), 960-978. doi: 10.1007/s10943-017-0475-0.

Larrivée, D., & Gini, A. (2014). Is the philosophical concept of 'habitus operativus bonus' compatible with the modern neuroscience concept of human flourishing through neuroplasticity? A consideration of prudence as a multidimensional regulator of virtue. *Frontiers in Human Neuroscience,* 8, 1-4.

Larson, D. B., Sawyers, J. P., & McCullough, M. E. (Eds.). (1998). *Scientific research on spirituality and health: A report based on the scientific progress in spirituality conferences.* Rockville, MD: National Institute for Healthcare Research.

Lazar, S. W., Bush, G., Gollub, R. L., Fricchione, G. L., Khalsa, G., & Benson, H. (2000, May 15). Functional brain mapping of the relaxation response and meditation. *Neuroreport.* London, U.K.: Lippincott, Williams, & Wilkins.

Lazar, S. W., Kerr, C. E., Wasseman, R.H., Gray, J. R., Greve, D.N., Treadway, M. T., et al., (2005). Meditation experience is associated with increased cortical thickness. *Neuroreport,* 16(17), 1893.

Leaf, C. (2021). How are the mind and the brain different? A neuroscientist explains. *Integrative Health.* Retrieved from http://www.mindbodygreen.com

Lee, B., & Newberg, A. (2005). Religion and health: A review and critical analysis. *Zygon: Journal of Religion and Science, 40,* 443-468.

Lehmann, K., Raffelt, A., & Egan, H. D. (Eds.). (1993). T*he best of Karl Rahner's Theological Writings*. NY: Crossroad.

Lehmann, K., Raffelt, A., & Egan, H. D. (Eds.). (2000). *The content of faith: The best of Karl Rahner's theological writings*. New York: Crossroad.

Lehtonen, J. (2010). Dimensions in the dialogue between psychoanalysis and neuroscience. Routledge: *International Forum of Psychoanalysis, 19*(4), 218-223. doi: 10.1080/0803706X.2010.499136.

Lejeune, J. (1992). A geneticist's point of view. In G. del Re (Ed.), Brain research and the mind-body problem: Epistemological and metaphysical issues. Vatican, Rome: Pontifical Academy of Sciences.

Leman, J., Hunter, W., Fergus, T., & Rowatt, W. (2018). Secure attachment to God and trust with psychological health in a national, random sample of American adults. The International *Journal for the Psychology of Religion, 28*, 116-123.

Leo XIII, Pope. (1879). *Aeterni Patris:* On the Restoration of Christian Philosophy. Retrieved from https://www.vatican.va/content/leo-xiii/en/encyclicals/documents/hf_l-xiii_enc_04081879_aeterni-patris.html

Letheby, C. (2017). Naturalizing psychedelic spirituality. *Zygon: Journal of Science and Religion,* 52(3), 623-642.

Lewis, R. (2019, February 24). What actually is a thought? And how is information physical? *Psychology Today.* Retrieved from http://www.psychologytodaycom/us./blog/finding-purpose/201902/what-actually-is-thought-ahd-how-is-information-physical.

Lex, B. W. (1979). The neurobiology of ritual trance. In E. G. d'Aquili, C. D. Laughlin, Jr., and J. McManus (Eds.), *The Spectrum of Ritual* (pp. 117-151). New York: Columbia University Press.

Li, H., Chen, Q., Lu, J., & Qiu, J. (2017, December). Brain structural bases of tendency to forgive: evidence from a young adults sample using voxel-based morphometry. *Scientific Reports,* 7, 16856-16856.

Libet, B. (1999). Do we have free will? *Journal of Consciousness Studies,* 6(8-9), 47–57.

Ling, S., Umbach, R., & Raine, A. (2019). Biological explanations of criminal behavior. *Psychology, Crime, and Law, 25*(6), 626-640. doi: 10.1080/106831 6X.2019.1572753

Lombard, J. (2017). *The mind of God: Neuroscience, faith, and a search for the soul.* New York: Harmony.

Lonergan, B. (1957/1992). *Insight: A study in human understanding.* (F. Crowe & R. Doran, (Eds.). Toronto, Ontario, Canada: University of Toronto Press.

Lonergan, B. (1967). *Collection: Papers by Bernard Lonergan.* Montreal, Quebec, Canada: Palm Publishers.

Lonergan, B. (1972/2017). *Method in theology.* Toronto, Ontario, Canada: University of Toronto Press.

Lonergan, B. (2002). *The ontological and psychological constitution of Christ.* In *Collected Works of Bernard Lonergan.* Lonergan Research Institute. Toronto, Canada: Regis College.

Lou, H. C., Kjaer, T. W., Friberg, L., Wildschiodtz, G., Holm, S., & Nowak, M. (1999). A 150-H20 PET study of meditation and the resting state of normal consciousness. *Human Brain Mapping*, 7(2), 98-105.

Ludwig, D., & Ruphy, S. (2021, Winter). Scientific pluralism. In E. N. Zalta (Ed.), Stanford Encyclopedia of Philosophy. Retrieved from https://plato.stanford.edu/archives/win2021/entries/scientific-pluralism

Lutz, A., Greischar, L. L., Rawlings, N. B., Davidson, R. J., et al. Long-term meditators self-induce high-amplitude gamma synchrony during mental practice. (2004, December). *Proceedings of the National Academy of Sciences*, 101(46), 16369-16373.

Maas, A. (1912/2021). Salvation. In *The Catholic encyclopedia*. New York: Robert Appleton. In *New Advent Catholic Encyclopedia*. Retrieved from https://newadvent.org/cathen/13407a.htm.

MacIntyre, A. C. (1984/2007) *After virtue: A study in moral theory.* Notre Dame, IN: Notre Dame University Press.

MacLean, C. R. K., Walton, K. G., Wenneberg, S. R., Levitsky, D. K., Mandarino, J. P., Wziri, R., & Schneider, R.H. (1997). Effects of the transcendental meditation program on adaptive mechanisms: Changes in hormone levels and responses to stress after four months of practice. *Psychoneuroimmunology*, 22, 277-295.

Madden, J. (2013). Thomistic hylomorphism and philosophy of mind and philosophy of religion. *Philosophy Compass, 8*, 664-676.

Manalili, M. M. C. (2018). On neurotheology? Why engage empirical studies on theological concepts. *Lumen et Vita, 9*, 35-45.

Mandel, A. (1980). Toward a psychobiology of transcendence: God in the brain. In J. Davidson & R. Davidson (Eds.), Psychobiology of consciousness (pp. 379-464). New York: Plenum Press. Marcel, G., & Fraser, G. S. (1950-1951/2001). *The mystery of being. Gifford Lectures (1949-1950). Vol 1: Reflection and Mystery; Vol 2: Faith and Reality.* South Bend, IN: St. Augustine's Press.

Maritain, J. (1932/1959/1995). *The degrees of knowledge.* (Trans. G. B. Phelan). Notre Dame, IN: University of Notre Dame Press.

Maritain, J. (1953). *The range of reason.* Retrieved from https://maritain.nd.edu/jmc/etext/range05.htm.

Maritain, J. (1954/1962). *Approaches to God.* New York: Colliers.

Markie, P., & Folescu, M. (2021, Fall). Rationalism vs. Empiricism, In E. N. Zalta (Ed.), *The Stanford Encyclopedia of Philosophy.* Retrieved from https://plato.stanford.edu/archives/fall2021/entries/rationalism-empiricism.

Marmion, D. (1996). The notion of spirituality in Karl Rahner. *Louvain Studies, 21*, 61-86.

Martinez Selio, A. (2009). Neuroteologia, Neurologia Suplementos 51(1), 21-27.

Maturana, H. R., & Varela, F. J. (1992). *The Tree of Knowledge: the Biological Roots of Human Understanding (revised edition).* Boston: Shambala.

McAndrew, F. T. (2019). Costly signaling theory. In T. K. Shakelford & V. A. Weekes-Shackelford (Eds.), *Encyclopedia of Evolutionary Psychological Science.* doi.org/10.1007/978-3-319-16999-6_3483-1.

McCabe, D., & Castel, A. (2008). Seeing is believing: The effect of brain images on judgments of scientific reasoning. *Cognition, 107*, 343-352.

McCarthy, M. H. (2015). *Authenticity as self-transcendence: The enduring insights of Bernard Lonergan.* South Bend, IN: University of Notre Dame Press.

McCauley, R. N. (2001). Ritual, memory, and emotion: Comparing two cognitive hypotheses. In J. Andresen (Ed.), *Religion in mind* (pp. 115-140). Cambridge, UK: Cambridge University Press.

McGilchrist, I. (2021). *The matter with things.* Vol 2: *What then is true?* Padstow, Cornwall, U.K.: TJ Books.

McGilchrist, I. (2021). *The matter with things.* Vol. 1: *The ways to truth.* Padstow, Cornwall, U.K.: TJ Books.

McGinn, B. (2006). *The essential writings of Christian mysticism.* New York: Random House.

McGoldrick, T. A. (2012, September). The spirituality of human consciousness: A Catholic evaluation of some current neuro-scientific interpretations. *Science and Engineering Ethics, 18*(3), 483-501. doi: 10.1007/s11948-012-9387-2.

McGonigle, T. D. (1993). Union, unitive way. In M. Downey (Ed.), *The new dictionary of Catholic spirituality* (pp. 987-988). Collegeville, MN: Liturgical Press.

McIlhenny, R. (2011). "God is in your head": Neurotheology and religious belief. *American Theological Inquiry, 3*(2), 29-44.

Meissner, W. W. (1984). Transformative Processes in *The Spiritual Exercises.* In J. J. Heaney (Ed.), *Psyche and Spirit: Readings in Psychology and Religion.* NY: Paulist Press.

Meissner, W. W. (1992). *Ignatius of Loyola: The psychology of a saint.* New Haven, CT: Yale University Press.

Menary, R. (2014). Neural plasticity, neuronal recycling, and niche construction. *Mind & Language, 29*(3), 286-303. Retrieved from https://doi.org/10.1111/MILA.12051.

Merkur, D. (1999). *Mystical moments and unitive thinking.* Herndon, VA: State University of New York Press.

Merton, T. (1949/2015). Is mysticism normal? In P. F. O'Connell (Ed.), *Thomas Merton; Early Essays, 1947-1952* (pp. 50-58). Collegeville, MH: Liturgical Press.

Merton, T. (2003). *The inner experience.* San Francisco: HarperCollins.

Messer, N. (2017). *Theological neuroethics: Christian ethics meets the science of the human brain.* New York: Bloomsbury Publishing.

Mesulam, M. M. (1998). From sensation to cognition. Brain, 121, 1013-1052. https://www.vatican.va/archive/hist_councils/ii_vatican_council/documents/vat-ii_const_19631204_sacrosanctum-concilium_en.html

Michaud, D. (Ed.). (2005). Karl Rahner (1904-1984). In *Boston collaborative encyclopedia of Western theology,* W. Wildman (Ed.). Retrieved from https://people.bu.edu/wwildman/bce/rahner.htm

Miller, J. B. (2012, September). Haunted by the ghost in the machine. Commentary on "The spirituality of human consciousness: A Catholic evaluation of some current neuroscientific interpretations." *Science of Engineering Ethics, 18*(3), 503-507. doi: 10.1007/s11948-012-9389-0.

Miller, L., & Kelley, B. S. (2005). Relationships of religion and spirituality with mental health and psychopathology. In R. F. Paloutzian & C. Park (Eds.). *Handbook of the psychology of religion and spirituality*. New York: Guilford.

Miller, L., Balodis, I. M., McClintock, C. H., Xu, J., Lacardie, C. M., Sinha, R., & Potenza, M. N. (2019, June). Neural correlates of personalized spiritual experiences. *Cerebral Cortex, 29*(6), 2331-2338. doi: 10.1093/cercor/bhy102.

Miller, L., Wickramaratne, P., Hao, X., McClintock, C. H., Pan, L., Svo, C., Weissman. M. M. (2021, September). Altruism and "love of neighbor" offer neuroanatomical protection against depression. *Psychiatry Research: Neuroimaging, 315*, 1-9. doi: 10.1016/j.pscychresns.2021.111326.

Milstein, G., & Manierre, A. (2012). Culture ontogeny: Lifespan development of religions and the ethics of spiritual counseling. *Counseling and Spirituality, 31*, 8-29.

Miner, M., & Dowson, M. (2012). Spiritual experiences reconsidered: A relational approach to the integration of psychology and theology. *Journal of Psychology and Theology, 40*, 55-59.

Mitchell, S. (2003). *Biological complexity and integrative pluralism*. Cambridge, U.K.: Cambridge University Press.

Mitchell, S. D. (2009). *Unsimple truths: Science, complexity, and policy*. Chicago: University of Chicago Press.

Mitchen, S. (2000). Mind, brain, and material culture: An archeological perspective. In P. C. Caruthers & A. Chamberlain (eds.), *Evolution and the human mind: Modularity, language, and metacognition*. Cambridge, U.K.: Cambridge University Press.

Moberg, K. U. (2003). *The oxytocin factor: Tapping the hormone of calm, love, and healing*. Lebanon, IN: Da Capo Press.

Moghadosi, A.N. (2014). Ability to gain religious experiences as a part of cognitive abilities. *Iranian Journal of Neurology, 13*, 191-192.

Moll, J., de Oliveira-Souza, R. (2007). Moral judgments, emotions, and the utilitarian brain. *Trends in Cognitive Sciences, 11*, 319-321. doi:10.1016/j.tics.2007.06.001.

Moll, J., de Oliveira-Souza, R., Garrido, G.J., Bramati, I. E., Egas, M. A., Caparelli-Daquar, E. M. A., Paiva, L. M. M. F, et al. (2007). The self as a moral agent: Linking the neural bases of social agency and moral sensitivity. *Social Neuroscience, 2*, 336-352. doi:10.1080/17470910701392024.

Moll, J., Kreuger, F., Zahn, R., Pardini, M., de Oliveira-Souza, R., & Grafmar, J. (2006, October 17). Human fronto-mesolimbic networks guide decisions of charitable donation. *Proceedings of the National Academy of Sciences*, U.S.A., 103(42), 15623-15628.

Moloney, R. (2004). Conversion and spirituality: Bernard Lonergan (1904-1984). *The Way, 43*(4), 123-134.

Mouch, C. A., & Sonnega, A. J. (2012). Spirituality and recovery from cardiac surgery: a review. *Journal of religion and health, 51*(4), 1042–1060.

Mueller, J. J. (1984). *What are they saying about theological method?* New York: Paulist Press.

Muller, J., Middleton, D., Alizadeh, M., Zabrecky, G., Wintering, N., Bazzan, A. J., Lang, J., Wu, C., Monti, D. A., Wu, Q., Newberg, A. B., & Mohamed, F. B.

(2021). Hybrid diffusion imaging reveals altered white matter tract integrity and associations with symptoms and cognitive dysfunction in chronic traumatic brain injury. *NeuroImage, Clinical, 30,* 102681. Retrieved from https://doi.org/10.1016/j.nicl.2021.102681

Muller, R. J. (2008, May). Neurotheology: Are we hardwired for God? *Psychiatric Times, 25*(6). Retrieved from http://www.psychiatrictimes.com/view/neuro theology-are-we-hardwired-god

Murphy, B. (2023). The development of doctrine. Simply Catholic. Retrieved from https://www.simplycatholic.com/the-development-of-doctrine/#:~: text=in Newman's view

Murray, P. (2012). *In the grip of light.* London, U.K.: Bloomsbury.

Murray, P. D. (2000, April). [Review of the book *The shaping of rationality: Toward interdisciplinarity in theology and science,* by J. W. van Huyssteen (pp. 215-217). *Reviews in Religion & Theology, 7*(2), 215.

Nairn, A. K. (2017). [Review of the book *Theological neuroethics: Christian ethics meets the science of the human brain,* by Neil Messer]. International Society for Science and Religion. Retrieved from https://www.issr.org.uk/blog/ theological-neuroethics-christian-ethics-meets-science-human-brain-neil-messer

National Catholic Bioethics Center. (2020, May 11). FAQ: On the determination of death using neurological criteria (brain death). Retrieved from https://www. ncbcenter.org/resources-and-statements-cms/faq-on-the-determination-of-death-using-neurologica-criteria-brain-death

Navarini, C. (2020). The likelihood of actions and the neurobiology of virtues: Veto and consent power. *Ethical Theory and Moral Practice, 23,* 309-323. Retrieved from https://doi.org/ 10.1007/s10677-020-10081-4.

Neher, A. (1962). A physiological explanation of unusual behavior in ceremonies involving drums. *Human Biology, 34,* 151-161.

Nelson, J.A., Kirk, A. M., Ane, P., Serres, S. A. (2011, April). Religious and spiritual values and moral commitment in marriage: Untapped resources in couples counseling? *Counseling and Values, 55*(2), 228-246.

Newberg, A. (2018). *Neurotheology: How science can enlighten us about spirituality.* New York: Columbia University Press.

Newberg, A. B. (2013). How does meditation change our brains? Retrieved from https://andrewnewberg.com/research-blog/how-does-meditation-change-our-brains

Newberg, A. B. (2014). The neuroscientific study of spiritual practices. *Frontier on Psychology, 5*(215), 1-6.

Newberg, A. B., & Halpern, D. (2018). *The rabbi's brain: Mystics, moderns, and the science of Jewish thinking.* Nashville, TN: Turner.

Newberg, A. B., & Iversen, J. (2003). The neural basis of the complex mental task of meditation: neurotransmitter and neurochemical considerations. *Medical Hypotheses, 61*(2), 282-291.

Newberg, A. B., & Lee, B. Y. (2005). The neuroscientific study of religious and spiritual phenomena: Or why God doesn't use biostatistics. *Zygon, 40*(2), 469-489.

Newberg, A. B., & Newberg, S. (2008, January). Hardwired for God: A neuropsychological model for developmental spirituality. In K. K. Kline (Ed.),

Authoritative communities: The scientific case for nurturing the whole child (pp. 165-186). New York: Springer.

Newberg, A. B., & Waldman, M. (2009). *How God changes your brain: Breakthrough findings from a leading neuroscientist.* New York: Ballantine.

Newberg, A. B., & Waldman, M. R. (2016). *How enlightenment changes your brain: The new science of transformation.* New York: Penguin Random House.

Newberg, A. B., & Waldman, M. R. (2018b). A neurotheological approach to spiritual awakening. *International Journal of Transpersonal Studies, 37,* 119-130.

Newberg, A. B., Wintering, N., Yaden, C. B., Zhong, L., Bowen, B., Averick, N., & Monti, D. (2018). Effect of a one-week spiritual retreat on dopamine and serotonin transporter binding: A preliminary study. *Religion, Brain, and Behavior, 8*(3), 265–278. Retrieved from https://doi.org/10.1080/2153599X.2016.1267035

Newberg, A., Alavi, A., Baime, M., Pourdehmed., M., Santanna, J., & d'Aquili, E. (2001, April 10). The measurement of regional cerebral blood flow during the complex cognitive task of meditation: A preliminary SPECT study. *Psychiatry Research, 106*(2), 113-122. doi: 10.1016/s0925-4927(01)00074-9.

Newberg, A., d'Aquili, E., & Rause, V. (2002). *Why God won't go away: Brain science and the biology of belief.* New York: Random House.

Newberg, A., Wintering, N., & Waldman, M. (2019, November). Comparison of different measures of religiousness and spirituality: Implications for neurotheological research. *Religions, 10*(11), 637. doi: 10.3390/rel10110637.

Newberg. A. B. (2010). *Principles of neurotheology.* Burlington, VT: Ashgate Publishing.

Newen, A., Gallagher, S., & De Bruin, L. (2018). 4E cognition: Historical roots, key concepts, and central issues. In A. Newen, L. De Bruin, & S. Gallagher, *Oxford Handbook of 4E cognition* (pp. 1-16). Oxford, UK: Oxford University Press.

Newman, J. H. (1845/2023). *Essay on the development of Christian doctrine.* Chapter 8. Application of the Third Note of a True Development—Assimilative Power. In Newman Reader. Retrieved from https://www.newmanreader.org/works/development/chapter8.html

Noble, W., & Davidson, I. (1996). *Human evolution, language, and mind.* Cambridge, U.K.: Cambridge University Press.

Noe, A. (2010). *Out of our heads: Why you are not your brain and other lessons from the biology of consciousness.* New York: Hill & Wang.

Nola, R. (2018). Demystifying religious belief. In H. van Eyghen, R. Peels, & G. van den Brink (Eds.), *New developments in the cognitive science of religion* (pp. 71-92). New York: Springer International.

Northoff, G. (2014). *Unlocking the brain. Vol. 1: Coding.* Oxford, U.K.: Oxford University Press.

Northoff, G. (2014). *Unlocking the brain. Vol. 2: Consciousness.* Oxford, U.K.: Oxford University Press.

Northoff, G., & Bermpohl, F. (2004). Cortical midline structures and the self. Trends in *Cognitive Sciences, 8*(3), 102-107.

O'Callaghan, J. (2000). From Augustine's mind to Aquinas' soul. Jacques Maritain Center: Thomistic Institute. Retrieved from https://maritain.nd.edu/jmc/ti00/ocallagh.htm

O'Dougherty, J., et al. (2000). Abstract reward and punishment representations in the human orbitofrontal cortex. *Nature Neuroscience*, 4(1), 95-102.

Oomen, P. M. F. (2003). On brain, soul, self, and freedom: An essay in bridging neuroscience and faith. *Zygon: Journal of Religion and Science, 38*, 377-391.

Otto, R. (1923/2010). *Idea of the holy*. London: Oxford University Press.

Otto., R. (1932/2016). *Mysticism East and West: A comparative analysis of the nature of mysticism*. Eugene, OR: Wipf and Stock.

Pace, U., Cacioppo, M., & Schimmenti, A. (2011). The moderating role of father's care on the onset of binge eating symptoms among female late adolescents with insecure attachment. *Child Psychiatry and Human Development*, 43(2), 282-292.

Pargament, K. I., Koenig, H. G., Tarakeshwar, N., & Hahn, J. (2004, November). Religious coping methods as predictors of psychological, physical, and spiritual outcomes among medically ill elderly patients: A two-year longitudinal study. *Journal of Health Psychology, 9*(6), 713-730. doi: 10.1177/1359105304045366.

Park, C. L. & McNamara, P. (2006). Religion, meaning, and the brain. In P. McNamara (Ed.), *Where God and science meet* (pp. 67-90). Westport, CT: Praeger.

Paul VI, Pope. (1963). Dogmatic constitution *Sacrosanctum concilium*. Retrieved from Sacrosanctum Concilium (vatican.va)

Paul VI, Pope. (1964). *Lumen Gentium:* Dogmatic constitution on the Church. Retrieved from https://www.vatican.va/archive/hist_councils/ii_vatican_council/documents/vat-ii_const_19641121_lumen-gentium_en.html

Paul VI, Pope. (1965). *Dei Verbum*. Dogmatic constitution on Divine Revelation. Retrieved from *Dei Verbum* (Vatican.va)

Paul VI, Pope. (1965). *Gaudium et spes:* Pastoral Constitution on the Church in the Modern World. Retrieved from https://www.vatican.va/archive/hist_councils/ii_vatican_council/documents/vat-ii_const_19651207_gaudium-et-spes_en.html

Payne, S. (2022). Some definitions of spirituality, Christian spirituality, and spiritual theology. [Handout for course, Introduction to the History of Spirituality, First Semester 2022-2023]. Washington, DC: Catholic University of America.

Peacock, B. (2022, September). A-118 Psychedelic interventions for neuropsychological conditions. *Archives of Clinical Neuropsychology, 37*(6), 1270. doi: 10.1093/arclin/acac060.118.

Peacocke, A. (2002). The sound of sheer silence. In R. J. Russell, N. Murphey, T. C. Meyering, T. C., & M. A. Arbib, (Eds.). *Neuroscience and the person: Scientific perspectives on divine action* (pp. 215-247). Notre Dame, IN: University of Notre Dame Press.

Pearce, M. J. (2013). Addressing religion and spirituality in health care systems. In K. I. Pargament, A. Mahoney, & E. P. Shafranske (Eds.), *APA handbook of psychology, religion, and spirituality*, Vol 2 (pp. 527-541). Washington, DC: American Psychological Association.

Peres, J. F. P., Moreira-Almeida, A., Nasella, A. G., & Koenig, H. G. (2007). Spirituality and resilience in trauma victims. *Journal of Religion and Health*, *46*, 343-350. doi: 10.1007/s10943-006-9103-0.

Persinger, M. A. (1983). Religious and mystical experiences as artifacts of temporal lobe function: A general hypothesis. *Perceptual Motor Skills*, *57*, 1255-1262.

Persinger, M. A. (1987). Neuropsychological bases of God beliefs. New York: Praeger.

Persinger, M. A. (1997). I would kill in God's name: Role of sex, weekly church attendance, report of a religious experience, and limbic lability. *Perceptual and Motor Skills*, *85*, 128-130.

Peters, K. E. (2001, September). Neurotheology and evolutionary theology: Reflections on *The mystical mind. Zygon*, *36*(3), 493-500. doi: 10.1111/0591-2385.00376.

PEW Research Center. (2012, December 18). The global religious landscape. Washington, DC: PEW Research Center. Retrieved from https://www.pew research.org/religion/2012/12/18/global-religious-landscape-exec/

Phelps, E. O. C., Gatenby, C. J., Gore, J., Grillon, C., & Davis, M. (2001). Activation of the left amygdala to a cognitive representation of fear. *Nature Neuroscience*, *4*(4), 437-441.

Picard, F. (2023). Ecstatic or mystical experience through epilepsy. *Journal of Cognitive Neuroscience*, *35*(9), 1372-1381.

Pigliucci, M. (2004). God in the brain. *Skeptic*, *10*(4), 82-83.

Pike, N. (1992). On the possibility of theistic experience. In *Mystic union* (pp. 116-153). Ithaca, NY: Cornell University Press.

Pinsent, A. (2015a). Neurotheological eudaimonia. In J. Clausen & N. Levy (Eds.). *Handbook of neuroethics* (pp. 1603-1617). Dordrecht, Germany: Springer Science and Business Media. doi: 10. 1007/978-94-007-4707-4_100.

Pinsent, A. (2015b). *The second-perspective in Aquinas' ethics: Virtues and gifts.* New York: Routledge.

Planche, V., Manjon, J. K., Mansencal, B., Lanuza, E., Tordias, T., Catheline, G., Coute, P. (2023, February 7). Structural progression of Alzheimer's disease over decades: The MRI staging scheme. *Brain Communications*, *4*, fcas109. Retrieved from https://doi.org/10.1093/braincomms/fcas109

Podgorny, P., & Shepard, R. N. (1978). Functional representations common to visual perception and imagination. *Journal of Experimental Psychology: Human Perception and Performance*, *9*, 380-393.

Polanyi, M. (1966). *The tacit dimension.* Chicago, IL: University of Chicago Press.

Poldrack, R., & Yankoni, T. (2016). From brain maps to cognitive ontologies: Informatics and the search for mental structure. *Annual Review of Psychology*, *67*, 587-612.

Poldrack, R., Kittur, A., Kalar, D., Miller, E., Seppa, C., Gil, Y., & Bilder, R. (2011). The Cognitive Atlas: Toward a knowledge foundation for cognitive neuroscience. *Neuroinformatics*, *5*(17), 1-11.

Polger, T. W., & Shapiro, L. A. (2016). *The multiple realization book.* New York: Oxford University Press.

Poulin, A. (1901/2016). *Graces of interior prayer: A treatise on mystical theology.* Jeffersonville, IN: Caritas Publishing.

Premack, D. (2007). Human and animal cognition: Continuity and discontinuity. *Proceedings of the National Academy of Sciences, 104*(35), 13861-13867. Retrieved from http://www.pnas. org/cgidoi/10.1073/pnas.0706147104

Pressman, P., Lyons, J. S., Larson, D. B., & Strain, J. J. (1990). Religious belief, depression, and ambulation status in elderly women with broken hips. *American Journal of Psychiatry, 147,* 758-760.

Price, C. J., & Devlin, J. T. (2011, June). The interactive account of ventral occipitotemporal contribution to reading. *Trends in Cognitive Sciences, 15*(6), 246-253.

Puderbaugh, M. & Emmady, P. D. (2022). Neuroplasticity. *StatPearls.* Retrieved from http://www.ncbi.nom.nih.gov/books/NBK557811

Pulvermuller, F., Garagnani, M, & Wennekers, T. (2014, October). Thinking in circuits: Toward neurobiological explanation in cognitive neuroscience. *Biological Cybernetics, 108*(5), 573-593. doi: 10.1007/s00422-014-0603-9.

Purves, D., Augustine, G. J., Fitzpatrick, D., Hall, W. C., Lamantia, A-S. Mooney, R. D., White, L. E. (2019). *Neuroscience.* International Sixth Edition, New York: Sinauer.

Pylyshyn, Z. W. (1973). What the mind's eye tells the mind's brain. *Psychological Bulletin.* 80: 1–24. doi:10.1037/h0034650.S2CID 145431092.

Pyysiainen, I. (2006). Amazing grace: Religion and the evolution of the human mind. In P. McNamara (Ed.), *Where God and science meet: How brain and evolutionary studies alter our understanding of religion* (pp. 209-225) Westport, CT: Praeger.

Quartz, S., & Sejnowski, T. J. (2002). *Liars, lovers, and heroes: What the new brain science reveals about how we become who we are.* Mosaic, PA: HarperCollins.

Quirin, M., Frohlich, S., & Kuhl, J. (2016). Implicit self and the right hemisphere: Increasing implicit self-esteem and implicit positive affect by left hand contractions. *European Journal of Social Psychology* Retrieved from http://dx.doi.org/10.1002/ejsp.2281

Quirin, M., Kent, M., Bokeem, M. A. S., & Tops., M. (2015, July). Integration of negative experiences: A neuropsychological framework for human resilience. *Behavioral and Brain Sciences,* 38.

Rachlin, H. (2012, July). Is the mind in the brain? A review of the book *Out of our heads: Why you are not your brain, and other lessons from the Biology of consciousness* by Alva Noe. *Journal of Experimental Analysis of Behavior, 98*(1), 131-17. doi: 10.1901/jeab.2012.98-131.

Rahm, C., & Sorman, K. (2019). From brain to symptom: Introduction to neuroscientific psychiatry. [Online Course, Coursera]. Karolinska Institute, Sweden.

Rahner, K. (1941/1994). *Hearer of the Word.* New York: Continuum Books.

Rahner, K. (1958). *Happiness through prayer.* Dublin, Ireland: Conmore and Reynolds.

Rahner, K. (1961-1992). *Theological investigations.* 23 vols. Baltimore, MD: Helicon.

Rahner, K. (1963/2010). *The mystical way in everyday life.* Maryknoll, New York: Orbis Books.

Rahner, K. (1964). *Nature and grace.* New York: Sheed and Ward.

Rahner, K. (1966). Dogmatic reflections on the knowledge and self-consciousness of Christ. In *Theological investigations,* Vol. 5. Oxfordshire, U.K.: Helicon Press.

Rahner, K. (1967/1974). Theology of the spiritual life. In *Theological investigations,* Vol. 3. Oxfordshire, U.K.: Helicon Press.

Rahner, K. (1968/1994). *Spirit in the world.* New York: Continuum.

Rahner, K. (1974). The theology of the spiritual life. In *Theological investigations,* Vol. 3. New York: Seabury Press.

Rahner, K. (1979). Experience of the Spirit: Source of theology. In *Theological investigations,* Vol. 16. New York: Seabury Press.

Ramachandran, V. S., & Blakeslee, S. (1998). *Phantoms in the brain: Probing the mysteries of the human mind.* New York: William Morrow.

Rao, T. S. S., Asha, M. R., Rao, K. S. J., & Vasedevaraju, P. (2009). The biochemistry of belief. *Indian Journal of Psychiatry, 51*(4), 230-241. doi: 10.4103/0019-5545.58285.

Rappaport, R. A. (1999). *Holiness and humanity: Ritual in the making of religious life.* Bridgewater, NJ: Cambridge University Press.

Rappaport, R. A. (1999). *Ritual and religion in the making of humanity.* London, UK: Cambridge University Press.

Ratcliffe, M. (2006). Neurotheology: A science of what? In P. McNamara (Ed.), *Where God and science meet: How brain and evolutionary studies alter our understanding of religion.* Vol 2. Westport, CT: Praeger.

Ratzinger, J. (1989). Letter to the bishops of the Catholic Church on some aspects of Christian meditation. Vatican City: Congregation for the Doctrine of the Faith.

Rausch, T. P. (1998, January 31). Divisions, dialogue, and the catholicity of the church. *America* Magazine, pp. 20-29.

Reddy, V., & Uithol, S. (2016). Engagement: Looking beyond the mirror to understand action understanding. *British Journal of Developmental Psychology, 34*(1), 101-114. doi: 10.1111/bjdp.12106.

Reddy, V., & Uithol, S. (2016, March). Engagement: Looking beyond the mirror to understand action understanding. *British Journal of Developmental Psychology, 34*(1), 101-114.

Redemptorist Spirituality. (2023) Retrieved from https://redemptorists.net

Redfern, C., & Coles, A. (2015, July 15). Parkinson's Disease, religion, and spirituality. *Movement Disorders in Clinical Practice, 2*(4), 341-346. doi: 10.1002/mdc3.12206.

Reeves, J. (2020, September). Methodology in science and religion: A reply to critics. *Zygon, 55*(3), 824-836. doi: 10.1111/zygo.12630.

Reimao, S. (2020). A window into the mind? Neuroimaging and our understanding of the human being [Audio recording]. Retrieved from https://soundcloud.

com/thomisticinstitute/a-window-into-the-mind-neuroimaging-and-our-understanding-of-the-human-being-pro-sofia-reimao.

Reiner, P. (2011). The rise of neuroessentialism. In J. Illes & Shhakian, B. J. (Eds)., *The Oxford handbook of neuroethics* (pp. 161-175). Oxford, U.K.: Oxford University Press.

Reniers, R. L. F. P., Corcoran, R., Vollm, B. A., Asha, M., Richard, H., & Liddle, P. F. (2012). Moral decision-making, ToM, empathy, and the default mode network. *Biological Psychology, 90*, 202-210. doi.10.1016/j.biopsycho.2012.03.009.

Riordan, P. (2015, July). [Review of the book, *The second-person perspective in Aquinas' ethics*, by Andrew Pinsent]. *Heythrop Journal, 56*(4), 694-696. doi: 10.1111/heyj.12250_10.

Rites of the Catholic Church. (2023). Catholic News Agency. Retrieved from http://www. catholicnewsagency.com/resources/56009/the-rites-of-the-catholic-church

Ritvo, E., Haji, L., Baker, L, & Albright, J. (2021, June 2). The pandemic's impact on well-being. *Psychology Today.* Retrieved from https://www.psychology today.com/us/blog/vitality/202106/the-pandemics-impact-well-being

Rixon, G. (2001). Bernard Lonergan and mysticism. *Theological Studies, 62*, 479-497.

Roache, R. (2014, April). Can brain scans prove criminals unaccountable? *AJOB Neuroscience, 5*(2), 35-37. doi: 10.1080/21507740.2014.884188.

Roberts, R. (2021, Spring). Emotions in the Christian Tradition. In E. N. Zalta (Ed.). *The Stanford encyclopedia of philosophy.* Retrieved from https://plato.stanford.edu/archives/spr2021/entries/emotion-Christian-tradition.

Roberts, T. B. (2006). Chemical input, religious output—entheogens: A pharmatheology sampler. In P. McNamara (Ed.), *Where God and science meet* (pp. 235-267). Westport, CT: Praeger.

Robillard, R., Naismith, S. L., Smith, K. L., Rogers, N. L., White, D., Terpening, Z., & Hickie, I. B. (2014). Sleep-wake cycle in young and older persons with a lifetime history of mood disorders. *Plos One,* 9(2), 1-8.

Robles, T. F., & Kiecolt-Glaser. (2003, August). The physiology of marriage: Pathways to health. *Physiology and Behavior, 79*(3). 409-417.

Robson, J. A. (1983). The morphology of corticofugal axons to the dorsal lateral geniculate nucleus in the cat. *Journal of Comparative Neurology, 216*, 89-103.

Rohlf, M. (2020, Fall). Immanuel Kant. In E. N. Zalta (Ed.), *The Stanford encyclopedia of philosophy.* Retrieved from https://plato.stanford.edu/archives/fall2020/entries/kant .

Rolls, E. T. (1999). *The brain and emotion.* Oxford, U.K.: Oxford University Press.

Rose, E., Westefield, J., & Ansley, T. (2008). Spiritual issues in counseling: Clients' beliefs and preferences. *Psychology of Religion and Spirituality, S*(1), 18-33.

Rosok, I. (2011). Unconditional surrender and love: How spirituality illuminates the theology of Karl Rahner. *The Way, 50*(4), 121-132.

Rosok, I. (2017, January). The kenosis of Christ revisited: The relational perspective of Karl Rahner. *Heythrop Journal, 63*(1), 51-63. doi: 10.1111/j.1468-2265.2012.00773.x.

Rossano, M. J. (2007). Did meditating make us human? *Cambridge Archaeological Journal, 17*(1), 47-58. doi: 10.1017/S0959774307000054.

Roth, G., & Dicke, U. (2005). Evolution of the brain and intelligence. *Trends in Cognitive Sciences, 9*(9).

Rottschaefer, W. A. (1999, March). The image of God of neurotheology: Reflections on culturally based religious commitment or evolutionarily based neuroscientific theories? *Zygon, 34*(1), 57-65. doi: 10.1111/0591-2385.19219 99192.

Rowe, C. (1999). Receiver psychology and the evolution of multi-component signals. *Animal Behavior, 58,* 921-931.

Roy, L. (2001). *Transcendent experiences: Phenomenology and critique.* Toronto, Canada: University of Toronto Press.

Ruczaj, S. (2022). Grace contra nature: The etiology of Christian religious beliefs from the perspective of theology and the cognitive science of religion. *Theology and Science.* Retrieved from https://www.tandfonline.com/loi/rtas20

Runehov, A. L. (2007). *Sacred or neural? The potential of neuroscience to explain religious experience.* Gottingen: Vandenhoeck & Ruprecht.

Russell, R. J., Murphy, N., Meyering, T. C., & Arbib, M. A. (1999/2004). Neuroscience and the person: Scientific perspectives on divine action. Castel Gondolfo, Italy: Vatican Observatory.

Ryan, T. (2014, April). Second-person perspective, virtues, and the gifts in Aquinas' ethics. *Australian eJournal of Theology, 21*(1), 1-14.

Sanguineti, J. J. (2011). Can free decisions be both intentional and neural operations? In J. J. Sanguineti, A. Acerbi, & J. A. Lombo (Eds.), *Moral behavior and free will: A neurobiological and philosophical approach* (pp. 179-202). Morolo, Italia: IF Press.

Sanguineti, J. J. (2013). Can the self be considered a cause? In G. Auletta. I. Colage, & M. Jeannerod (Eds.), *Brains top down: Is top-down causation challenging neuroscience?* (pp. 121-142). Hackensack, NJ: World Scientific.

Sanguineti, J. J. (2013). Neuroscience, philosophical relevance of. In R. L. Fastiggi [Ed.]. *New Catholic encyclopedia supplement 2012-2013: Ethics and philosophy.* Vol. 3 (pp. 1065-1068). Detroit, MI: Gale.

Sanguineti, J. J. (2015). The relevance of neuroscience in the study of religiosity. *Scientia et Fides.* Retrieved from http://www.academia.edu

Sanguineti, J. J. (2019). Freedom. In Philosophica: *Enciclopedia filosofica.* Retrieved from http://www.philosofica.info/archivo/2019/voces/libertad/libertad.html

Sanguineti, J. J. (2022). For a philosophy of the human brain. Retrieved from http://www. academia.edu

Sanislow, C., Pine, D., Quinn, K., Kozak, M, Garvey, M., Heinssen, R., & Cuthbert, B. (2010). Developing constructs for psychopathology research: Research domain criteria. *Journal of Abnormal Psychology, 199*(4), 631-639.

Sapolsky, R.M. *Determined: A science of life without free will.* New York, NY: Penguin Press, 2023.

Sarbacker, S. (2016, August 31). Rudolf Otto and the Concept of the Numinous. Oxford Research Encyclopedias. Retrieved from https://doi.org/10.1093/acrefore/9780199340378. 013.88.

Sattler, D. (2022). Being Roman Catholic today in a worldwide context: Ecumenical perspectives on confessional reform efforts. *Ecumenical Review, 74*(1), 84-97.

Sbarra, D. A., & Hazan, C. (2008). Coregulation, dysregulation, self-regulation: An integrated analysis and empirical agenda for understanding adult attachment, separation, loss, and recovery. *Personality and Social Psychology Review, 12*(2), 141-167.

Scaramelli, G. B. (1913/2005). *A handbook of mystical theology.* Berwick, ME: Nicolas-Hays.

Schall, J. D. (2009). Actions, reasons, neurons, and causes. In V. P. Gay (Ed.), *Neuroscience and religion: Brain, mind, self, and soul* (pp. 175-198). Lanham, MD: Rowman & Littlefield.

Scherer, K. R., & Zentner, M. R. (2001). Emotional effects of music: Production rules. In J. Juslin & J. Sloboda (Eds.), *Music and emotion* (pp. 361-3920. Oxford, U. K.: Oxford University Press.

Schleiermacher, F. (1799/1996). *On religion: Speeches to its cultured despisers. Cambridge texts in the history of philosophy.* Cambridge, U.K.: Cambridge University Press.

Schmidt, S. N. L., Hass, J., Kirsch, P., & Mier, D. (2021, May). The human mirror neuron system—A common neural basis for social cognition? *Psychophysiology, 58*(5). Retrieved from https://doi.org/10.1111/psyp. 13781.

Schmidt, S., & Walah, H. (eds.). (2014). *Meditation: Neuroscientific approaches and philosophical implications.* New York: Springer.

Schore, A. N. (2003a). *Affect regulation and the repair of the self.* New York: Norton.

Schore, A. N. (2021, April 20). The interpersonal neurobiology of intersubjectivity. *Frontiers in Psychology, 12*:648616. Retrieved from http://doi.org/10.3389/fpsyg.2021.648616.

Schwartz, M. E. (2012). Consciousness, spirituality, and postmaterialist science: An empirical and experiential approach, In L. Miller (Ed.), *Handbook of Psychology and Spirituality.* New York: Oxford University Press.

Science Council. (2023). Science. Retrieved from https://sciencecouncil.org/aboutscience/our-definition-of-science.

Scott, B. (2004). Second-order cybernetics: An historical introduction. *Kybernetes, 33*(9), 1365-1378.

Seligman, M. E. P., & Csikszentmihalyi, M. (2000). Positive psychology: An introduction. *American Psychologist, 55,* 5-14.

Sevine, G., & Spreng, R.N. (2014). Contextual and perceptual brain processes underlying moral cognition: A quantitative meta-analysis of moral reasoning and moral emotions. *Plos One, 9,* c87427. doi:10.1371/journal.pone.0087427.

Shae, H. (2021, July). Internal difficulties in the theology of Karl Rahner. *Modern Theology, 37*(3). doi:10.1111/moth.12652.

Shamay-Tsoory, S. G., Tomoer, R., Goldsher, D., Berger, B. D. & Aharon-Peretz, J. (2004). Impairment in cognitive and affective empathy in patients with brain lesions: Anatomical and cognitive correlates. *Journal of Clinical and Experimental Neuropsychology 26*(8), 1113-1127

Shannon. N. D. (2017, September). Believe and confess: Revisiting Christian doxastic intentionality. *Heythrop Journal, 58*(5), 749-761. doi: 10.1111/j.1468-2265.2012. 00795.x.

Shantz, D. H. (2010). The place of religion in a secular age: Charles Taylor's explanation of the rise and significance of secularism in the West. Calgary, Canada: University of Calgary. Retrieved from https://arts.ucalgary.ca/sites/default/files/teams/2/CLARE/ Chair Christian_Thought/2009march16_schantz _charles_taylorlecture.pdf.

Sharifi, S. (2018). Relationship between attachment style to God and depression in female breast-cancer patients: The mediating role of illness perception. *Pakistan Journal of Medical and Health Sciences, 61*(1), 27-35.

Shear, J., & Jevning, R. (1999). Pure consciousness: Scientific exploration of meditation techniques. *Journal of Consciousness Studies, 6*(2-3), 189-210.

Shukla, S., Acharya, S., & Raiput, C. (2013). Neurotheology: Matters of the mind or matters that mind? *Journal of Clinical and Diagnostic Research, 7*, 1486-1490.

Siegel, D. J. (1999/2020). The *developing mind: How relationships and the brain interact to shape who we are. (3rd. ed.).* New York: Guilford.

Siegel, D. J. (2006). An interpersonal neurobiology approach to psychotherapy. *Psychiatric Annals, 36*, 248-256. Retrieved from http://www.healio.com/psychiatry/journals/psycann/2006-4-36-3

Siegel, D. J. (2007). *The mindful brain: Reflection and attunement in the cultivation of well-being.* New York: W. W. Norton.

Siegel, D. J. (2012). *Pocket guide to interpersonal neurobiology: An integrative handbook of the mind.* New York: W. W. Norton.

Siegel, D. J., & Drulis, C. (2023, February 3). An interpersonal neurobiology perspective on the mind and mental health: Personal, public, and planetary wellbeing. *Annals of General Psychiatry, 22*(5). Retrieved from doi: 10.1186/s1991-023-0043405

Simmonds-Moore, C., Rice, D. L., O'Gwin, A., & Hopkins, R. (2019). Exceptional experiences following exposure to a sham "God helmet:" Evidence for placebo, individual difference, and time of day influences. *Imagination, Cognition, and Personality: Consciousness in Theory, Research, and Practice, 39*(1), 44-87.

Simmons, J. A. (2019). Robert Cummings Neville, Defining religion: Essays in philosophy of religion. *International Journal for Philosophy of Religion.* Retrieved from https://research-ebsco-com.eresources.cuyahogalibrary.org/e/oeuzzwh/viewer/html/dvcohi4liv

Singh, N., & Telles, S. (2015). Neurophysiological effects of meditation based on evoked and event-related potential recordings. *BioMed Research International*, 1-11. Retrieved from http://dx.doi. org/10.1155/2015/406261

Sisters of Notre Dame. (2023). Retrieved from http://www.snd1.org

Skrzypinska, K. (2021). Does spiritual intelligence (SI) exist? A theoretical investigation of a tool useful for finding the meaning of life. *Journal of Religion and Health, 60*(1), 500-516. doi: 10.1007/s10943-020-01005-8.

Smith, D. W. (2013, Summer). Phenomenology, In E. N. Zalta (Ed.), *The Stanford encyclopedia of philosophy. Retrieved from* https://plato.stanford.edu/archives/sum2013/entries/phenomenology.

Smith, E. E. (2017, Summer). How does the brain experience God? Interview on neurotheology with Andrew B. Newberg. *Sufi,* 31-37.Snead, O. C. (2020, December 1). The anthropology of expressive individualism. *Church Life Journal: A Journal of the McGrath Institute for Church Life.* Notre Dame, IN: University of Notre Dame. Retrieved from https://churchlifejournal.nd.edu/articles/the-anthropology-of-expressive-individualism

Society of Catholic Scientists. (2023). Retrieved from http://www.catholic scientists.org

Sohn, Y. H. I., Kaelin-Lang, A., & Hallett, M. (2003, July). The effect of transcranial magnetic stimulation on movement selection. *Journal of Neurology, Neurosurgery, and Psychiatry, 74* (7), 985-987. doi: 10.1136/jnnp.74.7.985.

Song, Y., Tian, M., & Liu, J. (2012, August 29). Top-down processing of symbolic meanings modulates the visual word form area. *Journal of Neuroscience, 32*(35), 12277-12283. doi: https://doi.org/10.1523/JNEUROSCI.1874-12.2012.

Sorenson, S. J. (2013). Depression and God: The effect of major depressive disorder on theology and religious identity. *Pastoral Psychology, 62*(3), 343-353. doi: 10.1007/s11089-012-0479-3.

Sosis, R. (2000). Religion and intragroup cooperation: Preliminary results of a comparative analysis of utopian communities. *Cross-Cultural Research, 34,* 70-87.

Sosis, R. (2003). Why aren't we all Hutterites? *Human Nature, 14*(2), 91-127.

Sosis, R., & Bressler, E. (2003). Cooperation and commune longevity: A test of the costly signaling theory of religion. *Cross-Cultural Research, 37,* 211-239.

Sosis, R., & Ruffle, B. (2003). Religious ritual and cooperation: Testing for a relationship on Israeli religious and secular kibbutzim. *Current Anthropology, 44,* 713-722.

Sosis, R., & Ruffle, B. (2004). Ideology, religion, and the evolution of cooperation: Field experiments on Israeli Kibbutzim. *Research in Economic Anthropology, 23,* 87-115.

Sousa, D. A. (2011). *How the brain learns. (4th ed.).* Thousand Oaks, CA: Corwin.

Spezio, M. (2000, March 1). [Review of the book *Whatever happened to the Soul? Scientific and theological portraits of human nature* by W. S. Brown, N. Murphy, & H. N. Malony (Eds.)]. *Zygon: Journal of Religion & Science, 35*(2), 202-204.

Spezio, M. L. (2011, March). The neuroscience of emotion and reasoning in social contexts: Implications for moral theology. *Modern Theology, 27*(2), 339-356. doi:10.1111/j.1468-0025.2010.01680.x

Spezio, M. L. (2013, June). Social neuroscience and theistic evolution: Intersubjectivity, love and the social sphere. *Zygon: Journal of Religion and Science, 48*(2), 428-438. doi: 10.1111/zygo.12005.

Spirituality: Canons Regular of Premontre. (2023). Retrieved from https://www.norbertines.org.uk/the-order/spirituality

Spitzer, R. (2015) *The soul's upward yearning: Clues to our transcendent nature from experience and reason.* San Francisco, CA: Ignatius Press.

Sporns, O. (2016). *Networks of the brain.* Cambridge, MS: MIT Press.

Stace, W. (1960). *Mysticism and philosophy.* London, U.K.: Macmillan.

Stanton, S. (2023). Epistemology and how we come to know. Retrieved from magiscenter.com/blog/epistemology.

Statistics & Data. (2022). "Most popular religions in the world—1945-2022." Retrieved from www.statisticsanddata.org/data/most-popular-religions-in-the-world

Stein, E. (2000). Individual and Community. In E. Stein & M. Sawicki et al. (Eds.), *Philosophy of psychology and the humanities: The collected works of Edith Stein, vol. 7.* Washington, DC: ICS Publications.

Steup, M. (1997). [Review of the book *Perceiving God. The epistemology of religious experience* by W. Alston]. *Nous, 31*(3), 408-421.

Stinson, C. (2016). Mechanisms in psychology: Ripping nature at its seams. *Synthese, 193*(5), 1585-1614.

Stockigt, B., Jeserich, F., Walach, H., Elies, M., & Brinkhaus, B. (2021, December). Experiences and perceived effects of rosary praying. *Journal of Religion and Health, 60*(6), 3886-3906. doi: 10.1007/s10943-021-01299-2.

Stoeber, M. (1992). Constructivist epistemologies of mysticism: A critique and a revision. *Religious Studies, 28*, 107-116.

Stone, J. A. (2000, June). J. Wentzel van Huyssteen: Refiguring rationality in the postmodern age. *Zygon: Journal of Religion and Science, 35*(2), 415-426. doi: 10.1111/0591-2385.00284.

Stovall, P. (2011). Professional virtue and professional self-awareness: A case study in engineering ethics. *Science and Engineering Ethics, 17*, 109-132. doi:10.1007/s11948-009-9182-x.

Strawn. B. D., & Brown, W. S. (2013). Liturgical animals: What psychology and neuroscience tell us about formation and worship. *Liturgy, 28*(4). Fuller Theological Seminary. doi: 10.1080/0458063X. 2013.803838 Retrieved from http://www.tandfonline.com/loi/ultg20

Stuckey, H. L., & Nobel, J. (2010, February). The connection between art, healing, and public health: A review of current literature. *American Journal of Public Health, 100*(2), 254-63. doi: 10.2105/AJPH.2008.156497.

Stucky, K., Kirkwood, M. W., Donders, J., & Liff, C. (Eds.). (2014/2020). *Clinical neuropsychology study guide and board review.* New York: Oxford University Press.

Stuhlmeuller, C. (Ed.). (1996). *The Collegeville pastoral dictionary of Biblical theology.* Collegeville, MN: Liturgical Press.

Sullivan, J. (2016a). Construct stabilization and the unity of the mind-brain sciences. *Philosophy of Science, 83*, 662-673.

Sullivan, J. (2016b). Stabilizing constructs across different research fields as a way to foster the integrative approach of the research domain criteria project. *Frontiers in Human Neuroscience, 10*, 309.

Sullivan, J. (2016c). Neuroscientific kinds through the lens of scientific practice. In C. Kendig (Ed.), *Natural kinds and classification in scientific practice* (pp. 47-56). New York: Routledge.

Sullivan, J. A. (2017, June). Coordinated pluralism as a means to facilitate integrative taxonomies of cognition. *Philosophical Explorations, 20*(2), 129-145. doi: 10.1080/13869795.2017.1312497.

Swaab, D. F. (2001, August 20-24). Plasticity in the adult brain: From genes to neurotherapy. *Proceedings of the 22nd International Summer School of Brain Research.* (M. A. Hoffman et al., Eds.). University of Amsterdam: Elsevier.

Sweet, W. (2019). Jacques Maritain. In *Stanford encyclopedia of philosophy.* Retrieved from https://plato.stanford.edu/entries/maritain

Tangney, J. P. (2009). Humility. In S. J. Lopez & C. R. Snyder (Eds.), *Oxford Handbook of Positive Psychology, 2nd Edition* (pp. 483-490). New York: Oxford University Press.

Taylor, C. (1989). *Sources of the self: The making of modern identity.* Cambridge, MA: Harvard University Press.

Taylor, C. (2003). *Varieties of religion today: William James revisited. Series: Institute for Human Sciences Vienna Lecture.* Cambridge, MA: Harvard University Press.

Taylor, C. (2018). *A secular age.* Cambridge, MA: Belknap, Harvard University Press.

Taylor, K. I., et al. (1999). Qualitative hemispheric differences in semantic category matching. *Brain and Language, 70*(1), 119-131.

Taylor, K., Zach, P., & Brugger, P. (2002). Why is magical ideation related to leftward deviation on an implicit line bisection task? *Cortex, 38*(2), 247-252.

Teresa of Avila, St. (1577/1980). *The collected works of Teresa of Avila, vol. 2, The Way of Perfection and Interior Castle.* Washington, DC: ICS Publications.

Thielicke, H. & Louth, A. (2022). Theology, In *Encyclopedia Britannica.* Retrieved from http://www.britannica.com/topic/theology.

Thurston, H. (1911/2023). Relics. In *The Catholic encyclopedia.* New York: Robert Appleton. In *New Advent Catholic encyclopedia.* Retrieved from https://www.newadvent.org/cathen/12734a.

Titus, C. S., & Moncher, F. (2009). A Catholic Christian positive psychology: A virtue approach. *Edification: Journal of the Society for Christian Psychology,* 57-63.

Tranel, D., Hathaway-Nepple, J., & Anderson, S. W. (2007). Impaired behavior on real-world tasks following damage to the ventromedial prefrontal cortex. *Journal of Clinical and Experimental Neuropsychology, 29*(3), 319–332. Retrieved from https://doi.org/10. 1080/13803390600701376

Traska, B. (2017, March). [Review of the book *Brain, Consciousness, and God* by D. A. Helminiak]. *Zygon: Journal of Religion and Science, 52*(1), 282-284. doi: 10.1111/zygo.12323.

Trepanier, L. (2017). Culture and education in Josef Pieper's thought. Retrieved from http://www.voegelinview.com/culture-education-josef-piepers-thought

Trevena, J., & Miller, J. (2010). Brain preparation before a voluntary action: Evidence against unconscious movement initiation. *Consciousness and Cognition, 19*(1), 447-456.

Tucker, D. M. (2013, August). [Review]. Neuropsychological foundations of conscious experience. *The Journal of Nervous and Mental Disease, 201*(8), 724-725. Retrieved from http://www.jonmd.com

Turner, L. (2020). Isolating the individual: Theology, the evolution of religion, and the problem of abstract individualism. *Zygon: Journal of Religion and Science, 55*(1), 207-228. doi: 10.1111/zygo.12580.

Turner, R. (2016). Uses, misuses, new uses and fundamental limitations of magnetic resonance imaging in cognitive science. *Philosophical Transactions B, 371*(1705), 1-11. doi: 10.1098/rstb.2015.0349. Retrieved from http://www.rstb.royalsocietypublishing.org

Turner, V. (1967). *The forest of symbols.* New York: Cornell University Press.

Turner, V. (1969). *The ritual process.* Chicago, IL: Aldine.

Turri, J., Alfano, M., & Greco. J. (2021, Winter). Virtue Epistemology, In E. N. Zalta (Ed.), *The Stanford encyclopedia of philosophy.* Retrieved from https://plato.stanford.edu/archives/win2021/entries/epistemology-virtu.

Uddin L. Q. (2020). Bring the noise: Reconceptualizing spontaneous neural activity. *Trends in Cognitive Sciences,* 24(9), 734–746.

Umpleby, S. A. (2016). Second-order cybernetics as a fundamental revolution in science. *Constructivist Foundations,* 11(3), 455-465.

Underhill, E. (1911). *Mysticism: A study in the nature and development of man's spiritual consciousness.* New York: E. P. Dutton and Company.

University of Edinburgh. (2016). Science and religion: Three views. [Online course, Module Two: *Philosophy, Science, and Religion*]. Retrieved from https://www.coursera.org/ learn/philosophy-science-religion-3

Uttal, W. (2001). *The new phenomenology: The limits of localizing cognitive processes in the brain.* Cambridge, MA: MIT Press.

van Dongen, J. D. M. (2020, April 6). The empathic brain of psychopaths: From social science to neuroscience in empathy. *Frontiers in Psychology, 11,* 1-12. Retrieved from https://doi.org/10.3389/fpsyg.2020.00695

von Hildebrand, D. (2001). *Transformation in Christ: On the Christian attitude.* San Francisco, CA: Ignatius Press.

van Huyssteen, J. W. (1999). *The shaping of rationality: Toward interdisciplinarity in theology and science.* Grand Rapids, MI: William Eerdmans.

van Huyssteen, J. W. (2006). *Alone in the world? Human uniqueness in science and theology.* Grand Rapids, MI: William Eerdmans.

van Inwagen, P., & Sullivan, M. (2021, Winter). Metaphysics, in E. N. Zalta (Ed.). *Stanford encyclopedia of philosophy.* Retrieved from https://plato.stanford.edu/archives/win2021/entries/metaphysics/

Varela, F., & Singer, W. (1987). Neuronal dynamics in the visual cortico-thalamic pathway as revealed through binocular rivalry. *Experimental Brain Research,* 66(1), 10-20.

Varela, F., Thompson, E., & Rosch, E. (1991/2017). *The embodied mind: Cognitive science and human experience.* Cambridge, MA: MIT Press.

Verheinjde, J. L., & Potts, M. (2010). Commentary on the concept of brain death within the Catholic bioethical framework. *Christian Bioethics, 16,* 246-256.

Vicini, A. (2012). Imaging in severe disorders of consciousness: Rethinking consciousness, identity, and care in a relational key. *Journal of the Society of Christian Ethics, 32,* 169-191.

Vicini, A. (2014). Neuroscience and bioethics. *La Civilta Cattolica, 2,* 143-158.

Vieten, C., Scammel, S., Pilato, R., Ammondson, I., Pargament, K. I., & Lukoff, D. (2013). Spirituality and religious competencies for psychologists. *Psychology of Religion and Spirituality, 5*(3), 129-144. doi: 10.1037/a0032699.

Vieten, C., Wahbeh, H., Cahn, B. R., MacLean, K., Estrada, M., Mills, P., Delorme, A. (2018). Future directions in meditation research: Recommendations for expanding the field of contemplative science. *PLoS One, 13*(11), 1-30. doi: 10.1371/journal.pone. 0205740.

Vincelette, A. (2011). *Recent Catholic philosophy: The twentieth century.* Milwaukee, WI: Marquette University Press.

Vincelette, A. (2020). *A reader in recent Catholic philosophy.* St. Louis, MO: Enroute.

Vincentian Spirituality. (2023). Retrieved from https://vinformation.org

Vita, P. C., Nordling, W. J., & Titus, C. S. (Eds.). (2020). *A Catholic Christian meta-model of the person.* Sterling, VA: Divine Mercy University Press.

Vitz, P. C. (2009). Reconceiving personality theory from a Catholic Christian perspective. *Edification, 3,* 42-50.

Vitz, P. C. (2011). Christian and Catholic advantages for connecting psychology with the faith. *Journal of Psychology and Christianity, 30,* 294-306.

Vogt, C. P. (2016). Virtue: Personal formation and social transformation. *Theological Studies, 77,* 181-196.

Von Hildebrand, D. (2001). *Transformation in Christ.* San Francisco, CA: Ignatius.

Wahlberg, M. (2020, Fall). Divine revelation. In E. N., Zalta (Ed.), *The Stanford encyclopedia of philosophy.* Retrieved from https://plato.stanford.edu/archives/fall2020/entries/divine-revelation

Wainright, W. J. (1981). *Mysticism: A study in its nature, cognitive value, and moral implications.* Madison, WI: University of Wisconsin Press.

Wainright, W. J. (2011). The spiritual senses in Western spirituality and the analytic philosophy of religion. *European Journal for the Philosophy of Religion, 3,* 21-41.

Walch, J. (2015). Nested narratives: Interpersonal neurobiology and Christian formation. *Christian Education Journal, 12,* 151-161.

Wall, T. (2015, April). Resurrection and the natural sciences: Some theological insights on sanctification and disability. *Science and Christian Belief, 27*(1), 41-58.

Walter, V. J., & Walter, W. G. (1949). The central effects of rhythmic sensory stimulation. *Electroencephalography and clinical* neurophysiology, 1, 57-86.

Watts, F. (2002). Cognitive neuroscience and religious consciousness. In R. J. Russell, N. Murphey, T. C. Meyering, T. C., & M. A. Arbib, (Eds.), *Neuroscience and the person: Scientific perspectives on divine action* (pp.327-346). Notre Dame, IN: University of Notre Dame Press.

Weaver, E. (2023). *Overcoming the darkness: Shining the light on mental illness, trauma, and suicide.* Retrieved from www.overcomingthe darkness.com/eric -weaver

Weisberg, D. S., Keil, F. C., Goodstein, J., Rawson, E., & Gray, J. R. (2008). The seductive allure of neuroscience explanations. *Journal of Cognitive Neuroscience, 20,* 470-477.

Weissenbacher, M. C. (2015, March). Ten principles for interpreting neuroscientific pronouncements regarding human nature. *Dialogue: A Journal of Theology, 54*(1), 41-50. doi: 10.1111/dial.12153.

Weker, M. (2016, December). Searching for neurobiological foundations of faith and religion. *Studia Humana, 5*(4), 57-63. doi: 10.1515/sh-2016-0024.

Werk, R. S., Steinhorn, D. M., & Newberg, A. (2021). The relationship between spirituality and the developing brain: A framework for pediatric oncology. *Journal of Religion and Health, 60*(1), 389-405. doi: 10.1007/s10943-020-01014-7.

White, C. (2017). What the cognitive science of religion is (and is not). In A. W. Hughes (Ed), *Theory in a time of excess: Beyond reflection and explanation in religious studies scholarship* (pp. 95-114). London, U.K.: Equinox Publishing.

Whitehouse, H. (2000). *Arguments and icons: Divergent modes of religiosity.* Oxford, U.K.: Oxford University Press.

Wildman, W. & Brothers, L. (2002). A neuropsychological-semiotic model of religious experiences. In R. J. Russell, N. Murphey, T. C. Meyering, T. C., & M. A. Arbib, (Eds.). *Neuroscience and the person: Scientific perspectives on divine action* (pp. 347-416). Notre Dame, IN: University of Notre Dame Press.

Wildman, W. J. (2013). Spiritual experiences: A quantitative-phenomenological approach. *Journal of Empirical Theology, 26*(2), 139-164. doi: 10.1163/157092 56-12341274.

Wilson, C., Bungay, H., Munn-Giddings, C., & Boyce, M. (2016, April). Healthcare professionals' perceptions of the value and impact of the arts in healthcare settings: A critical review of the literature. *International Journal of Nursing Studies, 56*, 90-101. doi: 10.1016/j.ijnurstu.2015.11.003.

Wilson, E. O. (1998). *Consilience: The unity of knowledge.* Visalia, CA: Vintage Press.

Winkleman, M. (2000). *Shamanism: The neural ecology of consciousness and healing,* Westport, CT: Bergin.

Wintering, N., Yaden, D. B., Conklin, C., Alizadeh, M., Mohamed, F. B., Zhong, L., Newberg, A. B. (2021). Effect of a one-week spiritual retreat on brain functional connectivity: A preliminary study. *Religions, 12*(1), 23. doi: 10.33 90/rel12010023.

Wiseman, J. A. (1993). Mysticism. In M. Downey (Ed.), *The new dictionary of Catholic spirituality* (pp. 681-692). Collegeville, MN: Liturgical Press.

Wolff, H. W. (1974). *Anthropology of the Old Testament.* Philadelphia, PA: Fortress Press.

Woodward, G. (2023). Karl Rahner (1904-1984). *Internet encyclopedia of philosophy: A peer-reviewed academic resources.* Retrieved from http://iep. utm.edu/rahner

Worthington, E. L. (1989). Religious faith across the life span: Implications for counseling and research. *The Counseling Psychologist, 17*(4), 555-612.

Yaden, D. B., & Newberg, A. B. (2022). *The varieties of spiritual experiences: 21st century research and perspectives.* Oxford, U.K.: Oxford University Press.

Yaden, D. B., Haidt, J., Hood, R. W., Vago, D. R., & Newberg, A. B. (2017, June). The varieties of self-transcendent experience. *Review of General Psychology, 21*(2), 1-18. doi: 10.1037/gpr0000102.

Yaden, D. B., Le Nguyen, K. D., Kern, M. L., Belser, A. B., Eichstaedt, J. C., Iwry, J., Newberg, A. B. (2017, July). Of roots and fruits: A comparison of psychedelic and nonpsychedelic mystical experiences. *Journal of Humanistic Psychology, 57*(4), 1-16, 338-353. doi: 10.1177/0022167816674625.

Yamane, D. (2007). Introduction: *Habits of the heart at 20*: Symposium on the 20th Anniversary of *Habits of the Heart. Sociology of Religion, 68*(2), 179-187.

Yasinski, E. (2021, July 12). Religion on the brain. *The Scientist.* Retrieved from https://www. the-scientist.com/news-opinion/religion-on-the-brain-68969

Zagzebski, L. T. (2009). *On epistemology.* Belmont, CA; Wadsworth.

Zagzebski, L. T. (2021). *The two greatest ideas: How our grasp of the universe and our minds changed everything.* Princeton, NJ: Princeton University Press.

Zarzycka, B., & Zietek, P. (2019, August). Spiritual growth or decline and meaning making as mediators of anxiety and satisfaction with life during religious struggle. *Journal of Religion and Health, 58*(4), 1072-1086. doi: 10.1007/s109 43-018-0598-y.

Zinnbauer, B. J., & Pargament, K. I. (2005). Religiousness and spirituality. In R. F. Paloutzian & C. Park (Eds.), *Handbook of the psychology of religion and spirituality* (pp. 21-42). New York: Guilford.

Zohar, D., & Marshall, I. (2000). Spiritual Intelligence: The Ultimate Intelligence. London: Bloomsbury.

Further Reading

Anderson, E. B. (1997, Summer). Liturgical catechesis: Congregational practice as formation. *Religious Education, 93*(3), 349-363.

Anscombe, G. E. M., Schneewind, J. B., & Reiman, J. H. (1958/2004). O'Hear, A. (Ed.), *Modern Moral Philosophy.* Cambridge, U.K.: Cambridge University Press.

Augustine, St. (400/1947). *De libero arbitrio voluntatis.* Richmond, VA : Dietz Press.

Benedict XVI, Pope. (1988/2007). *Eschatology: Death and eternal life.* 2nd ed. Washington, DC: Catholic University of America Press.

Bouyer, L. (2017). *Mysterion: De mystère à la mystique.* Paris, France : Edition du Cerf.

Byrne, P. (2016). [Review of book *Authenticity of self-transcendence: The enduring insights of Bernard Lonergan* by M. H. McCarthy). Retrieved from https:// ndor.nd.edu/reviews/

Carlson, J. W. (2012). *Words of wisdom: A philosophical dictionary for the perennial tradition.* South Bend, IN: University of Notre Dame Press.

Catholic Church. (1983/2022). *Code of Canon Law* (4th ed.) Arrieta, J. I. (Ed.). Montreal, Quebec, Canada: Librarie Wilson & Lafleur.

Catholic Church. Council of Trent, Session XXV. (2023). Retrieved from http:// www.thecounciloftrent.com/ch25.htm

Cuthbert, B., & Kozak, M. (2013). Constructing constructs of psychopathology: The NIMH research domain criteria (RDoC). *Journal of Abnormal Psychology, 122*(3), 928-937.

dal Covolo, E. (1999, March 17). The encounter of faith and reason in the Fathers of the Church. Vatican City: *L'Osservatore Romano,* 9-10.

Deely, J. (1997). Quid sit postmodernismus? In R. T. Ciapalo (Ed.), *Postmodernism and Christian Philosophy*. Washington, DC: Catholic University of America Press.

de Longchamp, M. H. (1997). *Lectures de Jean de la Croix : Essai d'anthropologie mystique*. Paris, France : Beauchesne éditeur.

Dixon, T. (2003). *From passions to emotions: The creation of a secular psychological category*. Cambridge, U. K.: Cambridge University Press.

Doran, R. M. (1990). *Theology and the dialectics of history*. Toronto, Ontario, Canada: University of Toronto Press.

Eckstrom, R. R. (1982/1995). *The new concise Catholic dictionary*. Mystic, CT: Twenty-Third Publications.

Edwards, J. S. (1977). Pathfinding by arthropod sensory nerves. In G. Hoyle (Ed.), *Identified neurons and behavior of arthropods* (pp. 484–493). New York: Plenum.

Elian, M., Hoerl, C., McCormack, T., & Koesler, J. (Eds.). (2005). *Joint attention: Communication and other minds: Issues in philosophy and psychology*. Oxford, U. K.: Clarendon Press.

Fairbairn, W. R. D. (1952a). *An object relations theory of the personality*. New York: Basic Books.

Fairbairn, W. R. D. (1952b). *Psychoanalytic studies of the personality*. London, U.K.: Routledge & Kegan Paul.

Feyerabend, P. (1975). *Against method*. New York: New Left Books.

Fizzotti, E. (2008). *Introduzione alle psicologia della religione*. Milano, Italy: FrancoAngeli.

Gilson, E. (1919/2002). *Thomism: The philosophy of Thomas Aquinas*. Toronto, Ontario, Canada: Pontifical Institute of Medieval Studies.

Gilson, E. (1941/2002). *God and philosophy*. New Haven, CT: Yale University Press.

Hall, C. R., Dixon, W. A., & Mauzey, E. D. (2004). Spirituality and religion: Implications for counselors. *Journal of Counseling & Development, 82*(4), 504–507.

Hardon, J. A. (1980). *Modern Catholic dictionary*. New York: Doubleday.

Harre, R. S., & Secord, P. F. (1972). *The explanation of social behavior*. Oxford, U.K.: Blackwell.

Hodge, D. R., & McGrew, C. C. (2006). Spirituality, religion, and the interrelationship: A nationally representative study. *Journal of Social Work Education, 42*(3), 637-654. doi: 10.5175/JSWE.2006.200500517

Jewett, P. K., & Shuster, M. (1996). *Who we are: Our dignity as human: A neo-evangelical theology*. Grand Rapids, MI: William B. Eerdmans.

Johnson, S. (1996/2004). *Creating connection: The practice of emotionally focused marital therapy*. New York: Brunner/Mazel (now Brunner/Routledge).

Jones, R. H. (2013). *Analysis and the fullness of reality: An introduction to reductionism and emergence*. New York: Jackson Square Books.

Jones, R. H. (2016). *Philosophy of mysticism: Raids on the ineffable*. Albany: State University of New York Press.

Jones, R. M. (1909). *Studies in mystical religion*. London, U.K: Macmillan.

Kelly, M. (2002/2014). *Rediscover Catholicism: A spiritual guide to living with passion and purpose.* North Palm Beach, FL: Blue Sparrow Books.

Kenny, A. (1988). *The self: Aquinas lecture.* Milwaukee, WI: Marquette University Press.

Kristjanson, K. (2014). Phronesis and moral education: Treading beyond the truisms. *Theory and Research in Education.* doi:10.10.1177/1477878514530244.

Kruger, F. P., & de Klerk, B. J. (2017, Jan.). The mediating influence of liturgy on the way of life: Disposing oppressing powers in oneself and appropriating compassion toward the other. *HTS Theological Studies, 73*(1).

Lambek, M. (2002). *A reader in the anthropology of religion.* Oxford, U.K.: Blackwell.

Lamm, J. A. (2013). *The Wiley-Blackwell companion to Christian mysticism.* West Sussex, U. K.: John Wiley & Sons.

MacIntyre, A. (2016). *Ethics in the conflicts of modernity: An essay on desire, practical reasoning, and narrative.* Cambridge, U.K.: Cambridge University Press.

Maritain, J. (1946). *The twilight of civilization.* Andesite Press. https://open library.org/publishers/Andesite Press

Maritain, J. (1951). *Philosophy of nature.* New York: Philosophical Library Publishing.

McGinn, B. (2001, Fall). The language of inner experience in Christian mysticism. *Spiritus: A Journal of Christian Spirituality, 1*(2), 56-171. Baltimore, MD: Johns-Hopkins University Press.

Melina, L. (2001, Spring). Christ and the dynamism of action: Outlook and overview of Christocentrism in moral theology. *Communio: International Catholic Review, 28, 112-139.*

Mittlestrass, J. (2011). On transdisciplinarity. *Trames 4,* 329-338. doi.org/10.31 76/tr.2011.4.01

Moodley, R. (2007). (Re)placing multiculturalism in counseling and psychotherapy. *British Journal of Guidance & Counselling, 35*(1), 1-22. doi: 10.1080/0306988 0601106740

Morel, G. (1960). *Le sens de l'existence selon Saint Jean de al Croix.* Aubier, Paris : Presses Universitaires de France.

Muñoz, C. P. D. (2012). En torno a dos lecturas posibles sobre el conocimiento de las esencias en Tomas de Aquino. *Topicos: Revista de Filosofia (Mexico),* 43: 123– 151.

Nédoncelle, M. (1942). *La réciprocité des consciences : Essai sur la nature de la personne.* Paris, France: Aubier.

Nédoncelle, M. (1946/1966). *Love and the person.* New York: Sheed and Ward.

Nicolescu, B. (2014, May). Methodology of transdisciplinarity. *World Futures: The Journal of General Evolution, 70*(3-4), 186-199.

Paul VI, Pope. (1963). *Sacrosanctum concilium.* Decree on the Sacred Liturgy. Retrieved from https://www.vatican.va/archive/hist_councils/ii_vatican_council/documents/vat- ii_const_19631204_sacrosanctum-concilium_en.html

Paul VI, Pope. (1964). *Orientalium Ecclesiarum:* Decree on the Churches of the Eastern rite. https://www.vatican.va/archive/hist_councils/ii_vatican_council/documents/vat- ii_decree_19641121_orientalium-ecclesiarum_en.html

Paul VI, Pope. (1965). *Presbyterorum ordinis.* Decree on the life and ministry of priests. Retrieved from Presbyterorum ordinis (vatican.va)

Paul VI, Pope. (1971). *Divinae consortium naturae.* Apostolic Constitution on the Sacrament of Confirmation. Retrieved from https://www.vatican.va/content/paul-vi/la/apost_constitutions/documents/hf_p-vi_apc_19710815_divina-consortium.html

Paul VI, Pope. (1974). *Marialis cultus.* Apostolic exhortation for the right ordering and development of devotion to the Blessed Virgin Mary. Retrieved from https://www.vatican.va/paul-vi/en/apost_exhortations/documents/hf_p-vi_exh_19740202_marialis-cultus.html

Peterson, G. R. (2012). Exemplarism: Some considerations. In *Theology and the science of moral action.* Philadelphia, PA: Routledge.

Piccinini, G., & Craver, C. (2011). Integrating psychology and neuroscience: Functional analyses as mechanism sketches. *Synthese 183*(3), 283-311.

Pico della Mirandolla, G. (1486/1996). *Oration on the dignity of man.* Southlake, TX: Gateway Publishing.

Pius IX, Pope. (1870/2023). Dogmatic constitution *Dei filius.* Retrieved from https://www.vatican.va/content/pius-ix/la/documents/constitutio-dogmatica-dei-filius-24-aprilis-1870.html

Pius XII, Pope. Encyclical *Humani generis.* Retrieved from https://www.vatican.va/content/pius-xii/en/encyclicals/documents/hf_p-xii_enc_12081950_humani-generis.html

Plantinga, A. C. (2000). *Warranted Christian belief.* New York: Oxford University Press.

Rahner, K. (1976/1982). *Foundations of Christian faith: An introduction to the idea of Christianity.* New York: Herder & Herder.

Rahner, K. (1982). Theology of freedom. In *Theological investigations.* Vol. 6 (pp. 178-196). New York: Crossroad.

Rubia, F. J. (2009). *La conexion divina: La experiencia mistica y la neurobiologia.* Barcelona, Spain: Critica.

Sandok, T. H. (1993). *Person and community: Selected essays: Catholic thought from Lublin.* Lausanne, Switzerland: Peter Lang International Academic Publishing.

Sanguineti, J. J. (2007). *Filosofia de la mente.* Madrid, Spain: Palabra.

Sanguineti, J. J. (2014). Neurosciencia y filosofia del hombre. Madrid, Spain: Palabra.

Sanguineti, J. J. (2018). La relevancia de al neurociencia en el estudio de la reliosidad. *Scientia et Fides, 6,* 85-99.

Shaw, S. M. (1999). *Storytelling in religious education.* Birmingham, AL: Religious Education Press.

Slatcher, R. B. (2010, June). When Harry and Sally met Dick and Jane: Creating closeness between couples. *Personal Relationships, 17*(2), 279-297.

Smith, J. K. A. (2009). *Desiring the kingdom: Worship, worldview, and cultural formation.* Grand Rapids, MI: Baker Academic.

Solomon, M. F., & Tatkin, S. (2011). *Love and war in intimate relationships: Connection, disconnection, and mutual regulation in couple therapy.* Scranton, PA: W. W. Norton.

Stuhlmueller, C., Bergant, D., Dumm, D., et al. (Eds.). (1996). *The Collegeville pastoral dictionary of biblical theology.* Collegeville, MN: Liturgical Press.

United Nations. (1948). *Universal declaration of human rights.* Retrieved from https://www.un.org>udhr_booklet_en_web

von Balthasar, H. U. (1990). *The glory of the Lord.* 7 vols. San Francisco, CA: Ignatius Press.

von Glasserfeld, E. (Ed.). (1991). Editor's introduction. In *Radical constructivism in mathematics education.* Dordrecht, Netherlands: Kluwer.

von Hildebrand, D. (1953). *Christian ethics.* Philadelphia, PA: David McKay Publishing.

von Hildebrand, D. (2016). *Liturgy and personality.* New York: Hildebrand Books. HarperCollins.

Wolfson, H. A. (1956/2022). *Philosophy of the Church Fathers: Vol. 1: Faith, Trinity, Incarnation.* Cambridge, MA: Harvard University Press.

Wojtyla, K. (1960/1993). *Love and responsibility.* San Francisco, CA: Ignatius Press.

Wojtyla, K. (1969/1979). *The acting person.* Dordrecht, Netherlands: D. Reidle Publishing.

Index

A

Absolute Unitary Being (AUB), 310, 313–15, 317, 328
action understanding, 140, 155, 213
Aeterni patris, 26, 29
affective neuroscience, 153
aging, 159, 162, 240
Alberic, St., 222
Albert of Mt. Carmel, St., 223
Albert the Great, St., 222
Alexandria, 2, 74
Alston, William, 246
Angela of Foligno, St., 221
Anointing of the Sick, 133, 154
Anthony of Padua, St., 222
altruism, 119, 142, 226, 274
amygdala, 31, 33–34, 102, 108, 136, 138, 140, 150, 153, 167, 170, 175–76, 200–201, 210–12, 214–15, 220, 226
Anscombe, Elizabeth, 28, 103
anterior cingulate cortex (ACC), 97, 137–39, 162, 168, 170, 294
anterior insula, 138
anxiety, 21, 113, 116–17, 119, 162, 173, 180, 184, 212, 237, 298
apophatic prayer, 236
Aquinas, St. Thomas, 19, 26–28, 30, 38–39, 45–47, 53–54, 59, 66-67, 75, 89–90, 100, 102, 105, 107–8, 131, 164, 191–92, 194, 222, 252–53, 256, 270–71, 292–93
Aristotle, 26, 30, 38, 53–54, 56, 63, 73, 89, 194, 273, 279
atheism, 87, 112, 294, 319, 325

atheists, 10, 73, 180, 184, 256, 265, 294
attachment to God, 297–98
attention, 32, 34–35, 40–41, 50, 55, 62, 67, 143, 150, 152, 156, 162, 165, 251, 253–54, 256
attunement, 14, 137–38, 196, 247, 283, 291–94, 296, 302–4
auditory cortex, 33, 146–47, 171, 215, 219
Augustine of Hippo, St., 27, 37, 63, 102, 104, 122, 127, 191, 205, 221, 225, 236, 253, 256-257, 264, 280, 298
autonomic nervous system, 32–33, 108, 119, 123, 136, 148–49, 201, 215
autonomous beings, 43, 90, 286, 305

B

baptism, 2, 14, 101, 106, 117, 129–33, 135–36, 138, 141, 154–56, 174, 189, 195, 254–55
Barbour, Ian, 4, 67, 316
basal ganglia, 150, 152–53, 181, 216, 220
Basil, St., 221
Beatific Vision, 64, 66
beatitudes, 15, 127, 255–56, 262, 271
Beauregard, James, 12
Beauregard, Mario, 233–35, 238, 250, 308, 311
Bednar, Gerald, 235, 270, 273, 310
behaviors
complex, 20, 83, 102

criminal, 103
cult, 179
being, 49, 56–59, 64–66, 75–76, 89–
   90, 93, 99–100, 120–22, 132,
   140–41, 200–201, 205–6, 216–
   17, 234–35, 247–48, 253, 257,
   271–74, 283–84, 288–89, 313–15
beliefs, 9, 11, 13, 23, 38–39, 64, 74,
   78–81, 85–86, 108–9, 112, 114,
   116–17, 143–46, 167, 184, 216–
   17, 246, 266–68, 278
   spiritual, 21–22, 80, 182–83
belief system, 2, 24, 150, 163
believers, 39, 73, 125, 132, 135,
   148, 170, 196, 258, 280, 285,
   298, 301, 306
Benedict, St., 221–22
Bernard of Clairvaux, St., 288
blessings, 65, 174, 176, 178
blood pressure, 119, 123, 162, 215
body and soul, 18, 27–28, 38–39,
   43, 53–54, 70, 191, 237, 326
body of Christ, 140, 189, 273
body's response to religious
   experience, 13, 15, 113–23
Bonaventure, St., 127, 221-222
Bonhoeffer, Dietrich, 101–2
Bosco, St. John, 223
brain activity, 40, 87, 94–95, 102–3,
   153, 239–41, 249, 316
brain and free will, 93-96
brain changes, 103, 144, 174, 255
brain death, 14, 277
brain functions, 36, 78, 88, 91, 95,
   139, 142, 175, 180–81, 197, 199,
   209, 234, 238
brain imaging, 84, 209, 244, 261,
   264, 274, 319
brain scans, 44, 48, 77, 84–85, 88,
   153, 182–83, 199, 210, 300, 313–
   14
brain sciences, 5

brainstem, 31–33, 231
brain structures, 10, 34, 155, 179,
   211–12, 241, 260, 274–75, 280,
   307, 311, 327
Brueggeman, Walter, 324
Brugger, Christian, 44, 188–91,
   193–94
Buddhism, 20, 41, 81, 84, 93, 236,
   243, 312, 325
Burns, Charlene, 265–66, 270, 272,
   278, 313–14

C

Carmelites, 219–20, 223
Catechesi tradendae, 8
*Catechism of the Catholic Church
   (CCC)*, 1-2, 15–16, 24–26, 37–39,
   65, 70, 75–76, 96, 100–106, 121–
   22, 129, 131–42, 159–62, 172–
   74, 176–77, 190, 264–65, 278,
   287–88, 290, 304
Catholic belief, 19, 60, 112, 176,
   186, 219, 294
Catholic Church, 1–2, 8, 15, 17, 23,
   37–39, 96, 118, 121, 159–60,
   185, 280, 287, 296
Catholic faith, 15, 26–27, 66, 75,
   90, 112, 133, 136, 160, 172, 176,
   186, 326
Catholic neurotheology, 1–15
Catholic practices, 14–15, 159–77
Catholic rituals, 6, 14–15, 125–57
Catholic sacramental system, 125,
   129, 135, 154–55, 157
Catholic spiritualities, 14, 159,
   218–20, 226–27, 229
Catholic theology, 5, 9, 15, 64–66,
   68–70, 74–75, 79, 109–10, 185,
   192, 194, 294, 298, 301–2, 305,
   326–27

charisms, 218–19, 225, 229, 250, 261
charity, 29, 64–66, 102, 106, 164–65, 172–73, 190, 192, 219, 223–24, 249, 255–56, 258, 287, 290, 292
Christ Jesus, 2, 125, 171, 181, 222, 224, 280
Christian anthropology, 7, 189, 192, 194, 306
Christian beliefs, 6, 38, 170, 268, 279–80
Christian doctrine, 9, 24, 185, 246
Christian ethics, 28
Christian faith, 8, 25, 102, 117, 192, 265, 267–68, 289, 291
Christian mysticism, 235, 246, 249, 261
Christian philosophy, 26, 194
Christian spirituality, 155, 218, 229
Christian theology, 6, 69, 102, 108, 258, 268, 272, 280, 307
cingulate cortex, 34, 136, 220, 226, 295
    anterior, 97, 137–39, 162, 170, 294
    posterior, 169, 274, 294
circadian rhythms, 160
Clare of Assisi, St., 222
clinical psychology, 44, 190, 192–93, 197
Cloninger, Robert, 208
Code of Canon Law, 75
cognition, 44, 46, 53, 55, 57, 62–64, 69, 163, 168, 175, 183, 189, 193, 198, 227, 232, 318–19
cognitive behavioral therapy (CBT), 44, 188, 192, 197
cognitive neuroscience, 20, 31, 40, 82, 84–85, 163, 325–26
cognitive operators, 312, 315
cognitive science theory, 63, 111, 186

Colette, St., 222
commandments, 15, 109, 187
communication, 76–77, 121, 137, 142, 146, 153, 156, 160, 196, 198, 217, 220, 222, 225, 227
communion, 2, 26, 114, 132–33, 135, 141, 143, 148, 154, 162, 177, 225, 270, 272
compassion, 11, 20, 46, 104, 142, 207, 213, 215, 233, 274, 296
complexity, 79, 95, 161, 168, 175, 201, 265, 306, 322, 326
connaturality, 14, 64, 68, 255, 259, 262, 292, 302–3
conscience, 103, 133, 205, 255, 257, 262, 285, 290
consciousness
    mystical, 128, 250
    subjective, 202, 232, 245, 314
contemplation, 2, 64, 74, 121–22, 161, 222–23, 253
contemplative neuroscience, 159, 161–63
conversion, religious, 118, 125–26, 251
cross, 131, 143, 172–75, 178, 221–24, 252–54, 262, 298, 300
culture, 38, 46, 149, 156, 161, 172, 176, 185, 205, 207, 268, 300, 306, 316

D

Damasio, Antonio, 99, 138, 200, 228
default mode network (DMN), 86, 169, 273–74, 279
Dei filius, 104, 265
Dei verbum, 160, 268, 280
de Montfort, St. Louis, 198

depression, 21, 23, 80, 84–85, 87,
    113, 116–17, 162, 180, 210, 228,
    27
Descartes, René 18, 28, 47
destiny, 2, 60, 76, 105, 273
development, lifespan, 164, 195
devotion, 171–73, 175, 190
dialogic model, 308, 327
dialogue
  constructive, 74
  neuroscience-theology, 45, 68,
    309, 329
  transversal, 324
diffusion tensor imaging (DTI), 85
Dionysius the Areopagite, 221, 236
divine, 64, 66–67, 99, 104–5, 126,
    128–29, 204–6, 217, 235, 237,
    248, 253, 263, 268, 287, 291, 298
divine action, 196, 272
divine plan, 100, 313
Divinae consortium naturae, 130
doctrine, 3, 9, 24, 76, 104, 126–27,
    131, 162, 191, 220, 268, 272,
    301, 310
Dodds, Michael, 26, 36, 46, 59–60,
    73, 89, 242, 260
dopamine, 87, 100, 150, 181, 201,
    216, 237

E

electroencephalography, 87, 91
emergence, 18, 187, 213, 226
emotional centers, 35, 103, 108,
    173, 180, 200–201, 210, 216
emotional disorders, 192–93
empathy, 11, 103–4, 136, 138–40,
    151, 155, 165–66, 168, 212–15,
    237, 241, 276, 280, 295–96
enlightenment experiences, 245,
    249
epilepsy, 311

epistemological considerations
    and faith, 13, 45–69
epistemology, 13, 15, 21, 45, 49–50,
    52–53, 55, 58–59, 65, 68, 76, 79,
    238, 242, 246, 320, 323
Evangelii Gaudium, 90
Evermode, St., 225
existential, 20, 197, 295
exorcism, 174–75, 178

F

faith
  expressing, 156, 225
  religious, 39, 68, 113, 150, 156,
    323
faith and reason, 2, 26, 30, 64, 74
faith and science, 23, 300
faith traditions, 216, 248–49, 302
Ferguson, Michael, 33, 183, 209
Fides et Ratio, 2, 30, 64, 74–75,
    299–300
flourishing, human, 188–89, 192,
    301
forgiveness, 104, 133, 139, 172,
    218, 235, 257, 293
Fowler, James, 188, 195, 198
Francis, Pope, 8, 10–11, 90, 177,
    287, 296, 299, 306, 327
Francis of Assisi, St., 222–23
Franciscans, 173, 220, 222
free will, 6, 13, 22, 29, 38, 78–79,
    93–100, 102, 104–7, 109–10,
    188, 195, 198, 241
Freud, Sigmund, 179, 187–88, 190,
    198
frontal, 34, 119, 143, 147, 149, 165,
    174, 193, 201, 215, 294, 296, 311
frontal lobes, 32, 35, 94, 97, 142–
    43, 165, 169, 180–81, 240–41,
    251

G

Gabriel of Our Mother of Sorrows, St., 224
Galgani, St. Gemma, 224
gamma aminobutyric acid (GABA), 202
Gaudete et exsultate, 287
Gaudium et spes, 25, 185, 286, 299-300
Gilson, Etienne, 29
God
  brain experience, 48
  fear of, 101, 105
  living, 268, 270, 289
  love, 257
Gonzaga, St. Aloysius, 223
grace, 8, 13–15, 24, 65–67, 69–70, 101–2, 127, 129, 131, 133–35, 141, 154–56, 159–64, 172–73, 218–19, 232, 254–58, 262, 268, 283–304
Gregory of Rimini, St., 221
Groome, Thomas, 218
Guzman, St. Dominic, 173, 222–23

H

Haidt, Jonathan, 97
Harding, St. Stephen, 222
Hardon, John, 1, 104
health outcomes, 12–13, 115–17, 123
hermeneutics, 73, 323
Hildegaard of Bingen, St., 221
hippocampus, 31, 33–34, 63, 108, 138–39, 167, 170, 201, 211–12, 215–16, 226–27, 240, 272, 296
Holy Trinity, 65, 288, 290
Hugh of St. Victor, 160
human, 49, 144, 156, 287
human body, 38, 59, 270

human condition, 19–22, 67, 70, 163, 203
humanism, 258, 306
human nature, 7, 17, 25, 28, 64, 127, 149, 190, 205, 287, 291, 327
human relationships, 14, 99, 119, 163, 194, 212
human soul, 46, 52–53, 55, 60, 65, 69, 90–91, 253, 262, 267, 279, 300–301, 320, 328
human understanding, 30, 64
human virtues, 106, 289
Humanae generis, 265
hylomorphic, 26-27, 127-128, 154, 261, 271
  Aristotelian-Thomistic, 27, 156, 244, 266
  metaphysics, 48
  unity, 237, 286
hymns, 145–46, 171
hypothalamus, 32–34, 136, 150, 160, 201, 220, 226, 295

I

identity, 9, 36, 61, 134, 190, 227, 232, 272–73, 278, 301, 324
Ignatius of Loyola, St., 7, 207, 221, 223, 237, 258, 264
ineffability, 237, 248, 313
insula, 102–3, 136, 138, 153, 165, 180–82, 214–16, 220, 251, 274
integrative pluralism, 322
intelligence, 49, 53, 56, 59–60, 106, 152, 189, 271
intentional consciousness, 55–56, 59, 62, 259
interoception, 138, 155
interpersonal dynamics, 256
interpersonal neurobiology, 14, 137, 211, 214, 220, 226, 295–97, 302

Islam, 84, 114, 268, 325

J

James, William, 208, 237, 248, 312
Jesuit, 153, 220, 223, 264, 291
John of the Cross, St., 223, 252, 262
John Paul II, Pope St., 2, 8, 15, 24,
    30–31, 43, 50, 74–75, 90, 173,
    221, 225, 269, 270, 275, 277,
    281, 286, 299, 302
Johnson, Joel, 13
Jogues, St. Isaac, 223
Judaism, 114, 263–64, 268, 278,
    325
judgment, moral, 44, 97, 294, 303
Jung, Carl, 187

K

Kant, Immanuel, 28, 70
knowledge
    empirical, 307
    human, 56, 235, 292, 316
    metaphysical, 51–52, 64
    scientific, 77, 185, 322
Koenig, Harold, 21, 115
Kolbe, St. Maximilian, 222
Kuhl, Julius, 231–32, 259

L

language abilities, 3, 41, 147
language and symbols, 149, 237
language areas, 147
laterality, 166
Lehmann, Kevin, 166, 205
lesion network mapping, 209, 228
Libet, Benjamin, 94-95, 105, 109,
    198
life, mystical, 67, 70, 135, 237, 288,
    298

Liguori, St, Alphonsus, 224
limbic system, 33–35, 97, 103, 162,
    169, 172, 180–81, 212, 214, 216,
    220, 226, 237, 241
liturgy, 14, 18, 76, 81, 123, 125, 129,
    131–32, 134–35, 155, 159, 177,
    219, 221
Lonergan, Bernard, 30, 45, 52, 54–
    59, 61–62, 69, 76–79, 125, 154,
    206, 228, 234, 257–59, 262, 269,
    284–85, 289
Lumen gentium, 7, 250, 287

M

MacIntyre, Alasdair, 104, 107, 110
magnetic resonance imaging
    (MRI), 85–86, 180, 313
Marcel, Gabriel, 28
Maritain, Jacques, 29, 45, 49–53,
    60, 64–67, 254, 292
martyrdom, 8, 256, 296
Mary, mother of Jesus, 121, 172-
    173, 175-176, 223
mathematics, 49, 51, 59, 85, 281,
    319
Mazzarello, St. Mary, 223
McGilchrist, Iain, 166–68, 178
meditation
    contemplative, 163
    individual, 171
    verbal/mantra, 166
meditation and prayer, 118–19,
    181–82, 216, 251
meditation practices, 86–87, 114,
    119, 162, 240
meditation research, 162
memory
    autobiographical, 136, 170
    episodic, 151, 170
    explicit, 138
    long-term, 211, 216

memory networks, 142, 193
mental experiences, 232, 243–44
Merton, Thomas, 222, 288
Messer, Neil, 97, 102, 307
metacognition, 163
mind, conscious, 56
mind and soul, 164
mind-body problem, 264
mindfulness, 163, 178, 207, 213, 296
miracles, 121–22, 250
mirror neurons, 140, 155, 166, 193, 198, 213–14, 220, 226, 228, 296
Mitchell, Sandra, 322, 329
models, neuropsychological, 231–32
models of neurotheology, 305–6, 327
Moltmann, Jurgen, 272
morality, 6, 13, 20, 25, 29, 35, 37, 68, 99, 107–8, 185, 195, 272–73, 275
moral reasoning, 97, 263, 273, 275, 280
moral theology, 25, 273
moral virtues, 1, 106, 247, 255, 262, 274, 276
Mormonism, 325
music, 96, 146, 150–51, 154, 166
mystery, eternal, 298
mystery of Christ, 2, 26, 159, 177, 288
mystery of prayer, 161
mystical, 32, 50, 232–34, 238–39, 242, 248–49, 253, 259, 261–62, 284, 288, 298, 302, 310–11
mystical experiences, 6, 42, 67, 74, 80–81, 207, 231–33, 235–52, 254–55, 259–62, 288, 303, 312–16
mystical states, 14, 128, 209, 232, 236–39, 260

mystical theology, 64, 220, 236
mystical transformation, 253–54, 262
mystical union, 122, 232, 250–51, 253, 303
mysticism, 14–15, 29, 49, 64, 126, 231–61, 288, 290, 312, 316, 326

N

near-death experiences, 41, 112, 116, 183
Nédoncelle, Maurice, 29
Neri, St. Philip, 223
nervous system
  parasympathetic, 32, 123
  sympathetic, 32–33, 123
Neumann, St. John, 224
neural binding problem (NBP), 264, 278
neural networks, 151–52, 165, 175, 178, 181, 186, 209, 215, 217, 243, 250, 279, 315
neuroscientific perspective, 20, 94, 97, 202, 273
neuroscientific research, 238, 266, 271, 275, 303
neurotheological investigations, 17, 164, 194, 245, 309
neurotheological investigations in Catholic thought, 13, 15, 19–43
neurotheological perspective, 5, 14–15, 24, 62, 81, 87, 104, 111, 125, 177, 179, 183–84, 199–229, 327
neurotheological studies, 21–22, 288, 321
neurotheology, interdisciplinary, 301
neurotheology and free will, 107
neurotheology and metaphysics, 45

neurotheology studies, 265, 318

neurotransmitters, 68, 87, 98, 106–7, 139, 201–2, 216, 228, 238, 266

Newman, St. John Henry Cardinal, 8-9, 223

Newberg, Andrew, 19–20, 22, 37, 39, 42, 44, 149, 165, 167, 169, 194–95, 215–16, 226–27, 232–35, 240–41, 243, 245, 264–66, 309–15, 317

New Testament, 64, 100, 160, 249, 278, 280, 288

Norbert, St., 225

numinous, 233–34, 248, 259, 312, 328

O

occipital lobe, 34, 36, 41

optimism, 120, 188, 192, 223, 324

Orientalium ecclesiarum, 7

original sin, 6, 99–102, 109, 265

Otto, Rudolf, 175, 204, 312

P

Papcsyznski, St. Stanislaus, 225

paradigms, 13, 71–72, 74, 77, 81, 325

paradoxicality, 248

Pargament, Kenneth, 206, 295

parietal lobe, 35–36, 63, 103, 143, 147, 149, 169, 182, 186, 202, 215, 288, 296, 298

passions, 44, 46, 68, 103, 133, 160, 172, 224, 280

pastoral care, 134, 185, 192, 198, 223, 225, 301, 325

Paul of Tarsus, St., 145, 163, 224, 250, 264, 268, 273, 288, 300

Payne, Steven, 12, 248, 262, 268, 281, 284

peace, 117, 132–33, 136, 139, 146, 169, 196, 256, 258, 313

penance, 118, 129, 133, 138–39, 141, 155, 222

perceiving God, 246

perceptions, sensory, 36, 232, 246, 254, 320

periaqueductal gray, 33, 136, 183, 201, 209, 226

Persinger, Michael, 311

personalism, 29, 189

perspective of neurotheology, 11, 59, 316

phenomenology, 28, 30–31, 126, 245

philosophers
  moral, 103
  political, 103
  pre-Socratic, 91

philosophical anthropology, 14, 59

philosophical criticism, 242

philosophical psychology, 103, 191–92

philosophy, natural, 45, 51–52, 65

physical health, 111–15, 119, 122, 311

physics, 2, 72, 78, 82, 92, 203, 237, 285, 306

Pike, Nelson, 126

Pinsent, Andrew, 256, 262, 292-294, 303

Pio of Pietrelcina, St., 222

pilgrimages, 14, 129, 176, 178

placebo effect, 270

Polanyi, Michael, 93

positive psychology, 186, 197

positron emission tomography (PET), 86, 98, 153

posterior cingulate cortex (PCC), 169–70, 274, 294

practices
  ascetical, 148

devotional, 15, 178
liturgical, 2, 134, 152
meditative, 164
prayer
apophatic, 236-237
centering, 232, 313
contemplative, 123, 161–62
individual, 159
intercessory, 112, 312
kataphatic, 236
liturgical, 133, 221
meditative, 251, 253
prayer and meditation, 149, 165,
251, 253
praying, 76, 85, 143, 161, 173
precuneus, 102, 170, 274, 294
prefrontal cortex, 97, 102–3, 137–
39, 141, 147, 162, 165, 168, 170,
172, 210–13, 220, 226, 294–95
Presbyterorum ordinis, 141
prophets, 8, 141, 177, 263
Protestants, 2, 8, 102, 250
psychological health, 153, 179–81,
188, 197, 303
psychological problems, 84, 160,
180–81
psychological science, 174, 213
psychological theories, 186, 189,
192, 197–98, 231
psychoneuroimmunology, 142
psychotherapy, 84, 190, 193, 275,
296
PTSD (post-traumatic stress
disorder), 185, 210–11, 228
pure consciousness, 236, 241–42,
244, 260–61

R

Rahner, Karl, 29–30, 74, 93, 127–
28, 154, 205–7, 228, 247, 255–
57, 262, 283–85, 287–92, 302–4

mysticism, 290
spirituality, 207
theology, 302, 304
rationality, 47, 53, 323–25, 329
transcend, 216
transversal, 323
realism, 45, 50, 191
realness of mystical experience,
261
reason
human, 65, 267, 300, 316
natural, 25, 190, 264–65
Reconciliation 133, 154
redemption, 131, 189, 220, 226,
268
reductionism, 48, 308, 326
Reformation, 47, 187
relationality, 198, 207, 214, 228,
295
relationships
causal, 123
complex, 90
husband-wife, 293
social, 38, 116, 212
relativism, 25, 28, 189, 309
religion
ancient, 238
folk, 325
religion and health, 111–12, 115,
117, 122–23
religiosity, 80, 114–16, 122, 297,
321
extrinsic, 297
intrinsic/extrinsic, 297
religious activities, 143, 182, 311,
321, 328
religious beliefs, 5, 80, 83, 87, 113–
16, 122, 134, 144–45, 156, 174,
181–83, 196, 246, 251
religious coping, 297
religious experiences, 13, 15, 67,
111–23, 163, 167, 178–79, 181–

84, 195–97, 203, 205–6, 208–9,
    233–35, 258–62, 266, 270–71,
    278–79, 308, 310–23, 328
religious individuals, 73, 115, 163,
    303
religiousness, 112–14, 116, 164,
    183, 208
religious perspectives, 4, 24, 83,
    107, 182, 211, 311
religious rituals, 112, 150–51, 153,
    156, 232
religious studies, 279, 306–7, 325–
    26
religious traditions, 15, 73, 81,
    111–12, 117–18, 183, 188, 240–
    41
representations
    abstract, 153
    cognitive, 153
    complex, 36, 170
    visual, 144, 214
research, neurotheological, 20, 22,
    251, 329
resonance, neurological, 213
resurrection, final, 39, 52, 60, 70
resurrection of Christ, 172, 177
revelation
    biblical, 220, 286, 305
    explicit, 128
    extraordinary, 267
    implicit, 128
    ordinary, 267
    transcendental, 154
revelatory experiences, 312
rhythms, 86, 146, 151, 159–60, 169
right hemisphere, 32, 41, 130, 146,
    166–68
Rita of Cascia, St., 221
rites
    liturgical, 174
    sacramental, 131, 135, 145
    sacred, 214

rituals, 1, 3, 6, 11, 13, 125–26, 129,
    134–35, 148–52, 154, 156, 166–
    67, 169, 171, 173–74, 176, 205–
    6, 265, 267, 323
Rodriguez, St. Alphonsus, 223
Runehov, Anne, 307, 313
Ruysbroeck, 221

S

sacramentals, 14–15, 129, 159,
    172, 174–78, 217–18, 277, 298
sacraments of healing, 133
sacraments of initiation, 130, 135,
    154
sacredness, 218, 224, 248
sacred symbols, 150, 154, 172
sacred texts, 3, 10, 73, 144, 179,
    259
Sacrosanctum concilium, 16, 131,
    159
salvation, 6, 75, 129, 133, 216, 267,
    329
Sanguineti, Juan José, 54, 59, 99,
    107–8, 316, 320–21, 328
Scholastica, St., 221
science and faith, 23, 52, 265, 299,
    303, 306
scientific discoveries, 23–24, 309
scientific falsifiability, 310
scientific investigation, 15, 79, 269
scientific method, 18, 54, 69, 71–
    74, 76–77, 79, 90, 205, 242, 266–
    67, 270, 316, 319
scientific model, 321
self
    autobiographical, 231
    moral, 274, 279
    observing, 119
    religious, 142
    spiritual, 119
self-actualization, 207, 286

self-awareness and free will, 29
selfishness, 241
selflessness, 208, 216–17, 239
self-transcendence, 43, 93, 163, 178, 182, 188, 198, 206–8, 217, 219, 229, 234, 257–58, 266
sense of self, 259
serotonin, 87–88, 100, 184, 201, 216, 227
Seton, St. Elizabeth Anne, 224
sexual behavior, 44, 295
single-photon emission computed tomography (SPECT), 86, 91, 243, 313
Smith, James, 152
social brain, 212, 295–96
social cognition, 138, 140, 155, 171, 193
social neuroscience, 82
soul
 enduring, 190
 immaterial, 270
 intellectual, 39
 rational, 38–39, 43, 59–60, 98, 271, 278
 spiritual, 38–39, 52, 60, 144, 266, 270
soul and body, 37, 48, 60, 111
soul and brain, 79
Spezio, Michael, 7, 275
spirit and matter, 38
"spirit in the world," 128, 154
spiritual, 42, 55–56, 185, 200, 218, 233, 269
spiritual awakening, 208
spiritual capacities, 36, 46, 57, 75, 254, 265, 293, 301
spiritual development, 161–62, 169, 197, 220, 226
spiritual experiences, 6, 32–33, 36, 68, 81, 83, 88, 91, 164, 183–84, 199–202, 215–17, 227–28, 233–34, 240–41, 244, 259, 311–12
 survey of, 81, 184, 234
spirituality
 apostolic, 219
 human, 201
spirituality and health, 43, 115
spiritual life, 11, 68, 123, 160, 218–20, 225, 262, 287, 290
spiritual practices, 35, 85, 88, 166, 168–69, 178, 181, 199, 201, 211, 240–41, 243, 247, 251
spiritual theology, 161, 220
spiritual transformation, 152, 154, 157, 163–64, 177–78, 245
split-brain conditions, 40
Stace, William, 237, 248, 261
stages of faith, 194
Stein, Edith, St., 28, 221, 223
stimuli, visual, 40, 175–76
stress, 117, 119–20, 137, 139, 173, 295, 299
Sullivan, Jacqueline Anne, 187, 322
Summa Theologica, 39, 45
supernatural aptitude, 255
supernatural beings, 267
supernatural capacities, 64, 255
supernatural connaturality, 29
supernatural faith, 65–66, 69, 106
supernatural order, 65–66, 141, 287
symbols
 abstract, 150
 affective, 125, 159
 anthropomorphic, 144
 religious, 86, 130, 144
 visual, 172
sympathetic nervous system (SNS), 32–33, 123

T

Taylor, Charles, 130, 187, 197, 258
temporal lobe epilepsy, 182
temporal lobes, 35, 147, 174, 182,
    193, 214–16, 270, 311
Teresa of Avila, St., 126, 188, 221,
    223, 246–47, 250, 261, 288, 298
Teresa of Calcutta, St. Mother, 114,
    200, 224, 300, 314
theological approaches, 19
    early, 6
theological closeness to God, 145
theological disciplines, 9, 19, 220,
    229
theological implications, 14–15,
    189, 269
Theological Investigations, 128,
    205, 290, 292, 309, 317
theological principles, 6, 13, 185,
    301, 324
theological virtues, 65–66, 68–69,
    106, 254, 289
Thérèse of Lisieux, 221
Thomas Aquinas, 18, 24, 26, 29,
    104, 313
Thomism, 18, 28–29, 75
Thomistic philosophy, 26–27, 54
Thompson, Evan, 63
Tillich, Paul, 58, 200, 272
traditions
    apostolic, 2
    cultural, 242–43
    devotional, 75
    liturgical, 2
transcendence, 42, 115, 187, 197,
    204–5, 209, 228, 233, 283, 285,
    296, 302, 316
transcranial magnetic stimulation
    (TMS), 88, 91, 95–96
Transformation in Christ, 123
traumatic brain injury (TBI), 123
trauma victims, 211
truth
    absolute, 324
    faith-based, 299
    moral, 24, 265
    scientific, 305

U

ultimate questions, 67, 69, 120,
    169, 186, 211, 226, 323
ultimate truth, 43, 75, 205–6, 280,
    317
Underhill, Evelyn, 234, 246–47,
    251–52, 259, 261–62

V

van Huyssteen, J. Wentzel, 323–25,
    329
Varela, Francisco, 94
Veritatis splendor, 24, 30, 275
Vega, Margarita, 12
Vincent de Paul, St., 223
Vitz, Paul, 44, 186-193, 198
vesicular monoamine transporter
    2 (VMAT2), 266
von Balthasar, Hans Urs, 127, 154
von Hildebrand, Dietrich, 23, 28,
    123

X

Xavier, St. Francis, 223

Z

Zagzebski, Linda, 70

www.ingramcontent.com/pod-product-compliance
Lightning Source LLC
Chambersburg PA
CBHW072044020426

42334CB00017B/1378